Emerging from the Shadows

SUNY series on the Presidency: Contemporary Issues

Robert P. Watson, editor

Emerging from the Shadows
Vice Presidential Influence in the Modern Era

RICHARD M. YON

Cover image from the U.S. National Archives (from the Vice Presidential Records Photography Office of White House Management)

Published by State University of New York Press, Albany

© 2024 State University of New York

All rights reserved

Printed in the United States of America

No part of this book may be used or reproduced in any manner whatsoever without written permission. No part of this book may be stored in a retrieval system or transmitted in any form or by any means including electronic, electrostatic, magnetic tape, mechanical, photocopying, recording, or otherwise without the prior permission in writing of the publisher.

For information, contact State University of New York Press, Albany, NY www.sunypress.edu

Library of Congress Cataloging-in-Publication Data

Name: Yon, Richard, author.
Title: Emerging from the shadows : vice presidential influence in the
    modern era / Richard M. Yon.
Description: Albany : State University of New York Press, [2024] | Series:
    SUNY series on the presidency : contemporary issues | Includes
    bibliographical references.
Identifiers: LCCN 2023019208 | ISBN 9781438496092 (hardcover : alk. paper) |
    ISBN 9781438496115 (ebook) | ISBN 9781438496108 (pbk. : alk. paper)
Subjects: LCSH: Vice-Presidents—United States—History. | United
    States—Politics and government—1945–1989. | United States—Politics
    and government—1989–
Classification: LCC JK609.5 .Y66 2024 | DDC 320.47309/04—dc23/eng/20230925
LC record available at https://lccn.loc.gov/2023019208

10 9 8 7 6 5 4 3 2 1

Contents

Acknowledgments		vii
Introduction		1
1	Defining Influence and the Four Dynamics that Shape It	15
2	Nelson Rockefeller: A Case of Marginalized Influence	39
3	Dick Cheney: A Case of Unprecedented Influence	91
4	Mondale, Bush, Quayle, Gore, and Biden: Tales of Vice Presidential Influence	173
Conclusion		253
Appendixes		277
Notes		283
References		361
Index		383

Acknowledgments

Writing a book requires the support of many. I wish to express my deepest gratitude to several individuals without whom this project simply would not have materialized. Several faculty mentors invested considerable time in helping me transform an idea into a dissertation and then a book manuscript. Words cannot express the appreciation I have for Drs. Beth Rosenson, Larry Dodd, Sharon Austin, Robert Watson, and Elizabeth Dale for standing by me through this long and arduous process. Beth Rosenson particularly helped salvage this project in the early days and was a voice of reason at a time when its completion seemed impossible. I am forever grateful for the countless hours she spent reviewing drafts and providing unvarnished critiques that contributed to a better product. This project would not have been conceived without the journal article I coauthored with Robert Watson in 2006 on vice presidential selection. He has been a pillar of strength and support since my days as a graduate student, and I am proud to call him a mentor and dear friend.

Thank you to the amazing and dedicated archivists at the Gerald R. Ford Presidential Library, the Jimmy Carter Presidential Library, the Ronald Reagan Presidential Library, the George H. W. Bush Presidential Library, the Minnesota State Historical Society, and the Rockefeller Archive Center. They opened their records and assisted me in my quest to uncover documents pertaining to the vice presidency. Very special thanks also go to the more than seventy individuals that I interviewed for this project. Their willingness to spend time with me to provide depth and context to my theory on the vice presidency was indispensable to advancing my research. It was my distinct honor to learn from Vice Presidents Mondale, Quayle, and Cheney, as well as President Biden, in preparation of this book. These leaders were exceptionally generous with their time, and their viii / Acknowledgments

support for my work served as a constant inspiration during the writing of this manuscript.

I would also like to thank several former students. Michael Ferro and Hope Landsem transcribed countless hours of recordings. Miles Manney assisted with formatting and citations and did so with great speed and accuracy. Without the tireless efforts of Kai Youngren, this book would not be where it is today. His sound judgment and editorial skills were invaluable. Thank you for taking such great interest in the project and being an invaluable partner during the book's development. I am proud to have taught and mentored you, and I am excited for all you will accomplish as you begin your new journey as an army officer and Rhodes Scholar.

I would also like to give special thanks to Krissy Hummel, a dear colleague at the Combating Terrorism Center. A consummate professional whose attention to detail and editing prowess are legendary, she helped scale back this behemoth of a manuscript and the quality of the final product is a testament to her hard work.

Last, I would like to thank my family for always believing in me and being so supportive. To Linda and Ricky Yon, the most wonderful and selfless parents anyone could ever hope for—your unrelenting support instilled in me a belief that I could accomplish anything with hard work and passion. My wife, Dr. Rachel Yon, is the glue that holds our family together, and without her, I would have been unable to complete this book. Thank you for the countless hours you listened to me, read my work, and offered your guidance and support. My daughters, Reagan and Kennedy, are the most important people in my life, my guiding lights who helped me to see the light at the end of this long tunnel. Thank you for always inspiring me and helping me get through countless moments of doubt. This book is dedicated to you.

Introduction

John Nance Garner, one of Franklin D. Roosevelt's vice presidents, equated the vice presidency to being "not worth a pitcher of warm spit," or as others have quoted him as stating, "not worth a pitcher of warm piss."[1] Garner goes on to say, "Worst damn-fool mistake I ever made was letting myself be elected vice president of the United States. . . . Should have stuck with my old chores as Speaker of the House. I gave up the second most important job in the Government for one that didn't amount to a hill of beans."[2] Yet, much has changed since the 1930s when John Nance Garner made those derogatory statements. In the last several decades, the vice presidency has reformed partly through those who have followed in the office and partly through the efforts of the presidents themselves. Garner's comments fail to capture the reality of the vice presidency today. For instance, Dick Cheney's role in the first year of the Bush administration was consequential and created the blueprint for the biggest governmental reorganization since the creation of the Department of Defense and advocated for new executive powers needed to fight the war on terror. Now, in the twenty-first century, the Office of Vice President has transformed into a position of tremendous influence.

The Evolution of the Vice Presidency

Presidents, realizing the demands of the office were so great due to the increasing size of the bureaucracy and executive branch, sought relief by delegating some of their presidential functions.[3] President Woodrow Wilson described the position of president prior to taking office as "the most heavily burdened officer in the world."[4] Likewise, Truman, contemplating

2 / Emerging from the Shadows

his tenure of office as president stated, "I think no absolute monarch ever had such decisions to make or the responsibility that the President of the United States has. . . . No one man can really fill the Presidency. The Presidency has too many and too great responsibilities. All a man can do is try to meet them. He must be able to judge men, delegate responsibility and back up those he trusts."[5] Because of such burdensome tasks, it is no wonder that the vice presidency can no longer be characterized as insignificant. Presidents have the authority to delegate powers in the exercise of their responsibilities, and the Supreme Court has ruled that the delegation of powers to others within the executive is implied "and acts performed by such officials, if pursuant to law, will be presumed to be the President's acts."[6] Vice presidents, and willing presidents, stretched the boundaries of the office by instilling it with more authority and stature. For instance, Kennedy chose Vice President Johnson to chair the Space Council, which included an increase in staff.[7]

The changes in American politics during the twentieth century such as the New Deal, new domestic and foreign policy roles of the presidency, and increased power of the president created the ideal environment for changes to occur in the vice presidency.[8] More specifically, the creation of numerous federal agencies under the auspices of the New Deal enlarged the executive branch and provided the president with greater authority in domestic policy. Recognizing the enormous growth in the executive branch, "Congress expressly gave the president broad authority to delegate to Department and Agency heads, and to certain lesser officials, functions vested in him by law if such law did not affirmatively prohibit delegation."[9] This express authority by Congress enabled the president to delegate duties, not prohibited by law, to agents such as the vice president. Due to the responsibilities given to the presidency in domestic and foreign policy, the vice president began to play a more active role by chairing committees for specific programs, acting as a liaison between the White House and Congress, attending cabinet meetings, traveling to foreign countries as "surrogate head of state," serving as a spokesman for the administration, and being actively involved in party politics.[10]

In 1949, Congress authorized an increasing role for vice presidents by making them statutory members of the National Security Council.[11] This action further enhances the vice president's foreign policy credentials and makes him or her a critical member of the president's team. The increased responsibilities given to the vice president are quite evident in the following quote from President Carter regarding Vice President Mondale. "I see Fritz [Walter Mondale] four to five hours a day. There is not a single aspect of my own responsibilities in which Fritz is not intimately associated. He is the only person that I have, with both the substantive knowledge and political stature to whom I can turn over a major assignment."[12]

Perhaps one of the greatest roles of the modern vice presidency is that of adviser to the president. With ever increasing demands on the office, the president must surround him- or herself with capable advisers that have the necessary skills and experience to assist the president in executing his or her constitutional duties. As the presidency has grown over time, so too has the vice presidency. With the increase in staff, budget, and responsibilities as well as the proximity of the vice president to the president (whose office is now located within the West Wing), vice presidents in the modern era are important advisers to the president.[13] Because influence depends on access, this role enables them to be influential and therefore, wield more influence than the vice presidents of yesteryear. In other words, proximity breeds influence, and the nature of the modern vice presidency is predicated on an assumption that the position carries influence, but the degree of that influence can vary. Both internally and externally, the vice president is perceived as being more influential because of this proximity and advisory role.

However, access does not guarantee that presidents will listen. Just because the vice president advises the president, and has weekly one-on-one meetings, does not mean that the president will take the vice president's advice.[14] Nonetheless, the greater access, visibility, location of the vice president's office in the West Wing, and the willingness of recent presidents to cultivate a more hands-on role for the vice president provides ample opportunity for access to become influence. A relatively large staff and independent budget provides the vice president with the latitude to independently staff his or her offices in a similar fashion to the president, thus further enhancing the vice president's capacity for influence.[15]

The Vice Presidency

Understanding the limitations that exist, presidents routinely turn to resources and tools that at times put them in direct conflict with the Constitution and open them up to criticism by the public and the media for

4 / Emerging from the Shadows

overstepping their boundaries. One aspect of the presidency that receives rather limited attention, yet can prove to be an important and strategic influence that can assist presidents in overcoming the restrictive nature of the office without giving rise to questions of constitutionality, is the vice presidency. As a constitutional officer, the vice president occupies a unique position as a nationally elected officeholder to assist the president with his or her duties. However, studies of the presidency inadequately address the nature of vice presidential influence. As argued by Neustadt, presidents must utilize informal powers to be effective. Presidents rely on their vice presidents in both formal and informal manners to transcend the obstacles they encounter. As a result, a greater opportunity for the exercise of vice presidential influence exists now more so than at any other time in history.

If we apply the fundamentals of Neustadt's argument to the vice presidency several things become clear. First, like the president, the vice president encounters a constrained office that is quite limited in terms of constitutional responsibilities. Second, some vice presidents are more effective than others, providing evidence that informal powers, informal institutional arrangements, and the politics in which they govern can offer vice presidents greater influence. Thus, good bargaining, negotiating, and persuasion skills are critical for a vice president to possess in order to play a significant role within a presidential administration. And once in office, employing these same skills to further the administration's policy objectives is crucial as well.

Finally, those vice presidents who make significant use of their existing skill sets to the benefit of the president become indispensable partners in the administration; further, in many cases, they take on greater responsibilities beyond the limited powers bestowed by the Constitution. While no specification exists in the Constitution for vice presidents to be given significant influence or responsibilities or that vice presidents should be men or women of influence, presidents in recent decades rely on their vice presidents to a greater degree, and with this comes greater influence and responsibility resulting in the vice presidency emerging from the shadows.

Although once derided as an insignificant office, the vice presidency in the last forty years has witnessed an increase in stature, prominence, and influence. It is difficult to argue against the fact that Vice Presidents Mondale, Gore, Cheney, and Biden have significantly altered the traditional views of the office and have assisted in advancing the president's objectives and their own influence and power with it.

Why Study the Vice Presidency?

At its most basic level, presidential scholars should consider the individual vice presidents and the institutional dynamics of the vice presidency for several reasons beyond just its constitutional position within the presidency. At least ten reasons exist for closely examining the vice presidency. First, the vice president is part of the Constitution and significant debate existed among the founding fathers as to the functions of his or her office. Second, the vice president maintains a crucial position within the executive branch as well as the presidential selection system (presidents and vice presidents appear together on the ballot). Third, the vice presidency is one of only two nationally elected offices created by the founding fathers. Fourth, as president of the Senate, the vice president is vested with the constitutional authority to issue a tie-breaking vote. Thus, he or she holds the ambiguous position of serving in the leadership hierarchy of two different branches of government. Fifth, in case of the president's death, resignation, and removal from office, or inability to execute the duties of the presidency, he or she is first in line of succession. In our nation's history, nine vice presidents have assumed the presidency due to assassinations (4), natural death (4), or resignation (1).[16]

Sixth, in our nation's history, fifteen vice presidents, mostly in the modern era, have become their party's frontrunner in the next presidential election. "Since 1953, four of the 11 VPs became presidents, and another four were their party's nominee for the presidency but lost the general election. In recent years, both George H. W. Bush and Al Gore spent eight years viewed by the public as essentially the president-in-waiting."[17] Seventh, examples of vice presidential selection failures have been widely criticized and lamented, thus careful study of the office is necessary in order to attempt to avoid future mishaps.[18] Eighth, a notable expansion of influence and importance has characterized the vice presidency in the post–World War II era. Ninth, the selection of a vice presidential candidate is considered by many to be the first major decision by a presidential nominee.[19] Last, focused attention on the vice presidential nominee by the media and the public occurs at least twice during the presidential campaign season (nominating convention and the vice presidential debate).[20]

Due to the nature of the office and the position it plays in American politics (elections and governing), attention should focus not only on the president, but also on the vice president. As a critical actor within the administration, and one who in recent years has displayed significantly more influence and responsibility in the presidency, vice presidents warrant increasing attention. More importantly, they deserve consideration because of how they contribute to presidential administrations and how they have helped expand the authority of the presidency. Furthermore, the way their role has changed over several decades fosters questions about how their role will continue to change in the future.

Most studies of the vice presidency tend to evaluate the role of the vice president or vice presidential nominee in elections. However, the role of the vice president in governing is often overlooked and warrants scrutiny because it is crucial in fully understanding the presidency in action. In particular, vice presidents function as the president's cheerleader and attack dog and in many cases act as the president's surrogate during their term in office. Furthermore, vice presidents serve as a lightning rod to mitigate potential criticism of the president.

Purpose of Study

This study analyzes the vice presidency from a constitutional, behavioral, electoral, and institutional perspective. It focuses on explaining variation in vice presidential influence over time, between vice presidents and within individual vice presidencies. This study is particularly interested in what causes vice presidential influence to increase or, more importantly, diminish over the course of a term, with an assumption that all vice presidents in the modern era have the capacity to exercise influence. While attention has shifted in recent years to the importance of the vice presidency, the need to address the ambiguous nature of the vice presidency and the rather unique position it occupies in national politics still exists. Great strides have been made in assessing the different aspects of the presidency (e.g., individual presidents, Executive Office of the President, the cabinet, etc.), yet a clear deficiency exists in those studies because they fail to examine a vital component—the vice president or the Office of the Vice President. This book intends to fill a noticeable void in the literature on politics within the executive branch.

Despite critical moments in vice presidential influence, academics have largely ignored the topic. One explanation is the challenging nature of the topic. In order to tackle the topic, I conducted extensive archival research and in-depth interviews with senior officials from presidential administrations to understand the imprecise nature of vice presidential influence. The research that follows distinguishes itself from the scholarship of others by conceptualizing how the informal roles of the vice president provide an outlet for exercising influence within an administration, the factors that affect the capacity for and exercise of vice presidential influence, and the fairly predictable phenomenon of diminishing influence over the course of an administration. To showcase vice presidential influence and fully understand its origins, the impact of vice presidential selection, electoral incentives, institutional arrangements, and the personal/professional relationship between the president and vice president on influence, and the political time in which these dynamics play out are analyzed.

Furthermore, a framework is developed for understanding vice presidential influence and the different ways it can impact the capacity of a vice president to exercise influence. This will assist the reader in understanding the unique nature of vice presidential influence and the ways in which it may be enhanced or marginalized from vice president to vice president or even within vice presidencies. Vice presidential influence seems to follow a certain trajectory with the same outcome for most vice presidents (diminishing influence). While no two vice presidents are the same, regardless of the level and capacity of their influence, one thing is certain—he or she will become marginalized and influence will diminish. This predicament can be attributed to personal, political, and professional decisions of the two principals (president and vice president), their surrogates, or circumstances in which they find themselves governing within.

Theory

The institutional development of the vice presidency in the modern era combined with precedent has provided all vice presidents with the capacity to exercise influence. As stated earlier, the developments that have occurred during the modern vice presidency justifies the assumption that the capacity for vice presidential influence exists and this is where the research will commence. What distinguishes one vice presidency from another is the interplay of four dynamics—interpersonal, situational, institutional, and electoral—(see figure 1) and its effect on vice presidential influence. This research will also demonstrate that within a vice presidency these four dynamics can shift, resulting in a change in the capacity for a vice president to exercise influence. The focus will not be on the direct consequences of vice presidential influence on decision making since influence,

8 / Emerging from the Shadows

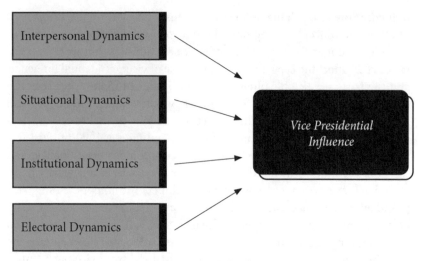

Figure 1. Vice presidential influence and the four dynamics. Author provided.

as some suggest, may not invoke change as a necessary component.[21] Vice presidential influence is not dependent on converting the president's position. Influence may be subtler. Vice presidential influence might still be present despite no change occurring in the position of the president that can be attributed to the vice president. Instead, the vice president might be influencing the process or influencing the definition of alternatives.[22] Furthermore, the direct consequences of a vice president's influence are less palpable since a lot of advice given to a president is done in private with only the two principals present. Above is a small diagram for the purposes of illustrating the focus of the research as it pertains to vice presidential influence.

Scope of Study

In an attempt to assess an understudied area of the presidency, this study will analyze the evolution of the vice presidency, the unique relationship of presidents and vice presidents in the modern era, vice presidential influence, and the role of vice presidents in governing. This research examines the modern vice presidency beginning with the vice presidency of Nelson Rockefeller. Nelson Rockefeller's vice presidency was selected as the inception of what is termed the "modern vice presidency" due to the nature of his involvement in the Ford administration. Admittedly, Rockefeller's vice presidency was short-lived; however, in that short period of time President Ford entrusted Rockefeller with responsibility over domestic policy. Ford named Rockefeller chair of the Domestic Council, to bring his vice president into the administration as a partner and provide him with definitive responsibilities. This was the first time a vice president took an active role in policy making.[23]

In addition to Rockefeller, this study will analyze the vice presidencies of Walter Mondale, George H. W. Bush, Dan Quayle, Al Gore, Dick Cheney, and Joe Biden. These vice presidents were selected for the case study in order to assess vice presidents of different political parties, as well as to study those vice presidents who have seen their influence wax and wane over the course of their terms due to changing interpersonal, situational, institutional, and electoral dynamics. Particular emphasis will be placed on the vice presidencies of Rockefeller and Cheney, because Rockefeller's vice presidency ushered in the possibility for an influential vice presidency to exist and is the start of the modern vice presidency as defined in this study, and Cheney epitomizes the apex of vice presidential influence at play. These two vice presidencies will allow for a greater understanding of vice presidential influence and its fleeting nature, because even though Rockefeller laid the foundation to exercise influence he still encountered obstacles to exercising that influence, and while Cheney is considered the most influential vice president in history, he too faced similar constraints. As a result, two very detailed chapters are dedicated to fleshing out the importance of their respective vice presidencies to our understanding of vice presidential influence.

The institutional structures, the situational dynamics, the electoral dynamics, the interpersonal dynamics, and precedent handed down by previous vice presidents will be studied in order to understand how the office transformed from an irrelevant and disdained office to one of considerable influence. To understand this phenomenon, specific attention will be paid to the president's and vice president's relationship and how the uniqueness of each relationship shapes the vice presidency. In addition to the unique relationship that exists between each president and vice president, the role of precedent in sustaining the influence and prominence experienced by vice presidents over the last forty years demands attention.

The object of this study is to analyze and understand the influence of the vice president in the modern era. Many mistakenly equate influ-

10 / Emerging from the Shadows

ence with power, but a clear difference exists. And in terms of the vice presidency, discussions tend to revolve around the ascendant power of the office. However, no two vice presidencies are created equal. Thus, it is important to distinguish between power and influence to accurately characterize the vice presidency. While power, in a social science context, is best defined as the ability of an individual to exert real control over his or her environment, influence is a trait that is much more indirect, and thus quite difficult to measure. Influence produces an effect without direct action and is intangible in nature. Influence is also more passive. Despite the differences, both power and influence require an individual to have the capacity for some type of an effect, whether direct or indirect.

To get at the heart of vice presidential influence archival research was conducted at the Ford, Carter, Reagan, and George H. W. Bush presidential libraries. In addition, the papers of Walter Mondale and Nelson Rockefeller were examined at the Minnesota State Historical Society and the Rockefeller Archive Center, respectively. The archival research provided insight into the day-to-day activities of the vice presidents under study and was useful in examining any institutional changes to the office across vice presidencies in terms of organization and responsibilities. As is expected from archival research, information can be quite hit or miss. While the research offered a picture of the contextual environment that each vice president governed within, not all information sought was available. To overcome this dearth of information, extensive in-depth interviews were conducted with individuals from each presidential administration from Presidents Gerald Ford through Barack Obama. The interviews helped clarify some of the information gathered from the archival research and assisted in framing the working relationship between each president and vice president and the changes in influence over time. Over seventy interviews have been conducted with vice presidents, cabinet secretaries, press secretaries, chiefs of staff, national security advisers, and other presidential/ vice presidential advisors.[24] This study is one of the first major efforts utilizing both in-depth interviews with political practitioners and extensive archival research to examine changes in vice presidential influence and the evolution of the office in the modern era. Furthermore, it is the first of its kind to ascertain the true nature of vice presidential influence and how that influence diminishes over time because of changing dynamics.

Every vice president's influence faces challenges that either advance or marginalize influence. I contend that while the modern vice presidency can be characterized as influential, the degree of influence is highly dependent on the relationship between the principals, the manner of selection, precedent, institutional arrangements, electoral incentives, and the political and social context in which the president and vice president find themselves governing. One conclusion that can be drawn from most if not all the vice presidencies under study is that influence, despite any disparities among vice presidents, declines over the course of an administration. Therefore, this study will examine the possible reasons for its decline over time.

Access to the president provides the opportunity and the capacity to exercise influence; thus, one would expect that if a president and vice president meet frequently there is a greater opportunity for a vice president to exercise influence. In the last several decades, many presidents have realized the importance of having regularly scheduled meetings with their vice presidents. For instance, President Gerald Ford and Vice President Nelson Rockefeller, as well as each of their successors, have had weekly scheduled lunch meetings. Although some of these meetings may not be considered substantive in terms of policy discussions, they have proven instrumental in keeping the vice presidents informed about activities within the administration while simultaneously allowing them the opportunity to share ideas about critical matters and policy decisions. This differs substantially from those vice presidents who barely met with their president. For instance, when Harry S. Truman became vice president at the start of Franklin D. Roosevelt's unprecedented fourth term, Roosevelt had met with him very infrequently. No substantial policy discussions occurred, and Truman was left in the dark about the conduct of World War II. Upon Roosevelt's untimely death in April 1945, Truman, only vice president for a short time, was sworn in as the nation's president with little to no idea of the current conditions of the war effort. Truman was unaware of the Manhattan Project, which was responsible for building the atomic bomb or critical negotiations that occurred between the US and its allies, specifically Winston Churchill and Joseph Stalin.[25] As a result, Truman as vice president was considered weak and did not play a critical role within the presidency. The frequency of contact and the proximity of the vice president to the president is a testament to the degree to which the president feels it necessary to include the vice president in critical discussions for the purposes of providing the vice president with an opportunity to assist in managing the executive branch, thus providing him or her the chance to exert influence.

One would expect that the greater the size of the office of the vice president, in terms of staff and the size of the budget, the greater is the

12 / Emerging from the Shadows

capacity for exerting influence. The increasing demands levied on the president with the establishment of the modern presidency have caused the executive branch to significantly increase in size over the last sixty to seventy years. In recent decades, where the influence of the vice president is noticeable, the vice president's staff has increased as well and, in many ways, resembles the president's staff in terms of organization and resources.[26] The increase in staff attests to the number and types of varied responsibilities the vice president is now involved in. It makes sense that the more active the vice president, the larger the staff needed to fulfill his or her obligations, and the more opportunity arises to exert influence. The increase in staff also signifies the influence of the office and its occupants.

Last, vice presidential influence can be affected by a host of different factors, including changing interpersonal relationships (interpersonal dynamic—how a presidential/vice presidential relationship is affected by scandal, election, etc.), changing political context (situational dynamic—issues facing the country), changing institutional structures (institutional dynamic—staff changes, chief of staff), and the electoral cycle and pressures (electoral dynamic). A vice president's capacity to exercise influence may be positively or negatively affected by the departure and arrival of staff and chiefs of staff, issues that arise that the vice president has an expertise on or does not, the presence of a scandal (vice presidential or presidential), and the demands of an election. In most cases, the vice president is utilized as a political emissary during election contests. During a president's reelection, the vice president crisscrosses the country to champion the administration's successes and win a second term for the ticket. However, electioneering can diminish the vice president's capacity for influencing policy since the vice president is so removed from the day-to-day activities of the White House while on the stump. The same is true of a vice president who is seeking election to the presidency in his or her own right. Not only does the vice president suffer from the same issues found in a reelection campaign but this is further intensified because the vice president may distance him- or herself from the administration, which could result in changes to the president's and vice president's relationship, thus resulting in a further diminishment of influence.

Regarding vice presidential influence in the modern era, one thing is certain—influence will diminish over the course of an administration. Regardless of the vice president, all vice presidents face the same phenomenon—diminishing or marginalized influence. Even with vice presidents who are considered the most influential in history (i.e., Vice Presidents Al

Gore, Dick Cheney, and Joe Biden), influence is negatively affected by the changing interpersonal, situational, institutional, and electoral dynamics, which will be explored in this study.

Chapter 1

Defining Influence and the
Four Dynamics that Shape It

Influence versus Power

Two of the most perplexing terms are *influence* and *power*. While at face value they seem to be rather simple concepts, political scientists and social scientists still struggle to understand their nuances. So fine is the distinction between these two terms, they are often considered the same concept or it is thought that one begets the other.[1] This section demonstrates the distinctiveness of these two concepts to develop a better understanding of what influence is, and what it is not, as these terms are "notorious [for being] difficult to operationalize."[2]

INTERCONNECTEDNESS OF INFLUENCE AND POWER

Before moving into a discussion of how influence differs from power, it is worth discussing how some consider influence and power to be interconnected. Many view "conceptions of power and influence [to be] fundamental to the understanding of society."[3] It should be added that they are also fundamental to the understanding of the institutions and organizations that comprise society. Because of the importance of these two concepts, some sociologists view influence as an "aspect of power." Important questions asked by sociologists attempt to determine the nexus of influence and power (does one produce the other?).[4] Some of the conclusions drawn are that a "theoretical distinction between power and influence may or may not be warranted" and that "power produces influence."[5] Dennis Wrong states, "power is the capacity of some persons to produce intended and foreseen effects on others."[6] Likewise, other scholars view influence as encompassing power.[7] Just as these two concepts are nuanced, so too are the possible distinctions and interconnectedness. There is no single theory that best captures the theoretical distinctions or interconnectedness of the two concepts and no two scholars share the same view of power and influence. Nonetheless, while this might be important to an understanding of these terms, it tends to blur the concepts, thus creating the impression that power and influence are the same.

INFLUENCE AND POWER: DISTINCT CONCEPTS

It is possible that power and influence can exist separate from each other and that the existence of one does not automatically confer the presence of the other.[8] Power can be conceived as a consequence of "positive or negative sanctions."[9] Similarly, power involves the exertion of "force, coercion and sanctions."[10] In other words, the exertion of power is a much more deliberate and direct force, as opposed to influence, which is rather indirect and at times more circumspect. This makes sense since power is usually conferred by a position, authority, office, or some other structural arrangement that provides the ability to exert some sort of sanction to achieve a specific outcome. Power can be thought of in terms of the Weberian theory of authority and hierarchy. Weber defines power as the probability of carrying out one's own will despite resistance and is dependent on the resources of the position.[11] This conference of power is derived by one's authoritative position or place in the hierarchy.[12] These positions provide the "capacity" and "particular resources, which some members control and others desire" that make power possible.[13]

Influence is also multidimensional, which means it possesses "both magnitude and direction, making it a 'vector' rather than a 'scalar' measure [which] only [consists of] magnitude."[14] Adding to the multidimensional view of influence is the subject of proximity and social cohesion. The proximity model espouses that "influence is enhanced when political discussants are close to each other in one dimensional space."[15] While the social cohesion model specifies that influence is embedded in "genuine discourse" between intimates or respected individuals.[16] Therefore, "influence will be greatest when communication is frequent and correctly understood."[17] Furthermore, the quality of interaction, in addition to the frequency of contact, matters as a well.[18] Influence may also "be conceived

Defining Influence and the Four Dynamics that Shape It / 17

of as the use or anticipated use of resources. . . . The actual use by an actor of authority, expertise, information, or other resources will depend upon the perceived importance of the issue."[19] Furthermore, one would expect that individuals with more resources would have the capacity to exert greater influence.[20]

RELATION TO THE VICE PRESIDENCY

Vice presidential influence is very difficult to ascertain because of its intangible nature. While the two concepts of power and influence seem to be similar there are significant differences. And since vice presidential influence is highly dependent on the adviser role, the observability of influence may be "covertly suppressed," "insensible or invisible . . . without the employment of material force, . . . [or] formally or overtly expressed."[21] Thus, influence is predicated on the existence of access. Influence manifests itself through the exercise of informal powers of the vice president. Every vice president since Mondale viewed their chief responsibility as serving as a senior adviser to the president.[22] Influence is a more indirect function than the exercise of power, and as such it is more nuanced and harder to conceptualize.

There is little the vice president can do to exert a positive or negative sanction based on his or her position, statutory role, or constitutional powers, which vice presidential power would imply. The vice presidency has one role that confers power on the office and that is as president of the Senate. Conversely, influence occurs with persuasion or the provision of information or advice.[23] It does not require the exertion of sanctions as found in the concept of power.[24] Instead, "influence derives from expectations that group members have for each other's competence."[25] This seems to fit the description of the vice presidency.

In many ways, the capacity to exercise influence is more important than the actual exercising of influence by the vice president. The capacity for influence brings with it certain expectations, which contributes to the power and influence of the vice president. If a vice president is seen as having access to the president, then other political players will seek out him or her as a conduit to the president for the sake of influencing. This provides the vice president with a personal cache of political power. This does not mean that a vice president can go rogue. All vice presidents since Mondale have cautiously balanced these expectations with the actual access they have been given. They are cognizant that the capacity for influence is tenuous and can shift in undesirable ways due to scandals, personnel changes, onset of war, and other such events that might be beyond their control. Vice presidents cautiously safeguard their relationship with the president to maintain access and the capacity to exercise influence.

While vice presidents might lack the ability to exert positive or negative sanctions, they do rely heavily on the expectations of others in influencing the president. Since vice presidential influence is highly dependent on the adviser role, the "directional model" is particularly important to consider when assessing vice presidential influence because the direction of one's influence is just as important as the magnitude of said influence.[26] With a few exceptions, most advice provided by vice presidents is given in private to the president when just the two principals are present, usually in their weekly lunch meetings, thus making the subject of vice presidential influence even more perplexing. Robb Willer, Lisa Troyer, and Michael Lovaglia assert that "influence relies on advice."[27] Therefore, the importance of the adviser role should not be discounted nor the fact that institutionalized mechanisms exist to provide the vice president the necessary resources to serve as a chief adviser to the president, which can advance vice presidential influence.

Stephen Skowronek, in *The Politics Presidents Make*, emphasizes the critical importance of resources to the presidency. These resources are termed "secular time" and are very much applicable to the vice presidency as well.[28] Skowronek states, "Presidential leadership in secular time will refer to the progressive development of the institutional resources and governing responsibilities of the executive office and thus to the repertoire of powers the presidents of a particular period have at their disposal to realize their preferences in action."[29] How does this relate to the vice presidency? Just as the development of institutional resources and governing responsibilities were important for the presidents of a particular era, so too is it important to the vice presidents of a given era and to our understanding of vice presidential influence. This research examines the modern vice presidency, which benefits greatly from the institutional developments and new resources available to vice presidents in this era. While vice presidents may not have the same resources available to presidents, such as leader of the party or even the bully pulpit, vice presidents rely on resources that are unique to the vice presidency and enable the capacity for influence to exist. The establishment of an office in the West Wing, the integration of presidential and vice presidential staffs, the creation of

Defining Influence and the Four Dynamics that Shape It / 19

an independent budget for the Office of the Vice President, and the ability for vice presidents to be intimate advisers of the president have provided a greater capacity for influence. These resources, while relatively new to the vice presidency, have been reinforced by successive vice presidents over the course of the last thirty to forty years.

Proximity is an important resource at the vice president's disposal as well and an important precondition of influence according to the proximity model. Since Walter Mondale, every vice president has maintained an office in the West Wing, thus making him or her an integral part of the day-to-day activities at the White House. In addition, the weekly lunches between the two principals, first started by Rockefeller and Ford, have built into the vice presidency an institutionalized mechanism to ensure proximity between the two principals that has continued with subsequent presidential administrations. This feature also demonstrates the applicability of the social cohesion model of influence to the vice presidency, which "stresses the importance of frequent communication between intimate, respected, and trusted associates."[30] Because of the institutionalization of the weekly lunches and the establishment of a vice presidential office in the West Wing, the foundation for influence, according to the proximity and social cohesion models, has been firmly established and thus provides the vice president with a platform by which to exert influence, more than could ever have been possible before these precedents were established in the late 1970s.

Vice presidents may utilize the resources of the office, particularly the interpersonal, situational, and institutional dynamics to influence the president—or at least they possess the capacity to influence. Influence can be viewed as conditional.[31] This helps explain why the nature of the interpersonal, situational, institutional, and electoral dynamics for each vice president will differ not only between vice presidents but within vice presidential terms as well, and perhaps why vice presidents prior to the modern era were unable to exercise any influence at all. However, a question arises—does the office confer influence or is it determined by the individual?[32] I would argue both are important determinants of influence. The office provides the resources and institutional structures by which influence can be exerted; however, the individual is an indispensable component because influence can vary according to the actor.[33] In the case of the vice president, the interpersonal dynamic matters, but also the institutional dynamics within which the principals operate matters as well. Precedent may be established by the actions of previous presidents

20 / Emerging from the Shadows

and vice presidents and a strong interpersonal dynamic may exist, yet the institutional dynamic and the constraints imposed may reduce vice presidential influence. This also provides some explanation as to the variability of influence across and within administrations.

Vice presidential influence is not solely predicated on this interpersonal dynamic in which the president sets the rules of the game for the vice president. Instead, the character and personality of the principals are important. In other words, while the level of influence exerted by the vice president is very much dependent on what the president will allow the vice president to do, it is also very much dependent on how comfortable the vice president is in exercising influence or how aggressive he or she is in terms of advocating and acquiring influence. James David Barber offers a useful matrix for understanding presidential character that could in many ways be applied to the vice president as well. Barber examines a president's worldview, style, and character to predict their respective performances in the White House across an active-passive spectrum and positive-negative spectrum.[34] Activity and passivity references the amount of activity that the president invests in his or her presidency, and positivity and negativity references how the president feels about the job of being president.[35] The intersection of these four patterns results in four different categories of presidential character: active-positive, active-negative, passive-positive, and passive-negative.[36] The usefulness of Barber's analysis to the vice presidency is found in two arguments,

> First, a President's personality is an important shaper of his Presidential behavior on nontrivial matters. . . .
> Third, a President's personality interacts with the power situation he faces and the national "climate of expectations" dominant at the time he serves. The tuning, the resonance—or lack of it—between these external factors and his personality sets in motion the dynamic of his Presidency.[37]

This research does not attempt to predict vice presidential performance or character, but instead it strives to understand the capacity for vice presidential influence to exist within and across vice presidencies. As a part of the interpersonal dynamic it is important to understand how vice presidential psychology might affect the capacity for influence. Therefore, Barber's analysis is a good starting point for discussing the willingness of a vice president to be active, assertive, or desirous of influence and

Defining Influence and the Four Dynamics that Shape It / 21

whether some vice presidents are more prone to a restrained view of influence given their own character or proclivity to exercising influence.

In further applying Barber's analysis to the vice presidency, we could also examine the activity or passivity spectrum according to issues that are important to the vice president. For instance, Vice President Cheney played a more active role during the George W. Bush administration because the issues were ripe for him to assert his influence. Cheney had spent his career dealing with foreign policy and continuity of government and when those issues arose with the aftermath of 9/11, he was willing to exercise influence in those domains.[38] This means that the level of activity or passivity in a vice presidency depends partly on his or her character and personality (aversion to exercise influence, as was the case with George H. W. Bush) and partly on his or her interests (does an opportunity exist to exert influence on issues important to the vice president, as was the case with Cheney?).

In addition to the resources available to an individual, influence can be affected by the political context.[39] Context matters and in assessing vice presidential influence it is important to understand the political and societal context. For instance, the political context of post-9/11 provided an ideal opportunity for Cheney to exercise greater influence within the Bush administration. Given the vice president's extensive career in government (chief of staff to President Gerald Ford, member of Congress from Wyoming who worked on continuity of government plans in the 1980s, and secretary of defense during President George H. W. Bush's administration), his skills were indispensable to President Bush. Some might even argue that had 9/11 not happened, Dick Cheney's vice presidency would have looked much different.

E. E. Schattschneider argued that "the definition of alternatives is the supreme instrument of power."[40] While influence is more indirect than power, there are varying techniques and levels of influence. Controlling the context by defining the alternatives available to the decision-making authority is a very discreet and indirect means by which to influence, but it greatly enhances the ability to exercise influence.[41] It is also important to be able to "control the terms of debate or the way an issue is perceived [as this] can go a long way toward controlling the . . . outcome."[42] William Riker refers to this as heresthetical influence or persuasion in which an actor structures the playing field to win.[43] Some scholars argue that because Vice President Cheney was considered a "policy wonk," and President Bush was reticent to delve deep into large briefing papers, Bush relied on Cheney to

22 / Emerging from the Shadows

refine or condense material to frame the discussion in the president's daily intelligence briefing.[44] He would routinely ask questions to ensure that Bush was apprised of issues he thought were important.[45] Cheney controlled the context of briefings and influenced decision making by framing the discussion in terms of what he felt were the important issues. By defining the discussion, and possibly the alternatives available to Bush, Cheney was exercising much greater influence than previous vice presidents.

DEFINITION OF INFLUENCE

Given the state of the literature on influence and power and for the sake of this research, I will define influence as being a concept that is distinct from power. Although this study does not refute the notion that some interconnectedness exists between the two concepts, I believe that the presence of one does not automatically evidence the existence of the other. While one's position might provide the ability to exert either positive or negative sanctions, it fails to guarantee that those actions will produce the desired effect. Similarly, the exertion of influence does not have to be dependent on one's position, but instead could be understood according to informal resources available and the interpersonal, situational, institutional, and electoral dynamics. Therefore, influence is a subtle and indirect force that exists due to the interplay of these various dynamics. One's influence might be positively or negatively affected depending on the unique alignment across all four dynamics, which will differ across vice presidencies and even within a vice presidency.

Framework for Understanding Vice Presidential Influence

Conceptualizing and understanding influence is an age-old puzzle that has baffled scholars for decades, and by no means does this study present itself as the panacea to understanding the elusive nature of influence. Instead, this research attempts to provide a new framework by which to understand influence within the context of the vice presidency.

Despite the differences, both power and influence require an individual to have the capacity for some type of an effect, whether direct or indirect. It is this capacity that I am most interested in; specifically, identifying the conditions that foster or marginalize influence. In assessing vice presidential influence, this research provides a framework for under-

Defining Influence and the Four Dynamics that Shape It / 23

standing fluctuations in influence, both within and across vice presidencies, by laying out a scheme for characterizing vice presidential influence and capturing the conditions that effect and alter it.

The research conducted demonstrates that the capacity to exert vice presidential influence has increased during the modern era. Several reasons exist for the more influential role for vice presidents: the makeup of the president's and vice president's staff, the personal and professional relationship between the principals, the management style of the chief of staff, the selection of vice presidents based on their capacity to govern, the politics in which they govern, and the institutionalization of the advisory role of the vice president. Just as much as these factors enhance vice presidential influence, the presence of scandal, tensions between presidential/vice presidential staffs, an assertive chief of staff, and electoral incentives can have a dramatic impact on the nature of vice presidential influence. Regardless of how influential a vice president may be, one thing is certain—influence will diminish over the term of the administration, creating difficulties for the vice president and his or her ability to serve as a trusted adviser. For the sake of this research and the nature of *modern* vice presidencies an assumption will be made that all vice presidents have the capacity to exercise influence. The degree of influence, the dynamics that might affect vice presidential influence, and the trajectory of influence may differ across vice presidencies and even within vice presidencies.

In no way, does this research prescribe a manner for acquiring and developing more influence in the vice presidency, nor does it attempt to predict the type of influence a vice president will exert. Instead this study develops a conceptualization of vice presidential influence in which the effects of various dynamics on vice presidential influence can be understood, thus providing the tools necessary for evaluating vice presidencies and the dynamic nature of vice presidential influence. I assert that influence is better understood as contingent influence—influence that is dependent on several intervening elements that may or may not be in the vice president's complete control and represents the potential influence of the vice president. Furthermore, it is natural for contingent influence to become marginalized and diminish over the course of a vice presidency despite the best efforts of individual vice presidents. Contingent influence in the vice presidency is shaped by interpersonal dynamics (personal/professional relationship of the president and vice president), situational dynamics (the political conditions of the time and events), institutional dynamics (staffing arrangements and presence or absence of a strong chief of staff), and electoral dynamics. Any changes in these conditions or dynamics can usher in a corresponding change to vice presidential influence, which could very well result in influence diminishing or becoming marginalized.

Before moving forward, it is important to define the various factors categorized as interpersonal, situational, institutional, and electoral dynamics, which shape vice presidential influence. These dynamics are predicated on the historical conditions and precedents that gave rise to influential vice presidents. For instance, the constitutional and statutory roles of the vice president, and informal roles or powers acquired by precedent through the actions of previous vice presidents matter and are a starting point from which vice presidential influence can emerge.

Interpersonal Dynamics

The interpersonal dynamic is the bedrock for vice presidential influence and interplays with the other dynamics discussed. Interpersonal dynamics consist of the most important factors in determining vice presidential influence though. These include the presidential/vice presidential relationship (including pre-presidency), the principals' perspectives on the role of the vice presidency, the president's management/leadership style, the president's and vice president's respective personalities, and the respective capacity and skills of the president and vice president.[46] As stated earlier, the personal and professional relationship between the president and vice president is a precursor to the establishment of vice presidential influence.

For most of history vice presidents were chosen for one reason—to get the ticket elected. Making vice presidential selections for electoral reasons results not only in a treasure trove of stories alluding to poor presidential/vice presidential relations characterized by mutual disdain and a lack of trust, but also to a much-marginalized vice president who lacks influence and thus occupies an insignificant office. History is replete with examples of vice presidents undermining their presidents or vice versa, especially in an era when parties chose the vice presidential nominee, not the standard bearer of the party. For instance, Vice President John Nance Garner refused to support President Franklin Roosevelt's policy toward labor union strikes and the court-packing proposal, even coming out to publicly oppose FDR's campaign for reelection to a third term.[47] John F. Kennedy's selection of Lyndon Johnson seems to support the notion of balancing the ticket for electoral purposes. Meeting with a southern

Defining Influence and the Four Dynamics that Shape It / 25

delegation of party leaders during the Democratic Party Convention, Kennedy, informed of his problem of winning the South, was urged to add Johnson to the ticket.[48] Distrust of Johnson permeated Kennedy's staff, and once elected to office, the vice president served a mere ceremonial function.[49] Those that knew Lyndon Johnson as a senator witnessed a huge transformation in his persona. No longer was he the epitome of strength and power, instead he was a diminished man with little to no capacity to exert influence.[50] These anecdotes demonstrate the flawed relationships that historically existed between presidents and their vice presidents, and the seeds of distrust sown between them, as well as potential reasons for the vice presidents' limited influence.

In recent years, presidential candidates increasingly choose running mates who will assist them in governing as evidenced by Jimmy Carter's selection of Walter Mondale, Ronald Reagan's selection of George H. W. Bush, Bill Clinton's selection of Al Gore, George W. Bush's selection of Dick Cheney, and Barack Obama's selection of Joe Biden. This consideration creates the conditions for a strong partnership. Most presidential candidates, prior to inception of the modern vice presidency, believed strongly that their own election depended greatly on their selection of a running mate. "Implicit in this belief is the assumption that voters may cast their vote for president on the basis of the person selected for vice president."[51] Despite these beliefs, evidence fails to support this assumption.[52] Therefore, presidential candidates increasingly look for running mates who will complement them once elected to office and assist them in governing. From the start, this translates into an increasing opportunity for the vice president to exercise influence in the day-to-day activities of the administration. Since presidential candidates are increasingly searching for running mates to help govern, they are more attuned to their own strengths and weaknesses, as well as those of their vice presidential candidate. Therefore, when they assume office they will utilize their vice presidents to complement their own shortcomings, especially in the beginning of the term, when the new president might be a Washington outsider while his vice president might be a Washington insider, and when circumstances arise that necessitate the skills of the vice president.

Since Walter Mondale, most if not all vice presidents developed an understanding with their running mate regarding their role in the White House. For instance, before Senator Joe Biden accepted Senator Barack Obama's offer of the vice presidency, Biden solicited a promise from him that he would be included on "every critical decision."[53] In recalling their

26 / Emerging from the Shadows

conversation, Biden stated in an interview with ABC's *This Week*: "I said, I don't want to be picked unless you're picking me for my judgment. I don't want to be the guy that goes out and has a specific assignment. . . . I want a commitment from you that in every important decision you'll make, every critical decision, economic and political, as well as foreign policy, I'll get to be in the room."[54] These discussions, which seem rather routine today, help preclude any potential turf battles once in office and provide vice presidents with a greater capacity for exercising influence. If the principals contemplate differing visions for the role of a vice president and never come to an agreement, it will almost always end in confusion, misunderstanding, and distrust and result in a severely marginalized vice president, as was the case of Nelson Rockefeller.

An understanding regarding the proper role of a vice president, however, is predicated on the president's and vice president's individual personalities and the president's leadership/management style. Several examples throughout history demonstrate the importance of the president's personality and management style in determining the role of their vice president. President Lyndon Johnson, a larger than life individual, whose domineering personality tended to alienate those who challenged his views, treated his vice president, Hubert Humphrey in less than a complimentary fashion. As the war in Vietnam raged on, Humphrey became concerned about the administration's escalation of hostilities in Vietnam. As vice president, he saw it as his duty to offer candid advice to the president and argued that escalations would divert precious resources from his Great Society and might draw China and the Soviet Union into the conflict. Even though his advice was given privately, the president admonished Humphrey and increasingly froze him out of critical war policy meetings and discussions.[55] Johnson's penchant for bullying his vice president was clearly on display during a meeting of the National Security Council. According to Alexander Haig, "In at least one White House meeting that I attended, with members of the NSC and congressional leaders present, President Johnson allotted the loquacious Hubert H. Humphrey five minutes in which to speak ('Five minutes, Hubert!'); then Johnson stood by, eyes fixed on the sweep-second hand of his watch, while Humphrey spoke, and when the Vice President went over the limit, pushed him, still talking out of the room with his own hands."[56] Johnson's overbearing personality made it very difficult for Humphrey to develop a true partnership with him in the administration, and attempts to offer advice were quickly dismissed. Therefore, the opportunity for Humphrey to develop or acquire any semblance of influence within the Johnson administration was rather limited.

Situational Dynamics

Situational dynamics form the backdrop of the environment in which the vice president acts. This includes national and international events and political conditions. In some cases, political conditions will affect vice presidential influence significantly, in both positive and negative ways. The reality of political conditions may force a reluctant president to take certain actions that might curb the vice president's influence or in some cases enable said influence. Political conditions include the shifting alliances presidents need to govern successfully, state of the congressional/presidential relations, political timing, and the presence of both presidential and/or vice presidential scandal. The ever-changing partisan landscape poses significant challenges. Just because a president's party controls one or both chambers of Congress does not guarantee success on behalf of the president and his agenda. Today, presidents must rely on shifting alliances to govern effectively. The nature of these shifting alliances demands different strategies at different times. For instance, after the Democratic Party's loss of the House in the 2010 midterm elections and the resulting lame-duck Congress, Vice President Biden was quickly deployed to salvage the administration's agenda, which included Obama's New START Treaty and the repeal of Don't Ask, Don't Tell. "In fact, Biden's influence remained at an all-time high both inside the administration and beyond."[57]

> Biden worked the phones and used connections he built over his long Senate career to lobby Republicans to achieve the two-thirds vote necessary to ratify the treaty [New START Treaty]. Moreover, the White House and congressional Republicans reached consensus over the fate of the Bush tax cuts, which enabled Congress to proceed with ratification of the treaty and passage of a repeal of Don't Ask, Don't Tell. This was a remarkable feat given the stalemate that existed and the resulting productivity of a lame-duck Congress.[58]

While at other times vice presidents may be more of a liability than an asset, as they witness their influence wane and become marginalized. Vice

28 / Emerging from the Shadows

President Cheney recognized the diminishing role he occupied in the last two years of the Bush administration. Cheney states,

> I think the role was diminished in the latter part of the administration. Partly, I think it also reached a point where I was more of a liability just because of the controversies I was involved in. I had lost my image as a warm and fuzzy guy because I was for water boarding terrorists for example, and so there were probably fewer opportunities for sticking me in some sort of an assignment. It wouldn't necessarily get a lot of people nodding their heads and applauding.[59]

The presence of scandal demoralizes an administration, regardless of where it emanates. In instances in which presidents are encumbered by personal scandal, vice presidents, faced with protecting their own images and political futures, distance themselves from the scandal and the person in attempts to remain unscathed. However, the tendency to distance one's self jeopardizes the degree of influence a vice president exercises. The personal and professional relationship between the president and vice president often sours, resulting in either vice presidential influence increasing or waning, depending on the situation. "Most president's/vice president's relationship becomes strained somehow, sometimes to the disruption of a relationship at all."[60] This was particularly true of the relationship between Bill Clinton and Al Gore. Despite the strong interpersonal relationship between the principals, the relationship suffered due to Gore running for the presidency in 2000. He needed to demonstrate that he was his own man and distanced himself from the administration's policies and from the personal scandals that plagued Clinton toward the end of the administration. In addition, the demands of the campaign kept Gore from being near the decision-making process in the West Wing. As a result, their personal relationship suffered, and some suggest that it has yet to be repaired.[61] When scandal originates from the vice president, the situation will almost always result in diminished influence.

Institutional Dynamics

Another determinant of vice presidential influence is institutional dynamics. Institutional dynamics within the White House will shape vice presidential influence and can either make it much easier for a vice president to exercise influence within the administration or not. Institutional dynamics include such factors as: input on and changes in staffing (presidential and vice presidential), the chief of staff and his management style, and the office of the vice presidency's institutional resources (budget, vice presidential staffers, office space, etc.).

Staffing decisions represent one of the most critical decisions made by an administration. White House staffers can greatly affect all aspects of an administration from the development of policy to the management of relations. Vice presidents who enjoy the confidence of their presidents often play an instrumental role in staffing decisions, and in many instances, get their top choice to fill a coveted slot in the cabinet or on the president's staff. For instance, Ronald Reagan's selection of James Baker as chief of staff spoke volumes to Bush's role in the new administration, given Bush and Baker's longtime friendship and the fact that Baker managed his 1980 presidential campaign against Reagan. Chiefs of staff can foster vice presidential influence and at other times marginalize the vice president as well.

The administration of George W. Bush ushered in a new first for the vice presidency regarding staff decisions. For the first time, members of a vice president's staff held dual appointments—presidential as well as vice presidential.[62] According to Cheney, "I had two people carry both the commission from my operation and one for the president. One was Scooter [Libby]. The other was Mary Matalin."[63] The meshing of presidential and vice presidential staffs not only reduces the tendency for interstaff warfare, but it also places the vice president in a position to exercise greater influence as well. Cheney elaborated by recognizing that a lot of the time problems developed at the staff level. "I ended up consciously looking for ways to tie my staff to the Presidents."[64] This helped a great deal in reducing the number of turf battles typically found between the respective staffs in other administrations and ensured that the vice president had someone on the president's staff looking out for their interests.

The chief of staff can negatively or positively affect vice presidential influence. Just as a chief of staff can make or break a president, so too can he or she make or break a vice president. The types of roles played by the chief of staff determine the nature of vice presidential influence, and the chief of staff's roles are quite varied. For instance, chiefs of staff manage the policy process, settle disputes within the administration, serve as gatekeeper, and coordinate all White House functions.[65] David Cohen conceptualizes the role of chief of staff as an administrator of

White House process, political and policy adviser, and guardian.[66] The roles can be condensed to two major functions—managerial and advisory. Under the managerial role, the chief of staff is expected to hire White House staffers and oversee their performance, provide structure to the staff system, control both people and information into the Oval Office, and manage information and advice for the president. The advisory role includes providing policy, political, and administration advice to the president; protecting his interests at all times; and managing relations with Congress, cabinet secretaries, and other key stakeholders inside and outside the White House.[67]

The two critical functions performed by a chief of staff that can affect a vice president's influence involve their role as gatekeeper and protector. In these roles, a chief of staff can severely limit the vice president by blocking his or her proposals. It may appear as purposefully obstructing the vice president. However, the chief of staff is fulfilling his role by "staffing out" policy proposals. When the vice president's policy proposals get "staffed out" and fail because they are inconsistent with the president's policy goals and agenda, the chief of staff becomes the lightning rod. Cheney, recalling his time as chief of staff to President Ford, contends, "From the standpoint of the vice-president, you are the bad guy, an obstacle to his opportunity to have a significant impact on policy. The ultimate result is great personal hostility between, in my case, myself and the vice-president."[68] Utilizing the chief of staff in this way enables the president to maintain good relations with the vice president while simultaneously limiting the vice president's influence in policy inconsistent with the president's agenda. Cheney, elaborating on the relationship, stated, "It was unfortunate, it was difficult, but from the standpoint of the president, it was absolutely essential. He [President Ford] ended up having a good relationship with Nelson Rockefeller."[69] The detrimental effect on vice presidential influence can also emanate from a chief of staff who views himself as a "deputy president" based on their own management style.[70]

As a result, the chief of staff's management style further complicates things. A very protective, domineering, and territorial chief of staff who thinks in terms of his own ambition and less about what is in the best interests of the president can limit access and marginalize staffers, including the vice president. However, vice presidents may circumvent particularly domineering chiefs of staff during the private weekly lunch meetings, which have become a tradition. Nonetheless, these heavy-handed personalities can place limits on anyone attempting to exercise influence. Furthermore,

Defining Influence and the Four Dynamics that Shape It / 31

the efforts of the chief of staff may be overt in their quest to alienate and isolate the vice president. As history demonstrates, a domineering chief of staff creates problems.[71] Consider the failure of Donald Regan as President Reagan's second chief of staff. Scholars often view Regan's tenure as dictatorial.[72] Donald Regan's approach to management included complete domination over the White House staff with an unprecedented centralization of power.[73] Even Reagan commented on Regan's autocratic management style: "He [Regan] resisted having others see me alone and wouldn't forward letters or documents to me unless he saw them first. In short, he wanted to be the only conduit to the Oval Office."[74] A controlling and manipulative chief of staff results in poor staff relations, diminishes morale, and increasingly isolates a president; all power and influence rests in the hands of the chief of staff and anyone who challenges that influence becomes a threat that must be diffused.

President Obama's first chief of staff, Rahm Emanuel provides an example. He was known to be a bit prickly, abrasive, and domineering. He made it clear from the onset that he thought Joe Biden was the wrong choice for vice president. Emanuel was frequently dismissive of Biden and has been quoted as chastising him because of his outspokenness in meetings. As a result, Biden played a much smaller role and had less capacity to exert influence during Rahm Emanuel's tenure as chief of staff.[75] Nonetheless, as soon as Emanuel left the administration, a power void existed, and the situational and institutional dynamics changed in favor of the vice president. He stepped in after dramatic Democratic losses in the House of Representatives to be the president's point person on Capitol Hill to help usher through the New START Treaty, the repeal of Don't Ask, Don't Tell, and an extension of the Bush tax cuts—all under the political realities of a lame-duck session of Congress.[76]

Even the vice president's chief of staff can impact the capacity for influence. A good example lies with Vice President Dan Quayle's chief of staff, William Kristol. Over the course of the interviews conducted of members of the George H. W. Bush administration, one frequent comment heard from the president's staff is that Quayle's chief of staff could not be trusted. He was viewed as the source of the administration's leaks and subsequently was alienated and locked out of sensitive discussions.[77] This indirectly affected the type of role Quayle would continue to play in the administration.

Alternately, those chiefs of staff who embrace the role of "honest broker" foster a collegial workplace with no ambition beyond serving

32 / Emerging from the Shadows

as a guardian, administrator, and adviser.[78] For instance, Jim Baker, Reagan's chief of staff, "did not seek complete control over access to the president . . . and he exercised his power in a subtle rather than a heavy handed way."[79] "Jim [Baker] never tried to become 'prime minister.' Rather, he fit the more traditional role of a strong White House chief of staff, keeping assignments straight, knocking heads, and serving as the major point man on the outside. As it turned out, he was ideally suited for the job and . . . emerged as the best chief of staff in the modern presidency."[80] In assembling the White House staff, Baker ensured that Reagan received the best advice and was not afraid to surround himself with the most qualified Washington insiders. Regan, the president's subsequent chief of staff, on the other hand, remained skeptical of staffers beneath him, in the hierarchical structure he created, and chose subordinates that were "yes-men." Regan's staffing decisions ensured no rivals would challenge his own influence.[81]

> The experience of Ronald Reagan over two distinct administrations is well known. In the first Reagan term, a "troika" including a strong and capable chief of staff, James Baker, headed a fractious but effective White House staff in the service of a president who depended upon staff more than most. In the second term, Donald Regan, seemingly trying to operate after the fashion of Haldeman, failed both to keep track of the "trains" (most notably Iran-Contra events) and to please the president and his wife.[82]

As these two contrasting approaches show, the type of chief of staff affects the entire operation. Style can either foster a smooth working enterprise marked by collegial relations or create a divided White House that suffers from conflict and poor morale. A vice president might find themselves blocked at every turn by a particularly aggressive and autocratic chief of staff who limits the vice president's own influence for the sake of protecting and ensuring their own. On the other hand, a vice president might be in a situation where the chief of staff, as an "honest broker" and unconcerned about their own influence, makes certain that their president receives the best advice from the most qualified staffers, including the vice president. Since the average tenure of a chief of staff clocks in at two years, a vice president's influence may fluctuate during an administration in response to different chiefs of staff and their personal styles.[83]

Defining Influence and the Four Dynamics that Shape It / 33

The replacement of Andy Card as chief of staff with Josh Bolten in 2006 exemplifies the impact that changes in the chief of staff could have on the vice president, and this was clearly a turning point for Cheney's influence.[84] Cheney noticed palpable differences in the White House operation shortly after Card's departure, partly because Card and Cheney had a long history together going back to the George H. W. Bush administration, when they both served in the cabinet.[85] Bolten and Cheney clearly lacked a similar relationship, and this had recognizable consequences on the role Cheney played in the latter part of the Bush administration.

The last feature of institutional dynamics revolves around institutional features found within the vice presidency. Just as the organization of the presidency has grown considerably since the inception of the modern presidency, so too has the vice presidency. Once relegated to the shadows of the executive branch with little to no formal staff or budget, the Office of the Vice President in the last several decades is unrecognizable from its earlier days. Although the office falls under the auspices of the presidency, the vice presidency has developed in many ways to resemble the organization of the presidency in terms of the type of advisers and the chain of command. The emergence of these features equips vice presidents in the modern era with a greater ability to leverage contingent influence to their advantage.

While a great many studies exist that examine the organization of the presidency, few evaluate the Office of the Vice President in the depth required to evaluate its effects on the presidency and presidential power. John Burke, in his study of the organization of the presidency, dedicates only one paragraph to the Office of the Vice President.[86] Stephen Hess provides a bit more coverage of the office but fails to make the link between the institutional vice presidency and presidential power.[87]

In recent years, the vice presidency has come to resemble the Office of the President regarding its organization. Vice presidents, following precedent, have sustained and fostered continued growth in the office.[88] They maintain key staff positions that mimic the president's own staff, to include: a chief of staff, press secretary, national security advisers, legal counsel, domestic policy advisers, and scheduling and advance offices.[89] Corresponding with these staff changes was a larger budget and new offices, to include the most coveted West Wing office.[90] For fiscal year 2020, the budget request for the vice president was approximately $4.6 million.[91]

The Office of the Vice President has become institutionalized over time as a result of the precedents established by various vice presidents in

34 / Emerging from the Shadows

the modern era and the increasing responsibility given to its occupants.[92] The vice presidency has evolved to assume the responsibility of several roles outside his or her constitutional duty to preside over the Senate and succeed to the presidency in the event that the president dies, resigns from office, or is incapacitated in some way. In fact, one of the main reasons for the creation of the vice presidency was to act as a "ready-made stand-in available if accident befell the Chief Executive."[93] Vice presidents of the modern era now have the staff and resources to effectively assume these responsibilities, with many modern vice presidents distinguishing themselves as significant players within an administration.

Electoral Dynamics

The last dynamic is electoral, and before we discuss the consequences of electoral dynamics on vice presidential influence it is important to discuss briefly vice presidential selection. As mentioned before, vice presidential selection transformed in the modern era from a condition based solely on electoral benefit to one of balancing the ticket for governing purposes. Subsequently, the likelihood of witnessing influential vice presidents has become more prevalent. The selection of every vice president since Walter Mondale attests to this fact.

As discussed, the presidency witnessed significant growth that makes it more likely that presidents will tap their number two to assist in governing. Conventional wisdom held that ticket balancing occurred to maximize the chances for victory, catering to a specific wing of the party, or at the very least—to do no harm.[94] However, studies have shown that vice presidential candidates do not decide the election and instead presidential candidates need to look beyond the election to select someone who will become a true partner in governing.[95]

> Presidents can no longer politically afford to slight their choice of vice presidential running mate. Expectations about what type of person is capable and competent to serve as vice president, and potentially as president, have changed. Presidential candidates in the modern era, who are solely responsible for the selection of vice presidential nominees, have responded to these changes. They can no longer afford to select someone who is not perceived as being of presidential caliber, and generally have

paid a great deal of attention to the experience and ability of potential running mates in the selection process.[96]

Vice President Mondale echoed these sentiments when he stated the following:

> I think it is important that the ticket is balanced in a way that the president is helped. In other words, you might have a president with a strong Congressional background like Gerry Ford so you might need less of that so you might need someone [to] help you more at the political level or governors' level or something like that. The president brings these strengths to the office, but the president has these gaps in what he will be good at the outset and you need to find someone who can help fill out the picture. Every president has strengths and gaps so you kind of have to look at each president as a nominee and figure out how you can best help.[97]

Carter argued, "It was important for me to choose a member of Congress as my running mate in order to provide some balance of experience to our ticket. Without ever serving in Washington myself, I needed someone who was familiar with the federal government and particularly with the legislative branch."[98]

While these considerations generally increase the likelihood of vice presidents playing a greater and more influential role in their respective administrations once elected, electoral considerations can also marginalize vice presidential influence once the president seeks reelection or the vice president considers running for president in his or her own right. Unlike the president, vice presidents do not have the benefit of traveling with the White House. In other words, if a vice president is removed from the White House for extended periods of time he or she has less proximity to the president, and this is important because the president is the center of decision making at the White House. Thus, the vice president can be quickly sidelined due to the realities of running for office. Sitting presidents running for reelection generally use their vice presidents to do extensively more electioneering and travel to help secure reelection. Furthermore, vice presidents are routinely used as the president's attack dog to enable the president to remain above the fray. Vice presidents are uniquely positioned to sing the praises of the president and the administration. "Presidential candidates cannot sing their own praises publicly to the extent they might like. Their running mates need show no such inhibitions. They can be the unabashed champions of the presidential candidates, lavishing them with praise or defending them from attack."[99] These realities make it highly likely that the vice president will spend more time on electioneering than on governing, which can marginalize his or her influence due to being separated from the day-to-day decision-making process.

A similar reality affects vice presidents who are seeking election to the presidency, but with an additional difficulty—they must demonstrate how they are different from the president. Not only does the electioneering activities take the vice president away from the White House for extended periods of time, as is the case of reelection efforts, but a campaign for president alienates the vice president from the president on a personal level. In many ways, the concerted efforts of the vice president to distance him- or herself can create the appearance of disloyalty. However, aligning oneself too closely to a president runs the risk of creating the image that the president is due all the credit, not the vice president.[100] A case in point is the 2000 presidential election when Al Gore was running against George W. Bush. "His [Al Gore's] biggest difficulty probably lay in successfully defining himself in relation to the president."[101] Al Gore had to walk a tightrope that enabled him to take credit for the successes of the administration while simultaneously distancing himself from the various scandals and policies of President Clinton, so he could be seen as his own man. This is very difficult for any vice president to manage and ultimately it strains the relationship of the principals. Thus, vice presidents who are running for president face a double blow to their influence—personal as well as professional.

The various factors discussed above (interpersonal dynamics, situational dynamics, institutional dynamics, and electoral dynamics) combine to impact the character of vice presidential influence. These different arrangements provide an understanding of the fluctuations found in vice presidential influence, why certain vice presidents are more influential than others, and how quickly influence can become marginalized or diminished within a vice presidency. Facing different contextual environments and changing interpersonal and institutional dynamics (mostly out of the vice presidents' control), the influence that vice presidents wield, transform into different conceptualizations. As such, vice presidents experience waxing and waning influence over the course of their term(s) in response to changing dynamics and conditions. The following chapters will illustrate

Defining Influence and the Four Dynamics that Shape It / 37

the interplay of these various dynamics by applying them to specific vice presidencies. Chapter 2 will examine Rockefeller's vice presidency, which represents the start of the modern vice presidency. This will be followed by chapter 3 on Cheney, whose vice presidency represents the apex of influence. Chapter 4 will examine the vice presidencies of Mondale, Bush, Quayle, Gore, and Biden with particular attention focused on demonstrating the manner in which influence can be fostered or marginalized when viewed through the lens of the various dynamics.

Chapter 2

Nelson Rockefeller

A Case of Marginalized Influence

I never wanted to be Vice President of anything.

—Vice President Nelson Rockefeller

The above quote attributed to Vice President Nelson Rockefeller evokes images of a frustrated vice president who never aspired to the office. Rockefeller experienced a rather difficult start to his term in office that would plague him throughout his tenure and serve as a source of consternation. In many respects, Vice President Rockefeller encountered institutional dynamics that affected his capacity to exercise influence. He faced two extremely strong chiefs of staff—Donald Rumsfeld and Dick Cheney—who he often cited in interviews as undermining him at every turn.[1] Cheney even admitted that the chief of staff could be a hindrance when he stated, "Certainly from the stand point of the vice president, if you don't have a good relationship with the chief of staff, it can be a miserable experiment because in the end, he has everything from office space to slots to budgets."[2] This chapter will analyze the Rockefeller vice presidency by focusing on the nature of his selection, the strengths and weaknesses he brought to the vice presidency, the strengths and weaknesses of President Ford, and his role in the administration. Rockefeller's limited vice presidential influence and frustrating term in office becomes easy to understand when viewed through the lens of the four dynamics (interpersonal, situational, institutional, and electoral).

40 / Emerging from the Shadows

Nelson Rockefeller's Selection as Vice President

Nelson Rockefeller was no stranger to the presidency. Due to his family's name recognition and his involvement in politics as far back as the Franklin D. Roosevelt administration, Rockefeller worked intimately with both Democrats and Republicans. He was appointed by Roosevelt to lead the Office of Inter-American Affairs and later to be the assistant secretary of state for Latin America.[3] After taking a short hiatus from government to work in the family business, Rockefeller returned to government service when President Harry Truman appointed him to chair a committee advising the president on the implementation of the Point Four Program, which sought to "bring technology to underdeveloped countries."[4] Rockefeller's service to the country continued when Dwight Eisenhower won the presidency and he was tasked, along with the president's brother, Milton, and Arthur Flemming, to provide recommendations for reforming the federal bureaucracy.[5] One recommendation resulted in the creation of the Department of Health, Education, and Welfare, with Rockefeller named the agency's first undersecretary.[6] In a matter of one year, Rockefeller persuaded President Eisenhower to appoint him as a special assistant to the president for foreign affairs, a position he left in 1955 to return to the family business.[7]

He worked so well with members of both the Republican and Democratic Parties that President Truman tried to convince him to join the Democratic Party and Hubert Humphrey asked him to join the Democratic ticket in 1968 as the vice presidential nominee, both of which he quickly turned down.[8] While serving as a governor, Rockefeller was approached by the Nixon campaign in 1960 about serving on the Republican ticket as the vice presidential nominee. He told Vice President Richard Nixon that "it [vice president] was standby equipment and I just wasn't cut out for it."[9] Rockefeller describes the meeting with Nixon when he turned him down: "That's when he [Nixon] came to talk about that and then, having finished that, he gave me the figures that I could help him 2½ percent, Cabot Lodge could help him 1 percent. And I thanked him very much and just said that I was interested in doing things, that I would like to be president, frankly, because that's where I felt I could be most useful."[10]

This desire to be president would remain with Rockefeller throughout the rest of his political career and through his failed attempts to win the Republican nomination in 1960, 1964, and 1968.[11] After running as a presidential candidate in three consecutive national election cycles, why did Rockefeller finally capitulate to being vice president when President Ford asked him in 1974, even though he had been adamantly opposed to being "standby equipment" in the past?[12] The simple answer is that the circumstances changed.

For most of Rockefeller's political career he was averse to serving in the number-two spot as vice president. Rockefeller had never served as number two to anyone.[13] However, three factors converged to push Rockefeller to seriously consider being vice president in 1974. First, the nation faced a constitutional crisis that began when Vice President Spiro Agnew resigned from office due to an investigation into whether he accepted bribes while serving as a Baltimore County executive, governor of Maryland, and vice president of the United States.[14] This was the first in a series of events that would undermine the presidency and the vice presidency. After Agnew's resignation from office, President Nixon nominated Representative Gerald Ford of Michigan to serve as Agnew's replacement and within eight short months Ford became our first and only unelected president due to the Watergate Crisis and the resignation of Richard Nixon in August 1974.[15] This constitutional crisis plunged the nation deep into discussions over the survival of the presidency and the republic and greatly increased public cynicism toward the government and public officials.[16] This crisis weighed heavily on Rockefeller and he felt it his duty to serve his country by assisting the new president in whatever way possible.[17] Rockefeller explained, "Having known all the Vice Presidents since Wallace, having turned it down twice, not wanting the job but feeling this was a moment in national history, a constitutional crisis, a crisis of confidence in the Executive branch and if I could help President Ford in any way reestablish confidence and respect and decency in the White House that I would do it."[18] These series of events forced Nelson Rockefeller to reconsider the vice presidency for the sake of the country and his own personal patriotism.[19] As Joseph Persico notes, "Nelson Rockefeller was an unabashed patriot of the self-proclaiming breed who tends to make sophisticates uncomfortable. The country then stood at a fragile nexus, with constitutional power passing over a divide never before crossed. Nelson saw Ford's appeal as a call to duty. If Ford wanted him, he could not see how he could say no."[20] He clearly thought that he had the experience and skills to assist Ford in navigating the country through the crisis of confidence and his sense of duty weighed heavily on him.

Second, Rockefeller also became convinced in his conversations with Ford that he would have a meaningful and substantive role to play as vice

42 / Emerging from the Shadows

president. Recalling his conversations with Ford prior to the nomination, Rockefeller stated, "He [Ford] wanted [me] to give him the support in the domestic field and wanted me to head it up as Henry [Kissinger] was in the foreign field. And he wanted me to help him on recruitment which he said that I was known as having attracted good people and that I could be very helpful to him on that."[21] Rockefeller elaborated by stating that Ford told him, "I want you to be a partner in this thing."[22] Having been vice president and recalling how unhappy he was in the role, Ford envisioned something different for his own vice president.[23] President Ford stated, "I told him [Rockefeller] that I thought we could work together very well. I would give him meaningful assignments. I wouldn't let him just carry out the routine functions of a Vice President, which involved presiding over the Senate and going on ceremonial trips around the world. . . . I thought his input, whether it was in the cabinet or in the National Security Council, would be invaluable."[24] Therefore, with both Ford and Rockefeller wanting a more meaningful role for the vice president, Rockefeller's fears of being just "standby equipment" were somewhat allayed. They both came from the same position—"they wanted to maximize the vice presidency for the benefit of the country . . . and the vice presidency [would] be used to [its] full advantage."[25] Although he did recognize that "it [vice presidency] may just be what I've always thought it was. And I've known all the Vice Presidents since Henry Wallace. They were all frustrated, and some were pretty bitter. So, I was totally prepared to go down and just be there."[26] This aligns with his sense of duty. The fact that there was a glimmer of hope for a more fruitful role eased the transition in Rockefeller's mind from complete refusal to full acceptance.

Third, Rockefeller understood the political realities and the prospects for his own political future. A direct path to the White House seemed elusive given his failure to receive the Republican nomination in three consecutive presidential elections. After all, "Watergate had destroyed his latest presidential timetable. Ford, now the incumbent, had an apparent lock on the 1976 presidential nomination."[27] Perhaps a more indirect path was possible—the vice presidency.[28] Even though history has not been kind to vice presidents, nine vice presidents have assumed the presidency due to death, assassination, or resignation. Furthermore, some vice presidents (Martin Van Buren, Richard Nixon, and Hubert Humphrey) have become the standard bearer for their parties by serving as the party's nominee in subsequent elections, and this is especially true after Rockefeller's tenure in which Walter Mondale, George H. W. Bush, Al Gore, and Joe Biden received their party's respective nominations.[29] His prospects for political office were rather limited having served in various capacities in state and national government. "The Vice-Presidency was the only game in town left for him."[30] These three conditions (existence of a constitutional crisis, the possibility for a meaningful role for the vice president, and prospect of attaining the presidency) seemed to provide Nelson Rockefeller with significant reason to finally take the offer of the vice presidency seriously. Despite these conditions, Rockefeller would become discouraged and frustrated in his role as vice president.

Strengths and Weaknesses—Rockefeller and Ford

When considering a vice presidential nominee, presidential candidates, or in the case of Ford as president, must take inventory of their own shortcomings and strengths not only from an electoral perspective but in terms of governing. In the case of Rockefeller and Ford, their distinct backgrounds complemented each other well. Despite the relatively short time-span in which Ford found himself elevated from vice president to president, he gave considerable thought to his vice presidential nominee, knowing that the gravity of the situation made the selection even more important.[31] Ford stated, "I felt it was awfully important that in the selection of a Vice President if there was any way that I could assure the world of stature in the administration, [it] would be extremely beneficial."[32] Ford was also concerned with selecting the "strongest possible partner in restoring the strength and credibility of the Presidency."[33]

The vice presidential search involved seeking the advice of members of Congress, talking with Republican and Democratic Party leadership and "a score of political advisors," consulting a political chart with mathematical computations devised by Bryce Harlow, and reviewing surveys and polling of the Republican National Committee.[34] The process resulted in a total of sixteen candidates, and with Bryce Harlow's assistance, the list was narrowed to five candidates by the end of Ford's first week as president.[35] The recommendations from cabinet members, counselors, Republican members of Congress, governors, members of the Republican National Committee (RNC), personal friends, and senior staff of the Nixon and Ford White Houses were tracked, and in total the White House received 911 suggestions.[36] Bush received 255 votes and Rockefeller 181 votes, all other candidates received fewer than 100 votes.[37]

44 / Emerging from the Shadows

Even with all the input Ford received for potential nominees, he needed to sit down and think about what he truly wanted in his vice president. According to Ford,

> What I was really looking for was someone who I thought in case my death or any other disability who could really do the job in the best way. Number two, I felt it was awfully important that in the selection of a Vice President if there was any way that I could assure the world of stature in the administration, would be extremely beneficial and of the potentials on a worldwide basis, Nelson Rockefeller stood out. He'd been Governor of the State of New York for fifteen years, part of every Administration since FDR. Name was extremely well-known on a global basis. That was a very influential factor.[38]

James Cannon added that the president also sought "a moderate Republican to balance his own conservative philosophy and record."[39] Ford was also concerned with nominating the best Republican with the necessary experience to govern in both domestic politics and the international arena.[40]

In interviews given after he left office, Ford recalled the decision-making process. "Well, as I looked at the three that came down to be the last three, Rockefeller, Bush and Reagan, there were elements certainly in the case of Rockefeller and Reagan who would oppose either one. Liberals certainly would not be happy with Reagan. Conservatives would not be happy with Rockefeller. George Bush had no enemies in a philosophical sense. He was more of a neutral candidate."[41] Cheney, who had served on the transition team for Ford and would later serve as his chief of staff, remembered the decision centering on a choice between Rockefeller, Bush, or Don Rumsfeld.[42]

Regardless of the last remaining candidates on the list, Nelson Rockefeller was becoming a top contender despite the low ranking given by Harlow. Nonetheless, Harlow offered a caveat to his ranking of Rockefeller, which Ford discusses in his memoirs.

> The fifth name on the list—with a total of 35 points—was Nelson Rockefeller. He was, Harlow pointed out, "professionally the best qualified by far with the added strengths of (a) proving the President's self-confidence by bringing in a towering number two, (b) making available superb manpower resources to

staff the Administration and (c) broadening the Ford political base." But he had drawbacks too. One was his age; he was sixty-six. A second was the fact that his name was anathema to conservatives. A third was the acute discomfort that I was sure he'd feel to find himself functioning as the number two man for someone else. In sum, Harlow continued, "it would appear that the choice narrows to Bush and Rockefeller. For party harmony, plainly it should be Bush, but generally this would be construed as a weak and depressingly conventional act, foretelling a Presidential hesitancy to move boldly in face of known controversy. A Rockefeller choice would be hailed by the media normally most hostile to Republicanism, would encourage estranged groups to return to the Party, and would signal that this new President will not be a captive of any political faction."[43]

James Cannon recalls that on Saturday morning, August 17, 1974, Ford sat in the Oval Office to make the final decision.[44] Ford needed Rockefeller for all that he represented, for all that he could bring to the administration, and for all his experience domestically as well as internationally. Ford lacked executive experience and did not produce notable legislative accomplishments during his twenty-five years in Congress, thus lacking policy expertise.[45]

Rockefeller, despite potential negatives, offered Ford a solution to his weaknesses and the difficult circumstances his new presidency encountered. Rockefeller had state experience where Ford had none, and he also had considerable Washington experience.[46] Given the country's circumstances in 1974, the administration needed to balance Ford, who was relatively unknown domestically and internationally, with a recognizable individual like Rockefeller. "Internationally, everyone who was in the political class knew about the Rockefellers but very few people knew about Ford."[47] Rockefeller was also a "long-time political figure who inspired confidence" and was a "reassuring figure" and one who had the kind of "stature and recognition" needed for Ford's vice president.[48]

While Ford wanted someone more liberal than him to counter his conservative positions, there was some concern over whether Rockefeller would be too out of step with the president on domestic issues. Many on the far-right viewed Rockefeller as the "Republican anti-Christ," due to his fifteen-year record as governor of New York.[49] Ford saw this as a mischar-

46 / Emerging from the Shadows

acterization of Rockefeller. "That was the most unfair political charge I've ever known. Because . . . basically he was a moderate to the right Governor. . . . And the allegation that he was a wild-eyed liberal was totally unfair and a cross that he should not have had to bear. And I never understood why the far right considered him an ogre."[50] While they sometimes differed on domestic priorities and policy, they almost always found agreement on foreign policy.[51] Ford stated, "In his [Rockefeller] early days, he was probably more liberal than I in domestic problems. With international policy, I believe our view coincided 100 percent, including our view on national defense methods."[52] The more liberal stance that Rockefeller represented on domestic policy could prove to be an asset for Ford and his administration, specifically in reaching out to certain segments of the Republican and Democratic Parties. While governor of New York, Rockefeller successfully "made the Republican party and important segments of the Democratic party into extensions of his person and money."[53] As Bryce Harlow put it, "It would encourage estranged groups to return to the party and would signal that the new President will not be captive of any political faction."[54] Ford felt politically compatible and personally comfortable with him.[55]

Another potential negative with a Rockefeller selection had to do with his larger than life personality. There was fear by some in the Ford administration that Rockefeller would outshine the president. Even Rockefeller recognized how some people might see his personality as potentially problematic for Ford. "Now, I think that it took, because I am a reasonably strong personality and have been in this business a long time and so I think that it took a lot of strength or showed that President Ford had a great deal of strength and confidence to pick somebody who had been a candidate and who was a political figure and who had had a great deal of experience."[56]

Ford knew that Rockefeller had a strong and dominating personality but felt he was secure enough in his own being that it would not pose a problem.[57] Rockefeller's selection was hailed by the media as a terrific pick. A *Washington Post* article specifically referenced the ability of Rockefeller to generate political excitement where it had been lacking with Ford.[58] In this sense, it seems that his personality paid dividends early in the administration.

Ford viewed Rockefeller as an asset when it came to domestic policy and attracting strong people to staff his administration. Ford told Rockefeller when he offered him the vice presidency, "You [Rockefeller] have a reputation and a record of always getting the best people and you could be very helpful."[59] Ford summed up his thoughts when he stated, "I was looking more at trying to strengthen the team, because right at that moment, not only domestically but internationally, we needed to have not image but the substance of real strength as an Administration. I thought Rockefeller contributed in that way more meaningful than any other of the possibilities."[60]

Ford paid particular attention to how a vice president could help him govern. The characteristics he looked for in a nominee focused on governing rather than electability. This may be a concern of typical presidential candidates but the manner in which Ford assumed the office meant that the selection clearly centered on the vice president's ability to assist with governing, compensate for the president's shortcomings, and broaden his base of support. By no means was Rockefeller a "cautious choice."[61] If Ford wanted a "cautious choice" he would have chosen George H. W. Bush, who on paper, according to Harlow's calculations, garnered the highest score.[62] The fact that Ford chose Rockefeller demonstrates an important consideration when it comes to vice presidential selection—ultimately, the decision rests with the presidential nominee, or in this case the president. Despite numerous polls and discussions with friends and advisers, Ford went with his gut feeling and sat in the Oval Office alone to make the final decision.[63] Ford embraced his decision and would routinely comment that one of the best actions he ever took during his time in office was in asking Rockefeller to be vice president.[64] On December 10, 1974, the Senate voted 90 to 7 to confirm Rockefeller as vice president and on December 19, 1974, the House voted 287 to 128 in favor of Rockefeller's confirmation.[65] After a lengthy four-month confirmation process, Rockefeller was eager to jump into the role of vice president.

Role of Nelson Rockefeller as Vice President

The Ford transition team advised the president that a vice president "should have an advisory role in policy areas, a role that went beyond the traditional one of ceremony and symbolic duty."[66] Regardless of who would become vice president, it was universally understood that Ford needed help on the domestic front. Despite his legislative career, he had few legislative achievements to call his own and lacked domestic policy chops.

When Ford offered the nomination to Nelson Rockefeller on the phone, he briefly discussed the role he envisioned for his vice president.

In particular, he wanted Rockefeller to have oversight of domestic policy and assist with staffing the administration. Rockefeller recalled that the president went as far to state that "he wanted me to give him the support in the domestic field and wanted me to head it up as Henry [Kissinger] was in the foreign field."[67] In alluding to the role Ford envisioned for Rockefeller in domestic policy, he stressed the need for Rockefeller's help in crafting a legislative package.[68] Ford needed Rockefeller's experience to help his "fledgling" administration.[69] "The Vice President had some thirty-four years of experience and achievement in domestic and for-eign-policy development and implementation at federal and state levels of government, as well as excellent access to corporate heads of the banking and industrial worlds."[70]

Ford thought they would have a good working relationship and promised to "give him meaningful assignments" and not to simply impose the "routine functions" of the office, which included president of the Sen-ate and ceremonial excursions across the world.[71] Statements like these created expectations, not only from Rockefeller's point of view, but from the media and the public that Rockefeller's vice presidency would be dif-ferent than those who came before him. In the first couple of months of his vice presidency, a news article ran a story regarding Rockefeller's role. The headline read, "Rockefeller Aiming at Major Role in Administration."[72] The article went on to state, "There has been nothing traditional about the role he has begun to play during his month on the job. Already there are signs that Rockefeller will have far more to do in the No. 2 post than any of his predecessors."[73] Another news article in the *Detroit Free Press* stated that Nelson Rockefeller was positioned to become "the most influential vice-president in many years" because of the commanding role he would undertake on the Domestic Council.[74] Richard Allison, an assistant to Vice President Rockefeller, recalling his time in the Ford administration, stated, "It is my notion that [Vice President] Cheney is the kind of vice president that Rockefeller would have wished he could have been and involved in everything like an assistant president. I think there were some plans of that with the Domestic Council in the Ford White House."[75]

After Rockefeller's confirmation, Ford and his staff sat down with the newly confirmed vice president and his staff to draw up the specifics regarding the vice presidential role Ford envisioned. According to notes from the meeting, Ford asked Rockefeller to undertake the following assignments:

One, to be a member of the National Security Council, acting
as Vice Chairman.

Two, to be Vice Chairman of the Domestic Council, with a
strong emphasis on working with the White House to find
a new Executive Director to replace Ken Cole.

The Vice President also expressed his special interest in handling the Domestic Council's role in coordinating activities
with the Governors and mayors.

The President said that he wanted Vice President Rockefeller,
because of his wide association in and out of Government,
to help with the recruiting of top people for the Ford
Administration.

The President also asked the Vice President to become a member of the so-called Murphy Commission. The purpose of
the commission is to analyze American foreign policy and
to make recommendations on implementing and improving
American foreign policy.

The President asked the Vice President to study the question
of whether the system of a White House science adviser, or
board of advisers, should be revived, and if so, in what form.

The President also asked Vice President Rockefeller to help in
presenting and explaining the President's programs throughout the country.

Also, it was decided that members of the Vice President's Staff
will be attending regular White House Staff meetings.

The President felt strongly that he has an open door, as he put
it, to the Vice President.[76]

At first blush this does not seem to represent a robust role given past
assignments that other vice presidents undertook; however, a few responsibilities stand out. First, Rockefeller serving as vice chair of the Domestic
Council would be seen on paper to be more of a figurehead position that
would involve more oversight than operational control. However, Rockefeller understood the post of vice chair of the Domestic Council would
provide him "operational direction" of the Council, or at least that is what
he wanted.[77] If the position held true to the discussions that Ford had
with Rockefeller about the latter serving in domestic policy in the same
manner that Henry Kissinger served in foreign policy, then operational

50 / Emerging from the Shadows

control could be implied.[78] Rockefeller saw the Council as an instrumental body for the president in developing a "coherent domestic policy," and in this capacity it transcended "Cabinet lines" because domestic problems more than likely cut across multiple cabinet departments.[79]

Second, Rockefeller was asked to assist in recruiting top-quality individuals to staff the administration.[80] Up until this point in history it was quite unusual for a vice president to be consulted on appointments and staffing issues. This could potentially be the biggest boon to a vice president and his or her influence. By recommending intimates in key positions, a vice president could successfully augment his or her own influence by leaning on those loyal to him or her for their position, thus situating the vice president into the daily processes of the White House through those loyal surrogates.

Third, Rockefeller was guaranteed access to President Ford. Not only did Ford have an open-door policy and weekly meetings with his vice president but he also insisted that Rockefeller's staff participate in daily White House staff meetings.[81] Rockefeller was the first vice president to have a weekly scheduled meeting with his president.[82] This enabled Rockefeller to have a voice, and one that could be heard by the president directly. Ford encouraged his vice president to be frank and honest with him about policy, staffing, and politics.[83] Ford stated, "One of the things I said to him [Rockefeller], when I asked him to be Vice President, 'We have to have the opportunity to be very frank with one another.' He was always totally frank, sometimes brutally frank. I can't remember specifics but if he didn't like an appointment or if he didn't like a policy or if he didn't like our campaign organization, he was very frank about saying so."[84] Rockefeller met on average once a week with the president and he drew up the agenda.[85] The Ford Library archive now holds the agendas that Rockefeller drafted for their weekly meetings. Topics of discussion usually centered on the various assignments with which Rockefeller was actively involved, such as the Murphy Commission, CIA Commission, Domestic Council, Energy Independence Authority, and foreign policy issues (e.g., Turkish Aid). On rare instances Rockefeller advised on political matters such as the allocation of convention delegates in 1976, recommendations for State of the Union Address, selection of a political counselor, intergovernmental relations, and the bailout of New York City's bankruptcy.[86] As referenced by Dick Cheney, these meetings presented the vice president with an opportunity to "lobby" the president for his ideas and proposals, such as the Energy Independence Authority. His access to the president was such that Rockefeller could go into the Oval Office at any time of day and call the president on the phone day or night.[87] The access and unvarnished input provided Rockefeller with a greater capacity to assert influence than had existed prior to his vice presidency. Rockefeller made clear in an interview on the *Today Show* that if he disagreed with President Ford in any respect he intended to voice his opposition publicly and had received "Ford's approval to do so."[88] Rockefeller would address any differences in policy with Ford privately but once a decision was made by the president, he would support the administration's decision except where significant disagreement might exist.[89] Ford was completely miserable as vice president.[90] Thus, Ford made a concerted effort to include Rockefeller in the day-to-day activities of the administration and to provide him with an opportunity to speak openly and candidly, even if it involved significant disagreement over policy.

CIA Commission

When Ford asked Rockefeller to serve as chair of the Commission on CIA Activities within the United States, he was entrusting his vice president with a politically sensitive, high visibility assignment.[91] The CIA Commission, which became known as the Rockefeller Commission, was established by President Ford on January 4, 1975, in response to allegations of illegal activities conducted by the CIA.[92] The commission was to determine if the CIA "had acted illegally and beyond the scope of its charter, and to make appropriate recommendations to the president."[93] Accusations were made that the CIA had, over a long period of time, violated its statutory authority by eavesdropping on phone conversations of American citizens, breaking into homes and offices without a warrant, and conducting domestic surveillance.[94] The political timing could not have been any worse because the *New York Times* article by Seymour Hersh that broke the news to the American public was written not long after Watergate.[95] Ford stated, "In the aftermath of Watergate, it was important that we be totally aboveboard about these past abuses and avoid giving any substance to charges that we were engaging in a 'cover-up.' At the same time, I realized that unnecessary disclosures could cripple the agency's effectiveness, lower its morale and make foreign governments extremely wary about sharing vital information with us."[96] Ford grappled with the decision of who he should name to head the commission. He narrowed

52 / Emerging from the Shadows

the choice to Henry Kissinger, Brent Scowcroft, or Nelson Rockefeller. He decided that Rockefeller was the best candidate. He stated, "There was no question he was qualified. I told him I saw the investigation as part of the healing process that I had begun in August. The sores of discontent would break out again if we didn't treat them quickly."[97] This assignment demonstrated the regard in which Ford held Rockefeller.

Within six months, Rockefeller made several recommendations to Ford regarding the CIA Commission's findings.[98] The recommendations were broken down into various actions to include submission of legislation to Congress, executive orders, presidential directives, and explicit endorsements by the president.[99] The Commission urged the president to explicitly endorse the following recommendations: CIA should adhere to "legal procedures governing access to Federal income tax information," CIA should not "engage in the testing of drugs on unsuspecting persons," and the CIA should "guard against allowing any component or special operation to become so self-contained and isolated from top leadership that regular supervision and review are lost."[100] The CIA Commission made twenty-eight recommendations to the president for actions related to the investigations into CIA activities in the United States.

However, before the recommendations even went to the president, Donald Rumsfeld, the president's chief of staff, intervened in the matter. Rumsfeld did not want Ford to take the vice president's recommendations and so he asked a White House adviser, Jack Marsh to get involved.[101] Rumsfeld felt these types of recommendations should come from the White House staff, not an outside commission, even though Rockefeller was part of the commission.[102] This ended up dragging out the process for four months and resulted in Jack Marsh asking the vice president for help in presenting the same recommendations he had given earlier.[103] Ironically, during this same meeting, Rockefeller went over his committee's originally devised recommendations and everybody in the meeting, including Ford, agreed to them.[104]

Shortly after the June 19, 1975 memo to the president on the CIA Commission recommendations, the Commission released its report. The principle recommendations listed in the report included the establishment of a "Joint Committee on National Security," which would be a counterpart to the National Security Council in Congress.[105] In addition, the final report discussed "restricting claims of executive privilege to those of the president himself," reestablishing the CIA as a "Foreign Intelligence Agency," and restricting the Agency's covert activities and mandating that those activities are reported to the "proposed Joint Committee."[106] Rockefeller's influence was felt in the recommendations the administration ultimately made regarding the CIA. Ford stated, "Drawing essentially on the excellent recommendations of the Rockefeller commission [CIA Commission], we had proceeded with plans to reorganize and reform the agency."[107] Approximately 90 percent of the vice president's recommendations were accepted and most of it was instituted by executive order.[108]

Despite the importance of the issue and Rockefeller's influence being asserted in the development and acceptance of the Commission's recommendations, he was very unhappy with the assignment for several reasons. First, Rockefeller was not consulted on the makeup of the Commission and its membership.[109] Thus, he lacked the authority to influence the Commission or direct its staff. Second, the assignment was extremely time consuming.[110] Rockefeller felt this distracted him from his main priority, which was tackling the work of the Domestic Council, the central focus of his vice presidency.[111] Relatedly, Rockefeller felt some people in the administration were conspiring against him by hampering his ability to fully engage in a policy role in the administration by inundating him with the Commission's work.[112]

Commission on the Organization of the Government for the Conduct of Foreign Policy "Murphy Commission"

Another important commission that had significant repercussions for the administration was the Murphy Commission. The Murphy Commission was created in response to the Vietnam War. Established in July 1972, its membership would be chosen by both congressional leadership and the president.[113] The purpose of the Commission was to review the objectives of the United States' foreign policy organization and to exert greater congressional control in the process.[114] Four subcommittees were created to examine four significant areas: "Congressional Oversight, National Security (Defense and Arms Control) and Intelligence, International Economics, and Public Diplomacy."[115] President Ford asked Rockefeller to join the Commission because one of the Commission's members, Anne Armstrong, resigned.[116] The president selected Rockefeller because he was worried that the Commission was contemplating several "critical and restrictive recommendations," which would be "unacceptable to the Administration."[117] These included "splitting CIA operations from analysis, the future of the

54 / Emerging from the Shadows

NSC and the dual role of the Assistant to the President [Kissinger serving as both NSC advisor and Secretary of State], Congressional Restrictions of the Executive, the Future of USIA (including the Voice of America), and White House Economic Arrangements and State versus Treasury leadership in international economics."[118] Rockefeller's role was to preserve the president's foreign policy powers.[119]

Whether or not Rockefeller exercised great influence in the final recommendations of the Commission is arguable. However, once Rockefeller was named to the Commission several restrictive measures were absent from the final Commission's report. First, no recommendation was made in the final report to split CIA operations from analysis.[120] Second, Vice President Rockefeller was specifically responsible for defending the dual role that Henry Kissinger held in the Ford administration as secretary of state and national security adviser. The final report made no mention of his dual role and did not recommend that this should be ceased.[121] Third, attempts to inject greater congressional involvement in the foreign policy process created significant discord between the Congress and the White House.[122] Rockefeller attempted to diffuse the situation by seeking a more balanced report that would be acceptable to both Congress and the president. He drafted a letter to the Commission, which focused the White House on addressing the problem by seeking a letter from the attorney general on issues of executive agreements and executive privilege.[123] Rockefeller drafted a completely new chapter for the Commission report on congressional-executive relations, which resulted in a compromise that was viewed as a "vast improvement" over the previous draft.[124] In the end, Rockefeller's proposals were accepted and incorporated in the report and the vice president and his staff recognized that he had a "strong and constructive moderating influence on the final recommendations."[125] Ultimately, the White House achieved what they had hoped—"The 'dreaded' Report was received favorably within the Executive branch and unhappily by its Congressional sponsor."[126]

The following subsections will examine in greater detail the vice president's activity related to congressional relations, his work on the Domestic Council, and his efforts to establish the Energy Independence Authority. These specific roles demonstrate Rockefeller's influence and its fluctuation over time. His lead role on the Domestic Council and his attempts to realize the Energy Independence Authority for the United States also demonstrates the policy process in the Ford administration that left Vice President Rockefeller frustrated, despite public comments made to the contrary.

Congressional Relations

The most basic constitutional responsibility of the vice president is serving as president of the Senate. In this capacity, he or she can serve as a conduit for the president in terms of congressional relations. Rockefeller genuinely enjoyed his role of presiding over the Senate, which was a surprise to many who had known him intimately.[127] H. Spofford Canfield, an aide to Rockefeller, stated—"He is on a very friendly basis with most of the Senators, even those he is not philosophically in tune with, . . . and [he] is unique [in that] he is very interested in the legislative process and enjoys the ceremonial aspects of the job."[128] Despite Rockefeller's statements regarding his constitutional duty, the archives demonstrate a rather limited and superficial role in congressional relations. After reviewing all the agendas that were crafted by Rockefeller for his weekly meetings with Ford, Congress or congressional relations was only mentioned seven times.[129] This is not to suggest that Ford and Rockefeller did not address congressional relations outside these meetings or even in meetings where it was not part of the official agenda. Nonetheless, only seven references could be identified as specifically articulated in the agenda. Rockefeller even admitted to his limited role in congressional relations. When pressed as to why he was not active, he stated—"I only do it if I'm asked."[130] He did, however, attend the weekly Republican Policy Committee meetings every Tuesday.[131]

It is not surprising that Rockefeller did not take on a more activist role when it came to congressional relations. After all, Ford was a product of the Congress, having spent approximately twenty-five years in the House of Representatives, with a portion of that time spent in the congressional leadership.[132] Rockefeller did have decades of experience dealing with Congress; however, he had spent the last couple of decades entrenched in New York State politics.[133]

While the record does not show a very robust role for Rockefeller in congressional matters during the Ford administration, Ford and his staff still made sure that the vice president received briefings from the president's staff on legislative efforts and the status of administration efforts

56 / Emerging from the Shadows

on Capitol Hill.[134] They ensured that the vice president was invited to all congressional meetings to include, the congressional leadership breakfasts, receptions with newly elected members from both political parties, and meetings with Republican congressional leaders. Rockefeller was not just a wallflower in these events. Rather, he was given marching orders to advance the administration's legislative program. The meetings varied to include discussions of domestic issues associated with nuclear fuel, the president's veto of S. 1849 (Emergency Petroleum Allocation Extension Act), the president's veto of a jobs bill and strip mining bill, strategies for advancing the administration's energy and economic packages, briefing members on the State of the Union message, and consumer protection legislation, among others.[135] Many of the meetings focused on foreign policy issues such as the Turkish Arms Embargo, Turkish Base Agreement, strife in Lebanon, and the Sinai Agreement.[136] His involvement in these meetings was simply to brief and cajole members of Congress.

On several occasions Ford asked Rockefeller to directly lobby members of Congress on specific issues. He was asked to intervene with three senators in regard to the Northern Mariana Covenant issue, which was an effort to give commonwealth status to the Northern Mariana Islands.[137] On another occasion, the vice president was asked to help sustain the president's veto of the ninety-day delay on imposition of tariffs on oil imports by contacting four New York Republican congressmen (Bob McEwan, Bill Walsh, Ben Gilman, and Norm Lent).[138]

Several meetings that the vice president personally took with members of Congress emphasized his work on the Domestic Council. He was asked to meet with members of the Senate Appropriations Committee to discuss the Domestic Council and budget issues.[139] On April 23, 1975, he was asked to meet with members of the Senate Subcommittee on Treasury, U.S. Postal Service, and General Government to discuss his role on the Domestic Council.[140]

Rockefeller was also sought out by members of Congress to intervene and press the administration. For instance, Senator James Abourezk sought increased humanitarian aid to Lebanon as quickly as possible, and he was concerned that the Office of Management and Budget and the White House would not be able to act in an expeditious manner.[141] Rockefeller brought the issue up with the president previously and told Senator Abourezk that he would be willing to do so again.[142] He made it clear that there was little support in the Congress, and he imagined that it would be difficult for the administration to "get out in front of this issue."[143] Furthermore, the vice president was often invited to events and sometimes these invitations were sent to the president's staff and concurrence was sought on whether the vice president should attend.[144] Most of Rockefeller's involvement in congressional relations comprised duties such as attending receptions and pressing certain members of Congress to support the administration's positions, none reflected the ability of the vice president to operate with his own discretion.

Energy Independence Authority and Domestic Council

The last roles Vice President Rockefeller undertook that require further examination are his involvement in the Domestic Council and the Energy Independence Authority. The role and influence Rockefeller exhibited pertaining to the Domestic Council and the Energy Independence Authority reveals both the highs and lows of his influence and will be a necessary precursor to understanding how each of the four dynamics can affect vice presidential influence. A discussion of the Domestic Council is perhaps the most important indicator of the volatile nature of vice presidential influence, especially given the great importance both the president and vice president initially placed on this role for Rockefeller.

Energy Independence Authority

During the Ford administration the country was in the midst of an energy crisis. This crisis was looming over the US since the 1950s, when the country's self-sufficiency in energy began to deteriorate.[145] Ford stated, "Until 1950, the U.S. had been self-sufficient in energy. Then demand exceeded our domestic supply of crude oil. . . . In 1952, President Eisenhower appointed a commission to assess the nation's future energy needs. Unless action was taken to stimulate the domestic production of energy, that commission concluded, we would face severe shortages within twenty years. The warning went unheeded."[146] By 1973, the US faced even greater shortages of oil due to the Arab oil embargo.[147] Not only was an oil embargo imposed against the United States by Arab members of OPEC in 1973 and 1974, but crude oil prices increased drastically during the same period.[148] As a result, Ford felt the need to act, and in a televised address he called for action on the energy crisis.[149] Ford used his State of

58 / Emerging from the Shadows

the Union message to call for three goals related to national energy. These included: the reduction of "oil imports by one million barrels per day by the end of this year [1975] and by two million barrels per day by the end of 1977," putting an end to "economic disruption" by foreign producers by 1985, and developing new technologies and resources so the country could significantly contribute to the world's energy needs by the end of the twentieth century.[150]

Rockefeller met with Ford on March 6, 1975, to discuss his thoughts on the problems and his proposal.[151] He discussed how the creation of a federal entity, the Resources Policy and Finance Corporation (RPFC), could induce private sector confidence and accelerate energy production.[152] Ford asked him to develop the proposal further but to do it in consultation with the Domestic Council. Several members of the Domestic Council, particularly the Treasury secretary (William Simon), chair of the Council of Economic Advisers (Alan Greenspan), and director of the Office of Management and Budget (James Lynn), voiced serious concerns over the size and extent of the RPFC, but did express interest in providing federal assistance to the private sector.[153] Ultimately, the presidential directive to consult with the Domestic Council reduced the scope of the RPFC to focus more on energy and less on economic issues.[154]

Sensing possible divisions within the administration over his proposal, Rockefeller recalled that "On the energy one . . . I thought that it was so important that I was willing to fight. On that I wrote the President a memo, I think, but I got his approval for what I wanted to do. And the overwhelming evidence was so great that he couldn't not go with it."[155] On May 2, Rockefeller outlined the functions of the proposed federal entity (RPFC) which were to "(1) achieve the president's goal of energy and self-sufficiency by 1985; (2) assure adequate supplies of essential raw materials . . . ; (3) assure the provision of essential transportation services; and (4) have the capacity to finance the conversion of vacant or underutilized plants" for production.[156] Rockefeller did not ask for outright approval of the RPFC; instead he sought approval for the creation of a review group within the Domestic Council titled "Energy and Resource Policy and Finance."[157] Rockefeller did not seek this review group for the purposes of stalling activity on his proposal; rather, he sought it to build support. "Within the Domestic Council's general framework, the review group would have access to the council's staff and financial resources."[158] The review group would provide "due process" to those who were "lukewarm and even hostile participants . . . on a basis controlled by Rockefeller."[159]

Ford gave Rockefeller the approval to create the working review group within the Domestic Council.

The establishment of the review group did not make things easier for Rockefeller. Instead, Simon, Greenspan, and Lynn found themselves in total opposition.[160] Despite this, Rockefeller proposed the creation of a federally sponsored Energy Resources Finance Corporation (ERFCO), rather than RPFC, which was its precursor during the development stage. Rockefeller saw ERFCO as a "financing vehicle" that would instigate private investment in the administration's energy independence goals.[161] Referring to the opposition he received to his proposal, Rockefeller stated, "It is very hard for people, particularly if they come from . . . more conservative backgrounds, to think on the scale that is required to meet the needs of the future. We were talking at the time of the commission of $800 billion needed to develop energy independence. A hundred billion dollars is nothing."[162] Rockefeller even faced opposition from those who approved of ERFCO. Frank Zarb, head of the Federal Energy Administration, thought that ERFCO should have oversight by the Office of Management and Budget and the Treasury, though Rockefeller disagreed.[163] Zarb also sought a smaller-scale proposal.[164] Rockefeller recommended that the president utilize a previously scheduled news conference on September 4, 1975, in Seattle for the purposes of outlining the initiative, but Ford declined because of the existing opposition.[165] Ford wanted to ensure that Zarb and Rockefeller were on the same page, and personally brokered a meeting between the two in hope of a resolution.[166]

The meeting was a success. ERFCO would be renamed the Energy Independence Authority (EIA). Its functions would include the development of new technologies to "support or directly produce, transport, or conserve energy," the development of new nuclear technology, and development of "conventional technologies" beyond the scope of private finance.[167] Zarb and Rockefeller agreed that the EIA would be an autonomous federal entity and that they would report directly to Ford, and after Rockefeller compromised and agreed to $100 billion financing level.[168]

Seven months from his initial conversations with Ford, Rockefeller was finally able to convince the president to publicly support of the EIA.[169] "On September 16, at his regular weekly meeting with the president, Rockefeller stressed the importance of the EIA as a stimulant to the economy and job creation and strongly urged Ford to decide affirmatively on the initiative."[170] Ford took several days before giving Rockefeller his approval to make it a formal administration program. Furthermore, Ford would

60 / Emerging from the Shadows

do so publicly at an address to the AFL-CIO Building and Construction Trades Department's Convention on September 22, 1975.[171]

Ford assented to the program and public support of it despite the opposition that still existed within his administration, particularly among Simon, Greenspan, and Lynn. Ford's chief of staff, Donald Rumsfeld, was also opposed to EIA. Rumsfeld stated,

> Ford brought it [EIA] out over [a] personal feeling that it would hurt . . . Nelson Rockefeller, if he didn't. I just have to believe that it was heavily weighted in respect for Nelson Rockefeller, in respect to the advisors Nelson Rockefeller has, in his sensitivity to his personal relationship to Nelson Rockefeller and that did it. My attitude was fine, he made a decision, that's the Administration position. If I'd had my choice, I would have sunk it. But I felt an obligation to see that it was honestly looked at and that the President had the best advice from those people.[172]

Rumsfeld's recollection implies the president was opposed to it as well but felt obligated to support it. And my interview with Rumsfeld confirms this. Ford felt a personal obligation to send up Rockefeller's EIA proposal to Congress even though Rumsfeld told the president it would fail because it was unrealistic.[173] The opposition did not end with Rumsfeld. Treasury Secretary Simon opposed EIA because he thought it was the "wrong way to finance research and development and implementation . . . and a bad way for the government to get into private business."[174] Ford said that Alan Greenspan and Jim Lynn "fought it tooth and nail" and that it was the "one program that Alan Greenspan vigorously opposed."[175] Rockefeller felt that Ford showed great courage in supporting it "despite all his other advisors" being opposed.[176] Rumsfeld had staffed the proposal out to cabinet secretaries and other White House officials and there was almost uniform opposition to it.[177]

Rockefeller's influence is quite clear. Despite the opposition from such heavyweights in the administration such as the Treasury secretary, director of the Office of Management and Budget (OMB), and chair of Council of Economic Advisers, Rockefeller was able to win over the president. Ford argued, "Nelson and I were isolated. Alan Greenspan, Jim Lynn, Frank Zarb and others were all opposed to it. I believe that it was a good approach, and frankly, had it been enacted four years ago, we would be much further along in the development of our synthetic fuel programs today."[178]

Rockefeller's success was short lived. Those opposed to the EIA persisted in lobbying Ford to reverse his decision. Ford stated, "As a matter of fact, those that didn't agree with Nelson after I'd made the decision persisted and wanted me to reverse my decision. So I listened not only in a group, but listened individually and that way I got the maximum input from talented people who were in the Oval Office."[179] Rockefeller was appalled that the staff would persist in their opposition after the president made his decision. Recalling the trip to San Francisco where Ford would announce his support for EIA, the vice president stated, "But right through the trip out to the West Coast where he was going to put it in his speech they were trying to cut it down, whittle it down. And then at the last minute Frank Zarb became a convert with me, at the last minute they canceled, the White House did, Frank Zarb's putting out background sheets which explained it so nobody ever knew what it was. And then the President never mentioned it again."[180] The inclusion of a fact sheet is considered a standard operating procedure when announcing a presidential program and this was surprisingly missing.[181] James Cannon, an assistant on the Domestic Council, also noted that those opposed did everything to undermine the EIA. "A handful of White House staffers berated the plan to the press, and we never got anywhere with it."[182] Ford was annoyed by the efforts of some of his staff to undermine the EIA. "They [Alan Greenspan and Roderick Hills] tried to kill [the EIA] out of the speech. . . . They rode all the way till the 'plane was on the landing field trying to cut it out.' Finally, he [Ford] just put his foot down and said: 'No, it is going to stay.'"[183] If significant opposition existed in the administration, it was even worse in Congress. "EIA legislation faced stiff opposition in a Congress that had shown itself throughout 1975 unwilling to enact Ford administration energy proposals."[184] Furthermore, an election year was quickly approaching, and the Democratic majority in Congress would be less willing to support proposals from a Republican administration.

Rockefeller was frustrated that the administration was not promoting the legislation publicly or with Congress. "Little was being done by senior members of the administration to push for legislative hearings."[185] Rockefeller was informed that "there is no evidence that an overall strategy for promoting EIA either on the Hill or among the public has been

62 / Emerging from the Shadows

developed."[186] Therefore, Rockefeller asked the president for permission in one of their weekly meetings to make a series of appearances in support of EIA and to seek support from the business sector and Congress, which Ford approved.[187]

Rockefeller undertook the lead role in lobbying Congress. His efforts with Congress were mixed. Even though Rockefeller "pressed hard, no hearings were forthcoming in the House committees."[188] He was more successful with the Senate. Senator William Proxmire, chair of the Committee on Banking, Housing and Urban Affairs, agreed to hearings. Rockefeller even made a "rare vice presidential appearance" as a witness and is one of only three vice presidents to give congressional testimony by this point in time.[189] His appearance was overshadowed by the conspicuous absence of Simon, Greenspan, or Lynn. "Given the massive nature of the administration's proposal, the absence of such influential witnesses (who would normally have been expected to appear in support of the administration) served to underscore the disputed nature of the EIA within the administration."[190] This impacted its chances in Congress when it was obvious that there was mixed support for EIA in the White House.

Unfortunately, Rockefeller's efforts were not enough, and the bill never moved forward in Congress. Peter Wallison, counsel for Rockefeller, argues that the delay in Rockefeller's confirmation as vice president negatively impacted the EIA. "Had the Energy Independence Authority proposal been developed for inclusion in the 1975 State of the Union Message, it would have been less vulnerable and isolated and would have been pushed into the legislative process much sooner."[191] Rockefeller also hurt his own proposal by insisting that a review group within the Domestic Council be created. While this was meant to provide legitimacy to the proposal and counter the opposition, instead it emboldened the opposition. It had the effect of "arousing instincts of 'territorial imperative' within units that perceived these efforts as trespass[ing] on their own areas of jurisdiction" and the opposition became especially intense and "time-consuming to overcome."[192] In essence, it caused great institutional conflict and delayed a presidential initiative.

Rockefeller's attempts to develop, promote, and establish the Energy Independence Authority is rather instructive about vice presidential influence. First, Vice President Rockefeller demonstrated significant personal influence when it came to the president. President Ford approved of Rockefeller's efforts on the matter, approved of the creation of a review group, approved of Rockefeller's proposal, and finally approved of his lobbying efforts on behalf of the program. However, this was not enough. Rockefeller's influence was countered by situational and institutional constraints, namely, a Democratic Congress unwilling to support a Republican administration in the lead-up to a presidential election year and an influential White House staff who sought to undermine the vice president's efforts. Where Rockefeller saw the system as "sandbagging" him, others in the White House saw it as their responsibility to staff out proposals to best serve the president. This was exactly how the White House staffing system operated.[193] Staffing out proposals is an important aspect of the policy process in normal White House operations, which ensures the president receives expert advice from the most senior advisers in an administration.[194] This process provides an opportunity for every assistant to the president who has a stake in the policy proposal to offer input.[195] Staffing out policy proposals can also move it beyond the White House to the cabinet departments that might have a responsibility to execute the policy, something that is normally carried out by the OMB.[196] These vetting procedures are in place to save the White House and the president from making careless mistakes.[197] Nonetheless, Rockefeller may have seen this as a personal slight but as Cheney recalled, "I was the source of much of his frustration, and from my perspective, it wasn't personal it was professional. I think from his perspective it was personal."[198] He went on to state, "He believed deeply that I was out deliberately to make life unpleasant for him."[199]

Domestic Council

The Domestic Council had its origins in the Nixon administration.[200] It was conceived in 1969 to bring together a small group of professionals in charge of domestic policy to evaluate competing policies "against each other and against available resources, and integrated for maximum effectiveness."[201] Similar to the National Security Council, the Domestic Council included statutory membership whereby the president would serve as chair, and Council members would include the vice president; the secretaries of Treasury, Agriculture, Commerce, Interior, Health, Education, and Welfare, Labor, Transportation, Housing and Urban Development; heads of several federal agencies; and the attorney general with an appointed executive director to manage the professional staffers.[202] An organization that spanned the whole scope of domestic policy for an administration had

64 / Emerging from the Shadows

the potential for great influence. After all, it was established to coordinate all domestic policy and be a "strategic policy-making" unit.[203]

Up until Rockefeller, vice presidential involvement in the Domestic Council was both shallow and empty; no opportunity existed for the vice president to coordinate or develop policy. Ford intended to change this when he promised Rockefeller meaningful responsibilities as vice president. Ford wanted to "harness" Rockefeller's decades-long executive experience and "long association with policy planning, working with problems, [and] problem solving."[204] "His [Ford] preliminary discussions with Rockefeller during the August 17 telephone conversation had essentially accorded to him the principal administration role in the development of domestic policy, a role that was to be the domestic counterpart to Henry Kissinger's in the areas of national security and foreign policy. As the principal actor in the domestic-policy area, Rockefeller's assumption of the vice presidency held high promise that the vice presidential office would become elevated to a much higher stature and status."[205] The position of vice chair was created to achieve Ford's intent and sent a message that the vice president would have more direct involvement in the Council than previous Vice Presidents Agnew and Ford.[206] Based on these conversations, Rockefeller saw his principal role being the development of policy proposals for the administration to address the needs of the country.[207]

One of Rockefeller's first tasks was to find a replacement for the departing executive director, Kenneth Cole.[208] This provided a terrific opportunity for the newly confirmed vice president to bring his own people into the organization and tighten his control over it. He brought in people like James Cannon, Dick Parsons, Dick Dunham, and Art Quern to serve as professional staff on the Domestic Council. James Cannon, a longtime aide, assumed responsibilities as executive director.[209] With his executive director selected, Rockefeller began the task of organizing the Council. According to Ford, "He [Rockefeller] also wanted to organize the council as an autonomous unit that reported directly to him."[210] In fact, before Rockefeller named his own people to the Council, he had hoped to serve as both the vice chair and the executive director, a proposal that was clearly untenable to the White House staff.[211] A memo from Dick Cheney through Donald Rumsfeld to the president outlines the difficulty of such a proposal as early as January 20, 1975. The ideas presented in the memo would in effect form the basis of Rumsfeld's opposition to all of Rockefeller's proposals regarding the organization and staffing of the Domestic Council.[212]

Rockefeller ran up against opposition on both these fronts from the president's chief of staff, Donald Rumsfeld.[213] According to Ford, Rumsfeld opposed Rockefeller's insistence on converting the Council into an autonomous unit that reported to the vice president, because he feared "there was not enough time in the day" for the vice president to do all the things he was required to do.[214] Rumsfeld argued, "My concern about the President having Nelson Rockefeller be the Domestic Council head, was that basically the same concern that I had with the President trying to be his own Chief of Staff. There weren't enough hours in the day."[215] Rockefeller wanted to have operational control so as to create an organization that was run by capable staffers who ensured "the paper work is run smoothly."[216] The process would not work for Rumsfeld and he told the vice president, "That is not the way we work around here."[217] He wanted to be involved in all the details and wanted the flow of paper going through him.[218] Rumsfeld felt it would be a mistake to allow it to operate outside "the organization that he [Rumsfeld] had set up and that he controlled."[219] He argued that as the person responsible for organizing and managing the White House, he had to have control.[220] Furthermore, Rockefeller was not strongly suited to coordinate because his experience as an executive required him to make decisions, not coordinate processes.[221]

Other White House staffers, beyond Rumsfeld, voiced significant concerns over the vice president running the Domestic Council and making decisions on policy.[222] Regardless, Rockefeller felt he knew much more than Rumsfeld and other White House staffers when it came to domestic policy and politics.[223] Therefore, Rockefeller bypassed Rumsfeld by writing a memo to the president on his ideas for organizing the Council, which included the appointment of James Cannon as executive director and Richard Dunham as deputy director, and with a concept that more closely aligned with its original intent.[224] When Rockefeller presented the memo to the president, Ford stated, "I want this. I want you to do this."[225]

Ford took the memo and within a short time Rockefeller received the memo back with a host of changes that he attributed to Rumsfeld.[226] Rockefeller went to the president and told him that he could not "do it on that basis, it won't work for you" and "I cannot be useful to you unless your staff is enthusiastic and supportive of what you want me to do." Ford ended up siding with Rockefeller and signed off on the original order created by the vice president by issuing an executive order.[227] Ford stated, "After three or four unhappy meetings, I made the decision to go

66 / Emerging from the Shadows

along with Nelson. The paper would have to flow through Don as chief of staff, but Nelson would be in charge of domestic policy."[228]

This win, despite the opposition, demonstrates Rockefeller's influence with Ford. However, Rumsfeld continued to "undercut" the vice president, as Rockefeller would state on numerous occasions.[229] A perpetual state of "tension" now existed between the vice president and the president's chief of staff.[230]

On the personnel front, Rumsfeld opposed the appointment of James Cannon as executive director and instead wanted his own person in the position.[231] As Cannon recalls, "After a contest that was brief but divisive, Rockefeller won, and I was appointed by the President."[232] It was not a complete win for Rockefeller. He wanted James Cavanaugh, a holdover from the Nixon administration, fired, and he tasked James Cannon with the responsibility.[233] After seeing Cavanaugh still present, Rockefeller asked Cannon, "Why haven't you gotten rid of Cavanaugh?" to which Cannon argued there was resistance from Rumsfeld.[234] Cannon stated, "Rummy [Rumsfeld] says that this would be a disaster to this whole operation, that he knows all this, that this stuff is all going through very smoothly," and "I have made a commitment to him that I would keep him and that we would have two deputies and that he would do the papers."[235] Rockefeller was furious that Cannon would back down and make a "commitment to Rumsfeld without talking to [him]."[236] Cannon told him that he could not change things without their being "a major break and a fight in the White House."[237] Rockefeller chose to do nothing and accepted Cavanaugh's position as deputy director of operations, which he viewed as a big mistake. Fractionalization that appeared in other parts of the White House would now exist in the Domestic Council and it pushed the "whole machinery in the hands of the organization who had been there before."[238] He found himself trying to make changes against an institutional framework led by Rumsfeld, who was resistant to change.[239] "There wasn't any meshing of Rumsfeld's West Wing organization and Rockefeller. Nothing. This developed into some tension."[240] This battle with Rumsfeld set the basic pattern for their relationship moving forward.[241]

While Rockefeller realized some early successes, the institutional constraints remained too difficult to overcome, and as time went on Rockefeller realized that Ford's intent would fail to materialize because of the institutional framework that was already in place when he arrived.[242] The fractionalization that Rockefeller observed in the White House organization had bled over to the Domestic Council and made it difficult to pull everything together under its auspices. Rockefeller stated, "[In] domestic policy you can't separate the economic side from the social side, you can't separate energy from economics. They all have to be pulled together somewhere and that is what this council was supposed to be."[243] Furthermore, he felt that Rumsfeld's intent was quite different, and that the president's chief of staff wanted the Domestic Council to be a "paper shuffling staff."[244]

Rockefeller had to face the reality that the Domestic Council had "lost its capacity for leadership and for service to the President."[245] He sought to use the Domestic Council to assert his influence and continue to serve the president. First, as mentioned earlier, Rockefeller utilized the Domestic Council to develop and propose the EIA, which took up a considerable amount of his time. Second, he also decided to give a series of speeches around the country on topics ranging from health care, welfare, foreign policy, and military affairs.[246] Ford gave permission to Rockefeller to give these speeches with the understanding that copies be given to the president after the speeches were completed.[247] Rockefeller stated, "He [Ford] was unique as a President to his Vice President. He let me go out and make a series of speeches. What other President of the United States would do this?"[248] This was especially unique because he made clear to Ford that at times the speeches would differ with the administration's positions.[249] Regardless, Ford was happy that Rockefeller would give the speeches, and even if they differed with the administration, he thought it would be "very useful" and he ended up being "crazy" about them.[250]

In coordination with the speeches, Rockefeller held meetings around the country, under the auspices of the Domestic Council to engage the public on their concerns and problems that the country faced.[251] The meetings were personally presided over by Rockefeller, and he made a point of bringing cabinet members to the meetings as well.[252] He saw the speeches and meetings as a two-prong strategy for bypassing the institutional constraints at the White House while still being able to present the president with policy statements and ideas.[253] Rockefeller assembled a book of his policy recommendations, including transcripts from the meetings, which allowed him to continue in his efforts outside of what he called "Rumsfeld's control."[254] Despite his efforts, he was left with the impression that the policy recommendations were taken from the president by Rumsfeld before the president had a chance to read them.[255]

The tensions that existed and Rockefeller's frustration with the Domestic Council's inability to meet the president's intent made it untenable for

68 / Emerging from the Shadows

him to continue serving as vice chair. Rockefeller felt he achieved, rather circuitously, his purpose, which was to provide policy recommendations to the president and develop proposals for the 1976 State of the Union address.[256]

Rockefeller came to the realization that Ford could not grant him authority over domestic policy.[257] James Cannon concluded that "no president can give up control over domestic policy any more than he can give up control over foreign policy."[258] Cannon suspects the decision to give control over domestic policy to the vice president was not well thought out, since the decision was made only ten days after Ford assumed office.[259] Rumsfeld confirmed this suspicion as well when he said Ford was making decisions as a legislator early on in his term and that he did not truly understand the consequences of making such an arrangement with Rockefeller.[260]

The reality of the situation became apparent early on when Roy Ash asserted that the Domestic Council did not assume responsibility for economic policy. This confirmed the fractionalization in policy development that Rockefeller witnessed early in his tenure, which made it difficult for him to assume control over the entire domestic apparatus. Rockefeller discussed the failure of the Domestic Council to achieve its intent in a memo to President Ford on December 16, 1975, the same day he resigned from the Domestic Council.[261] In the memo, he states that the president authorized the Domestic Council to be the "counterpart in the domestic field of the National Security Council."[262] However, the current organization does not allow for a consolidation of function; rather, the president is advised on domestic policy from disparate organizations such as the Economic Policy Board, Energy Resources Council, the Council of Economic Advisers, and the Office of Management and Budget.[263] Rockefeller states, "There is no overall conceptual planning and staff responsibility on the domestic front to assist you. Domestic problems and needs are not solely problems of economics or energy or finance or social needs. They . . . must be attacked by an organizational unit that also has these multi-faceted characteristics."[264] Having recognized that he achieved what he could among the constraints, and while he was still resigning from the Council, he addressed the role of the White House organization in domestic policy development.[265] He recommended that staff responsibilities be centralized for economic, social, and fiscal policies under the Domestic Council and that relationships be clarified in the future.[266] It is clear that the organizational constraints existed before Rockefeller even stepped foot in the vice president's office and only intensified over the course of his tenure. He argued that the Domestic Council was largely used to put out fires.[267] Given the constraints, it was impossible for Rockefeller to assume the pinnacle of vice presidential influence that so many had expected.

The next sections will analyze Rockefeller's roles against the four dynamics laid out in Chapter 2. This will provide a more comprehensive understanding of Rockefeller's influence and those factors that both increased and diminished it. The discussion above hints at the influence he attained early in his tenure; however, his influence quickly diminished as he faced institutional and situational constraints that challenged it.

Interpersonal Dynamic

The relationship between the president and vice president forms the foundation for the existence of influence in the vice presidency or lack thereof. As the precursor to vice presidential influence, it often works in conjunction with the other dynamics described. Up until the modern era, the president's and vice president's relationship could best be described as shallow and limited. Vice presidential selection usually followed an approach that was similar to the one used prior to the modern era—pick a running mate who will assist the presidential candidate in winning the election. Very little attention was paid to governing compatibility and, thus, vice presidents were quickly locked out of the process—just ask Harry Truman and Lyndon Johnson, among others.

Rockefeller was perhaps one of the first vice presidents chosen for the purpose of governing rather than winning an election. Recall the discussion earlier regarding Rockefeller's selection. Ford chose Rockefeller because he wanted someone who could help him heal the country and increase the American people's confidence in their government. In addition, he sought someone who he could feel comfortable with and who could assist him on domestic policy and staffing arrangements in the White House. Furthermore, Rockefeller's selection was unique in that he was appointed by a president who unexpectedly ascended to the presidency without an election. Therefore, vote getting was not part of the calculus. This does not mean that Ford was immune to public opinion in his selection of a vice president. Rather, Ford needed to gauge support among party elites, specifically members of Congress and the Republican Party leadership, as a proxy for public opinion.

The lack of electoral incentives allowed Ford to concentrate on who was the best person to govern with, who he could form a true partnership with, and who he was most comfortable with on a personal basis. News articles at the time picked up on how this might allow for greater vice presidential influence. Early on in Rockefeller's tenure, a *Washington Post* article stated, "The bedrock of Rockefeller's growing influence within the administration is a personal relationship with Mr. Ford that intimates of both men claim is unique in the modern presidency."[268] The personal and professional relationship of the two principal actors is the bedrock or foundation for influence.

While Rockefeller and Ford were no strangers to each other prior to the nomination and selection process, one could not argue that they were close friends, politically or otherwise. Ford stated, "I've never really been an imminent close political friend of Nelson Rockefeller. We sort of were on different tracks. . . . We had different paths that we were following."[269] Although they had different professional trajectories, their paths did cross from time to time, and it was in these interactions where mutual admiration developed. Rockefeller and Ford first became acquainted with each other after Rockefeller left the governorship in New York and was working on his Commission on Critical Choices.[270] At this time, Ford was serving as minority leader in the House of Representatives and proved to be very helpful to Rockefeller as he sought federal funding for the Commission. Ford provided him with political advice and referenced that the best way to ensure the feasibility of federal funding for the Commission would be to work with Mike Mansfield, the Senate majority leader, and Hugh Scott, the Senate minority leader, and Ford helped arrange the meetings.[271] Rockefeller, taken aback by Ford's cooperativeness and responsiveness, stated,

> So I was organizing this commission and I wanted to have the leaders of Congress and the key people in the administration and so I was considering the possibility of a legislative authorization. So I went to talk in both Houses to the two leaders, majority and minority, and of all the people in the Congress with whom I talked nobody was more responsive to or understanding of the objectives of the commission and its purposes as was then Minority Leader, Gerald R. Ford.[272]

Rockefeller formed the Commission without legislation and asked members of Congress to serve on the Commission, including Gerald Ford.[273] By the time of the Commission's first meeting, Ford had already become the vice president designate, and he showed a keen interest in the Commission and participated in the two-day session as well as a press conference at the end of the session.[274] Rockefeller stated, "And in the press conference he was very generous not seeking to take the limelight in terms of the Vice Presidential candidate but supportive of the efforts of the program."[275] Their brief encounters through the years at various Republican meetings and Republican coordinating committees, and their work together on the Commission of Critical Choices developed into what Ford stated was a "warm mutually affectionate relationship."[276] Ford also saw firsthand how diligent Rockefeller was in creating something from nothing, his passion for solving the nation's problems and garnering support for his programs— something that would come in handy in a very brief time, unbeknownst to him. These encounters set the stage for their mutual admiration, which would continue in the White House and beyond.

This does not mean there were not bumps along the way in terms of their relationship. Institutional arrangements and staffing issues at the White House, which will be discussed in a subsequent section, stressed their relationship, which for all intents and purposes was strong. Furthermore, Ford's management style proved to impede the fulfillment of the promises made to Rockefeller regarding the influence he would have over domestic policy. These challenges would strain the relationship; nonetheless they weathered those difficulties and their admiration for one another remained unchanged.

Ford's management style further aggravated Rockefeller's already tense relationship with White House Staff, in particular, Donald Rumsfeld. Rockefeller stated, "I think he wanted to be an efficient administrator and I think he recognized he had no real administrative experience or background in conducting of the affairs of the executive responsibility in either domestic or international affairs."[277] Based on their conversations, he knew that the president wanted to build structure into the White House, but his collegial management style made this quite difficult. As Rockefeller argued, "nobody [was] really in charge" and Ford's style made it difficult for him to be assertive which allowed jealousies to develop and intensify with time.[278] Rockefeller felt that it was impossible for "him [Ford] to achieve what he wanted simply because of the jealousies which would be aroused and because of the structure of the government—the structure of the White House which had been restructured from the centralized control under Nixon to a committee structure."[279] He believed that the

72 / Emerging from the Shadows

collegial system or committee structure approach opened Ford up to be taken advantage of by his staff.[280] His fear was that his staff "abused his patience" and abused his collegial approach to the presidency.[281]

Even though Rockefeller was quite vocal with the president in regard to the problems he saw with the White House structure and organization, he did not place blame with the president, and this enabled their relationship to continue on a good footing. Instead, he placed the blame on the president's White House Staff. Cheney argued,

> Ford was always sensitive to Rockefeller's situation, having counted his months as vice president as a generally miserable experience. But Rockefeller never blamed Ford for his disappointments in office. He decided that the cause of his troubles were elsewhere—with Don Rumsfeld and that deputy of his [Cheney]. In my case, I suppose it must have [been] a little galling to see his grand ideas sandbagged by some staff aide who was exactly half his age and who had never been elected to anything.[282]

Throughout this time, Rockefeller's frustration remained focused primarily on Rumsfeld, and to a lesser extent on Cheney, thus allowing the president and vice president to continue on good terms. Ford recognized this: "Our relations were always very good, and he never accused me of being a part of any of that."[283] Ford continued, "He knew he could be very tough, he could be in disagreement with me, but he knew that those disagreements and his strength never destroyed our personal relationship. I think basically, outside of some of the political things and his unhappiness with the way the staff operated, we always had a super, personal man-to-man relationship."[284] It was palpable to all, including the news media. An article in the *National Journal* states, "Indeed, Ford and Rockefeller continue to carry on an amiable personal relationship. The Vice President still meets privately with the President at least one hour each week. It is at the staff level, however, that the trouble is recognized."[285]

The archives show only glowing references to each other and include notes to each other that exemplify their mutual feelings. Whether it is Ford thanking Rockefeller for his counsel and outstanding leadership or Rockefeller praising Ford and thanking him for his kind comments, handwritten notes from both the vice president and president litter the archives.[286] Even those close to the president and vice president noticed the strength of their relationship. Hugh Morrow stated, "My observation was that no two men got along better in the world, as men" and Ford replied to Morrow's comment by stating "that's right. We had a super, super relationship."[287] Suffice it to say, their relationship was strong despite the turf battles and jealousies that developed. They had a comfortable relationship, in which they could talk openly.[288] Ford commented on numerous occasions that the best thing he did as president was nominating Rockefeller to be vice president.[289] Ford stated, "You know, there is a somewhat trite slogan that says, 'Ford has a better idea.' Well, I am here tonight to tell you that one of the best ideas this Ford ever had was nominating Nelson Rockefeller to be Vice President of the United States."[290] Rockefeller never regretted serving as vice president either and stated that his greatest satisfaction was serving the country during a critical time.[291]

The strength of their relationship despite any setbacks Rockefeller encountered demonstrates that the prerequisite for vice presidential influence is a strong personal and professional relationship between the principals. A strong relationship increases the likelihood that the vice president will have the capacity to exercise influence. In the case of Rockefeller, the relationship with Ford set the conditions for a more influential vice president. The archives demonstrate that there was not only an expectation of this among those in the media but also within political circles. Ford's ease with Rockefeller made it possible for him to grant authority to his new vice president to coordinate the formulation of domestic policy as vice chair of the Domestic Council. This was a first for a vice president. While Vice Presidents Spiro Agnew and Gerald Ford served on the Domestic Council, they did so only as council members and lacked a substantive role.[292] A president truly sets the stage for the vice president and the role he or she will play. Ford's personal feelings about the vice presidency made the prospect of a more influential vice president possible and led to high expectations that this would be the case, and for a short while Rockefeller demonstrated influence, but that influence would begin to wane.

Situational Dynamic

The political conditions and the circumstances at the time of Nixon's resignation and the subsequent ascension of Ford to the presidency, presented Ford with numerous challenges. A crisis of public confidence in the government plagued the country and seemed to be intensifying by the minute. Furthermore, the relationship between the presidency and the Congress had deteriorated in the latter part of the Nixon administration. This presented Ford with a conundrum—who should he nominate as vice president who could assist him in healing the country's wounds? As his first presidential act, he nominated Nelson Rockefeller. The situation was ripe for a candidate like Rockefeller. First, the President needed to nominate someone who had a certain level of gravitas. Rockefeller had been on the political scene for decades having served under both Republican and Democratic presidents. Furthermore, Rockefeller was a household name. There would be no need for the president to introduce and educate the public on his choice. Second, Rockefeller maintained good relations with members of both political parties and was someone who could easily make it through the nomination hearings in a body controlled by the opposing party. Furthermore, he could serve as a bridge to the more liberal wing of the Republican Party, since Ford was more conservative than Rockefeller. Last, he had significant executive and domestic policy experience, which Ford lacked. Rockefeller could simultaneously assist the president in tackling the problems of the country while working with the president to attract talented people to serve in the administration, which was one of the things Ford expressed to Rockefeller when he nominated him.[293]

The conditions produced the expectation that Rockefeller would be the most influential vice president at that time.[294] For the most part, that is exactly the footing his vice presidency started on. Political conditions and recent national events combined with the strong presidential–vice presidential relationship provided the foundation for exercising influence. As a result, Rockefeller achieved some key successes early in his tenure. First, he successfully received Ford's approval on the organization and structure of the Domestic Council, even against the opposition of Donald Rumsfeld. Second, Rockefeller was able to replace the executive director of the Domestic Council with a person of his choosing, even though Rumsfeld opposed his choice. These two early examples of Rockefeller's success demonstrate his influence with the president, especially considering that Ford went against the recommendations of his senior advisers to side with his vice president. However, within his first year, events began to shift away from Rockefeller's favor and his standing within the administration and the greater political world changed, contributing to his diminished influence.

While Rockefeller achieved some victories in his showdown with Rumsfeld on the Domestic Council, 1975 brought with it concerns over the economy and the burgeoning federal budget.[295] As a result, Rockefeller's input on new public policies to address the nation's issues, a key aspect of his job as vice president, was curtailed and resulted in a loss of influence. Neither Rockefeller nor the Domestic Council's executive director, James Cannon, were invited to the Sunday meeting.[296] The meeting was the brainchild of Don Rumsfeld and Alan Greenspan; at the meeting Rumsfeld argued that capping the federal budget for 1976 at $395 billion and including tax cuts and spending cuts would be a "great political boon."[297] This was a direct repudiation of Rockefeller's domestic policy operation and a reflection of the institutional constraints that Rockefeller faced. Rockefeller was an expansionist, a doer, an innovator. His interest was in solving public problems. That took money. But President Ford was determined to cut the cost of the federal government. "The two men had contradictory objectives."[298] Rockefeller was known as a big spender, and one who had executed numerous large policy projects as governor of New York.[299] Cheney recalled that the president issued a mandate known as "No New Starts," and that few exceptions to this order would be granted.[300] "I had to defend this policy many times, and against no one more often than the vice president."[301] Of course, Rockefeller would face this more than anyone in the administration, especially when the key function as vice chair of the Domestic Council was to evaluate policy proposals and make new recommendations to the president. This ran directly against Ford's and Rockefeller's agreement regarding domestic policy at the time of his nomination. Cheney stated, "When President Ford placed him in charge of domestic policy, new federal initiatives seemed to the vice president like the natural order of the day."[302] "Rockefeller was always initiating programs and Ford basically was very cautious of new programs and was more careful with the taxpayers' dollars."[303] Ultimately, the key driver in deciding the viability of any Rockefeller proposals submitted through the Domestic Council, or otherwise, was the budget and the "No New Starts" policy, making the viability of Rockefeller's proposals even more elusive.[304]

Facing a White House structure that was intent on executing the president's mandate, Rockefeller tried to bypass White House channels to propose his recommendations directly to the president. Instead of resulting in more favorable treatment, the end was almost always the same—inconsistent with the president's mandate.[305] Cheney recalled,

> Listening to a few of those pitches myself, I could see why Ford liked and admired this man, who had natural charm and a forceful personality. After his meetings with the vice president, Ford would often call me into the Oval Office, hand

76 / Emerging from the Shadows

> me Rockefeller's latest proposal, and say, "Dick, what do we do
> with this?" And each time I would reply, "Well, Mr. President,
> we'll staff it out." This meant that the idea would be circulated
> for general review, including a cost assessment by OMB, and
> that it would invariably come back with the answer that the
> proposal had been found inconsistent with our policy of No
> New Starts.[306]

While Rockefeller attempted to bypass the White House staff, which he viewed as hostile to him, he still faced the obstacle of working around the president's mandate of "No New Starts." Nonetheless, the vice president was still able to secure the president's blessings for his proposal on the Energy Independence Authority and the early stages of the domestic policy options review he undertook in 1975.[307] This demonstrates both Rockefeller's early influence with the president and why it precipitously declined over the course of 1975 and 1976.

The conditions that made Rockefeller so appealing from a political standpoint also led to his demise. The equation changed between the time of Rockefeller's appointment and Ford's nomination in 1976.[308] In 1974, Ford needed to ensure his vice presidential nominee would have no difficulty getting confirmed by Congress. As stated earlier, Rockefeller was considerably more liberal than Ford, thus endearing him to the more liberal wing of the Republican Party and even to some in the Democratic Party. Furthermore, his name recognition eased the confirmation process and made him even more palatable to the American electorate. However, less than a year later, Ford found himself in a difficult position in his election efforts in 1976. He was encountering a primary challenge from the former governor of California, Ronald Reagan, who was considerably more conservative than Ford, thus, now making Rockefeller a political liability and ultimately causing him to be dropped from the Republican ticket.[309] "The calculation was that Rockefeller would cost him votes in the southern states so that's why Rockefeller was asked to announce that he wasn't running as vice president [in 1976]."[310] He found himself increasingly estranged from the president's reelection efforts and Ford gave in to pressure from his campaign consultants and White House counselors who asked Rockefeller to remove himself from consideration, thus freeing the president to choose a nominee who would be more appealing to the conservative wing of the party, to weather the primary challenge by Reagan.[311] "Accordingly, it was argued by some of Ford's intimate advisers that it would be advisable for him to disengage himself from Rockefeller, in his pursuit of the nomination, to avoid alienating conservative delegates who still harbored resentment against Rockefeller for his staunch liberal campaigns against Nixon in 1960 and Goldwater in 1964."[312] Even before Rockefeller was forced off the ticket, Ford's campaign manager, Bo Callaway, began making more and more damaging public comments about the dangers Rockefeller posed to Ford's election effort.[313] Callaway referred to Rockefeller as the president's "number-one problem" in securing the Republican nomination.[314] While all of this was transpiring, Ford remained silent and failed to publicly put an end to the criticisms his vice president faced.

While facing diminishing influence because of the increasing likelihood that he would not remain on the ticket in 1976, Rockefeller also faced institutional obstacles within the White House that further reduced influence starting in 1975 and continuing through 1976. The new situation Rockefeller faced, a mere six months into his tenure as vice president, was an increasingly hostile White House staff and a White House structure that was opposed to his role in domestic policy, a "No New Starts" mandate that minimized his role as head of the Domestic Council, and a political effort to neutralize Rockefeller to assist Ford in winning the nomination. These efforts both from in and outside of the White House had the same effect—alienating the vice president and reducing his influence.

Institutional Dynamic

By the 1970s, vice presidents received their own line item in the federal budget, rather than relying on funds appropriated as president of the Senate.[315] The budget also increased dramatically during the Ford vice presidency.[316] These changes provided the vice president with a distinct institutional identity that enabled the office's occupants to exercise greater control over staff and resources, thus increasing their capability to exercise influence. Four institutional advantages were now available to modern vice presidents that previously did not exist: the ability to attract quality staff, "protection and a vantage point in the White House policy process," a stable stream of resources to assist the vice president with his or her advisory function, and the ability to prepare for emergency transitions should anything happen to the president.[317]

Rockefeller was a recipient of all these advantages and utilized his budget as a springboard from which to exercise influence. In 1975,

Rockefeller had a budget of $1,493,615 with a total of sixty-six salaried positions.[318] This number reached as high as seventy during his tenure.[319] He also had eight individuals, part of his military office, who were detailed to him but were not included in his budget because their salaries were paid for by their respective agencies.[320] Rockefeller also enticed fourteen of his aides from his gubernatorial office to join him at the White House, and all of them held top positions in the office.[321]

As president of the Senate, the vice president was authorized a $550,000 budget, which was required to be spent solely on personnel salaries.[322] Additionally, Rockefeller utilized the Domestic Council to supplement his staff and resources since many of his activities were tied to the Domestic Council.[323] His staff mirrored the president's staff in terms of organization and responsibilities, which has become accepted practice in the modern vice presidency.[324] Rockefeller's staff included a press secretary, national security adviser, counselors, a congressional affairs adviser, speech writers, domestic policy advisers, among others.[325]

President Ford also introduced opportunities for Rockefeller to take on a more influential role. Ford made it clear to his staff, before Rockefeller took office, that he was intent on giving his vice president a "meaningful role" in his administration.[326] White House staff who worked for Ford as vice president recognized the difficulties in achieving this intent if they continued the practices from the Nixon administration. Jack Marsh, an adviser to Ford, told his boss, "Based on my experience when you were Vice President, I feel there was a lack of communication and interrelationship with the Nixon White House."[327] Marsh went on to state, "I am of the view that considerable thought should be given to the relationship between the two offices with far broader contact and endeavors than have existed in the past. Basically, I think the Vice President and his people must be treated more as insiders than outsiders."[328] This advice echoed Ford's thinking on the matter, and he asked Marsh to come up with suggestions. Suggestions to achieve Ford's intent included: representatives of the vice president be included in junior and senior White House staff meetings, access provided for "exchange of information" between OMB, Domestic Council, and the vice president's office; close coordination between the president's and vice president's press offices; representatives of the vice president be included in meetings on congressional relations, energy, and economic issues; and vice presidential input on major presidential addresses, policy statements, and State of the Union message.[329] Marsh stated, "I would be one of the first to admit broader incorporation into staff operations of the Vice President would be a departure from the past; however, I am also of the view that greater incorporation is necessary to achieve greater effectiveness in that office."[330]

Ford incorporated all these recommendations in his approach to the vice president and his staff. In an interview, early on as vice president, Rockefeller commented on Ford's willingness to include his staff in critical meetings when he stated, "He has been extraordinary on that. He has invited members of my staff to attend his staff's meetings and he said to me this morning that every morning he wanted our representatives. That is unheard of."[331] As a result, Rockefeller's chief of staff, Ann Whitman, and James Cannon attended these morning meetings, and both contributed fully, never "hesitating" to provide input.[332]

Ford truly embraced the concept of including Rockefeller's staff and sought out the vice president's view and perspective. Rockefeller stated, "As Vice President, he has been very generous in giving me the opportunity at all times and on all subjects to express totally freely and openly my views."[333] He was given the opportunity to provide his views in private due to the standing weekly meeting between him and Ford, in which he drafted the agenda and he "adds his voice" in cabinet and NSC meetings, in which he is fairly outspoken.[334] As evidenced, this was not just empty rhetoric on Ford's behalf but a true desire to include the vice president and his staff in all aspects of the administration.

Initially, these institutional arrangements benefited Rockefeller and increased the likelihood that he would be a more influential vice president. His initial battles over staffing of the Domestic Council and its operation proved to many that the vice president could win these battles and had the president's ear. Despite Ford's intent and Rockefeller's early successes, institutional obstacles began to develop early in Rockefeller's tenure that limited the vice president's ability to exercise influence.

In many ways, the uniqueness of what was being proposed for the Ford/Rockefeller relationship, in terms of the vice president's role, represented a wholesale change from what had been done previously. Changes to political processes within an entrenched institution, such as the White House, are bound to face strong and powerful "vested interests" that are resistant to change.[335] Rockefeller (the reformer in this case), in order to institute a change in the normal processes of the White House, which rarely if ever allowed a vice president to assume significant responsibility over a policy domain, had to overcome resistance by White House staff. Both Rumsfeld and Cheney had a "vested interest" in ensuring that

Rockefeller did not upset the standard operating procedures that they oversaw. From their perspective, the vice president's new proposed role sought to circumvent existing processes, which would have changed the way the White House operated, threatening their roles as chiefs of staff.

Shortly after Rockefeller's nomination, Ford began to move his own presidential appointees into key White House positions and reorganize the White House's structure.[336] The institutional obstacles began during this reorganization and specifically with the replacement of Al Haig with Donald Rumsfeld.[337] The original agreement that was decided on by the president and vice president regarding the role of the vice president occurred while Donald Rumsfeld was still serving at NATO.[338] By the time Rockefeller was confirmed and took office, Rumsfeld was now serving as chief of staff (although his title was actually coordinator) and he had instituted an organizational structure that made it difficult for the vice president to meet the intent of the agreement.[339] Rockefeller tried to "negotiate" with Rumsfeld regarding a way to function as the president intended but was unsuccessful because their philosophies were diametrically opposed.[340] According to Rockefeller,

> Mr. Rumsfeld's concept of how the people in the White House should function was that they would all be staff people at the beck and call of the President through him. That he would meet with them at these 7:30 and 8 o'clock meetings and would discuss things and then he would take it up with the President and then tell them what the President said. Well . . . to me, this was just a structure for chaos. And, therefore, it became clear to me that for me, as Vice President, to function the way the President wanted as chairman of the Domestic Council and attending these meetings and acting as a staff assistant to Mr. Rumsfeld to get the word from the President through him, where he was not Chief of Staff but merely a coordinator therefore he didn't take responsibility, was out of the question.[341]

Rockefeller then purposefully bypassed Rumsfeld by taking actions directly to the president.[342] And Rumsfeld took an early position that he would "resist efforts by Rockefeller to bypass the system. Rumsfeld's opposition to Rockefeller's plan to personally operate the Domestic Council as a vehicle for coordinating domestic-policy was total and unyielding."[343]

Initially, Ford sided with Rockefeller on the staffing and operationalization of the Domestic Council, even on the EIA that Rumsfeld personally opposed. Nonetheless, although Rockefeller and Ford had a good personal relationship and the vice president had access, it was not enough. For policies to move from proposal to policy, they were required to move through the structure instituted by Rumsfeld, thus leading to changes, delays, and failure. This was seen in the structure of the Domestic Council in which Rockefeller had to capitulate on some of his operational and staffing ideas. This was seen in Rockefeller's recommendations regarding his work on the CIA Commission, which resulted in a drawn-out process but ultimately ended with his original recommendations being accepted. Last, it was seen with the EIA in which Rockefeller had to negotiate with White House staff, who was opposed to the initiative before receiving the president's acceptance and then watching the stated administration policy flounder due to lack of support and unwillingness by the White House staff to work with Congress to lobby for its passage.

To be fair, Rumsfeld was fulfilling his responsibility as chief of staff in which two of the functions is to serve as an administrator and guardian of the White House.[344] According to Richard Allison, an assistant to the vice president, both Rumsfeld and Cheney were looking out for what was in the president's best interest even if their actions seemed to undermine or block Rockefeller.[345] "The mission of Rumsfeld and then Cheney was to make sure Ford was in charge, not Rockefeller."[346] Rumsfeld realized that Rockefeller's experience as a decision maker and never serving in a number-two capacity did not work well with how he executed his role as chief of staff and how the White House worked.[347] Rumsfeld, just like Cheney, was responsible for delivering the bad news to Rockefeller and educating him on how the White House operated, and neither of these went over well. Instead, it increased his animosity toward them.[348]

Rockefeller and Rumsfeld were not friends. Ford stated, "He [Rockefeller] was awfully, firmly convinced that Rummy was the devil."[349] Rockefeller viewed Rumsfeld as a "very bright, able manipulator and maneuverer but not an administrator."[350] Rumsfeld viewed the vice president as a "hell of a guy and very well motivated."[351] Rumsfeld stated, "If there is one thing that I feel badly about during that time, somehow or other I wasn't brilliant enough to figure out how to make that work better."[352]

Rumsfeld was opposed to Rockefeller hiring "outside people" or Rockefeller's own people for the Domestic Council, which he was able to ultimately do with a concession to keep James Cavanaugh on the Council staff.[353] Even Rockefeller's handpicked executive director was no guarantee against Rumsfeld's involvement with the Domestic Council. Rockefeller was faced with the problem of either firing Cannon and risking under-

82 / Emerging from the Shadows

mining confidence in the Domestic Council or just acquiescing and he chose to acquiesce.[354] Cavanaugh's loyalty remained with Rumsfeld, not Rockefeller. Thus Cavanaugh "operated the paper work just exactly as Rumsfeld had wanted."[355] Ultimately, the Domestic Council did not reflect the organization in "shape or form" that the president had envisioned.[356] Rockefeller encapsulates his view of Rumsfeld's opposition and obstruction by stating, "He [Rumsfeld] had already built a structure and had a concept which made it impossible. And then he added the making of it impossible by his opposition and then when I did get through over his opposition he was able to undermine by his outmaneuvering Jim Cannon on the Cavanaugh thing."[357]

The institutional obstacles did not exist solely around Rumsfeld and Rockefeller. Instead, significant backbiting existed at the staff level. One Rockefeller aide, on a condition of anonymity, remarked to the press that "'things haven't gone as we had hoped . . . at times we feel as though our legs are being cut off.'"[358] A presidential assistant commented on Rockefeller and his staff: "'Let's face it, Rockefeller and his people have been a disappointment. They're just hanging on. Where can they go?'"[359] Some have attributed that the animosity on the president's staff was from a belief that "the vice president posed a distinct threat to the established positions" due to the nature of the proposed role for Rockefeller, one which had no precedent in history.[360] Furthermore, Rockefeller's efforts on domestic policy cut across numerous White House agencies and staffers. "He presented a challenge to the tight budgetary positions of the OMB, the CEA, and the treasury department. . . . Rockefeller's policy development activism put him in a challenging and competing posture at the outset."[361] Rockefeller felt that the obstacles he faced from Ford's staff were both "arbitrary and unimaginative."[362]

Rockefeller's views of Dick Cheney were no more flattering. He argued, "Mr. Cheney is just a shadow of Mr. Rumsfeld's."[363] When Cheney took Rumsfeld's position after he became secretary of defense, there was no change in the White House operation. Rockefeller stated, "Cheney was more efficient than Rumsfeld, but he never moved without Rumsfeld. And he was on the phone four or five times a day with him."[364] From Rockefeller's standpoint, no improvements had been made in White House operations. He considered it "amateurish" under Cheney and also felt that it "deteriorated" as well.[365] He felt Ford was becoming increasingly isolated from people by the actions of Cheney.[366] Even with Cheney as chief of staff, Rockefeller thought "Rumsfeld was running the White House from the

Defense Department."[367] Most of the disagreements with Cheney centered on the president's reelection efforts, which will be discussed in the next section, since by this point in his tenure Rockefeller had relinquished control over the Domestic Council.

Ultimately, the institutional constraints that hampered Rockefeller's exercise of responsibility and assertion of influence left him frustrated, not for himself, but for the president. He felt that the "amateurish" White House staff and organization failed in its ability to serve the president. From day one, Rockefeller cautioned Ford about his White House staff, especially Rumsfeld and Cheney. He stated, "I had been telling the President that there were those around him, there were those whom he thought were his friends, who, in my opinion, were not."[368] His statements became even more blunt when he told the president, "Mr. President, there are people who you think are friends who want to see your administration fail, who want to see you not nominated and who, if you are nominated, want to see you defeated."[369] Rockefeller offered to help the president reorganize the West Wing and "clean house," but Ford's response was that he did not agree with the vice president's assertion that it was "as badly run as you [imagine]."[370]

The institutional obstacles that Rockefeller faced were born out of an organization that felt threatened by the scope of authority granted to the vice president and that cut across different agency jurisdictions. The opposition to Rockefeller and his proposals was also born from his strength.[371] For some time, Rockefeller was adept at maneuvering past the institutional obstacles and it contributed to his early successes with the Domestic Council and the EIA. No matter what agreement existed between the president and vice president and no matter how strong their relationship, Rockefeller and Ford had to operate within the same White House system. Some argue that Ford's management style worsened the institutional obstacles for Rockefeller. "The vice president is dependent on the president for his place in the executive branch of government. That lesson is amply demonstrated in the vice presidency of Nelson Rockefeller. The problems and vicissitudes he encountered in his efforts to play an active role as a policy maker in the Ford administration sprang in large measure from the ambivalence, indecision, and imprecision that characterized Ford's leadership style."[372] The intent for the vice presidency and the strength of Ford's and Rockefeller's relationship was no match for an institutional framework that was resistant to change and a president who failed to exert the leadership to ensure it changed. For in the case

84 / Emerging from the Shadows

of the EIA, Ford had publicly endorsed Rockefeller's recommendation as administration policy, but the White House staff failed to support its passage. Rockefeller felt that once a president decided, the entire White House should support it.

Electoral Dynamic

The benefits of Rockefeller joining the Ford administration were apparent during the tumultuous crisis that plagued the country with Watergate and the resignation of a sitting president. However, the situational dynamic changed in the latter part of 1975. Ford, facing election in his own right in 1976, found himself battling the more conservative wing of the Republican Party, represented by Governor Reagan, who was mounting a primary challenge.[373] As a liberal Republican, Rockefeller was no longer an asset but proved to be a liability to Ford's election efforts.[374] Ford's campaign manager Bo Callaway made public statements to this effect in the summer of 1975 when he stated, "The Ford and Rockefeller campaigns are not one and the same" and implied that "Rockefeller was a liability."[375] It added fuel to the fire surrounding the Rumsfeld-Rockefeller relationship, especially since Rockefeller was convinced that Rumsfeld had selected Callaway as Ford's campaign manager and was taking his "marching orders" directly from Rumsfeld.[376]

After this incident, Ford recalled telling Callaway, "The Vice President is very sensitive to the kinds of things you are saying. He is important to us in getting the nomination. I personally have a great fondness for him and a strong allegiance to him. You can't do this anymore."[377] The damage was done. Rockefeller's political legitimacy was called out in the press by the president's campaign manager, thus diminishing his influence. One can understand Rockefeller's suspicions of Rumsfeld's involvement given that Callaway not only recommended that Rumsfeld serve as the White House liaison with the campaign, but Rumsfeld also did have a hand in Callaway's selection as campaign manager.[378] Furthermore, Callaway had made statements that he never did anything "without getting his marching orders from Don Rumsfeld."[379]

By all accounts Rockefeller was a political liability.[380] The political landscape had changed, and Reagan proved to be a legitimate opponent. The Ford campaign staff, as well as White House staff, saw the threat that Rockefeller posed to Ford's chances of winning the nomination. "Clearly, there has been a calculated attempt by the President and his political aides to put some distance between him and Rockefeller, and the vice president is in no position to do anything but go along."[381] Ford acknowledged this by stating, "Don [Rumsfeld] was a total pragmatist and I suspect Don felt that Nelson's potential as a running mate in '76, might have jeopardized my chance to get the nomination."[382] Ford needed to win over conservatives to secure the nomination, and Rockefeller was disliked by the conservative wing of the party.[383] Callaway theorized that the best way to defeat Reagan was to "undercut" his strength in the South, where Rockefeller was least popular, thus demonstrating the desire to drop him from the ticket.[384]

Ford was left with no choice but to ask Rockefeller to withdraw his name from consideration, which he stated was "one of the hardest, face-to-face meetings" he ever had.[385] Later in life, Ford admitted that Rumsfeld pushed the hardest to drop Rockefeller from the ticket; he "was hoping to succeed Rocky on the ticket—'Don was a major factor.'"[386]

Despite his removal from the ticket, the president still needed Rockefeller for his reelection effort. While he was not involved in the development of political strategy for the campaign, he did offer his unsolicited political judgment to Ford during the reelection process.[387] Cheney and the campaign tasked Rockefeller to make appearances in states where Ford was vulnerable and he was stronger,[388] such as New York, New Jersey, the upper Midwest, and West Coast.[389] Rockefeller delivered by securing the New York Delegation for Ford in 1976.[390] He was the linchpin for securing these key delegations.

Although publicly repudiated, Rockefeller maintained some level of influence since the campaign needed him to assist where he could. One sensitive area where Ford asked for Rockefeller's help was with his replacement. Rockefeller stated, "So he [Ford] then wanted to talk to me about working with him on picking a Vice President and he said that he was not taking or leaving any names out including my own. And I figured that he was going to come around which politically, of course, he should have."[391] Ford specifically needed him to act as a liaison with more progressive elements of the party to gauge their acceptance of possible candidates.[392]

Despite all his work to assist Ford's election efforts, the tension with the White House and campaign organizations persisted and resulted in Rockefeller feeling slighted at every turn. An anecdote from the convention demonstrates the treatment Rockefeller received, whether intentional or not. Cheney stated,

86 / Emerging from the Shadows

> Rockefeller let loose on me only once, later on at the 1976 Republican National Convention, after the sound system had mysteriously gone dead in the middle of his speech. Protocol issues earlier in the week—debates about whether it should be Rocky, the sitting vice president, or Bob Dole, the running mate, who joined Ford onstage after his acceptance speech— had left him feeling slighted one too many times. On the final night he spotted me in the corridor beneath the rostrum and saw a fitting target for all his frustrations. He leaned in close and really let me have it, even accusing me of sabotaging his speech. I took my verbal pounding, assured the vice president of my innocence, and got out of there as fast as I could.[393]

Those present during the confrontation recall Rockefeller pounding Cheney on his chest and the young chief of staff was "absolutely chalk white."[394]

After feeling undermined and watching his influence wane due to circumstances beyond his control, Rockefeller was sensitive to any appearance of his diminishment as a person and vice president. Recalling the night at the convention he stated, "And I said, 'look, you so and so, I know what has been going on and I have been taking this all the way through and now it is over. You tell the President for me what has happened here. You tell him I am not going to have anything further to do with his campaign. You can take full credit with Mr. Rumsfeld for what has happened."[395] "It was at that moment that all of his frustration and anger burst forth about what a miserable time he had had as vice president and he blamed a good part of that on me."[396] Rockefeller told Ford, "I have got to tell you the truth, I have had it. These are the final insults tonight that have happened. I love you but I am finished."[397]

Surprisingly, Ford's and Rockefeller's relationship remained strong throughout the administration and after, despite the repeated slights he experienced. Ford stated, "Our friendship continued right up until his death, and our friendship with Happy [Rockefeller's wife] has also continued. So there's never been any backing off in our relationship, and I suspect, that [even] if I didn't say it directly, he understood that I was embarrassed."[398] Ford was embarrassed that he did not stand by Rockefeller and support him for vice president, despite the vocal opposition to him by the conservatives in the party. He stated, "[I] was angry with myself for showing cowardice."[399] Many of the public accounts and public statements made at the time suggest that Rockefeller removed his name from consideration without any pressure from Ford. However, the archives suggest otherwise. Ford asked Rockefeller to submit a letter withdrawing his name from consideration and Rockefeller reluctantly agreed.[400] Ford also tried to convince himself that this was the best thing for Rockefeller, as well, because he felt that Rockefeller was restless and therefore could not see him happy continuing on as vice president for another four years.[401]

Rockefeller's influence diminished very publicly because of the changing situational dynamic and electoral conditions. While other vice president's experience challenges to their influence due to electoral dynamics, his experience was more overt and public. He owes the start of his political misfortune to when Ford's campaign manager stated that Rockefeller was Ford's greatest liability. From that point forward, his candidacy was ended, and efforts were made to marginalize him even further, contributing to his frustration and diminished influence.

Effects on Influence

Ultimately, Rockefeller's conclusions about Ford encapsulate his predicament as vice president: "He [Ford] was given to imprecision and could not always be relied upon to support his own previous decisions."[402] Rockefeller tried to protect himself from these "shifts in presidential positions or challenges to vice presidential actions from senior White House staff members" by ensuring that he always sought the president's approval by signature for every action he carried out.[403] However, even that was not enough to overcome the institutional, situational, and electoral dynamics that imperiled his vice presidency.

Recall that Rockefeller's vice presidency started on a very high note, which created the expectation that he would indeed be an influential vice president, and for a short time he was in fact influential. Rockefeller won key battles against the president's chief of staff, Don Rumsfeld, early on. Despite these successes, Rockefeller faced obstruction from a White House structure that was resistant to his efforts and recommendations. While Rockefeller was able to circumvent the structure to receive the president's support, those actions would still need to be carried out by the White House staff, which limited his influence, as was seen with his EIA proposal.

An evolution took place regarding his influence that was palpable to Rockefeller. Rockefeller stated, "At least, during the first two-thirds, three-quarters of the time I was Vice President I had never been busier

88 / Emerging from the Shadows

heading commissions, undertaking special projects for the President and traveling both at home and abroad."[404] He felt his vice presidency was unique in that he did not "think there is any Vice-President in the history of the United States who has been given as many responsibilities and as great a latitude as I have."[405]

An evolution to his role took place—one that all vice president's face at some point during their terms of office, which results in diminished influence. Rockefeller's role changed because of institutional, interpersonal, situational, and electoral dynamics that made it increasingly difficult for him to exercise sustained influence. Some of it was self-inflicted. Rockefeller resigned his supervisory authority over the Domestic Council, hampered by institutional turf battles between him and the White House staff, which was supposed to be the main source of his influence. The institutional dynamic, however, is only part of the story.

In terms of the interpersonal dynamic, Ford's management style enabled White House staff to obstruct the vice president and perpetuate conflicts that diminished Rockefeller's influence. While Rockefeller was influential enough to get the president to support his position or take a position advocated by him, "His problem was he [Ford] wouldn't tell people what to do."[406] Rockefeller continued, "He [Ford] was so used to this congressional business of trying to get a consensus that he couldn't get used to the fact that he was President."[407] Others, such as Melvin Laird, also noticed Ford's hesitancy: "I wish Jerry had some of the same drive and ambition. You have to kick Jerry in the ass usually to get him to do anything. Even in the House you had to keep prodding him."[408] This nonconfrontational approach allowed problems to persist and let the White House staff dictate the proper role for the vice president, even if it was contrary to what had been agreed on between the two principals.

The situational dynamic also impacted Rockefeller's influence. Prior to his selection, the political conditions and situation welcomed a figure like Rockefeller to the vice presidency. His experience as a fixer was a positive, since Ford sought to "fix" the country and restore public confidence in government after Watergate. Rockefeller was adept at proposing large and costly government programs to help solve problems. However, his style of governing would suffer a setback when conditions quickly changed. The country faced a declining economy, and the president instituted a policy of "no new starts." Tasked with developing, examining, and proposing new policies to address the nation's problems, the "no new starts" policy basically took the wind out of his sails. The new landscape made it difficult for him to gain support for grand proposals. And even when they did gain the president's support, as was the case of EIA, they failed to become law because White House staff was reluctant to fight for it and Congress lacked the political will to move forward on the initiative.

The electoral dynamic also reduced Rockefeller's influence. The political reasons for his selection would become a political liability to Ford and his election effort. Rockefeller's more liberal policy positions and record were a significant obstacle for Ford. Many of Ford's advisers, including his chiefs of staff and his campaign manager, lobbied for Rockefeller's replacement to win in the Deep South, which was seen as Reagan territory.[409] Cheney stated, "If we didn't replace Rockefeller on the ticket, we were going to have real trouble winning the nomination in Kansas City. He would be a rallying point for all the conservatives who would like to go with Reagan anyway."[410] Once the decision was made to drop him from the ticket, the campaign and the White House further distanced themselves from Rockefeller.

As demonstrated, the interpersonal, situational, institutional, and electoral dynamics adversely affected Rockefeller's vice presidency and ability to exercise influence in the same manner as when his vice presidency began. Rockefeller's influence peaked approximately six to eight months after his confirmation and precipitously declined from then on. Despite witnessing the jealousies and turf battles that existed in his administration, Ford failed to diffuse the situation; by committing to his agreement with the vice president, he further alienated Rockefeller. Despite the eventual decline in vice presidential influence, some argue that the Mondale vice presidency, which scholars believe was beginning of the modern vice presidency, was "largely formed by the Ford-Rockefeller relationship."[411] As James Cannon stated, "Up 'til that point he was as influential, probably more influential in his personal conversations with the president . . . Ford liked to have Rocky there and get his advice and views. Looking back Rocky was the most influential vice president up until that time."[412]

Chapter 3

Dick Cheney

A Case of Unprecedented Influence

> One of the things I was concerned about [was] I had seen other
> relationships between presidents and vice presidents not work out.
> And usually that started at the staff level, not at the principals' level.
>
> —James Rosen, *Cheney One on One*

In the various capacities he served over the course of his career in public
service, Dick Cheney witnessed firsthand how frustrating life could be
for a vice president. This was especially true of his time spent as chief of
staff during the Ford administration and the condition Nelson Rockefeller
found himself in as vice president—one of disillusionment.[1] "My chief of
staff experience was important in my thinking about how to operate as
vice president in terms of avoiding some of the pitfalls, some of the ways
that [I'd seen the] relationship [president/vice president] . . . damaged
over the years."[2] Cheney had never observed anyone truly happy as vice
president. "So the things I did as vice president and the way I operated
I think were certainly significantly influenced [by] what I had seen and
experienced as chief of staff in my own right."[3]

Yet, universally, by all accounts, Cheney's vice presidency was a success in terms of his ability to exert influence and separate himself from
recent vice presidents. He "transformed [the vice presidency] into a focal
point of presidential power."[4] Vice President Cheney goes down in history
as the most influential and powerful vice president.[5]

92 / Emerging from the Shadows

Dick Cheney's Selection as Vice President

For George W. Bush, Dick Cheney was an unconventional pick for vice president.[6] First, Cheney had not held political office in approximately ten years, and had instead developed a successful private-sector career as chair and chief executive officer of Halliburton, an oil service firm based in Texas.[7] Second, Cheney's selection brought very little of the typical "balancing" that is sought in a vice presidential pick—balancing based on geography, age, ideology, etc.[8] Third, Cheney's poor health was problematic, a concern that Cheney himself clearly articulated to Governor George W. Bush and his advisers.[9] Fourth, there was the potential for a constitutional conflict if Bush selected Cheney, since both principals resided in the state of Texas.[10] The Constitution stipulates that "under the Twelfth Amendment electors cannot cast ballots for both presidential and vice presidential candidates from their own state. Since Cheney at the time lived in Dallas and was a registered voter in Texas, that would mean Texas's electors could vote for Bush but not for Cheney."[11] In totality, Cheney seemed like a poor choice. As some have noted, "the choice of Dick Cheney as vice president struck many as a poor one. He had little charisma and was not a campaigner; he was, as one writer put it, 'a balding, overweight, middle-aged man who is not especially telegenic.' In his own brief bid for the presidency in 1994, Cheney had had to withdraw because of his uneasiness in the meet-and-greet side of campaigning. He didn't like fundraising, shaking hands at factories, and smiling at chicken-and-potato dinners, and he had difficulty asking supporters for money."[12] Last, Cheney was tapped by Bush to head up the governor's vice presidential search.[13] An extremely unlikely avenue for becoming vice president.

Bush envisioned "an intensive, but invisible process that would produce no surprises, no drama, no high-profile interviews, and no rushed decision."[14] Bush publicly announced Cheney as the head of his vice presidential search committee on April 25, 2000.[15] Bush praised Cheney, stating, "he couldn't think of a better person" to lead the search.[16] Cheney felt that he was uniquely qualified to lead the search: "When I thought about it, I realized I'd been observing or participating in the vice presidential selection process for nearly a quarter century, so I felt that I had a good sense of how an effective search should work."[17] Adding to the unconventional nature of Cheney's selection as the eventual nominee, no other vice presidential nominee in history had served as the head of a vice presidential selection committee, which raised questions regarding the propriety of the selection.[18]

Many critics of Dick Cheney's selection as vice president speculated that it was concocted by him, thus allowing him to avoid the normal rigors of the vetting process.[19] Others argued that Bush put him in charge of the vice presidential search, knowing full well he intended on picking Cheney, which Ari Fleischer, the president's press secretary, never saw evidence of.[20] Nonetheless, critics argued, "Amid stealth and misdirection, with visible formalities obscuring the action offstage, Cheney served as producer for Bush's first presidential decision. Somewhere along the way he stepped aside as head of casting, taking the part of Bush's running mate before anyone really auditioned. And he dodged most of the paperwork, bypassing the extraordinary scrutiny he devised for other candidates."[21] This notion assumes that Bush was "led to the decision" by Cheney's manipulation of the vetting process and his systematic elimination of other candidates, leaving him the only reasonable choice.[22] Cheney was involved in the interviews that Bush conducted with prospective candidates, however, it is not unusual for the head of the search committee to be present.[23]

The official version offered by those most involved in the selection process debunks the critics' theories. Karl Rove, then Governor Bush's chief political strategist, stated, "Some people have suggested that Cheney engineered his own selection. This is far-fetched. I saw the man squirm as Bush pressed him to accept."[24] Bush had approached Cheney, before he asked him to head up the vice presidential search, to inquire if he was willing to be a candidate for consideration, and Cheney adamantly stated no.[25] Shortly after Bush secured the Republican presidential nomination, he asked his campaign manager, Joe Allbaugh, to visit Dick Cheney to ask him two questions: "First, was Dick interested in being a candidate for vice president? [and] If not, was he willing to help me find a running mate?"[26] Bush recalled, "Dick told Joe he was happy with his life and finished with politics. But he would be willing to lead the VP search committee."[27] If the critics are correct and Cheney did actively want the vice presidency, he would have jumped at the chance when it was first offered, well before any lists were drawn up. Cheney confirms this by stating, "There was some effort to make a serious charge that I had conducted the search process so that I could position myself to be the nominee, but it ignored a pretty important fact. If I had wanted the job, I could have said yes back in March 2000 when Joe Allbaugh asked if

94 / Emerging from the Shadows

I'd be willing to be considered. It would have been a heck of a lot easier way to end up where I did."[28] Furthermore, Cheney would not have been as thorough in working his way through the potential candidates. Over thirty people were on the initial list, and Cheney discreetly visited each candidate to gauge interest and narrow the list.[29] Those people were then given an extensive questionnaire to complete, interviewed, and had their tax documents, writings, and speeches scrutinized by Cheney and his team.[30] In addition, he had much to lose by accepting the vice presidency. Cheney "was sitting on hundreds of thousands of Halliburton shares and options worth tens of millions of dollars. By joining the ticket, he would deny himself the opportunity to sell his shares and exercise his options when the market dictated the maximum price."[31] Even after committing to head the search, he reassured the Halliburton board of directors that he would not serve in a Bush administration.[32] He stated, "I have no plan, intention, desire under any circumstances to return to government."[33]

Although it is impossible to know what was going through Cheney's mind during the selection process, the events that transpired confirm the "official" explanation of how Cheney found himself the vice presidential nominee in 2000. Furthermore, Cheney knew vice presidents going back to Spiro Agnew and saw how frustrated they had been in the office.[34] He recalled that Ford "took delight in telling me it [vice president] was the worst job he ever had."[35] "Cheney viewed the vice presidency as a political black hole and had no interest in being trapped there."[36] In my interview with him, he stated his initial view was, "This is a crappy job, I liked running Halliburton a lot better."[37] However, after running the vetting process and working closely with Governor Bush, he became more amenable to the idea of being considered.

Several reasons demonstrate that Cheney transitioned from an adamant "no" to a resounding "yes." First, the vice presidential selection process that Cheney headed convinced him that not only was he qualified to be vice president but that he fit the model Bush was seeking for a nominee.[38] Cheney stated, "What happened, in effect, was he [Bush] had asked me to help him find somebody to be vice president. And walking through that process over a period of months, talking about various individuals and the traits and attributes he was interested in and what he needed, I developed an understanding of what he was looking for. And when we got through that whole process he concluded by saying, 'You're the solution to my problem.'"[39]

Cheney finally acquiesced to Bush's persistent efforts during a visit to the Bush Ranch in Crawford, Texas, in July 2000.[40] Cheney reviewed the search committee's final report with Bush.[41] After their session and a leisurely lunch with Laura Bush, Karen Hughes, and a Bush family friend, Bush and Cheney excused themselves to talk privately on the back porch.[42] Bush, once again, voiced his desire for Cheney to be considered. Cheney was noncommittal but seemed to be more amenable to the idea. Bush was tenacious to say the least. This is no surprise since, Bush, more than eight years earlier tried to make the case to his father, George H. W. Bush, to drop Dan Quayle from the ticket in 1992 and replace him with Dick Cheney.[43] Cheney joked that Bush wore him down.[44] Cheney argued that the "heat overcame his good sense because he finally agreed to consider joining the ticket."[45]

Second, Cheney's experience working with Bush during the vice presidential selection process instilled within him a deep admiration for his demeanor and vision for the country. "I [Cheney] had an experience that changed my mind this spring [2000]. As I worked alongside Governor Bush, I heard him talk about his unique vision for our party and for our nation. I saw his sincerity. I watched him make decisions, always firm and always fair. And in the end, I learned how persuasive he can be."[46]

Third, the vice presidential selection process brought Cheney back into the political world that he enjoyed most. Cheney was always an ideas man and would much rather spend time perusing briefing papers and reports rather than socializing with the political elite.[47] The aspect of politics he disliked greatly was the constant fundraising and scrutiny by the media.[48] He was a man content at spending time alone studying the issues and engrossing himself in policy.[49] Dick Cheney's wife, Lynne, "thought the way to understand him was to remember how much he loved fly-fishing, standing without a sound for hours casting for a bite—'not a sport for the impatient,' as she put it, and 'definitely not a sport for chatterboxes.'"[50] Cheney approached politics with a similar disposition—studying policy and issues in solitude. "For all of his skepticism, the vice presidency ultimately appealed to him because it offered the prospect of shaping policy without having to endure the hassles required to be elected president."[51]

Fourth, as Bush articulated what he wanted in a vice president, Cheney realized he was serious about finding a true partner in governing.[52] Cheney stated, "I was impressed and believed that he was serious . . . that he was looking for somebody of consequence to do the job and he wasn't just worried about the Electoral College."[53] "When the two men talked about the most important qualities of prospective candidates, Bush's answer in private was the same one he gave in public: someone who could help him govern."[54] This distinction mattered greatly to Cheney, who had seen other vice presidents languish in the job because they were granted no authority. Cheney delineated Bush's "wish list" to Alan Greenspan, the Federal Reserve chair, and a close personal friend, which included: "a person capable of commanding the presidency should need arise, yet satisfied to wait quietly in the wings; a confidant of sound judgment with experience in foreign affairs, in Congress, or in the corridors of the executive branch."[55] Not surprisingly, these attributes mirrored Cheney's own qualities.

Last, Cheney's "abrupt change of heart" was influenced by a sense of duty.[56] He stated, "If the president of the United States asks you to do something, you really have an obligation to try to do it if you can."[57] This is not unique to Cheney but is seen with other vice presidents who reversed their initial rejections. As we saw in chapter 2, one of the overriding motivations for Rockefeller to accept was the overwhelming sense of duty he felt to assist President Ford in restoring the nation's confidence in government after Watergate. Cheney had spent a lifetime in politics and his sense of service had not diminished over time.

With so many qualified candidates on Bush's short list, why did Bush persistently seek out Cheney as a contender even though he made it clear he was opposed to being considered? In short, Cheney met all the criteria Bush set for a vice president. His thinking on the vice presidency had not changed since he had offered Cheney's name to his father as a replacement for Vice President Quayle in 1992. Eight years later, Bush still thought he was the best candidate.[58] Bush explained, "I never completely gave up on my idea of a Bush-Cheney ticket."[59]

Cheney was, after all, the "résumé vice president."[60] He served as White House chief of staff at the young age of thirty-four, and then went on to serve ten years as the sole congressman from Wyoming.[61] In Congress he served in the leadership as the "No. 2 House Republican leader" before he was asked by George H. W. Bush to be secretary of defense.[62] He was considered one of the best qualified candidates in the Republican Party to run for president, which he considered doing in 1996, but was dismayed by the fundraising and media scrutiny.[63] Cheney's résumé obviously appealed to Bush. "He possessed the perfect combination of experience in Congress and the executive branch."[64] But Cheney's selection went beyond just the résumé.

Bush was not circumspect about his views on Cheney. During the lunch in July, Laura had asked her husband about the vice presidential search process. Bush stated, "The man I really want to be vice president is here at the table," referring to Cheney and surprising those at the lunch.[65] "George [Bush] liked Dick's thoughtful, measured demeanor . . . he liked to laugh and was funny, smart, and devoted to his wife, his daughters, and his grandchildren." Bush quickly realized that "the person who was best qualified to be my vice-presidential nominee was working by my side."[66] Cheney was part of Bush's "comfort zone."[67] "He [Bush] knew him [Cheney], his father knew him, and both trusted him. One of the hallmarks of the Bush family was their loyalty—and, as one commentator noted, 'it is no secret that the Bush clan values loyalty above nearly all else.'"[68] Cheney checked all the boxes for Bush. He was capable of being president, was loyal, added value, and Bush was comfortable with him.[69]

While vice presidential candidates do not decide elections, their selection should not damage the election effort. Although Cheney did carry some baggage of his own, in relation to others his baggage was relatively minor.[70] As a young man, Cheney had been arrested twice and charged with a DUI.[71] Furthermore, he was kicked out of Yale twice due to poor performance.[72] Neither of these incidents occurred during his time as an elected official or appointee and could easily be dismissed as the indiscretions of a misguided youth—something a campaign could explain away. "Cheney had a long marriage, no financial scandals, and deep experience in the federal government."[73] He was viewed as a strong conservative who presented very little in terms of political risk.[74] Thus, Cheney's personal history was unlikely to harm Bush's election effort.

One of the most appealing features of a Cheney candidacy was his lack of presidential ambition. "Although Cheney brought Beltway and policy experience to the ticket, his greatest appeal to Bush was considerably simpler: he posed no threat."[75] If Bush selected Cheney, he would not have to worry about his loyalty or that he had a separate agenda. Bush would be free to bestow a great degree of trust in his vice president and make him a true partner in governing, never having to look over his shoulder wondering if his vice president was going rogue. Cheney was particularly sensitive to the dangers of having a politically ambitious vice president in the White House. He had seen firsthand some of the turf battles that developed in his father's administration because of divided loyalties.[76] "Vice presidents with ambitions breed staffs whose principal interest is

98 / Emerging from the Shadows

the elevation of the VP at the expense of the president."[77] Cheney was the "least threatening" of the vice presidential candidates under consideration.[78]

Compatibility with his vice president was very important. Out of all the candidates, Cheney had the strongest working relationship with Bush. While not personally close, they had known each other since the late 1980s, but their relationship reached a new phase in 1994, when Cheney became involved in Texas state politics after becoming CEO of Halliburton.[79] In running a Texas-based corporation, his interaction with the governor and willingness to serve on government advisory councils was good for business.[80] Bush benefited by getting "free advice" from an "experienced political hand," which proved priceless.[81] After securing reelection as governor, Bush's political horizon broadened to the national stage, which would require him to brush up on national security issues. Bush began to consult with Cheney about running a campaign and eventually on questions of foreign policy.[82] They discussed the "mechanics" of a campaign including staffing, scheduling, and prioritizing.[83] Shortly after their meeting, Bush began inviting experts on national security policy, Cheney included, for frequent visits to the Governor's Mansion to help him prepare for a potential run.[84] "It is safe to assume that it was during these meetings that Bush's trust of Cheney developed and grew."[85] Cheney would join the "foreign policy advisory team," which included Condi Rice, Steve Hadley, Rich Armitage, and Paul Wolfowitz.[86] While Cheney was not officially a member of the "Vulcans," the name given to the group, his involvement was extensive, and he joined the team for strategy meetings.[87] "Bush understood that a neophyte on the world stage like himself could use a seasoned veteran like Cheney at his side."[88] Bush's praise of Cheney's demeanor from these meetings became effusive as time went on.

> Cheney came down to a lot of our policy meetings and he was the kind of guy that—he didn't speak a lot . . . But then when he spoke, everybody—like, the energy level in the room kind of shifted a little bit. . . . It was a very impressive group of people and impressive presentations. But the one guy that pretty much commanded, I felt, the respect of everybody around the table during these meetings was Cheney. And so he got my attention.[89]

Their relationship gave Cheney a leg up on other contenders. He "was the only recent vice president who had a strong working relationship with the president prior to his selection, as an important campaign advisor and then as the director of Bush's vice presidential selection process."[90]

Cheney would also make the case to Bush that he should consider other options because he may not be the best choice. However, Bush made up his mind. He told Cheney on that July afternoon, "Dick, you are the perfect running mate."[91] Bush recalled their conversation,

> While I had dropped hints before, he [Cheney] could tell I was serious this time. Finally, he said, "I need to talk to Lynne." I took that as a promising sign. He told me that he had had three heart attacks and that he and Lynne were happy with their life in Dallas. Then he said, "Mary [Cheney's daughter] is gay." I could tell what he meant by the way he said it. Dick clearly loved his daughter. I felt he was gauging my tolerance. "If you have a problem with this, I'm not your man," he was essentially saying. I smiled at him and said, Dick, take your time. Please talk to Lynne. And I could not care less about Mary's orientation.[92]

While Cheney finally succumbed to Bush's entreaties by stating he would consult with his family, he still needed to ensure that Bush and his team were fully aware of the extent of his health issues. Governor Bush asked Allbaugh, Rove, and Hughes to join him at the Governor's Mansion so Cheney could address his health with them. Cheney assured them that despite having had three heart attacks, he was still "active and vigorous" and that heart disease had not inhibited his ability to run a large multinational business.[93] Nonetheless, he made it clear that there was still an unknown quality to his health. They all agreed that they would need something from Cheney's doctors that would allay their fears.[94]

After the meeting, Cheney contacted the Halliburton board to let them know that he might be selected as the vice presidential nominee and then contacted his physicians to schedule a complete workup.[95] By July 12, 2000, Bush informed Cheney that he was given an all clear by his heart surgeon and "there was no reason why [he] could not run for and serve as vice president."[96] Despite the clearance on the health issues, Cheney still wanted an opportunity to make the case against himself.[97] Cheney stated, "I wouldn't be just going through the motions. There were solid reasons why I didn't think I made sense as George Bush's running mate, and I intended to put them on the table. I was so serious about talking

100 / Emerging from the Shadows

him out of picking me that my family was confident I would come back from the meeting having taken myself off the list."[98] Bush gave Cheney an opportunity to make the case against his own candidacy by scheduling a meeting on Saturday, July 15, and asking Karl Rove, knowing full well that he was particularly impassioned in his opposition to Cheney, to be present.[99] Not only was Cheney laying out the case against himself, but he expected that Rove would do the same.

Cheney methodically listed all the potential problems with his candidacy, to include his DUIs and Yale dismissals.[100] Although Bush was satisfied with the reassurances from the heart surgeon, Cheney reiterated the precarious nature of his health. He stated, "Heart patients have to be vigilant, and I told them that if I ever felt even a twinge in my chest during the campaign, I would go directly to a hospital. It would make no difference if I were in the middle of a speech or in the middle of a debate; minutes could mean the difference between life and death. There was simply no way to judge the impact of such an event on the outcome of presidential race, but it wasn't likely to be positive."[101] He then discussed their similar backgrounds, both having spent time in the oil business.[102] "It wasn't hard to imagine the negative charges our opponents would level at us based on that common denominator."[103] Bush's contest against the environmental activist Al Gore would be complicated by having two oil men at the top of a Republican presidential ticket. A looming constitutional dilemma complicated matters further for Bush. The Twelfth Amendment's Habitation Clause prohibits Electoral College electors from casting a vote for a president and vice president from the same state.[104] Last, Cheney was self-described as "deeply conservative" even though he had "a reputation of being somewhat moderate."[105] Cheney believed he was mischaracterized as a moderate because he was not considered a "bomb thrower," worked across party lines, and began his political career under the moderate Gerald Ford.[106] Cheney argued, "I had a very conservative voting record, more conservative than most people realized. The press never looked at my voting record. They thought I was all warm and fuzzy and they never looked to see."[107]

Bush turned to Karl Rove and stated, "Tell me why you think I shouldn't pick Dick Cheney."[108] Rove spent over thirty minutes laying out his argument.[109] He made a similar case as Cheney, but his concerns were more political. He argued that Bush would carry Wyoming regardless of whether Cheney was on the ticket or not—it had been solidly Republican for decades, therefore Bush should pick a candidate who might help with a swing state, in particular Danforth, who might put Missouri in Bush's corner.[110] This line of criticism did not resonate with Bush, who was seeking someone to help him govern best. By picking Cheney, Rove also felt he opened himself up to criticism that Bush was living in the shadow of his father.[111] Rove felt this point mattered to Bush; how much weight he gave it was another question entirely.[112]

Last, Rove elaborated on Cheney's point about Texas residency and the ticket being dominated by men who had careers in the oil industry. He felt the "press would badger us for having two Texans on the ticket even if Cheney changed his registration to Wyoming. And while changing the registration could be done legally, someone could file a frivolous lawsuit."[113] With the ticket being dominated by two "big oil" individuals, Rove argued it would hurt Bush in the Midwest and Northeast.[114] Rove stated, "Why . . . make our perception problem worse?"[115]

Rove's critique of Cheney's candidacy did very little to dissuade Bush from his preference for Cheney as his vice president. Bush recalled,

> I listened carefully to Karl's objections. Dick said he thought they were pretty persuasive. I didn't. Dick's old congressional record didn't bother me. I considered his experience on Capitol Hill an asset. His lack of impact on the electoral map did not concern me either. I believe voters base their decision on the presidential candidate, not the VP. . . . As for Karl's concern about picking Dad's defense secretary, I was convinced that the benefits of choosing a serious, accomplished running mate would compensate for any perception that I was falling back on Dad for help.[116]

Bush felt "the political downsides were more than offset by the advantages of having Cheney as vice president."[117] To Bush's credit, none of the issues became a persistent problem.[118] Bush told Rove the day after the meeting, "If things go well, it doesn't matter who the vice president is. But if the unknown happens, the country will need Cheney's steadiness."[119] Cheney was someone who was "eminently qualified" to assume the presidency, which was extremely important to Bush—"Cheney was his man."[120] Bush echoed a similar sentiment when he made his final decision and asked Cheney to be his running mate. He stated, "If times are good, I'm going to need your advice, but not nearly as much as if times are bad."[121]

On July 25, 2000, Bush called Cheney at his residence at 6:22 a.m. and made his official offer of the vice presidency.[122] Bush told Cheney,

102 / Emerging from the Shadows

in offering him the position, "I don't know what's going to come on my desk, but I'm going to need somebody who's seen things before, who can give me advice to make good decisions."[123] Cheney answered by stating that he would be honored to do it.[124] He then turned to his wife and told her, "Honey, let's sell the house. . . . I quit my job. We're going back into politics."[125]

Bush's decision sought to reassure voters that he had a partner who complemented his weaknesses, as well as someone who would add the necessary gravitas to the ticket that was noticeably missing.[126] If voters had concern about Bush's ability to govern, Cheney's extensive resume would sufficiently allay their concerns and "blunt criticism" about Bush's apparent lack of national experience.[127] The reaction to Cheney's selection confirmed this thinking. Donald Rumsfeld, a close friend and early mentor to Dick Cheney, reacted to Bush's decision by stating, "Unlike many presidential nominees, Bush selected an excellent running mate. He made a reasoned, sober choice of a well-known figure who might not offer him much near-term political advantage but would be both a source of sound counsel and well prepared to assume the presidency if necessary."[128] For conservatives, building on the Reagan legacy and the Reagan-Bush coalition was important, Cheney served as a link to that legacy.[129] "Cheney's record as a deficit hawk was an essential part of that appeal."[130] His selection reinforced Reagan's tenets, such as support for a strong military, interest in a "strategic defense initiative," and the importance of government deregulation.[131] Sean O'Keefe, a former aide of Cheney, called his boss "The most prominent adult in the room."[132] Bush, during Cheney's announcement, listed Cheney's experience and stated, "Even my opponent, the vice president, once said, 'Dick Cheney is a good man who is well-liked and respected by his colleagues,' and I agree."[133] However, praise for Bush's pick was far from universal. The *New York Times* called the selection of Cheney the "least adventurous and least sensational."[134] The *Times* continued, "It underscored that Mr. Bush is generally not a bold risk taker in his public life."[135] Nonetheless, Bush was very pleased that Cheney agreed to serve as his running mate.

Strengths and Weaknesses—Cheney and Bush

Cheney's selection demonstrated the importance of balancing a presidential ticket from an insider-outsider perspective, a norm that has developed in presidential elections during the modern era.[136] Bush stated, "Cheney was the kind of guy that would be a good fit for a two-term governor from Texas who, while he had a pretty good political pedigree, didn't have a lot of what they call 'Washington experience.'"[137] However, Cheney's selection went beyond this, instead Cheney balanced the ticket on various aspects of governing that Bush was weakest.

One of the greatest complements was his extensive experience in national security, an area in which Bush was a noticeable novice. It was quite clear that Cheney was the expert in this field.[138] Most importantly, Cheney understood the difficult decisions presidents were required to make because he "had stood next to presidents during the most gut-wrenching decisions that reach the Oval Office, including sending Americans to war."[139] No other candidate under consideration matched Cheney in this regard, thus providing Bush with solace, knowing that Cheney would be at his side when these decisions would be made.[140]

Cheney's expertise was not limited to foreign policy and national security though. Most of Bush's closest campaign advisers, such as Karl Rove, Karen Hughes, Margaret Spellings, and Dan Bartlett, lacked Washington experience or policy expertise.[141] "They were no match for Cheney, who easily captured Bush's ear as an expert on policy and legislation."[142] After all, Cheney's experience transcended two branches of government.[143] This appealed to Bush who never held a legislative position. Bush's experience in Congress was limited to helping his father's campaigns for the Senate in 1964 and 1970, and for the House in 1966, serving as an aide to Rep. Edward Gurney, working as the political director for Red Blount's Alabama Senate campaign, and undertaking his own failed bid for Congress in 1978.[144]

Cheney's experience in the executive branch spanned four presidential administrations.[145] During the Nixon administration, Cheney worked for Donald Rumsfeld at the Office of Economic Opportunity.[146] He went on to serve in the Ford administration as Rumsfeld's deputy chief of staff. Cheney later took over Rumsfeld's position as chief of staff during the latter part of Ford's term.[147] Although elected to Congress in 1978, Cheney served in the Reagan administration as a special envoy, developing continuity of government plans should the United States face a nuclear attack.[148] Last, as President George H. W. Bush's defense secretary, he led the Pentagon during the Gulf War.[149] These experiences provided him with the opportunity to see how small agencies, large bureaucratic departments, and the White House staff operate.

104 / Emerging from the Shadows

Whatever baggage Cheney had was mitigated by his impressive career and policy expertise. Bush also helped balance Cheney's seriousness and aversion to retail politics. Just as Cheney excelled where Bush was weakest, Bush excelled where Cheney was weakest—electoral politics.[150] Bush was gregarious and enjoyed interacting with people, whereas Cheney was more reserved and comfortable in his own private thoughts.[151] Bush found it quite amusing when Cheney told him once that a personality test "determined his ideal job would be funeral director."[152] Clearly, the two balanced each other, not only from a political perspective, but also from a personality perspective.

Role of Dick Cheney as Vice President

Dick Cheney and George W. Bush developed a unique arrangement for the role the vice president would play in the administration. Having witnessed other vice presidents in office, Cheney was determined to have a "consequential" vice presidency, and Bush made this possible.[153] A pivotal conversation that took place at Bush's ranch in July would have far-reaching consequences for the Cheney vice presidency and the Bush presidency. Cheney made clear that he "was not interested in the traditional portfolio of political fund-raisers and ceremonial trips."[154] Dan Bartlett, Bush's counselor and communications advisers, recalled Cheney telling Bush "If I'm going to do this I'm going to do this differently. . . . I'm not going to be the guy going to funerals. I want to be a real partner in helping you make decisions."[155] A consequential vice presidency meant that Cheney would be "a major participant in the process" and have the latitude to dip his hand in any issue he wanted.[156] It also meant that he would be at the center of the action in the administration—"shaping policy and working to strengthen presidential powers."[157]

Bush was receptive to the idea. Bush was a skilled fundraiser and someone comfortable with the ceremonial roles of the presidency, which allowed Cheney to focus on policy and the operation of government. "The result of that partnership was to give Cheney a large part of what he had sought from the job of president (a dominant role in running the federal government) while sparing him from the parts of the job he liked the least (the ceremonial and symbolic aspects of the presidency)."[158] Bush had witnessed his father's vice presidency and was determined to ensure his would not experience the same "indignities of the vice presidency" that his father may have suffered.[159] It appealed to Bush because he sought a partner to govern as president.[160] Cheney argued, "Ours [Bush and Cheney's perceptions of the role of the vice president] was, I think, a relatively unique arrangement. That's what President Bush 43 wanted. He wanted me to play a significant role, and he was true to his word."[161] Bush was fully on board with an expanded role for his vice president.

The uniqueness of their arrangement was fully apparent during the transition when they began entertaining contenders for the position of secretary of defense. It was so unique that Cheney and Bush even considered having the vice president serve as secretary of defense as well.[162] While no vice president in history ever served as vice president and cabinet head, the Constitution did not prohibit this sort of arrangement.[163] Donald Rumsfeld who was advising the Bush campaign on cabinet selections suggested the same scenario for Cheney, reasoning that he had served as defense secretary before and it would not be too much of a stretch for him to do both simultaneously.[164] "If anyone could handle both positions, it was Dick."[165] After consideration, Bush and Cheney felt it would be "unwise" to pursue.[166] Serving as a cabinet secretary would have interfered with the vice president's ability to provide objective advice on any subject he chose. It would keep him away from the West Wing, where he would be absent from the issues the president faced day-to-day.

Cheney was convinced that the only way the arrangement could work was "if it was clear there was only one agenda in the White House and that was his."[167] He continued, "It was essential if I was going to be effective working for him, to be able to have his total trust and confidence, and that of the people around him, that I didn't have my own agenda, that I wasn't trying to figure out what a particular proposal or speech was going to do for my image or my standing in Iowa caucuses in January of '08, that I was there specifically as part of a team."[168] Cheney's early decision not to run for president unshackled him from the normal constraints that other vice presidents faced in their attempt to exert influence. It eliminated the natural inclination of presidents and their staffs to wonder whether the vice president's actions benefited the administration or just the vice president's political future. Bush reflecting on this stated, "When you're getting advice from somebody . . . no matter who he or she is, if you think deep down part of the advice is to advance a personal agenda, if you're an observant person and obviously trying to do what's best for the country, you discount that advice."[169] Everyone in the Bush administration knew Cheney had Bush's complete and implicit trust.[170]

106 / Emerging from the Shadows

That trust was further cemented when Cheney asked Kathleen Shanahan, a friend of the Bush family, to serve as his chief of staff during the campaign.[171] Since Cheney was out of politics and in the private sector he did not bring with him the same "coterie of staffers" who other vice presidential candidates brought into existing campaigns, thus enabling the Bush campaign to fill out Cheney's staff.[172] "His deference to the campaign sent an early signal to Bush and his advisers that Cheney was willing to subordinate his interests to theirs."[173]

Bush also appreciated Cheney's lack of interest in the polls. "One thing about Dick Cheney is, you don't have to worry about him taking a political opinion poll and then trying to fashion his policy to make him popular."[174] If Cheney had his sights on the presidency, the polls would be a consistent worry. Cheney's lack of interest enhanced his trust with Bush and his staff. David Frum, a White House speechwriter, stated,

> There has never been a vice president like Dick Cheney, and there probably never will be again. He abjured any independent political existence from the president. He had no political operation at all. He employed only a single communications aide . . . he shared his sole speechwriter with the president. He built no power base within the party, and he shunned personal publicity. His strength depended entirely on Bush's trust in him—and he earned that trust by subordinating himself to Bush.[175]

Cheney's aversion to polls and disregard for his standing meant that his own image would suffer greatly over the course of his tenure, with unforeseen consequences for his vice presidency. Nonetheless, the trust that Bush placed in Cheney meant that he would defend Bush as they navigated "a hostile and bewildering capital."[176]

Attempts to define Cheney's role have resulted in various characterizations. Some like Joel Goldstein and Peter Baker define the role as that of a consigliere.[177] Others, like Shirley Anne Warshaw viewed Cheney's role as more of a copresident.[178] Nevertheless, the "division of labor" would allow Bush to focus on his compassionate conservative agenda such as education reform and faith-based initiatives and leave the fields of energy policy, national security, economic policy, and presidential power to his vice president.[179] In relation to other vice presidents, none affected policy in the same manner as Cheney.[180]

Joshua Bolten, Bush's chief of staff during his second term, referred to Cheney as a "true counsellor."[181] Bolten did not view him as a manager or even a decision maker; that designation belonged to Bush.[182] During the transition, Bolten studied previous vice presidencies to determine a role for Cheney and determined that vice presidents did not govern, instead they "kept an eye on how the rest of the government worked. They advised the president as the president saw fit. Sometimes they had niche projects. . . . They chaired commissions and laid out proposals for reform"—clearly a conception of a vice presidency that Cheney disavowed.[183] When word reached Cheney he made it clear that "he would engage in 'whatever area the vice president feels he wants to be active in' and Bush backed him."[184] "The president made it clear from the outset that the vice president is welcome at every table and at every meeting."[185]

Bolten was not the only one to mistakenly assume that Cheney would be a traditional vice president. On Inauguration Day, former vice president Dan Quayle paid a visit to Cheney's West Wing office to offer his unsolicited advice.[186] Quayle wanted Cheney to know what he "was in for."[187] Quayle said, "Dick, you know, you're going to be doing a lot of this international traveling, you're going to be doing all this political fund-raising. . . . I mean, this is what vice president's do. We've all done it."[188] Cheney responded, "I have a different understanding with the president."[189] Quayle came away thinking that the "different understanding" meant he would serve as a "surrogate chief of staff."[190] As Quayle put it, "He [Cheney] didn't want to do that much international travel. He wanted to be there all the time. And this was the deal he had."[191] Bush reinforced this view when he told a Republican senator, "when you're talking to Dick Cheney, you're talking to me. When Dick Cheney's talking, it's me talking."[192] "Everyone who worked with Cheney understood he spoke for Bush."[193]

Bush's and Cheney's conception of the vice presidential role, however, did not necessarily reach the level of "copresident" that Warshaw emphasized and his role was not as ominous as that of a "consigliere." The ability to freely offer his advice was his most valuable commodity. He stated, "I'm not a staffer, I'm the vice president, a constitutional officer, elected same as he [Bush] is, but my ability to contribute depends on basically my advice to him more than anything."[194] He may have viewed himself as an adviser, but he was not a typical adviser. For one, he was not a staffer who could be fired at will like other White House advisers.[195] Instead, he pointed out that he "did not serve at the pleasure of the pres-

108 / Emerging from the Shadows

ident."[196] There were limits though. Beyond his constitutional duties, he said, "my role depended on George W. Bush."[197] "I could give advice. And the impact of my advice depended first and foremost on my relationship with the president. At the end of the day, it wouldn't have mattered how many years of experience I had or how many other offices I'd held, if the president wasn't interested in what I had to say."[198]

Bush saw Cheney as one adviser, among many, who he sought input from in making his decisions. When Robert Gates met with President Bush about becoming secretary of defense during the second term, the topic of the vice president came up and Bush told Gates, "He is a voice, an important voice but only one voice."[199] However, some thought he had greater sway than others. Bush's own father felt he had "a disproportionate voice in the affairs of the son's administration—and Bush always believed in proportion."[200] Bush did not agree with his father's assessment though and would likely disagree with Wilkinson's as well. He stated, "I valued Dick's advice, but he was one of a number of my advisers I consulted, depending on the issue."[201] Cheney was no ordinary adviser though, as Bush stated, "Dick was the only one on a regular schedule [for private meetings]. He had put his name on the ballot and gotten elected. I wanted him to be comfortable with all the issues on my desk. After all, it could become his at any moment."[202] Cheney's unmatched depth of policy experience made him an invaluable asset to the president. Where Bush lacked the experience to "speak with authority" on foreign policy and national security, Cheney could easily step in and speak fluently and with gravitas on military matters, foreign policy, national security, missile defense, etc.[203] Rice viewed Cheney's role as "a bit of [a] very very high-level utility infielder for the president who could be deployed in numerous important areas."[204]

Cheney's indispensability as an adviser was proven early on when Bush took one of his first foreign trips to visit President Vincente Fox of Mexico on February 16, 2001. During that trip, Bush was alerted to bombings that took place in Iraq by American and British forces monitoring the "no-fly zones."[205] When Rice informed Bush of the bombings, the first thing he said was, "I'm going to call Dick."[206] "Rice was struck that in a moment of uncertainty the first person Bush thought to consult was Cheney."[207] She stated, "That said something to me, that he was sort of looking for reassurances."[208] This demonstrated the importance of Cheney's advice and Bush's own insecurities as a new president. Cheney at this point, clearly had no equals.

Advice was the commodity that Cheney could provide, and it served as the foundation for all roles he undertook as vice president. Bush ensured the primacy of his advice by setting up a White House that encouraged it at all levels and on all topics. Bush sought a flatter organizational structure at the White House, choosing a different arrangement from his father's administration, which had a vertical structure under the "domineering John Sununu," who served as George H. W. Bush's chief of staff.[209] The flatter structure would grant Bush greater access to his advisers, including his vice president.

The Vice President and Meetings

Many White House officials were surprised that Cheney, who was an intimidating force and held strong opinions, was so reserved in meetings.[210] His demeanor usually unnerved subordinates due to his steely blue gaze, emotionless expression, and "quiet, powerful certitude."[211] In cabinet meetings or other public settings with Bush, Cheney "rarely said a word."[212] He would keep quiet because as a "principal, by speaking up at a meeting, [he or she] can squash internal debate, and you won't necessarily get the best thinking."[213] He just did not feel the need to "pop up" all the time and speak up.[214] As a result, White House officials were often at a loss for what Cheney was thinking. If he did speak, it was to ask questions to "sharpen the discussion" and ensure Bush heard differing perspectives.[215] And if he made his preferences known in National Security Council meetings, he was careful about not putting Bush "in a corner," limiting his options.[216]

Cheney was a prolific meeting attendee.[217] Not only did he attend the usual meetings of most vice presidents (cabinet meetings, national security council meetings, and weekly private lunches with the president), but he also attended meetings considered below his pay grade, such as the Principals Committee meetings and economic meetings.[218] Even after 9/11, when Cheney was sequestered at an undisclosed location, he was still "omnipresent," frequently joining meetings through a secure video teleconferencing system (Secvid or SVTS).[219] Cheney stated, "I could set up a machine that looked like a very large laptop just about anyplace and be wired into meetings going on in the White House Situation Room or anywhere else around the world where the other participants had the same

110 / Emerging from the Shadows

technology."[220] "Cheney's specter . . . hovered over the administration's policy deliberations . . . its decision making . . . there always loomed the ghost of this balding, white-haired, slightly pudgy, bespectacled man . . . who took government seriously and worked as the consummate inside operator."[221] Additionally, someone from the vice president's staff would attend meetings in his absence, whether it was "presidential policy briefings, world leader meetings, [or] congressional meetings."[222]

Cheney took on new roles for the vice president. For one, Cheney's participation in Principals Committee meetings was a first for any vice president. The Principals Committee, an offshoot of the National Security Council, typically met in the absence of the president and vice president to iron out issues before being presented to the president.[223] Principals Committee meetings usually include the attorney general, secretaries of state, defense, and treasury, and director of central intelligence, the normal characters present during National Security Council meetings as well.[224] By tradition, other vice presidents had not attended these meetings.[225] Vice presidents were represented at the meetings by their national security advisers. However, Vice President Cheney preferred to go to these meetings himself.[226]

Another departure for the vice presidency was Cheney's participation in economic meetings. One of the vice president's interests, going back to his time in the House, was the economy and taxes.[227] As a result, he often attended meetings of the National Economic Council in order to understand the varying perspectives on the economy so he could counsel Bush accordingly, in some cases before proposals even reached the Oval Office.[228] Cheney even met regularly with his close friend and chair of the Federal Reserve, Alan Greenspan, throughout his vice presidency.[229] While it was unusual for a vice president to meet with the Federal Reserve chair alone, Cheney had a history with Greenspan that went all the way back to the Ford administration.[230] Greenspan's pace of visits increased from monthly during the Clinton administration to weekly as soon as the Bush administration took office.[231] "The Fed chairman was not usually there to see Bush or his economic team. Most of the time he came for Cheney alone. This was more than unusual; it was unique. As vice president, Al Gore never met with Greenspan alone, according to Gore's chief of staff, Ron Klain. Even Clinton knew, Klain said, that the treasury secretary "owned the relationship with Greenspan."[232] The long-term friendship between Greenspan and Cheney is partly responsible for the frequency of the meetings, however, it goes beyond that. Cheney was a policy guy. He enjoyed immersing himself in policy formulation and the operational side of government. As such, he often vetted policy proposals before they reached Bush.[233] He liked to "reach down," a term he used to describe reaching down through layers of the bureaucracy to access those responsible for developing policy.[234] He wanted to go to the source and preferred the "information direct, [and] unfiltered."[235] Vice presidents, up until this point, would join the president in meetings when it was time for a decision to be made.[236] Not Cheney, he was interested in involving himself much sooner, especially on issues of importance to him.[237]

Cheney also had "carte blanche" access to attend foreign and domestic policy meetings.[238] According to Bush's scheduling director, Cheney attended anywhere from 75 to 80 percent of the president's meetings.[239] Cheney was also a frequent attendee at "Terrorism Wednesdays (later Terrorism Tuesdays)" where the war cabinet (chief of staff, national security adviser, homeland security secretary, attorney general, director of national intelligence, CIA director, and director of the National Counterterrorism Center) met to discuss potential threats.[240] He also met weekly with top administration officials, to include the national security adviser and cabinet secretaries such as the secretary of defense and secretary of state.[241]

Cheney met with Bush with such frequency that Bush had a hard time recalling meetings he was not present for.[242] They met numerous times a day. As a result, the weekly lunches that most presidents and vice presidents shared were merely a formality, because he had numerous opportunities to offer advice.[243] However, the weekly lunches served as "an opportunity, sometimes, to argue issues [and the discussions varied greatly], sometimes it was family; sometimes it would be personnel matters related to the cabinet."[244]

Cheney's staff was just as plugged in. They attended "lower level interagency forums" to ensure that his voice was heard, and he was kept informed.[245] As a result, "Cheney got three bites at any major decision, his staff sat on committees that developed policies, the vice president participated in cabinet-level meetings that debated proposals, and then he had a chance to talk with Bush about them alone."[246] While other vice presidents had a similar ability to attend any meetings they wanted, what made Cheney unique is that he actually did.

Cheney's omnipresence in meetings contributed to the perception that he was a significant force within the walls of the White House, inside the bureaucracy, on Capitol Hill, and even in foreign capitals. For instance, "The British were struck that the vice president attended all the meetings,

112 / Emerging from the Shadows

including the one normally restricted to the leaders, which brought home 'as never before Cheney's influence in the Bush administration.'"[247] Cheney would frequently meet with foreign dignitaries, sometimes in advance of meetings with the president, because of the influence they assumed he exerted.[248] "For example, [when] British Prime Minister Tony Blair came to the White House for a meeting with Bush, he met with Cheney for an hour beforehand."[249] People sought Cheney out because it was understood that he "was almost always the last person that Bush talked to before a major decision was made."[250] Even when visitors did not seek out the vice president but rather "expected" to meet with the president, they often found themselves on Cheney's schedule.[251]

President's Daily Brief

Another unique activity had to do with Cheney's role in the President's Daily Brief (PDB). The PDB is a "highly classified" compilation of "intelligence and threat reporting" assembled by the intelligence community and presented to the president each morning.[252] Cheney was one of only a select few to be "entrusted" with the PDB.[253] He received the brief early in the morning at his residence before Bush received his, which was highly unusual for a vice president.[254] Interestingly, the CIA briefer tailored the brief to him in terms of answering questions he asked at previous briefings or providing additional information they thought the vice president would be interested in.[255] As Cheney recalled,

> My copy of the PDB quickly expanded to two sections. The first section was identical to the president's copy. The second section—"behind the tabs," we called it—contained responses to questions I'd asked or items my briefers knew I was interested in. Some mornings I would pull material from my section behind the tab. On at least one occasion, I asked to have material reinserted in the President's Daily Brief after others on the national security staff decided that he didn't need to see it.[256]

This suited Cheney given his interest in policy and his desire to immerse himself into its intricacies.[257] He was an "avid" consumer of intelligence.[258]

In discussing the arrangement, he remarked that he had the luxury of spending more time on intelligence than the president.[259] Asked whether the president sought this "unusual arrangement," Cheney responded, "Well, he obviously [wanted it this way]."[260] This role gave Cheney significant influence over the PDB. According to a Cheney biographer, "Information was power. Cheney sought it widely and creatively, and used it to shape what the president learned and when."[261] He would often highlight certain information or ask for information to be included that was missing so that Bush received what Cheney deemed important.[262]

Cheney always attended the president's briefing.[263] "If the vice president is in town he'll always be there. . . . If he's out of town, he'll almost always be on the SVTS. . . . Doesn't matter if it is five a.m. Cheney time, the vice president is going to want to be in, and that happens not infrequently."[264]

Presidential Power

Cheney, going back to his time as chief of staff, was a defender of presidential power, specifically against what he viewed as the encroachment of the legislative branch on the executive.[265] Even as a member of Congress, Cheney was a strong defender of the executive, arguing "not only that the executive branch had a right to restrict access to sensitive information, but that in some cases it had an obligation to do so."[266] Donald Rumsfeld articulated Cheney's position when he stated, "Vice President Cheney appreciates the importance of preserving the President's powers as commander in chief, especially when they were under assault for short-term political reasons. Cheney and his chief legal counsel and later chief of staff, David Addington, supported by senior lawyers from around the government, helped guard presidential authority as a matter of principle."[267] The first order he gave to David Addington, when he assumed office, was to "restore the powers of the presidency."[268] "Cheney's overriding goal was enlargement of presidential authority," which he had witnessed erode under previous administrations.[269]

His vision of presidential power was based on his view that the president had a very important and grave role, one that no other elected official shared. Cheney stated,

> I tend to think about it [the presidency] more in terms of there
> are certain things the nation has to do, things that have to get
> done. Sometimes very unpleasant things. Sometimes commit-

114 / Emerging from the Shadows

> ting troops to combat, going to war. And the president of the
> United States is the one who's charged with that. . . . The stuff
> you need the president for is the hard stuff . . . but when they
> earn their pay is when they have to sit down and make those
> really tough decisions that in effect are life-and-death decisions
> that affect the safety and security and survival of the nation.[270]

Cheney was certain that presidential power needed to be preserved, restored, and at times strengthened. He understood the need to make unpopular decisions in the "shadows" to safeguard the nation.[271] Yet, he was willing to suffer the consequences. One consequence was, that for many, he became "a dark and shadowy villain . . . the Darth Vader of his generation."[272] "If his chosen path meant leaving office as a symbol of belligerency and excess, he was willing to pay. . . . He claimed he didn't worry about it, said he had developed a pretty thick skin and just rolled with the punches."[273] His attempts to protect presidential power would put him in the middle of controversy but would also ensure an influential role for himself.

Vice Presidential Authority: Signing Statements, Executive Order Reviews, Budget Appeal Process, and Classification and Declassification of Documents

Cheney's expansive view of the presidency spilled over to the vice presidency and Bush provided him with the authority to assume new roles for the office. For instance, signing statements, used by the president to inform Congress of parts of a bill he would not enforce or deemed unconstitutional, were drafted by Cheney's office.[274] David Addington, Cheney's legal counsel, reviewed all bills to "determine whether any parts overstepped what he perceived as legislative authority. It was Cheney and Addington who decided whether Congress had overstepped its legislative authority—not George W. Bush or the White House staff."[275]

Additionally, his office undertook an exhaustive review of executive orders issued during the Clinton administration.[276] While this is a routine function of all incoming administrations, the fact that the effort was run out of Cheney's office was unique. Not only was this one of the first assignments he gave his staff, it was also done swiftly.[277] Cheney, who was well-versed in the intricacies of government, knew that the fast-track review of executive orders was a quick way to begin the process of exerting presidential authority.

Demonstrating Cheney's influence on internal process, the White House crafted a Budget Review Board, with Cheney serving as the panel's chair.[278] The panel provided guidance to agencies and cabinet secretaries on budget priorities and spending requests.[279] All appeals to budget decisions were decided by the Board, rather than the president.[280] In previous administrations, these appeals went directly to the president for a decision. Since the Office of Management and Budget turned down thousands of budgetary requests, this panel would eliminate a significant demand on the president's time.[281] After the board reached a decision on a budget issue, a cabinet secretary could appeal its decision to the president; however, this was not done.[282] According to Mitch Daniels, director of the OMB under Bush, "The sense people had was if that particular group didn't agree with them, then the president wasn't likely to either."[283] Board decisions stood without appeal for two reasons. First, everyone understood that Cheney spoke for the president. If Cheney said no, Bush would likely follow suit. Second, cabinet secretaries made it a point to run proposals by Cheney prior to submitting requests to the OMB or submitting appeals to the Board.[284] This demonstrates the influence Cheney had on internal White House processes.

Last, Cheney received authority no other vice president would receive during their tenure in office—the ability to classify or declassify documents.[285] He had been granted this authority by Bush in March 2003.[286] For all intents and purposes, as Charlie Savage stated, this presumably meant that Cheney was "the full equal to the president."[287] Bradford Berenson, who served as associate White House counsel in the Bush administration, stated, "[Cheney] has probably tasted from the cup of presidential power more than any other vice president in modern history."[288]

Despite the vast issues he took interest in, he did not feel the need to get involved on every issue. As Cheney's deputy chief of staff remarked, "The vice president didn't have to get involved in every issue. The president did. . . . This afforded the vice president a little more freedom."[289] Cheney did limit himself and his office reflected his desire to avoid a large portion of domestic policy. Out of four senior domestic policy staff, three were focused on energy issues, which demonstrated his desire to stay out of the president's pet issues (education and faith-based initiatives).[290] Moreover, the number of staff dedicated to foreign policy and national security issues far outnumbered those focused on domestic affairs.[291]

116 / Emerging from the Shadows

Press Relations

Cheney lacked an interest in press relations, his public profile, and communications in general. As vice president he was reluctant to engage, even though he had done this extensively as chief of staff and secretary of defense. In those capacities, he often met with the press to brief them on background or grant interviews with various reporters.[292] However, he stated, "I also decided to limit my exposure to the press. . . . as vice president I wanted a much lower profile. Members of the press were most often interested in what advice I had given the president on a particular issue, and he needed to know that I wasn't walking out the door of the Oval Office to brief reporters on what I'd just said."[293] He argued that his ability to play a meaningful role depended on his advice to the president, which needed to remain confidential. He stated, "The first time there is a lot of coverage of the vice president urging the president to do X, that starts to put a strain on the relationship and that linkage to him, that's crucial and needs to be protected."[294] Cheney understood that Bush's trust in him provided the vice president with a certain degree of independence.[295]

Some of Bush's staff reinforced Cheney's antipathy toward the press. There were concerns among some advisers, particularly Karl Rove and Karen Hughes, that the president might be upstaged by Cheney. They "privately worried that Cheney was overshadowing" Bush as president-elect.[296] Therefore, the White House communications shop encouraged Cheney's reluctance to engage the press and sought to downplay his role.[297] This was a legitimate concern because just after the election was decided, caricatures of Bush and Cheney began to appear on late night shows and comedy sketch shows. One skit from *Saturday Night Live* reinforced the concerns that the communications staff shared.[298] In their exchange, Bush played by Will Ferrell, tells Gore played by Darrell Hammond, "Dick Cheney's going to be one tough boss," to which Gore responds "Yeah, actually, George, you're going to be his boss," and Bush's retort was "Don't I wish."[299] The exchange was reflective of the public impression that the White House would continually try to dispel.

The White House press shop was able to keep his media exposure to a minimum because unlike other vice presidents, he did not have ambition to run for president and he did not need to continually generate buzz in the press.[300] Bush stated, "Dick didn't care much about his image—which I liked—but that allowed the caricatures to stick. One myth was that Dick was actually running the White House. Everyone inside the building, including the vice president, knew that was not true. But the impression was out there."[301] This was a quality of Cheney that Bush appreciated; however, it caused headaches for the administration's communications office, who had discouraged a more active public role. Dana Perino, Bush's press secretary, stated, "I don't know why he got so vilified early on, and part of it is he doesn't really care much what people think of him, and that's admirable on one level, but when it comes to good PR, it makes things difficult, difficult for everybody."[302]

Consequential Role

Cheney needed to keep the ceremonial aspects of the office to a minimum to be consequential. Normally, vice presidents log thousands of miles in air travel, but Cheney limited his international travel.[303] He took fewer foreign trips than most of his predecessors, and when he did, it was to gain support for the war effort or to visit troops abroad.[304] Cheney knew that distance from the White House for extended periods of time would diminish his ability to exert influence, and since he was interested in "reaching down" through the bureaucracy to gather information and stay involved in policy development, he would need to be close to the action. However, even if traveling, he was still able to stay connected, more so than any of his predecessors, because of the SVITS connections, thus maintaining his influence.

Cheney's role will be explored in greater detail in the following sections. Specific attention will be given to the following areas: the transition, energy policy, relations with Congress, homeland security and the attacks on September 11, and the War on Terror. Not surprisingly, these areas align with Cheney's personal interests and expertise. These areas also exhibit the nature of his influence and how it waxed and waned over the course of his tenure.

Transition

Immediately after Election Day, Cheney planned for the transition even as the election remained unresolved. He stated, "Whatever else happened, the forty-third president of the United States was going to be inaugurated at noon on the steps of the U.S. Capitol on Saturday, January 20, 2001. . . . I

118 / Emerging from the Shadows

reached for the nearest piece of paper [on November 9] and flipped it over and began listing what needed to be done in the seventy-one days between now and then."[305] He set up a privately funded office since the government provided office space and funding was unavailable because the election result was not officially declared.[306] Bush and Cheney felt it was important to operate as if the election would be decided in their favor and to immediately begin putting together an administration.[307] "The transition affects the quality of planning, the building of relationships between the administration and the Congress, the capacity of a new administration to develop and execute a legislative program, and even the ability of the new team to deal with that first crisis when it arises, as it inevitably will."[308] By the time they gained access to the GSA funded office in Washington, DC, it was already December 14, 2000, which meant they only had five weeks to fill thousands of jobs, with many requiring Senate confirmation.[309]

Cheney, who suffered another heart attack, had just been released from the hospital, but immediately went to work on the transition by announcing that Bush had designated him to run it.[310] He worked with Clay Johnson, the executive director of the transition and a Bush loyalist who had actually recommended Cheney for the transition, and a small staff, which included his two daughters, Scooter Libby (Cheney's chief of staff) and David Addington (Cheney's legal counsel) as well as Andy Card, the soon to be White House chief of staff.[311]

Bush felt it was important for Andy Card to be involved in the process since he would be responsible for overseeing the White House.[312] Both Card and Cheney had experience with outgoing transitions, too.[313] The trifecta of having Cheney, Card, and Johnson oversee the transition meant that their combined experience and knowledge of staffing "surpassed their counterparts in earlier transitions."[314] With most of the heavy lifting being done by them, they could avoid problems that beleaguered the Clinton transition in 1992, in which transition principals became cabinet secretaries.[315]

In the transition, Card ensured Bush loyalists were brought into key administration positions, while Cheney worried about the cabinet and the staffing of executive agencies.[316] Johnson, who reported to Cheney, broke down the fourteen cabinet departments between them, with Johnson focusing on subcabinet political positions and Cheney recruiting the cabinet and key subcabinet-level positions.[317] Joshua Bolten, the domestic policy director for the campaign, was brought in to set up policy transition teams.[318] These teams were meant to help incoming cabinet officials with the process of transitioning. "Cheney was unwilling, however, to relinquish his influence over the departments to the Bolten task forces."[319] He created advisory teams for the twelve domestic cabinet departments to advise incoming cabinet officials on policy.[320] Cheney kept a tight control over the Defense Department transition team by placing Zalmay Khalilzad, his deputy undersecretary for policy planning at the Pentagon, in charge of it.

Cheney's influence was very much apparent. He took the lead in filling out the administration and selecting key administration officials.[321] He vetted potential candidates based on two criteria—ideology and political compatibility with the White House.[322] While many of the key White House staff jobs went to Bush's Texas loyalists, Cheney selected nearly all the cabinet secretaries as well as deputy cabinet members, with the exception of Attorney General John Ashcroft and Secretary of State Colin Powell.[323] Thus, Cheney's "closest associates" would fill top positions, to include Donald Rumsfeld as defense secretary, Spencer Abraham as energy secretary, and Paul O'Neill as treasury secretary.[324] Cheney's part in this equation was bringing those with Washington experience into the administration. The result was that "Bush loyalists would manage the White House, but it would be Cheney allies who would manage the larger government."[325] This was particularly important in explaining the degree of influence Cheney would exhibit as vice president because the "key to controlling government decision structures . . . was to put people in place who could be trusted."[326] And Cheney did just that.

Meanwhile, Scooter Libby began filling out the vice presidential office, which he would lead as chief of staff.[327] Cheney made sure that his own allies found positions on his policy staff. Some of Cheney's staffers were given the designation of assistant to the president, further integrating the vice president's loyalists into the president's own staff.[328] Cheney's role in influencing the cabinet staff and cabinet deputy positions fueled speculation that Cheney was calling the shots.[329] In fact, his influence over the cabinet and his good working relationships with the top three cabinet secretaries (State, Defense, and Treasury) foreshadowed the expansive influence he would have over matters under their purview as vice president.[330] Moreover, his responsibility in crafting "governing strategies" meant that he would be intimately involved in procedures, operations, and governing in the administration, especially on matters of importance to him.[331] In essence, he was the "transition's chief architect."[332]

Cheney ensured that the key legal offices in the administration were filled with lawyers who shared his expansive view of presidential power.[333]

His groundwork during the transition would provide him access to the levers of government, which is a precursor for influence. "Cheney's transition role strengthened his position. Many kindred spirits landed important White House and departmental positions, and had reason to feel indebted to him in view of his role in staffing the administration."[334] His reach was all the greater because his loyalists found themselves in key positions. Examples include Paul Wolfowitz as deputy secretary of defense, Christine Todd Whitman at the Environmental Protection Agency, Robert Zoellick as US trade representative, Sean O'Keefe as deputy director of the OMB, John Bolten at the State Department, Stephen Hadley as deputy national security adviser to the president, Donald Rumsfeld at defense, Paul O'Neill at treasury, and Zalmay Khalilzad on the national security council staff.[335]

Cheney also took an active role in courting Congress. He stated, "I also spent a good deal of time during the transition on Capitol Hill. I would be the only person in the Bush 43 West Wing initially who had previously been a member of Congress, and I enjoyed the chance to renew old friendships. In addition, I knew that we would need good relations on the Hill."[336] While Bush met with individual groups such as educators, farmers, and business executives during the transition, Cheney spent considerable time fielding questions from members of Congress, keeping them updated, and soliciting their input.[337] He saw building good relations with Congress as the key to Bush's legislative success.[338]

Images from Cheney's Capitol Hill visits invoked the impression that he was an equal partner in governing with Bush and he could speak for the new president.[339] On the day Gore conceded the election, Cheney headed to Congress to discuss the Bush legislative agenda.[340] He met with the Senate first and then went over to the House to meet with the Republican Policy Committee chair, Christopher Cox, and the Speaker of the House Dennis Hastert.[341]

The transition was also unusual because of the attention paid to details. Cheney, who is known for this, understood the importance of subcabinet positions. He recommended stalwarts to positions that were second- and third-ranking and made sure that allies found homes even deeper in the bureaucracy on policy areas he had an interest in.[342] "Reliable people in mid-level posts would have the last word on numberless decisions about where to spend or not spend money, whom to regulate, [and] how to enforce."[343] He understood that a lot of decisions would not even make it to cabinet or deputy cabinet level.

The transition helped Cheney avoid some of the pitfalls that other vice presidents faced in exercising influence. He was a critical voice in the staffing of the administration. People who worked with Cheney in previous capacities in government, as well as his loyalists and friends, rounded out the administration, thus making it more likely that the executive branch would be receptive to having a more influential vice president. More importantly, it diminished institutional constraints, because he had eyes and ears in key positions in government.

Energy Task Force

The Bush administration took office as rolling brownouts plagued California and caused energy prices to soar.[344] The possibility of an economic disaster was real. The crisis was caused by the state's deregulation of the wholesale energy market in 1996.[345] While the wholesale energy market was deregulated, the retail market was left regulated. "The discrepancy contributed to an imbalance in supply and demand that allowed energy companies, including Enron, to manipulate prices."[346] As prices soared, shortages in power developed, resulting in blackouts throughout California.[347] Worried about the ripple effect, governors from surrounding states visited with the vice president to express their fears.[348] Even Alan Greenspan, the chair of the Federal Reserve, expressed concern to him.[349] He was worried "the shortages might sweep across the country, leaving a trail of doubts about the strength of the U.S. economy."[350] Given the gravity of the crisis, Cheney took Greenspan to meet with Bush to discuss the possible consequences for the greater US economy.[351] At the conclusion of the meeting, Bush agreed action was required.[352] And so, Cheney received his first assignment. Bush tapped Cheney to lead an energy task force (The National Energy Policy Development Group) to comprehensively review US energy policy.[353]

Just nine days after taking office, Bush announced that Cheney would take the lead in developing an energy plan for the administration.[354] Critics immediately questioned the decision given Cheney's ties to Halliburton. The *New York Times* argued that "Halliburton and its rivals would all probably benefit from an aggressive government push to promote exploration and to weaken environmental controls."[355] These stories implied that Cheney's leadership of the task force amounted to political payback for campaign contributions from the energy sector.[356]

One of the first assignments Cheney gave to David Addington was to investigate ways to strengthen presidential power.[357] On the same day as Bush's announcement, Addington wrote a memo explaining how the

122 / Emerging from the Shadows

task force could bring together a group who would not fall under the Federal Advisory Committee Act (FACA).[358] If they were not careful with the official membership of the task force, they would be required to provide all records from the task force to Congress, if requested.[359] To avoid FACA's reporting requirement, the task force would need to be comprised of government employees only.[360] The task force consisted of six cabinet secretaries and some staffers. Outside experts were solicited for their views, but they were not part of the official membership and as such, "Addington would argue, were not subject to disclosure rules."[361] As a result, the outside interests were "withheld" from the public.[362]

After meetings with outside experts, including environmental groups, the business community, and representatives of energy groups, the task force developed a recommendation that became the foundation of a national energy plan.[363] The plan called for increasing energy output and the diversification of energy resources.[364] The task force worked through over 100 proposals during a four-month period.

Critics complained the task force spent less time with environmental groups, denying them input.[365] Unlike the energy-producing companies, numerous "green" supporters were relegated to a single day to offer advice.[366] However, the importance of these stakeholder meetings was limited. The White House met with various interest groups to check a box since they already had a framework in mind.[367] "The meetings had been largely political, and the content of a plan a foregone conclusion. The meetings might produce an idea or two—or cause the staff to reconsider something already discarded—but nothing that came from them was going to have any real influence in shaping the final policy."[368]

In less than four months, on May 19, 2001, Cheney delivered the report, which he considered "lightning speed by government standards."[369] The report stated, "To achieve a 21st century quality of life—enhanced by reliable energy and a clean environment—we must modernize conservation, modernize our infrastructure, increase our energy supplies, including renewables, accelerate the protection and improvement of our environment, and increase our energy security."[370] Cheney also advised the president to go back on his campaign promise to lower emissions of carbon dioxide, which Bush agreed to.[371] With the energy crisis, he believed "it was the wrong time to add to industry's burden" by imposing a cap on carbon emissions that Bush promised during the campaign.[372] Cheney's advice on the reversal was to state that "given the incomplete state of scientific knowledge of the causes of, and solutions to, global climate change," further inquiry regarding "innovative options" was required.[373] In essence, Cheney and his staff argued the evidence was inconclusive and that it would be "premature at this time for the President to propose any specific policy or approach aimed at addressing global warming."[374] The reversal would demonstrate the depth of Cheney's influence.

The report created a backlash not due to its recommendations, but over the fact that Congress and the public were kept in the dark.[375] Two Democratic congressmen, Henry Waxman and John Dingell, sent a letter to Andrew Lundquist and David Walker, the comptroller general of the General Accounting Office (GAO), requesting access to the records.[376] The request went to Addington, who refused to turn over any records.[377] While this was occurring, Cheney traveled the country to explain the administration's energy plan, giving major speeches during the spring and summer of 2001.[378] The public campaign brought more attention to the administration's energy plan but failed to quiet critics. If anything, it emboldened the critics who felt the administration was hiding something by not releasing the records, and it "earned him [Cheney] a reputation for secretiveness."[379]

Meanwhile, Addington continued battling the GAO over the records until fall of 2001.[380] He argued "that the GAO, as a legislative body 'could not intrude into the heart of Executive deliberations.'"[381] Continually rebuffed by Addington, the GAO threatened litigation to get the records.[382] Cheney backed his aide. He stated, "I looked at it, looked to me like it was a pretty clear-cut case. We had in fact done what we said we were going to do, and we weren't subject to the advisory committee act. And so we fought it."[383] Cheney and Addington seemed to be the only ones interested in a fight, though. The White House communications office was tired of repeated inquiries from reporters on the release of the documents and argued for the records to be disclosed.[384] Even Lundquist, who understood Cheney's and Addington's position, felt the records should be released.[385] Bush sided with Cheney. Bush stated, "Stiff 'em," referring to the members of Congress requesting the information.[386]

Cheney was determined to restore presidential power, and this was an opportunity to aggressively guard against congressional encroachment. It was a matter of principle. He was opposed to turning over documents he felt the GAO and Congress had no right to. "Something larger was at stake: the power of the presidency and the ability of the president and vice president to carry out their constitutional duties."[387] "If citizens who come to the White House to offer advice have to worry about lawsuits or being called before congressional committees, it would pretty severely curtail

124 / Emerging from the Shadows

the counsel a president and vice president could receive."[388] It would have been far easier to release the documents, but he would not relent. Cheney explained, "One of the things over the years that I've been frustrated by is that government often took the easy way out. Somebody would come along and issue a subpoena or file a lawsuit—they'd cave, give it up. And I didn't like to do that. It struck me as an opportunity to fight all the way, and the president backed me up on it."[389] Cheney convinced Bush that it was important to go to court to protect his constitutional rights.[390] With Bush's support, he publicly demonstrated the administration's intent to curb the intrusion on presidential power and their "willingness to fight on behalf of executive power."[391] The case went all the way to the Supreme Court, which remanded it to a district court on a vote of seven to two, where it "died."[392] The GAO would cease to pursue the matter further.[393]

Cheney's work on the energy task force demonstrated his influence with the president. In addition to winning a critical battle over presidential power, he also used the task force to persuade Bush to "undo what he saw as an ill-advised campaign pledge," the carbon emissions cap.[394] On March 13, Cheney received a letter from Senator Chuck Hagel as well as three other Republicans who sought clarification of the president's energy policy position.[395] Cheney took the letter to Bush and told him that now was the time to reverse course on the campaign pledge while simultaneously rejecting the Kyoto climate change treaty.[396] Bush agreed and Cheney drafted a response letter for his signature.[397] The letter indicated that Bush opposed the Kyoto treaty because it did not include "rising economies" and would cause "serious harm to the U.S. economy."[398] The letter also elaborated on the president's position on carbon emissions by stating that he did not believe the "government should impose on power plants mandatory emissions reductions for carbon dioxide, which is not a 'pollutant' under the Clean Air Act."[399]

Cheney circumvented White House procedures by working the issue directly with Bush. Christine Todd Whitman, the president's Environmental Protection Agency director, was bypassed and the letter was never vetted by others.[400] Cheney admitted to circumventing the system but justified it due to the time sensitivity of the issue.[401] By the time Whitman had arrived at the White House, Cheney was departing for Capitol Hill with the president's response. She was visiting the president to advise him to keep his campaign promise, but was too late.[402] Furthermore, since the matter dealt with an international treaty, its importance went beyond the EPA director. The State Department and the national security adviser would normally be included on any deliberations, but in this case, neither Powell nor Rice were consulted ahead of time.[403] While Rice and Powell would later state that they did not necessarily oppose the position, they would have worked to tone down the language so it would be less provocative by stating that a "rejection of Kyoto was not a rejection of the issue altogether."[404] But Powell was annoyed for being cut out of the process. He stated, "They all got together . . . and said to hell with everybody else . . . no references to 'Let's work with them [allies] and find a way forward on carbon emissions.'"[405] Rice echoed this sentiment when she told Bush she was "appalled" that the vice president would take a letter regarding an important international policy to the Senate "without the input of the national security adviser or secretary of state."[406]

Congressional Relations

Cheney was the administration's go-to-guy for all congressional matters because of his career in the House, where he still had many friends and associates.[407] These relationships ensured that he was the first person in the White House to find out if there was a problem in Congress.[408] Cheney's friendships provided him with unprecedented access, and as a result he was the "principal source of information" about what could and could not be done in Congress.[409] And it was a two-way street. Members of Congress saw him as a reliable indicator to gauge the administration's receptivity to their ideas and they understood that Cheney spoke for the president. Rep. Bill Thomas, a longtime friend of Cheney's, stated, "I can pitch the specific structural modification, and he can give immediate assurance that the administration is supportive of what I want to do."[410] Thomas recalled that it was difficult to pinpoint a time in which Cheney failed to convince Bush of something that Thomas lobbied him for.[411] Senator Phil Gramm noted that what separated Cheney from others was "Dick could make a deal. He didn't have to check with the president, as far as I could tell. I'm sure at the end of the day, he would fill the president in on what had happened. But Dick had the agency of the president."[412] Bush reinforced these views. As mentioned previously, Bush had once told a Republican member of Congress, "When you're talking to Dick Cheney, you're talking to me. . . . When Dick Cheney's talking, it is me talking."[413]

Cheney's role with Congress as the person putting out fires, enforcing, informing, intervening, and compromising is best exemplified by a

126 / Emerging from the Shadows

discussion of key issue areas that he contended with in Congress. The issues Cheney spent the most time with as vice president included: the Iraq War authorization, the imminent attack on Iraq, the use of enhanced interrogation techniques, the Terrorist Surveillance Program, and the Bush tax cuts. It is no coincidence that these areas were some of the administration's top priorities. In all these areas, Cheney's involvement made a significant difference and demonstrated the influence he held on Capitol Hill and in the White House.

Iraq Authorization

When the Bush administration sought an authorization for war with Iraq from Congress, despite feeling that congressional approval was unnecessary, Cheney led the effort.[414] Cheney thought it was risky; if you failed to obtain the approval, it would be a major "political setback," although he was certain they could win.[415] After all, Democrats had approved of the Iraq regime-change policy, and Cheney thought it would be hypocritical for them to go against the authorization for war because Iraq posed an even greater danger.[416]

This did not mean it was smooth sailing. Rep. John Murtha, a great ally to Cheney on Capitol Hill while he was secretary of defense, was undecided on the vote. His support for the authorization was uncertain, despite having voted in favor of the first Gulf War.[417] Murtha was being lobbied by Brent Scowcroft, the former national security advisor to George H. W. Bush and an opponent of the authorization, to vote no.[418] Murtha requested a meeting with the vice president. He told Cheney that he believed Saddam Hussein had weapons of mass destruction (WMDs) and would not hesitate to use them on American soldiers if invaded, but he did not think there was a link to al Qaeda.[419] Cheney told him he would relay his concerns to Bush but then made a convincing argument for war.[420] After that meeting, Murtha decided to vote in favor of the authorization, and eighty of his Democratic colleagues joined him in the House to vote in favor of the resolution.[421]

Cheney was a proponent of swift action. He said that in an election year, the president "should demand quick passage of a resolution so voters would know before the election where every congressman and senator stood on Saddam Hussein."[422] Bush invited two separate delegations from Congress to the White House, one on September 4, 2002 (eighteen key

Senate and House members) and a dozen more on October 1, 2002.[423] The main argument the president used, was the vice president's: "Doing nothing is not an option."[424] Cheney elaborated by stating, "The key things are that we have always underestimated this guy."[425] Then Bush added that Congress had overwhelmingly voted in favor of regime change in Iraq back in 1998 and that his "administration embraces that policy even more so in light of 9/11."[426]

The full-court press by the vice president and now the president was showing signs of success. However, there was still an important holdout, the Republican House majority leader, Dick Armey.[427] Armey made public comments that he did not feel the need to mess with Saddam Hussein. Yes, he was a tyrant, but not "a menace to the United States."[428] Bush intervened directly by inviting him to the White House and Camp David, and even arranged a special briefing for Armey with the CIA director, to no avail.[429] Cheney was asked to intercede. The consequences were considerable, because if the majority leader from the president's own party opposed, it could jeopardize support among rank-and-file Republicans. Some could use it for cover to vote against the measure.

Cheney spent a full hour with Armey in the vice president's house office and provided "a blood-chilling narrative" with graphics.[430] He told Armey the threat posed by Hussein was much greater than acknowledged publicly.[431] After the meeting, Armey toned down his rhetoric and ended up reluctantly voting for the authorization, "weeping in the well of the House" as he cast his vote.[432] Cheney was the deciding factor. The vote was 296 to 133 in the House and 77 to 23 in the Senate.[433]

Enhanced Interrogation Techniques

Cheney, a proponent of enhanced interrogation, was dispatched to the Capitol to defend the program, which was coming under attack by Senator John McCain, a former POW who was tortured during the Vietnam War.[434] McCain argued that these techniques violated the Geneva Convention, but Cheney viewed the issue differently.[435] "Cheney explained that because al Qaeda was not a state—as Geneva Convention signatories are—that its members were not protected by the Convention."[436] He viewed the program as essential. Interrogations should continue as long as they did not violate the nation's laws.[437] However, McCain was pursuing legislation to restrict interrogation techniques, which put the program in jeopardy.[438]

128 / Emerging from the Shadows

Cheney tried to change McCain's mind, but he was unmovable.[439] He argued, "My view was that some techniques should never be used because they then damaged our image with people in the world. And in my view, it made us no different from them or hard to tell the difference between ourselves and them. And my belief is that if you inflict enough physical pain on somebody, then they're going to tell you whatever it is you want to hear."[440] In one meeting, Cheney recalled that McCain "stormed" out of the room and did not want to discuss the matter. He completely lost his temper.[441] McCain was convinced that the program amounted to torture. He said, "You can't tell me it's not torture, I have been tortured, I know what torture is."[442] Before McCain stormed out, Cheney attempted to provide him with substitute language that would maintain the administration's flexibility, which McCain rejected.[443] Cheney told "McCain [that he] would have blood on his hands."[444] McCain recalled, "Basically, they told me that if our legislation passes, I am going to have planes flying into buildings."[445] Despite the frequent meetings with McCain, Cheney was unable to convince him to drop the amendment. It passed by ninety to nine in the Senate on October 5, 2005.[446] This was a significant blow to the White House. While the program was not widely used, it did provide crucial information that led to determining Osama bin Laden's location.[447] "We waterboarded a total of three guys, most of it was focused on KSM [Khalid Sheikh Mohammed] but he was a gold mine of intelligence and the program worked very well."[448] Cheney said the program had been disclosed to key members of Congress and not once did he hear any objection.[449] While a loss, Cheney was able to ensure interrogators were protected from legal liability.[450]

Terrorist Surveillance Program

Cheney was worried that not enough was being done to safeguard the United States and prevent another 9/11-style attack, and so he had a meeting with Director George Tenet and his suspicions were confirmed.[451] Tenet asked Michael Hayden, director of the National Security Agency (NSA), who stated he was doing the most he could within current authorizations.[452] The NSA is responsible for "collecting intelligence about the communications of America's adversaries."[453] It was constrained in its ability to monitor al Qaeda's planning efforts by the bureaucracy of the Foreign Intelligence Surveillance (FISA) court. It was exceedingly difficult to have warrants issued in a timely manner, making surveillance efforts less effective.[454] "But with so many foreign telephone calls and e-mails now coming through American communications trunks, it was impractical, Hayden and his team concluded, to seek individual warrants."[455] Wait times averaged four to six weeks, and even with emergency authorization the lag time was still a day or more.[456] Tenet and Hayden met with the Cheney to present a plan to enhance the NSA's ability to monitor al Qaeda's planning operations and communications.[457] Cheney took Tenet and Hayden to see Bush immediately after the meeting and received the president's permission to move forward with new procedures.[458] Within one week of the meeting, the NSA was granted new authorities for the Terrorist Surveillance Program (TSP), which required that any phone calls under surveillance had to have at least one end of the conversation outside the United States, and probable cause had to exist for at least one person on the call to be suspected of having ties to al Qaeda.[459] The plan would bypass the FISA court.[460] This meant that the NSA could now monitor domestic communications but only if the above conditions were met.[461]

Absent congressional authorization, Cheney asked Addington to draft a document to create the TSP for the president to sign.[462] Addington worked with Hayden and the president's legal counsel, Alberto Gonzales, to create the new authorities for the NSA.[463] Cheney brought the document to Bush, who signed it just three weeks after 9/11; thus, the TSP was born.[464] Bush stipulated that the program needed to be kept on a "short leash," which meant that it needed to be renewed every thirty to forty-five days and required signatures of the attorney general, secretary of defense, and the director of the CIA before the president would grant the renewal.[465] The program was approved by the signatories as well as NSA lawyers, who deemed it legally sound.[466] Cheney became the chief architect of the controversial and confidential TSP.[467] This was something that was hard to imagine for other vice presidents, although the circumstances were extraordinarily different. The program was so secretive that according to Cheney, when it needed to be renewed, "Dave Addington carried the authorizing document in a locked classified documents pouch by hand to each of the officials involved."[468]

The administration decided to inform select members of Congress. Cheney stated, "Given the extreme fragility and sensitivity of the intelligence sources and methods involved, we briefed only the chair and ranking members of the House and Senate intelligence committees."[469] Cheney and Hayden hosted the briefings for a group of congressional leaders known as the "gang of eight."[470] The gang of eight included leaders from both

130 / Emerging from the Shadows

parties in both houses, as well as the chairs and ranking members of the intelligence committees.[471] First, Cheney specifically asked the lawmakers assembled if they should continue the program, to which they responded yes.[472] Second, he asked whether they needed legislation, to which everyone in the room said no.[473] Speaker Hastert recalls that "everybody looked around the room and said no, I don't think we need to."[474] The lawmakers asked few questions, and all agreed that the program was both important and should continue.[475] More importantly, they thought no more people needed to be informed about the program. By seeking legislative authority, the program risked being disclosed so they advised against it.[476] This became one of the cornerstone programs of the war on terror, and Cheney had not only been involved in its conception but also routinely briefed lawmakers in order ensure its continuation and their buy-in.[477]

Bush Tax Cuts

Cheney was instrumental in the formulation and passage of the Bush tax cuts, with the first cuts taking place in 2001, and the second in 2003.[478] The 2001 package was priced at $1.6 trillion, but opposition formed in Congress over the amount.[479] Nonetheless, bipartisan support for a tax cut existed.[480] Cheney was involved in the "behind-the-scenes negotiations" to ensure the tax cuts were passed by Congress.[481] A group of Senate Democrats were only willing to support a $1.25 trillion package.[482] On April 3, 2001, Cheney cast his first tie-breaking vote to halt passage of the smaller tax cut.[483] The next day he met in Senate majority leader Trent Lott's office, and wrote three numbers on a napkin: 1.6; 1.425; and 1.25.[484] Cheney circled $1.425 trillion, a compromise he stated that Bush would be able to support.[485]

After the April 4, 2001 meeting, he learned that Senator Jim Jeffords (R-VT) wanted $450 million diverted from the cuts to fund special education.[486] He threatened to leave the Republican Party and caucus with the Democrats if funding was not provided.[487] The switch would give the majority to the Democrats. Cheney refused to give in to the demands. "Acquiescence to Jeffords, as Cheney saw it, would mean the White House had already lost the Senate. Negotiation, in this context, was akin to surrender." Jeffords left the Republican Party but still voted for the tax cut, which would ultimately amount to $1.325 trillion in tax relief.[488]

In 2003, Bush sought additional cuts and proposed a $550 billion tax cut to stimulate the economy.[489] The cuts were intended to allow the country to weather a recession and to recover from the 9/11 attacks. The 2003 tax cuts faced more resistance mainly because of differences between House and Senate Republicans. Rep. Bill Thomas and Senator Chuck Grassley, chairs of the "tax-writing committees," were no longer on speaking terms owing to such differences.[490] Senator Bill Frist called in Cheney to negotiate a deal.[491]

Cheney mediated between the two Republicans, and with Bush, invited the members of Congress to the White House.[492] The House had already passed the $550 billion package so it would need to go to conference.[493] Before the meeting, Grassley said that he could not back a tax cut larger than $350 billion, because Senators Olympia Snowe and George Voinovich would not agree to anything larger.[494] "That created an impasse: what Grassley saw as honoring a commitment to his colleagues, Hastert and Thomas [in the House] viewed as intransigence."[495] During the meeting Hastert told Frist that Grassley should be banned from the conference because he was already locked into a plan.[496] Cutting the chairman of the Senate committee responsible for taxes out of the negotiations was a significant slight. Bush ended the meeting by saying that he wanted a bill to sign by Memorial Day.[497]

Cheney worked closely with Thomas but communication between Thomas and Grassley was strained, so Cheney asked Voinovich to meet with Thomas since the House had already agreed to the $350 billion cap and he was the linchpin for the tax cuts.[498] Voinovich was upset though, because Grassley felt he needed "sweeteners" to get the bill passed in the Senate, and these additions, which included state assistance and child-care refunds, would increase the tax cut to $382 billion.[499] Thomas said, "Cheney sits there and doesn't say a word. . . . He put me out there and I would perform, so that he wasn't making arguments, I was. It was classic good cop, bad cop routine."[500] They ultimately agreed to a $320 billion tax cut with a reduction of individual tax on dividends to 15 percent, which with the sweeteners would bring it to $350 billion.[501] Within two days, Cheney cast a tie-breaking vote for the tax cut in the Senate.[502] Thomas argued that Cheney was "kind of like a pastor coming in and settling a family dispute. . . . The Republicans are a unified congregation because of Vice President Cheney."[503]

Cheney was satisfied with the results. This was his baby.[504] He stated, "By the time I took my seat as president of the Senate on May 23, I felt I had earned my keep. And when I cast the tie-breaking vote to ensure

132 / Emerging from the Shadows

the bill's passage, I was sure I had."[505] Cheney's involvement in the second round of tax cuts demonstrates the degree of influence he exercised over Congress.

Cheney's relations with Congress represented several firsts for vice presidents. First, while all vice presidents maintain a ceremonial office on the Senate side of the Capitol, Cheney was the first vice president to be given an office on the House side. According to Cheney, Speaker Hastert had approached him to offer office space on the House side.[506] The chairman of the Ways and Means Committee offered the conference room, which was prime real estate, located right off the House floor.[507] Cheney would attend meetings of the House leadership, which was highly unusual for a vice president.[508] This was a testament to not only Cheney's influence but represented how well he was received by the Republican leadership and rank and file. They considered him a "man of the House."[509]

Attendance at the meetings and securing office space on the House side of the Capitol were instrumental in furthering his legislative liaison role for the White House and came particularly handy when Cheney was negotiating the tax packages. After all, the House office became a "strategic outpost for Cheney" and allowed him to keep a pulse on the lower chamber.[510] And since the House is where all revenue bills originate, it gave Cheney an advantage that other vice presidents lacked—the ability to be involved at the point of entry.[511]

Another first was Cheney's attendance at the weekly policy luncheons held by Senate Republicans.[512] These lunches are informal sessions where ideas are floated, and pending legislation is discussed.[513] Cheney's participation in the meetings was limited. He would usually sit in silence and just listen.[514] Senator McCain stated, "He's very quiet. . . . If it's an issue that he feels strongly about, then he stands up and speaks. But generally he doesn't speak up. He just has lunch, sits at a big table with guys, converses, and after lunch people talk to him."[515] He wanted to ensure that the Republican senators viewed him as an ally in the White House, which is why he abstained from lobbying.[516] It was highly unusual for a vice president to receive a standing invitation. Lyndon Johnson, a giant in the United States Senate, was barred from entering the Senate Democratic lunches as vice president.[517] "As an institution the Senate does not always take kindly to vice presidents, who have a foot in the executive branch as well as in the legislative."[518] That was the last time a vice president attempted to attend a party's lunch caucus.[519] Cheney truly had robust interaction with Congress and took the role of liaison to Congress and president of the Senate to historic levels in terms of the numbers of "firsts" he created for the vice presidency.

Homeland Security and Attacks on September 11

HOMELAND SECURITY

Cheney had a long-standing interest in homeland security as a result of his participation in continuity of government exercises in the 1980s, his membership on the House Intelligence Committee, and his service as defense secretary.[520] He was more than willing to undertake this line assignment because he viewed terrorism, rogue states, and weapons of mass destruction as serious threats to the homeland.[521]

Continuity of government had always been at the back of the vice president's mind so he asked his counsel, David Addington, to review the "formal procedures" in place for "leadership succession."[522] Addington uncovered a flaw with the Twenty-Fifth Amendment; no procedure existed to remove an incapacitated vice president from office.[523] The Twenty-Fifth Amendment specified that a vice president, in concert with the cabinet, was required to remove an incapacitated president.[524] If Cheney was incapacitated, and the president also became incapacitated, there was no mechanism to remove the president and thus the government would face a succession crisis. The result would be that either the president could not be removed from office or Cheney "might become an incapacitated acting president. Neither of these was a good outcome for the country."[525] Given Cheney's health history, this was a serious concern.

As a result, Cheney drafted a letter of resignation, which Addington held in a safe in his home.[526] It authorized him to provide the letter to the president as soon as the vice president was deemed incapacitated, allowing the president to decide whether or not to submit it to the secretary of state, thus removing the vice president from office.[527] Only the vice president, president, and Addington knew of the letter's existence.[528] This was an extraordinary act that had never been undertaken by any other vice president; however, Cheney's health and personal concern for continuity of government made him more conscious of worst-case scenarios.

Related to homeland security was Cheney's interest in intelligence. Cheney stated, "From my perspective, one of the things I wanted to do, and I told him [Bush] I planned to do, with his approval, obviously, was

134 / Emerging from the Shadows

as soon as I could I wanted to dig back into the intelligence community—because I had been out of the loop for eight years."[529] Bush agreed that Cheney would engage the intelligence community.

He was "a voracious discriminating consumer of intelligence since his days in the Ford administration, Cheney is rarely satisfied with the formal intelligence products he's given."[530] He pushed hard to get more information, which explains why his PDB briefing was more extensive than the president's. Cheney always pressed intelligence analysts to say more than what was in the formal product.[531] He understood that intelligence was the first line of defense.[532]

Bush welcomed Cheney's tenacity when it came to intelligence and encouraged him to continue this approach.[533] He was comfortable giving him such an important piece of the administration's portfolio and even made clear well before they took office that "there will be a crisis in my administration, and Dick Cheney is exactly the man you want at your side in a crisis."[534] And Cheney did just that. Bush asked him to examine the nation's susceptibility to terrorism, specifically the threat posed by biological and chemical agents.[535]

This assignment, as well as the role he would play in the war on terror, contributed to the shadowy image that Cheney became known for. After all, Cheney would be operating behind the scenes in an area in which information was classified. He knew this came with the territory because just days after September 11, Cheney admitted,

> We also have to work, though, sort of the dark side, if you will. We've got to spend time in the shadows in the intelligence world. A lot of what needs to be done here will have to be done quietly, without any discussion, using sources and methods that are available to our intelligence agencies, if we're going to be successful. That's the world these folks operate in, and so it's going to be vital for us to use any means at our disposal, basically, to achieve our objectives.[536]

Statements like these would earn him the nickname Dark Side.[537] He stated, "I suppose people sometimes look at my demeanor and say, well, he's the Darth Vader of the administration."[538] Cheney did not mind though and even embraced it. In 2007, he dressed up his dog for Halloween as Lord of the Sith, a reference to the Star Wars franchise in which Darth Vader is featured.[539]

In the first few weeks of the administration, Cheney spent considerable time focused on homeland security and intelligence. Cheney made the rounds of the intelligence community by visiting Secret Service Headquarters, the Central Intelligence Agency (CIA), the Federal Bureau of Investigation (FBI), the National Security Administration, National Reconnaissance Office, and the Defense Intelligence Agency (DIA).[540] These visits familiarized him with their leadership and allowed him to speak with the agencies' employees.[541] By the summer of 2001, Cheney wanted a dedicated staffer to oversee his homeland security portfolio, so he hired Steve Abbot, a retired admiral.[542] Bush made an announcement that Cheney would head "a comprehensive review of U.S. government homeland security" in order to assess "domestic preparedness against weapons of mass destruction."[543] However, Cheney's assignment was not to prevent an attack, but to develop "worst case scenarios" and to prepare responses to these crises.[544] It was known as consequence management and "was neither offensive or defensive, but responsive."[545]

Cheney's assignment also bought with it the creation of a new federal agency, the Office of National Preparedness, which was formed within the Federal Emergency Management Agency to coordinate the federal government's response to a WMD attack.[546] The intent was to examine existing policies and then for Cheney to offer new proposals, with a report due to the president by October 2001.[547]

The gravity of the assignment was not lost on Cheney. In an April 2001 interview with Nicholas Lemann of the *New Yorker*, Cheney stated, "I think we have to be more concerned than we ever have about so-called homeland defense, the vulnerability of our system to different kinds of attacks."[548] To eliminate or diminish threats, Cheney spoke of the need to ensure that intelligence was robust.[549] Even before the attacks on September 11, Cheney was concerned with the effects terrorism would have on the nation. He was worried by the potential attack on an American city with a "dirty bomb," a makeshift nuclear weapon.[550] A dirty bomb attack would result in thousands of fatalities and leave a city uninhabitable for many years.[551]

Cheney's focus on homeland security intensified during the summer of 2001 due to spikes in threat levels, which forced the government to a status of high alert.[552] The "chatter" did not specifically call for an attack on the homeland, instead it viewed likely targets to be in Europe, Israel, Saudi Arabia, or Jordan.[553] Cheney recalled that the intelligence community never produced actionable intelligence, the only warning they had was a vague threat of an attack.[554]

136 / Emerging from the Shadows

The task force was slow going.[555] Cheney's task was complicated by the fact that so many agencies had overlapping jurisdictions over homeland security.[556] Thus, the review included the existing plans of various federal agencies as well as those of the different task forces created.[557] The task force's report recommended improvements to the government's WMD attack response and offered ways to revise intelligence and terrorism policies, to improve intelligence gathering efforts.[558] "The list included crafting and implementing a national strategy for preparedness and response; improving the intelligence warning of a WMD attack; clarifying lines of federal authority for counterterrorism and emergency response between FEMA and law enforcement; integrating local, state, and federal emergency response agencies; and improving bioterrorism detection and the public health system's ability to respond to such an attack."[559] The importance of the vice president's role in the task force took on greater significance after 9/11. The report's recommendations helped to establish new policies and led to the establishment of the Department of Homeland Security.[560] Moreover, the report would serve as a road map for Cheney to guide the country's immediate response to 9/11.

Attacks on September 11

While the attacks on September 11, 2001 shocked the country, Cheney had prepared most of his career for such a horrific act and was ready to implement his recommendations from the homeland security task force. He started that day with his routine CIA briefing at his residence before heading to the White House for a day of scheduled meetings.[561] Cheney recalled that the CIA briefing was unremarkable and gave no hint at what would unfold that day.[562] He was meeting with his speechwriter, John McConnell, and the deputy director of the OMB, Sean O'Keefe, in his West Wing office when their meeting was interrupted by Cheney's secretaries, telling him to turn on the television.[563] According to McConnell, there was no sense of alarm at first when they heard a plane had crashed into the World Trade Center.[564]

Initially, they thought it was just an unfortunate accident, not an act of terror. Cheney presumed it had been a small private plane. He stated, "Boy, it's going to be a bad day at the FAA today. . . . This is a tragedy."[565] However, a Secret Service agent, would confirm that it was a passenger plane.[566] A mistake of this magnitude was unimaginable.[567] However, after Cheney turned on the television, they watched in disbelief as a second plane, United Airlines Flight 175, hit the South Tower.[568] At this point the reality of the situation sunk in and Cheney knew at that moment that this was a terrorist act.[569] Cheney immediately went to Andy Card's office and told his secretary that he wanted to speak to the chief of staff when he called in.[570] He rushed back to his office, picked up his direct line to the president's communication team and told them he needed to talk to the president.[571] After being led to a holding room at the elementary school in Florida, Bush's first move was to contact the FBI director and the vice president.[572] Bush told Karl Rove, who was traveling with him, "We're at war."[573]

While waiting for the call to be patched through, a stream of people began flowing into Cheney's office, including Scooter Libby (Cheney's chief of staff), Condoleezza Rice (national security adviser), Joshua Bolten (deputy chief of staff), Richard Clarke (director of counterterrorism), and Mary Matalin (Cheney's communication adviser), in order to assess the situation with Cheney.[574] This demonstrated his central role that day as he coordinated the government's response. He told those assembled, "The cabinet is going to need direction" and so he started doling out instructions while waiting for the call with the president to be connected.[576] Cheney was connected to Bush via secure phone at 9:15 a.m., and they went over what they knew and decided on what Bush should say in a public statement.[576] "Better to be cautious, they agreed, and decided that Bush would speak of 'an apparent' act of terrorism."[577]

While Cheney was conferring in his office, the Secret Service burst into the office with their guns drawn and demanded he leave immediately.[578] The Secret Service received a call from Reagan National's control tower that a third plane was "flying fast and low toward the White House."[579] Cheney did not immediately get up when his secret service agent demanded he leave, so the agent slammed his hand on the desk and shouted "now."[580] Before he knew it, the agent grabbed him and moved him to the Presidential Emergency Operations Center (PEOC).[581] Cheney stated, "He put his hand on my shoulder and grabbed me by the back of my belt . . . and propelled me out the door. They must practice it."[582] Cheney arrived in PEOC just as the third plane crashed into the Pentagon.[583]

While all this transpired, Addington made a call to the general counsel at the Pentagon to ensure the THREATCON had been raised.[584] This one act demonstrates the influence that both Cheney and his staff carried. Instead of the order coming from the president's staff, the first thing that the vice president's counsel thought to do was to contact the

138 / Emerging from the Shadows

Pentagon to raise the THREATCON level. Immediately thereafter, Addington began evacuating the vice president's staff from the Old Executive Office Building.[585]

Once inside PEOC, Cheney called Bush while he was aboard Air Force One and told him not to return to Washington, because they needed to ensure continuity of government.[586] In the same vein, Cheney also tried to reach Speaker Hastert to ensure succession and relocate the congressional leadership to a secure location, but he was unable to get through.[587] "Cheney was going through the drills he had learned concerning the continuity of government; he was playing defense, trying above all to prevent what the nuclear war experts had called decapitation—that is, the elimination of all of a country's top decision makers, leaving the nation leaderless and unable to respond."[588] Cheney knew it was too unsafe to allow Bush to return, with so much still unknown.[589] Bush reluctantly agreed and told Cheney that he would "make decisions from the air and count on him to implement them on the ground."[590] Cheney remembered Bush disliked the idea of not returning to Washington.[591] He was troubled that the optics would send a bad message—that terrorists were successful in keeping the president from the "seat of power."[592]

PEOC had less than stellar communications. Secure calls were consistently dropped, and they could only hear sound on one video monitor at a time, frustrating all those in bunker.[593] Furthermore, those who were in the Situation Room monitoring the events could only communicate with PEOC through one telephone number they had, which Cheney waited "impatiently" to connect with the president, the mayor of New York, and the secretary of defense through.[594] Given the poor state of communications, Cheney told the president he should head to Offutt Air Force Base, in Nebraska, which had secure communications in the emergency operations center and was home to U.S. Strategic Command (Stratcom).[595]

In all accounts of the government's response on 9/11, one feature stood out—Cheney's demeanor. He worked with those assembled in a cool and deliberate fashion.[596] He was executing the plans he had studied for decades. "Cheney was the dominant figure on September 11. It was he who urged the president to fly to Offutt Air Force Base in Nebraska. . . . It was he who ordered that House Speaker Dennis Hastert and other congressional leaders be taken out of town to one of the Eisenhower-era bunkers built for use if America was under nuclear attack."[597] Karen Hughes remarked on Cheney's command of the situation, "I was impressed by the strength and decisiveness I was witnessing as the vice president coordinated with the president and issued instructions to various agencies."[598] Cheney was the most senior member at the table that day, he was the one considered in charge.[599] Cheney stated that he did not think of his actions as taking charge. Instead, he stated, "I began to operate. Everybody responded to me; everybody came to me. I didn't have to say, 'I'm in charge here.' I think . . . part of it had to do just with the way I'd been operating as vice president, the way the president had treated me."[600] His influence was palpable long before 9/11, and as a result, those assembled deferred to him. He "was the coolest head in the room, working calmly to gather data, digest it, and direct the cabinet. In another administration, that would have been the national security adviser's job, or the chief of staff's."[601] Most of the government response was administered from PEOC under Cheney's discretion.[602]

Cheney kept his head down and worked, making sure not to upstage the president. He thought it was important for someone to deliver a statement about the attacks in the president's absence and argued that "It was also important to get the message out that the government is still in business."[603] He told Karen Hughes, the president's director of communications, she should give a statement to the press.[604] He stated, "I don't think I got any credit from his communications people for that. It was a very good decision. I would have really stolen his thunder if I had asserted myself publicly with the press as the guy who was sitting in the bunker in the White House running the world while the president was off at an Air Force base."[605] Nonetheless, he was very much involved in managing the crisis, although not publicly.

Due to the uncertainty regarding the number of planes hijacked, Secretary of Transportation Norm Mineta and Cheney spent significant time tracking planes by tail numbers.[606] To reduce the threat, Mineta ordered all aircraft grounded and closed US airspace.[607] The Federal Aviation Administration grounded a total of four thousand planes.[608]

One of the most controversial occurrences during that chaotic day was the order to shoot down passenger planes that were unresponsive and failed to comply with the order to land. The record is mixed regarding who issued the order. Cheney's official biographer contends that when Cheney was informed by the Secret Service that a plane was quickly heading to Washington, he immediately called the president and told him that a decision had to be made.[609] "Cheney told the president: should we give pilots [of the combat air patrol] an order authorizing them to shoot down civilian aircraft that could be used to conduct further attacks in

140 / Emerging from the Shadows

Washington?"[610] Cheney advised the president that he supported such an order and the president agreed.[611] Karl Rove confirms this sequence of events, arguing that as soon as they were airborne on Air Force One, the vice president called to ask the president what the rules of engagement would be for the Air Force.[612] Rove recalls that Bush forcefully ordered engagement to shoot down planes that were hijacked and could not be "controlled."[613] Rove contends that Cheney asked the president twice on the phone and the president told him, "You have my authorization."[614] Cheney would actually call back to reconfirm the order as well.[615]

Bush backed up this scenario, stating, "I told Dick that our pilots should contact suspicious planes and try to get them to land peacefully. If that failed, they had my authority to shoot them down."[616] Cheney had called back to confirm the shoot-down directive once he had been informed of an unresponsive plane heading for Washington, which Bush did.[617] Rice also confirms this narrative, recalling that Cheney called the president to ask if they should shoot down unresponsive planes, which the president approved. "The Vice President transmitted to the Pentagon: if a plane did not 'squawk' properly, treat it as a foe and shoot it down."[618]

However, outside those principals, there exists some uncertainty of when the order was given and whether Cheney received prior authorization from the president. Cheney insisted that he gave the order after conveying the situation of the approaching plane to Bush.[619] "But there was, and has remained conflicting testimony and evidence of any such notification. There was also the question of whether, beyond the imperative of immediate action, any authority ever existed for a vice president to issue such an order."[620] According to Joel Goldstein, none of the records from that day, official or unofficial, were able to document the conversation, and even after Cheney gave the order, Josh Bolten requested Cheney confirm the order with Bush, which he did.[621] This led "some to wonder later whether Cheney did get permission before deciding what to do about further attacks."[622] The 9/11 commission also questioned the veracity of Bush and Cheney's explanation of the event, although they could not confirm or deny it.[623]

If Cheney did indeed issue the order without getting prior authorization, it represented a case of "Cheney unhesitatingly [filling] the breach in behalf of the president and thereafter functioned more in the nature of an assistant president than any of his forty-five predecessors."[624] As Goldstein notes, "With Bush away and handicapped by poor communication, Cheney exercised some presidential prerogatives."[625] Regardless of whether Cheney received authorization prior to issuing the directive or not, the vice president transmitted the order without hesitation. With the hijacked plane rapidly approaching Washington, a military aide asked Cheney for authorization to take out the aircraft.[626] According to Scooter Libby, he responded as quickly as the "time it takes a batter to swing, maybe starting from the windup."[627] The military aide was so surprised by the swift response that he asked the vice president three times to confirm, which Cheney did.[628] When the order was given, silence fell over the room as those inside pondered the gravity of the situation.[629] Cheney remained calm and steady. "'He clearly had been through crises before and did not appear to be in shock like many of us,' Bolten said."[630] The consequences for inaction were too great. Cheney stated, "I don't want it to sound heartless, but there was no alternative. . . . It wasn't the kind of thing you agonized over."[631] There was not enough time to wrestle with the decision or "consider the gravity of the order."[632] He referred to it as "painful, but nonetheless clear-cut."[633]

Despite his swift transmission of the order, when hijacked United Airlines Flight 93 crashed in Pennsylvania, the decision sunk in.[634] Intense emotion spread over those in PEOC, including Rice and Cheney.[635] According to Rice, "His [Cheney's] first thought, my first thought—we had exactly the same reaction—it must have been shot down by fighters. And you know, that's a pretty heady moment, a pretty heavy burden."[636] Cheney and Rice worked feverishly to find out if Flight 93 had crashed or been shot down.[637] When Bush found out about the crashed flight, he felt the same emotion. He stated, "Did we shoot it down, or did it crash? I asked Dick Cheney. Nobody knew. I felt sick to my stomach. Had I ordered the death of those innocent Americans?"[638]

From that moment on, Cheney's vice presidency changed dramatically. The country was at war and Cheney's experience would be invaluable. Bush would lean even more heavily on Cheney in the coming years. Some would argue that Cheney seemed a bit paranoid after 9/11; however, Andy Card argued that this word does not accurately describe Cheney after 9/11.[639] Instead, Cheney was concerned with creating a "shadow government," something that as a former chief of staff he worried about, as all other chiefs of staff have done.[640]

On the evening of September 11, Cheney, with his wife, Libby, and Addington, departed the White House from the South Lawn on Marine Two.[641] "The departure itself was a violation of long-standing protocol: no one takes off from the South Lawn other than the president."[642] It was symbolic of the role he played that day and the influence he wielded.

142 / Emerging from the Shadows

They were heading to an undisclosed location, which happened to be Camp David, where another tradition was "discarded" as Cheney slept in Aspen Lodge, which is reserved exclusively for the president.[643] In order to ensure continuity of government, Cheney would work from undisclosed locations and participate in meetings via secure videoconference, his name was not to be mentioned on telephone calls, and his schedule would only be delivered over secure email and fax.[644] This was the "new normalcy" Cheney discussed.[645] After the attacks on September 11, Cheney became even more resolved to act. "It was clear to Cheney that the threat from terrorism had changed and grown enormously . . . defense alone wasn't enough. They needed an offense."[646] As the nation faced down the possibility of a war on terror of unknown scope and duration, Cheney's influence within the administration would grow considerably as he advised Bush on the prosecution of the war.

The next day, when he sat for the interview with Tim Russert—the first to give an interview following the 9/11 attacks—his understanding of what needed to be done impressed those who watched. Eric Schmitt of the *New York Times* wrote in his article that Cheney's interview demonstrated overwhelmingly why the president wanted him as his vice president.[647] However, those in the White House communications office thought Cheney's "commanding" performance could potentially fuel speculation that he was calling the shots and not the president.[648] This was a constant fear of some, although Bush never seemed to be bothered. After this interview, Cheney would drop out of public view, which was fine with him. He was more content working behind the scenes anyway.[649] The reduced frequency of public appearances, combined with his stays at undisclosed locations, created speculation among journalists that the threats against the United States might be more severe than the administration had led them to believe and also fueled gossip regarding Cheney's health, with some even wondering if he had died.[650]

Despite this, Cheney's influence was profound. The physical constraints posed no match for his influence within the administration. The secure feeds that allowed him to participate in meetings, kept him fully engaged in all deliberations.[651] His influence was remarkable. First, Cheney's work prior to 9/11 created the White House Office of Homeland Security, which Bush announced just nine days after the attack.[652] Governor Tom Ridge would be selected as director with retired Admiral Steve Abbot serving as deputy director.[653] Second, Cheney's role in creating a coherent "national security framework," would place a premium on expanding presidential power to deal with the new threats.[654] "These early efforts would [spur] some of the Bush administration's most controversial policies: The Terrorist Surveillance Program, military tribunals, the guidelines for interrogation of detainees, [and] programs for tracking the finances of terrorists. This was a time when Cheney's visibility was at its lowest and his influence at its greatest."[655] Third, Cheney's tour of the intelligence community when he first took office led him to prioritize the role of intelligence in thwarting future attacks. Cheney operated under the notion, which was shared by most in the administration, that you do whatever you can legally. Rice stated, "Anything that anybody told you you could do legally, you do it, because the thought that something else was coming was just ever-present."[656]

War on Terror

The United States' military response to the attacks on September 11 signaled the start of a new kind of war. Unconventional in its methods and unique in the sense that the enemy was a non-state actor, Cheney had the experience and the expertise to take the country to war. His experience made him the undisputed expert on all things related to homeland defense and national security. Moreover, in just nine short months, Cheney undertook a sweeping review of homeland security that culminated in the development of new plans for responding to an attack on the homeland. Cheney was at the center of the country's response to 9/11—directing cabinet secretaries, ensuring continuity of government, transmitting shootdown orders for hijacked planes, and putting the legal machinations in motion to deal with the new reality.

Cheney realized that unconventional methods would be required to successfully prosecute a war on terror. With Cheney's urging, the Bush administration would make no distinction between terrorists and the nations who supported them.[657] This decision set the stage for the war on terror to move beyond the geographic limits of Afghanistan, the country that had been al Qaeda's base of operations. On the first Sunday after 9/11, Cheney appeared on *Meet the Press*. In response to Tim Russert's question regarding whether Saddam Hussein was harboring terrorists, Cheney asserted that the administration would not be reluctant to move against Iraq, however, the initial focus remained on Afghanistan.[658]

When the war cabinet met at Camp David on Saturday, September 15, 2001, to discuss the way forward, Cheney was initially quiet.[659] After Tenet argued that Osama bin Laden was responsible for the attacks, some

144 / Emerging from the Shadows

in the meeting questioned whether he was capable of this level of sophistication.[660] When Paul Wolfowitz, the deputy defense secretary, raised the possibility of Saddam Hussein's involvement, Cheney spoke up to articulate the need to remain focused on what they did know—Afghanistan.[661] He said that Iraq was a distraction that would need to be dealt with at some point, but there was no doubt that al Qaeda was responsible for planning and executing the attacks.[662] He cautioned that if we go after Saddam Hussein, "we lose our rightful place as good guy."[663] He argued that the United States had to aggressively pursue targets in Afghanistan, which required "boots on the ground."[664] Rice, recalling this meeting, stated, "He was very firm that we had something to get done, which was Afghanistan. . . . and that any move in any other direction was not—you know, we had to get the country ready for a potential of another attack and we had to win in Afghanistan and that was enough."[665]

Cheney's advice on Afghanistan was significant and seems to have influenced Bush's strategy. He warned of the danger that the United States could become an occupying force and advised that the US needed to ensure that the Afghans had some "skin in the game." Efforts to overthrow the Taliban in Afghanistan were successful because coalition soldiers were operating alongside Afghans who provided logistical support and manpower.[666] Cheney "often spoke of the need to 'get locals into the fight.'"[667] As the war in Afghanistan showed progress and success, many started to shift their attention to Iraq, including the vice president.

Cheney's first trip outside the US took place in March 2002, when he toured the Middle East to meet with allies in the region about the subsequent phases of the war on terror.[668] Cheney was also trying to gauge and rally support for military action against Iraq.[669] For ten days, Cheney traveled to twelve countries, publicly cautioning against the removal of Saddam Hussein but privately advising otherwise.[670] "In private . . . several of the Arab leaders Cheney met with were much more supportive."[671] In reporting his trip to the president, Cheney stated that leaders in the region were "as concerned as we are when they see the work that [Hussein] has done to develop chemical and biological weapons, and his pursuit of nuclear weapons; the past history that we all know about, in terms of his having used chemicals."[672]

Iraq had been an area of concern for the United States since Cheney was defense secretary. The agreement with Iraq that ended the Gulf War required Hussein to give up his WMD program and submit to inspections. However, inspections broke down during the Clinton administration.[673]

More importantly, there was significant uncertainty surrounding the dangers that Iraq posed, given the terrorist threat the United States now faced. Cheney argued, "I also think it's unfortunate that we find ourselves in the position where we don't know for sure what might be transpiring inside Iraq."[674] Developing a new policy for Iraq was on the agenda before 9/11, but as a result of the uncertainty, Iraq became a priority. The policy that the administration had decided on for Iraq before 9/11 involved exerting external pressure on the regime and "exploiting fissures and encouraging new ones" to bring about regime change from within.[675]

The September 11 attacks changed everything.[676] The attacks changed the way the US managed Iraq, led to a reorganization of the federal government and intelligence community, spurred the creation of the Department of Homeland Security, reoriented spending priorities, and expanded the scope of presidential authority.[677] Cheney was immersed in all those changes. He became increasingly focused on the threat posed by Iraq. Cheney and his staff frequently visited CIA headquarters to receive briefings and explore the state of intelligence.[678] In these meetings, Cheney took command by asking most of the questions. As one participant in the meetings recalled, his focus, and the content of the briefings, centered on Iraq and its support of terrorism.[679] He was concerned that the CIA briefers were unable to answer basic questions about Iraq and its relationships. "In several instances, the team from Cheney's office seemed to know the CIA's own material better than the analysts who had prepared it."[680] Tenet recalled, "Libby and the vice president arrived with such detailed knowledge on people, sources, and timelines that the senior CIA analytic manager doing the briefing that day simply could not compete. We weren't ready for the discussion. We determined from that moment on we would have multiple lower-level subject-matter expert analysts—people who knew a lot about a narrow range of topics—meet with them."[681] Beyond intelligence, Cheney was often the most well-read person in the room. Dana Perino recalls a conversation with Lea McBride, a Cheney spokesperson, who told her "no matter how early she got up in the morning, and no matter how many articles she had read, when she went to brief the vice president every morning, he had always read more than she had."[682] Because of how deeply knowledgeable Cheney was, the CIA prepared extensively for his visits by holding practice sessions, which they aptly called "murder boards."[683]

As pressure built on Iraq the administration considered their options. Some in the administration, particularly Powell, were insistent that efforts

146 / Emerging from the Shadows

must be made to diplomatically resolve the issue and get inspectors back in Iraq by pursuing a UN resolution.[684] Cheney explained his feelings about pursuing the UN route in a speech he gave to the Veterans of Foreign Wars (VFW) convention on August 26, 2002.[685] Cheney cited Iraq's failure to uphold the agreement that ended the Gulf War and its unwillingness to abide by the UN resolutions that called for the destruction of WMDs and admittance of inspectors.[686] They were convinced that Iraq would acquire nuclear capabilities and that the UN had "done too little" to restrain Hussein.[687] Cheney argued that they had an obligation to safeguard the United States and that containing Hussein was no longer viable. "Containment . . . [is] not possible when dictators obtain weapons of mass destruction and are prepared to share them with terrorists who intend to inflict catastrophic casualties on the United States."[688] The speech demonstrated how important the issue of Iraq had become to Cheney, who warned that "Time is not on our side."[689]

Cheney's speech left the impression that the Bush administration would forego the UN route, which was a cause for concern since Cheney's speech came three weeks before Bush was scheduled to appear before the UN General Assembly.[690] To be fair, vice presidents are usually able to "lean a little more forward in . . . rhetoric than the president" and that is exactly what Cheney did in this case.[691] Those in the administration always knew exactly where Cheney stood on the issues.[692] For weeks, Cheney had battled it out with Secretary Powell, questioning the wisdom of going through the UN.[693] The VFW speech highlighted those differences between Cheney and Powell in public, and it was left to the president's press secretary, Ari Fleischer, to avoid internal feuds from becoming public, per Bush's instructions.[694] "In Cheney's view, the Security Council had already passed seventeen resolutions that Saddam Hussein had violated. Why get another one? If we try and fail, he argued, it will be much harder to do what we may need to do."[695]

The VFW speech put the administration in a difficult predicament. Scott McClellan concluded that this was an example of Cheney being unable to "stay on message."[696] "At times, he simply could not constrain his deep-seated certitude, even arrogance—to the detriment of the president."[697] Although Rice previewed the speech, she was unconcerned. She admitted, "I didn't think much of it, really. It wasn't the first time that I missed and others missed how it could be read."[698] Tenet claimed that no one at the CIA had given the speech clearance, something that would normally occur for a speech that included claims about intelligence.[699] Tenet does admit that the information the CIA provided in the briefings was very assertive regarding Iraq and WMDs.[700] Bush thought Cheney had "gotten out in front" of his position and asked Rice to intervene with Cheney.[701] Rice called Cheney to express her concerns for the speech's impact on the president. "I just told the vice president, I said I think it's cut off the president's options."[702] Cheney told her it was not his intention, but he was "dubious of the UN" and thought it was important to temper expectations on additional resolutions given Hussein's track record.[703] Bush would state in his memoirs, "To Dick's credit, it never happened again."[704]

Powell thought they should go "the extra mile" to reintroduce an inspection regime in Iraq, which Bush felt was necessary to demonstrate that he exhausted all options.[705] Cheney gave a similar speech after the one at the VFW, which was toned down.[706] Rice recalled that after she confronted Cheney, he told her to provide Scooter Libby with the exact language she wanted to see in his subsequent speech, and that Cheney "read the text verbatim."[707] Despite Cheney's reservations, the president decided, after consultation with the British Prime Minister, Tony Blair, to pursue another UN resolution on Iraq.[708] Bush felt he had no alternative but to pursue a UN resolution since all the allies he consulted recommended that the "UN resolution was essential to win public support in their countries."[709] This is a rare example in which Cheney's influence did not carry the day with Bush in the early years of the administration.

As the White House prepared to make the case against Iraq, Cheney sifted through intelligence. The intelligence community had been "uncharacteristically emphatic" and unified in its assessment of Iraq's WMD programs but less so in making a connection between Iraq's support of terrorism.[710] Yet, Tenet felt that the intelligence was strong, suggesting a link between al Qaeda and Iraq.[711] He tasked the Counterterrorism Center to review the reporting on Iraq and al Qaeda to determine if a relationship existed.[712]

Tenet's belief in the connection was further reinforced by "fresh intelligence" Cheney received regarding Ayman al Zawahiri, the leader of Egyptian Islamic Jihad. The intelligence reported that al Zawahiri had fled Afghanistan, where he operated training camps, and set up safe havens in Baghdad.[713] What made this report even more damning for Iraq was the fact that the Egyptian Islamic Jihad had merged with al Qaeda, thus providing a link of Hussein giving safe haven to al Qaeda.[714] Tenet would later report in a briefing with the president and vice president, the case against Iraq was a "slam-dunk."[715]

On November 8, 2002, the UN Security Council passed Resolution 1441, which made clear that Iraq's noncompliance would result in

148 / Emerging from the Shadows

"serious consequences."[716] The administration needed to make the case against Iraq, and Bush asked Powell to do so before the UN.[717] Cheney's office took the lead in preparing the case with Libby focused on weapons of mass destruction, Neil Patel dealing with Iraq's support of terrorism, and John Hannah reporting on Hussein's human rights abuses.[718] They produced "three six-inch binders for the presentation."[719] Powell rejected most of it and instead focused on Iraq's WMDs, reasoning that this was their strongest argument since the UN resolution dealt with WMDs.[720] Powell felt obligated to draft the speech based on his own research, so he spent several days at the CIA to examine the evidence.[721] Cheney's office felt the strongest information was Iraq's connection to terrorists and his record of abuses.

Meanwhile, Bush delivered his State of the Union address, in which sixteen words would stand out and lead to a scandal that would take down Cheney's chief of staff.[722] The speech, which was personally cleared by the CIA director, included the statement, "The British government has learned that Saddam Hussein recently sought significant quantities of uranium from Africa."[723] Almost one year earlier, Cheney received an intelligence briefing in which a classified report from DIA claimed that Niger had met with Iraqis and agreed to sell 500 tons of uranium per year to Iraq.[724] This was in direct violation of previous UN resolutions prohibiting Iraq from acquiring materials for WMDs. Cheney tasked his intelligence briefer from CIA to get more information, who then reported the findings back to CIA headquarters.[725] The CIA's Counterproliferation Division discussed how to proceed, and one of their employees, Valerie Plame Wilson, recommended her husband, a former U.S. ambassador to Gabon, be sent to Niger to investigate.[726] Neither Cheney nor the director of the CIA was informed of the trip.[727] Due to the controversy the statement provoked, many advised the president to issue a retraction, which Cheney vehemently opposed.[728] He believed that if the president disavowed those comments it would invoke long-term damage, plus he believed the statements were true, because the British reported the information and it was also found in the National Intelligence Estimate (NIE) produced by the intelligence community.[729] The simple statement uttered by the president would have significant ramifications for the vice president, which will be discussed.

In response to UN Security Council Resolution 1441, Iraq submitted an 11,807-page weapons declaration claiming it had no WMDs, which Cheney considered to be a material breach of the resolution.[730] Bush and

Cheney felt they had ample justification to go to war, but Tony Blair stated their coalition would be stronger if they sought a second resolution.[731] Blair was feeling pressure at home, so Bush decided to pursue another resolution, despite opposition from Cheney, Rumsfeld, Powell, and Rice.[732] Cheney conceded, "Britain was our major ally, and when the president decided to try for a second resolution, I understood his reasons."[733] Their efforts were unsuccessful, so Bush provided Hussein with forty-eight hours to leave Iraq.[734]

As Bush awaited the deadline, intelligence reports indicated that Hussein was at a complex called Dora Farms.[735] CIA sources confirmed sightings of his two sons and received word that Hussein would be returning in the evening.[736] Tenet confidently told Bush, "If we want to be sure to get him, this is our chance."[737] Cheney remained quiet but was skeptical; his meetings with the CIA left him with the impression that "sourcing in Iraq was weak."[738] Bush was concerned about collateral damage, but Cheney thought the benefits outweighed the risks. "It was a good signal to send to go after Saddam Hussein at the outset. . . . If he were there and we did get him, it could, in fact, save lives and shorten the conflict by a significant margin. And if he wasn't there and we didn't get him, it still wasn't a bad way to start the enterprise."[739]

Bush asked to speak with Cheney alone to make his decision.[740] Cheney advised that they should move ahead, and his private counsel proved decisive.[741] Bush gave the order and then prepared to give a televised address to inform the country of the start of the Iraq War.[742] After months spent seeking UN resolutions, Cheney's persistence paid off. He viewed Saddam as a significant threat to national security. He argued, "I think after 9/11 when you move to a situation where your biggest threat is the possibility of terrorists, state-sponsored terrorists, or a terrorist with a relationship with a rogue government able to get their hands on deadly technologies, Saddam Hussein is a hell of a problem. And he was a problem before 9/11, but he became a bigger problem after 9/11."[743] Bush and his national security team believed they had done everything diplomatically possible to avoid war and no alternative existed but to remove Hussein from power by force.[744]

In the weeks and months following 9/11, Cheney, together with Addington, crafted many of the controversial programs that developed during the Bush years.[745] Addington shaped the legal strategy used by the White House to execute the war on terror.[746]

> When Alberto Gonzales arrived as White House counsel . . . he found that Addington had memorized elements of national security law that he himself had never before encountered. And when lawyers around town called their friends at the White House with suggestions on legal strategy, they were invariably told that Addington had already considered them. Virtually every legal decision made by the administration after 9/11 that was related to the war on terror had at least crossed Addington's desk.[747]

This was remarkable for a vice president's legal counsel to play such a pivotal role superseding the White House counsel's office. The White House counsel's office worked tirelessly to produce legal justifications for many of the controversial programs that originated from Cheney and his office, to include: removing prisoner of war status from captured terrorists, the approval of enhanced interrogation techniques, the creation of the TSP, and the use of military tribunals for terrorist suspects.[748] For a vice president to be the go-to person for items of such importance was extraordinary and demonstrated Bush's confidence in his vice president and Cheney's influence within the administration. Rice argued that the NSC was frequently bypassed or "cut out" of the process, which meant that the "State Department, the military, and even the attorney general were outflanked on occasion."[749]

Cheney, Addington, and lawyers at the Office of Legal Counsel (OLC) in the Justice Department believed that al Qaeda terrorists did not warrant POW status since they failed to abide by the Geneva Convention, were non-state actors, and their targets were primarily civilians.[750] Cheney would contend that they did follow a policy throughout their tenure in office that the detainees would be treated humanely and "in a manner consistent with the principles of Geneva."[751] The enhanced interrogation techniques were based on the same training the military uses, the Survival, Evasion, Resistance, and Escape Program, and those techniques were deemed lawful by legal experts and did not amount to torture.[752] In addition to being waterboarded, "Detainees were stripped nude, forced to stand for prolonged periods, deprived of sleep for days on end, put on a liquid diet, slapped in the face or belly, and doused with water."[753] The OLC and the Justice Department drafted a memo arguing that these techniques did not constitute torture under existing law "as long as they did not result in pain equivalent to organ failure, impairment of bodily function, or death."[754]

Addington drafted a memorandum, which Bush signed, to authorize enhanced interrogation techniques.[755] Cheney's staff also drafted a directive for Bush to sign, which created military commissions to try detainees, however, the order was signed without being routed through the national security team and the national security adviser.[756] In fact, Powell would learn of the president's action from CNN.[757] It was reported that the attorney general was incensed that the Justice Department had been bypassed and that the Defense Department would control the commissions.[758] Addington drafted the order with John Yoo in the OLC, which is in the Justice Department, without the attorney general's consultation.[759] Cheney argued that military commissions fell outside the Justice Department's jurisdiction.[760]

Cheney's influence on the war on terror cannot be understated. He was the lead architect of enhanced interrogations, military commissions, denial of POW status to captured terrorists, and the TSP.[761] He also influenced Bush's preemption doctrine that resulted in the invasion of Iraq.[762] It was obvious that Bush leaned "heavily" on Cheney as he navigated 9/11 and the war on terror.[763] "Cheney freed Bush to fight the 'war on terror' as he saw fit, driven by a shared belief that the government had to shake off old habits of self-restraint."[764]

In the remaining sections, Cheney's influence will be discussed against the backdrop of the theory articulated earlier. Careful attention will be given to how Cheney's influence was either expanded or diminished by the various dynamics that form the heart of the theory on vice presidential influence. Cheney's influence will be examined through the lens of the interpersonal, situational, institutional, and electoral dynamics. Despite Cheney's high level of influence early in the administration, he experienced similar challenges that would result in diminished or marginalized influence over time.

Interpersonal Dynamic

A good relationship between the principals is essential for vice presidential influence. Cheney contends "that personal professional relationship is [a] very important part, sort of the foundation to build on."[765] In the case

152 / Emerging from the Shadows

of Cheney and Bush, that was apparent from the moment Cheney began engaging with Bush when he was governor of Texas. While they were personally very different, Bush outgoing, Cheney more introverted, their contrasting personalities complemented each other's strengths.[766] Dan Bartlett stated, "They were not the type that would hang out together outside of the office, from a different generational standpoint . . . they operated in different social circles."[767] Ari Fleischer stated, "[Their relationship,] it was professional. And the personal, the two of them have a very different nature, very different everything about them, really."[768] However, there were similarities. Bush and Cheney were from the West and "identified with the frontier spirit," attended Yale, had trouble with the law as young men, and both had a terrific sense of humor.[769] Their humor was rather different; Bush was goofy and Cheney was understated.[770] However, Cheney was usually the butt of both their jokes.[771] When Bush's daughter got engaged, Bush, eluding to Cheney's secretive nature, told his daughter that the vice president "sent over a gift I could tell he'd picked out personally . . . a paper shredder."[772] Cheney embraced his dark persona and even wore Darth Vader masks to pose for pictures with his staff.[773]

Cheney served as a good complement to Bush. The president was rather emotional and prone to cry, while Cheney was "almost devoid of passion."[774] To those who admired the vice president found him "contemplative, unshakable, discreet," while to critics he was "scheming, uncaring, and secretive."[775] Cheney's closest friends and family fail to recall a time that they saw Cheney lose his cool or even cry.[776] Bush wears his emotions on his sleeve and cares about the "soft issues" such as faith-based initiatives, while Cheney buries his emotions and cares about issues that are less sexy such as taxes and energy policy.[777] Cheney's demeanor reassured the president, especially during those trying days after 9/11. "He trusted Cheney's instincts, admired his loyalty, and valued his discretion."[778] Bush "valued his steadiness" and considered him a "good friend."[779]

"Bush and Cheney's relationship was close—and substantially private."[780] It was a "partnership which implies equality and mutual respect."[781] Rice echoed this sentiment as well.[782] Their strong relationship was forged during Bush's preparation for his run for president.[783] Cheney's consultations with Bush on a prospective run and his involvement in the foreign policy sessions of the Vulcans laid the groundwork for a relationship built on respect.

The greatest factor in the strong relationship they built, which guaranteed Cheney's influence, was Cheney's lack of ambition to run for president.

During the 9/11 investigation, Bush informed the commission that "his relationship with Cheney was like no other president and vice president because there is no political rivalry."[784] He argued, "The vice president isn't interested in my job and I'm not interested in his."[785] Cheney understood that the "impact" of his advice was dependent on the president's trust in him.[786] Bush trusted Cheney wholeheartedly, which enabled Cheney to be the most influential vice president in history.

Bush and Cheney's relationship remained strong leading up to the reelection campaign. Regardless, Cheney gave Bush an out. On three separate instances he offered his resignation to Bush.[787] Cheney thought it was important for the president to have the option to improve his reelection chances.[788] "I was a believer in the proposition [that] there weren't many things an incumbent president can do to make himself more attractive but one of the things was [to] get a new running mate."[789] By 2004, Cheney's popularity was suffering due to the growing unpopularity of the Iraq War and the war on terror, both of which he had a heavy hand in.[790] "Cheney had become a focal point of the Democrats' attacks on the Bush administration."[791] Even press reports were commenting on whether they believed Cheney would remain.[792]

Although Bush did initially consider Cheney's offer, he brushed it off. Bush did consider Senator Bill Frist as a replacement.[793] The president also broached the subject with Karl Rove and Andy Card, who expected the 2004 reelection to be extremely competitive.[794] After a few weeks, Bush decided to stick with his vice president. He stated, "The more I thought about, the more strongly I felt Dick should stay. I hadn't picked him to be a political asset; I had chosen him to help me do the job. That was exactly what he had done. He accepted any assignment I asked. He gave me his unvarnished opinions."[795] Cheney would continue as vice president.

Several developments placed a strain on their strong relationship in the second term. First, during the 2004 election, Bush came out in support of a constitutional amendment that would effectively ban gay marriage in the United States.[796] Cheney not only differed with his president but also differed with "conservative orthodoxy" in the Republican Party.[797] For Cheney, whose daughter was gay, the issue was deeply personal. As a supportive father who was "fiercely protective of his daughters," Cheney was unable to privately support Bush's position.[798] Cheney did, however, understand the political realities of the president's position. After all, in 2004, more than 64 percent of those polled were opposed to gay marriage, something that Rove was seeking to exploit for the reelection.[799] Before

154 / Emerging from the Shadows

Bush made an announcement of his support, he had a private meeting with Cheney to inform him of his decision.[800] Cheney recalled, "He was very gracious about it. I mean, I guess that would be the way I would describe it. I knew going in that this was a place where we differed."[801] Publicly, without protest, Cheney accepted the decision, but privately he was "pissed off," according to a friend, and blamed Rove, not the president, for the decision."[802] Cheney, in his vice presidential debate, made clear that he differed with Bush's position but acknowledged that the president "sets policy for this administration, and I support the president."[803] Despite their differences, Bush was very accommodating to Cheney, suggesting that he would have no problem if Mary wanted to make a statement in opposition to his position.[804] While this issue did not cause irreparable harm to their relationship, it did strain it.

The second, and far more damaging strain on Bush and Cheney's personal relationship was the president's refusal to pardon Cheney's chief of staff in the Valerie Plame Wilson scandal.[805] The scandal will be discussed in greater detail in a subsequent section; however, it arose from the intelligence Cheney received reporting that Iraq had met with Nigerien officials to acquire uranium.[806] The president included that intelligence, provided by the British, in his State of the Union address, which resulted in significant controversy.[807] In the course of investigating the claims of Iraq's desire to acquire Uranium from Niger, Valerie Plame Wilson, the wife of the US ambassador Joe Wilson (who was sent to Niger to investigate the claim), had her identity, as a covert agent of the CIA and an employee of the Counterproliferation Division, compromised.[808] A special prosecutor was assigned to investigate the source of the leak, which they mistakenly thought was Scooter Libby.[809] Although never charged with leaking Valerie Plame Wilson's name to reporters, Libby was indicted and convicted of obstruction of justice and lying under oath during his questioning by the independent prosecutor.[810]

This was a significant blow to Cheney, who considered Libby a loyal staffer and one who he relied on greatly to advance his expanded role. He felt that Bush, despite several personal appeals, was "making a grave error" in not pardoning him.[811] He told him, "I can't believe you're going to leave a soldier on the battlefield."[812] Bush said, "The comment stung. In eight years, I have never seen Dick like this, or even close to this. I worried that the friendship we had built was about to be severely strained, at best."[813] Cheney concurred with Bush's assessment because he felt that it was "probably the most tense aspect of our relationship," but was glad that Bush commuted his sentence.[814] However, it was still a major disappointment for Cheney.[815]

Bush's concerns were assuaged on January 20, 2009, when Cheney made remarks at Bush's farewell, in which he said, "Eight and a half years ago, I began a partnership with George Bush that has truly been a special honor. . . . If I have one regret, it is only that these days have ended and that all the members of this fine team, now, must go their way." Bush was relieved: "The man I picked that hot day in July remained steady to the end. Our friendship had survived."[816] However, many argued that the relationship was never the same. They have had limited contact since leaving office, and Bush in an interview for the opening of his presidential library, described their relationship as "cordial."[817]

The third and final incident that strained their relationship was related to the firing of secretary of defense Donald Rumsfeld. Cheney convinced Bush on several occasions to keep Rumsfeld because it was not wise to make a change during a time of war.[818] He also thought that it sent a bad message—"It looked like you were turning your back on your Iraq policy. It was better to have continuity there than it was to convey that impression that somehow you weren't happy."[819] In 2006, despite Cheney's warnings, Bush decided to fire Rumsfeld. Bush, knowing Cheney's position, "cut Cheney out of weeks of deliberations about what to do about Donald Rumsfeld, bringing him in only once the decision had been made."[820] Cheney contends that this decision did not strain the relationship. "It was a legitimate decision by the president. It might have been different than the one I would have made."[821] Despite Cheney's assertion, it had to be difficult because he was not part of the decision-making process and Rumsfeld was a close friend.

These three events added significant stress to an otherwise strong relationship. As stated previously, their relationship did suffer, probably most from the Valerie Plame scandal and the president's decision not to pardon Scooter Libby. Despite this, they remain friendly enough that Cheney does see the president and have dinner with him when they are in the same town.[822] More importantly, Cheney feels that he can reach out to him at any time.[823] Cheney describes the relationship as "'interesting'—I would say it was always primarily professional and not personal. We weren't buddy-buddies in that sense."[824] Despite what transpired, Bush and Cheney built a strong relationship that served as a foundation for the extraordinary influence Cheney would exert as vice president.

156 / Emerging from the Shadows

Situational Dynamic

When applying the situational dynamic to Cheney, the interesting phenomenon is that it helps explain why he was as influential as he was during the first six years of the administration, but it also explains why his influence began to diminish from that point forward. The main factors that contributed to Cheney's astonishing influence were the attacks on 9/11, the subsequent war on terror, as well as the war with Iraq. However, the situational dynamic also negatively impacted Cheney as support for the war in Iraq diminished and as Cheney found himself having to defend the controversial programs he helped create. Moreover, Cheney's penchant for secrecy and unwillingness to engage with reporters further fueled the criticism he faced and thus he became a primary target. Last, Cheney found himself at the center of several scandals that, regardless of their outcome, had a detrimental effect on his influence.

When Bush took office, it was assumed that his presidency would be mostly focused on domestic issues. However, less than nine months into his first term, the country was attacked, creating the conditions necessary for Cheney to take the lead and play a consequential role in the administration. Cheney even admitted that if 9/11 had not happened, his vice presidency would have looked much different.[825] "It would not have been as much a center piece, if you will, of our agenda during the time we were there."[826] No one in the administration was better prepared to deal with the 9/11 attacks than Cheney.

Cheney's influence was palpable throughout that first term as the administration crafted a response to the attacks, preemptively went to war with Iraq, established the Office of Homeland Security, and reorganized the intelligence community. Cheney's review of homeland security and the intelligence community in the first months of the administration became the blueprint for the Department of Homeland Security and the new powers the executive would need to fight the war on terror. Cheney, with the help of his two top aides, Libby and Addington, made the case for expanding executive authority, defended presidential power, and drafted the presidential orders that created military commissions, denied POW status to captured terrorists, advocated enhanced interrogation techniques, and created the TSP. No other vice president had as important a role as Cheney in such consequential areas. After 9/11, the entire focus of the administration was centered on fighting terrorism and safeguarding the country against future attacks. At this critical moment, Cheney became the preeminent adviser and architect on these areas. He also took charge on domestic matters that arose during the administration, such as the Bush tax cuts. Cheney would play an important role in all vital matters facing the administration Most telling, in the months after the attacks, when Cheney was relegated to an undisclosed location, his presence and influence was still felt via the SVITS system.[827] "Cheney's clout had endured, partly because of the national security issues suddenly thrust to the fore and partly because of his skill at advancing his viewpoint while remaining deferential to Bush."[828]

As time progressed, Cheney became increasingly unpopular. First, as an architect of controversial programs that critics decried, Cheney became the target of disdain. Second, his limited exposure to the press fueled further criticism of his secrecy. A 2006 CBS poll found his approval at 18 percent.[829] The *Washington Post* concluded that approval of Cheney was worse than Michael Jackson after he was accused of pedophilia and O. J. Simpson after his murder trial.[830] An *NBC News/Wall Street Journal* poll put his approval rating at 30 percent. Cheney was unfazed, a quality that Bush admitted he admired in his vice president.

Cheney's influence was also negatively affected by his involvement in scandal, whether direct or indirect. The first major scandal surrounded his work on the energy task force and his refusal to release the task force's records when members of Congress requested them through the GAO. The refusal, which Cheney and Addington argued was grounded in law and did not violate FACA, caused widespread suspicion.[831] In fact, many of Bush's advisers argued the records should be released because there was nothing to hide.[832] Cheney was adamant that they needed to stand up to principle. His intent was to protect the president's powers and push back against unwarranted encroachment.[833] While Cheney could have easily dispatched the issue by releasing the records, he refused and convinced the president that this was the right course of action. While the scandal by itself did not hurt Cheney, in fact his position and influence carried the day, it did set him up for criticism that would slowly erode his influence. For one, it convinced some members of the administration that Cheney was a hardliner. Second, it furthered speculation as to the vice president's penchant for secrecy, which would only increase after the 9/11 attacks. The refusal to release the records, combined with his avoidance of the media and behind-the-scenes modus operandi, only confirmed and fostered this cloud of secrecy. This ate away at his poll numbers, causing some in the administration to question whether he was the right person to take lead on issues of importance.[834]

158 / Emerging from the Shadows

The second scandal that impacted his influence involved Valerie Plame Wilson. While the scandal did not directly implicate Cheney, his office was affected because Libby was convicted of perjury and obstruction of justice. During the investigation to uncover the source of the administration official who disclosed Wilson's name to columnist Bob Novak, Libby was one of many to be interviewed by the federal prosecutor.[835] He denied being the source of the leak. As it would turn out, Richard Armitage, Powell's deputy, leaked her name, something the independent prosecutor had already known, yet continued investigating for over two years.[836]

Libby was indicted, not because of the leak, but because of information he provided during his interview with the independent prosecutor. It surrounded a conversation Libby had with Tim Russert. Russert, in his interview claimed that Libby had brought up Valerie Plame Wilson's name, however, Libby disputed this and claimed it was Russert who had brought it up instead.[837] Cheney stated, "I believed Scooter was innocent and should never have been indicted, much less convicted. It was hardly surprising that two busy men would disagree about what happened in a telephone conversation that occurred months before."[838] However, Libby was forced to resign his position. His subsequent conviction, and Bush's refusal to pardon him, would cause irreparable damage to the president and vice president's relationship.

The scandal would have repercussions for the role he would play in the coming years. The loss of his chief of staff was significant because Libby was such an important figure in the administration. Libby not only served as Cheney's chief of staff, but he also served as his national security adviser, something no other vice presidential staffer had done before. Libby also carried a presidential appointment because he was considered an assistant to the president, a first for a vice presidential staffer.[839] Many of Cheney's close associates felt the vice president was "lost" without him.[840] Libby was instrumental in establishing a robust role for the vice president. "Libby had done so much of the preparations for the vice president's meetings and events, and so much of the hard work. He had been almost part of Cheney's brain."[841] He was his eyes and ears on the president's staff, someone who gave voice to the vice president and who was equal to the president's senior staff. With Libby gone, that arrangement would no longer exist, further limiting Cheney's influence.

The last scandal involved Cheney directly. On February 11, 2006, Cheney was hunting on the Armstrong Ranch in Texas when he accidently shot a fellow hunter.[842] Cheney recalled, "The image of him [Harry

Whittington] falling is something that I'll never be able to get out of my mind."[843] Bird shot tore up Whittington's face, neck, and chest and for a seventy-eight-year-old man, he was badly hurt.[844] Cheney did not to release anything about the shooting until the next day. The Secret Service reported the incident to headquarters, and Card was only told that there was a hunting accident, but Cheney was unhurt. "No one mentioned it was the vice president who had pulled the trigger. Card passed along the incomplete version to Bush."[845]

Cheney's staff began receiving calls from the White House communications office, pressing him to disclose the information. This would be another instance where Cheney and the White House communications shop would bang heads.[846] Instead of consulting with them on the best way to handle things, Cheney consulted with his former communications adviser, Mary Matalin, who suggested that he pass along the information to a Texas reporter because they would have better access to the local sheriff.[847] Bush's aides were annoyed that they were being ignored.[848] Bartlett stated, "We couldn't get hold of him for quite a bit of time. They were strategizing on their own, which always got me worried."[849] When he finally connected with Cheney's staff, they told him that he was releasing the information to the *Corpus Christi Caller-Times*, which Bartlett argued against.[850] He thought it would convince the media that they were trying to "hide the situation and would only fuel the fire."[851] Bartlett appealed directly to Cheney to handle the reporting differently, but he told him, "This is how we're going to handle it."[852] Rove would also unsuccessfully appeal to Cheney.[853]

Whittington would make a full recovery and Cheney would make history as the second sitting vice president to shoot someone. Cheney and his staff's handling of the situation caused an uproar among the press, who had already accused him of secrecy. The national news media were upset that they were not given first access to the story. He dismissed their complaints as just the "arrogance of an elite media that felt entitled to be hand-fed."[854] He refused to meet with reporters to discuss the accident, further agitating the president's staff.[855] Concerned that the story was getting out of hand, and their appeals to Cheney were going nowhere, Bartlett, McClellan, and Nicolle Wallace (communications staffer) went to Bush and asked him to talk with Cheney.[856] Cheney relented and sat for an interview with Brit Hume of *Fox News*.[857]

The situation damaged his standing. The "episode diminished Cheney's clout within the West Wing."[858] It also demonstrated that Cheney was

160 / Emerging from the Shadows

becoming a political liability.[859] He was no longer a "sober and intimidating force," but the "butt of jokes that would have never been uttered aloud in the corridors of the White House in the first term."[860]

Taken together, the situational dynamic demonstrates that the circumstances that were thrust on the White House with the 9/11 attacks ushered in an opportunity for Cheney to exercise unprecedented influence. However, that same influence took a hit from the scandals he faced, his low approval ratings, and his poor press relations. Each of these contributed to the increasing view among White House staffers that the vice president had become a political liability. Cheney admitted, "I think also it reached a point where I was more of a liability just because of the controversies I was involved in. I had lost my image as a warm and fuzzy guy. . . . After you have been around for 8 years, you pick up scar tissue."[861]

Institutional Dynamic

One of the main components that explains Cheney's unprecedented influence as vice president involves the institutional dynamic. As mentioned earlier, Cheney's involvement with the transition, a first for a vice president, put him in a position to influence the shape and makeup of the new administration.[862] As a result, he was able to recommend loyalists, and others who had a history with him, for key positions in the White House. While Andy Card organized the White House staff, Cheney concentrated on the cabinet, taking the lead not only at the secretary level but also at the subcabinet level.[863]

This ensured a degree of access for Cheney across the executive branch that other vice presidents failed to realize. First, the recommendations he made to the president were largely accepted, and even those that Bush made directly, such as the selection of Colin Powell, involved a preexisting relationship with him. Second, his interest in the subcabinet level provided him greater access to the machinations of government, because that is where government processes take place. This provided Cheney with an opportunity to "reach down" through the bureaucracy and engage with those who would have a direct influence on the policy process.[864] And, as the record shows, it was not unusual for the vice president to personally call a lower-level bureaucrat directly to get information.[865] He did his homework and dug deep into the policy process. "I'm sure there was some, you know, in the bureaucracy that were surprised the VP was paying so much attention or getting down in the weeds or asking tough questions that vice presidents didn't ask in the past."[866] Since Cheney was responsible for so many hires in the administration, many felt indebted to him.[867] The transition set the conditions for providing him the opportunity to have key associates throughout the administration at various levels, gaining him unprecedented access. Cheney understood that "personnel is policy."[868]

Beyond the transition, Cheney's extensive knowledge of the workings of government gave him an advantage over the Bush loyalists who lacked national government experience. First, it allowed him to navigate complex bureaucracies with a fluency no one else in the administration commanded. As a result, he became the "go-to-guy" for getting things done, which further solidified his position as the president's top adviser. Second, he used his knowledge of processes to expedite action on many key programs of the war on terror. He "short-circuited" the system on numerous occasions and received the president's approval for programs that were not fully vetted, violating standard operating procedures.[869] Cheney would justify his action by stating that these issues were extremely important matters, and they did not have the luxury of time on their side.[870]

This ability to overcome obstacles put him in a unique position. Previous vice presidents routinely faced constraints imposed by long-standing institutional structures. Cheney knew how to boost his influence within the White House.[871] He understood those pivotal points where he would face opposition and used his experience and personal relationship with the president to circumvent them. He used his knowledge of process to vet policy options for the president, including him in lower-level policy meetings, thus becoming an instrumental voice in policy deliberations and the decision-making process.[872] Additionally, he "had direct access to the President, and he used it."[873] This circumvention and intimate involvement of process led to the creation of the TSP, military commissions, and withdrawal from the Kyoto Protocol.

While it was very effective in the short-term because his perspective usually won out, in the long-term it caused some damage to Cheney's relationships in the White House. For one thing, Cheney strained his relationship with Rice and Powell over both the military commissions and the Kyoto Protocol. Cheney admitted that his relationship with Powell "soured" in the Bush administration.[874] Furthermore, he faced criticism from the attorney general, John Ashcroft, over the establishment of military commissions outside of the Department of Justice. The successful attempts to bypass key figures in the administration would not only cause

162 / Emerging from the Shadows

tension but would have long-term implications for Cheney's influence in the second term. Furthermore, the vice president's relationship with the communications operation was never strong and deteriorated when his bridge to the president's staff, Mary Matalin, left the White House.[875] Cheney was never close with Dan Bartlett, the communications director, and Cheney would operate "independently on occasion," which usually sparked some backlash.[876]

The chief of staff can make or break a vice president. In the case of Card and Cheney, Card's "low-key, self-effacing approach" enabled Cheney to play a significantly more influential role.[877] At times this allowed his office to dominate the process almost to the point of rivaling the chief of staff as a "surrogate chief of staff," something Quayle would opine.[878] "Cheney, in effect, had played the role of chief of staff, dominating the White House operations set up to feed decisions to the president."[879] Most importantly, Card supported Cheney's deliberate effort to reduce tensions between his and the president's staff by comingling their staffs.[880]

The intermingling of the staffs was done for the purposes of reducing the internecine battles that were characteristic of other presidential/vice presidential staffs. Cheney stated, "I ended up consciously looking for ways to tie my staff to the president's."[881] The natural tension that exists starts at the staff level.[882] However, in the Bush administration case, "There aren't Cheney people versus Bush people," said Cheney.[883] The staffs of the president and vice president got along well.[884] According to Karen Hughes, "We weren't split into various factions or camps; we were all part of a team assembled to serve the president, and the team included the vice president and his staff, too."[885]

With Bush's approval, Cheney helped usher in a new White House structure that was unlike anything seen before.[886] Cheney's chief of staff was invited to all the meetings of Bush's chief of staff, and vice versa.[887] Libby argued that this arrangement was ideal for adding "depth to the decision-making process—'Two heads are better than one.'"[888] Cheney's office was included in all communication. "Routing slips within the White House never failed to include the vice president's staff. E-mails were copied to the vice president's staff. And even some internal e-mails, such as those within the National Security Council, flowed to Cheney's office."[889] John Bellinger, legal adviser to the national security adviser, recalled that every memo he wrote to Rice was blindly routed to Cheney's office, an arrangement Libby made with Rice's deputy.[890] Having paper flow through his office as part of the standard operating procedures was unique and it ensured that Cheney remained in the loop.[891]

The fusion of Cheney's and Bush's staff was evidenced by the unique directive Bush released in February 2001, in which he designated Cheney's chief of staff (Libby) and counsel (Addington) as members of the Principals Committee.[892] Not only was Cheney attending Principals meetings, which was unique for a vice president, but now two of his senior staff were designated as members.[893] Libby, in Cheney's absence, would represent him in world leader meetings, a unique arrangement to say the least.[894] Nicholas Calio, who headed the president's legislative affairs staff, recognized that Cheney's and Bush's staff acted as one team; there was no distinction between the two staffs.[895] These accommodations not only demonstrated Cheney's influence but ensured that his voice would he heard, directly or indirectly.

Further increasing his reach, it was agreed that several of the Cheney's staff would be assistants to the president. For instance, Matalin and Libby were given the title.[896] This carried great significance and responsibility. It meant that Libby and Matalin attended Andy Card's senior staff meeting and were involved in all senior White House discussions.[897] It also meant that they were privy to the same information that Bush's most senior advisers received, outranked most everyone on the Bush staff, and could challenge any speech, legislation, or executive order.[898] This was quite remarkable for a vice president and his staff, and it extended Cheney's influence. "Scooter was a power center unto himself, and accordingly, a force multiplier for Cheney's agenda and views."[899] For Libby, this meant that he would sit "atop two separate and parallel hierarchies in the White House."[900]

Below the senior level, John McConnell, Cheney's speechwriter, and Steve Schmidt, Cheney's counselor, were given the title of deputy assistant to the president.[901] McConnell would not only write speeches for Cheney but also for Bush.[902] Nancy Dorn, Cheney's director of congressional relations, would be an equal of the president's director, Nicholas Calio.[903] Furthermore, having Addington attend the White House counsel meetings, as well as establishing close working relationships between the staff, would go a long way in reducing tension, according to Cheney.[904] These unique arrangements ensured integration at multiple levels, thus extending Cheney's reach.

Cheney argued that it was important to tie the staffs together to "strengthen the operation."[905] Cheney recognized the importance of "dual-hatting."[906] Those who had dual hats remarked that it ensured there was no competition, which was a departure from the past.[907] They viewed their work as being "in tandem with the main White House staff, on behalf of a single client."[908] However, this minimizes the significance of

164 / Emerging from the Shadows

Cheney's influence. The unprecedented dual hatting of the vice president's staff inserted them into the policy process of the West Wing, thus arming them to "fight above their weight."[909]

Cheney modeled his staff off the White House structure.[910] This was no mistake. It made sense that a vice president who had served as chief of staff would try to duplicate an organization that he once oversaw. This decision ensured that he had the resources necessary to fully engage in policy development and decision making. Cheney appointed individuals to his office who had an expertise in national security affairs and foreign policy that at times rivaled those in the National Security Council (NSC).[911] He established a shadow organization, which operated separately from the NSC, and supported his influence, allowing him to play a more significant role in those affairs than any other vice president in history.[912] George H. W. Bush argued, "He had his own empire there and marched to his own drummer."[913] He viewed it as a "big mistake" to let "Cheney bring in kind of his own State Department" within the office of vice president.[914] However, George W. Bush approved of this arrangement.[915] "Cheney stated, "That's what President Bush 43 wanted. He wanted me to play a significant role, and he was true to his word. And I did set up a strong organization to focus on what it was that he wanted me to focus on, which was all the national security stuff."[916] The organization resembled the NSC so much, that it was even organized similarly by geographic desk assignments.[917]

Cheney's organization in the White House was a departure from all other vice presidents. His organization resembled the president's in more ways than just the NSC; his office had domestic and national security policy staffers, a press secretary, legislative advisers, legal counsel, a chief of staff, and detailees from other departments, which supplemented the vice president's permanent staff, particularly from the Defense Department.[918] This meant that the administration was overseen by both Bush and Cheney, "jointly running the government, making decisions and setting goals."[919] Since the White House staff lacked policy experience, a former White House staffer, John Dilulio argued, "Politics, not policy, was the focus of White House meetings. The vice president and his staff moved quickly to fill the policy vacuum."[920] His office included over eighty-five staffers, a number that would expand over time.[921]

Since the organizations mirrored each other and were so well integrated, it became common practice for any vacancies that arose on the president's staff, to be filled by the vice president's aides. For instance, Candida Wolff, Cheney's legislative aide, became White House legislative director.[922] Similarly, Cheney's deputy domestic adviser became the deputy director of White House domestic policy.[923] With the vice president's office serving as a recruiting ground for White House staff positions, barely no matter went untouched by Cheney. Cheney's influence was palpable in most policy areas.

The institutional dynamic also demonstrates the negative impact on Cheney's influence. As much as it helped expand his capacity to exert influence, it posed constraints later in his term. It is widely known that Cheney's influence changed dramatically during the second term. For a vice president who had the greatest influence in the modern era, the change was unmistakable. Several institutional forces came together that diminished his influence. We will discuss the loss of Scooter Libby, Addington's replacement of Libby, Card's departure and replacement by Bolten, staffing for the second term, Rice's elevation to secretary of state, and the loss of many of his allies and loyalists throughout the executive branch.

When Libby resigned as a result of the Valerie Plame Wilson scandal, Cheney experienced a profound loss. Libby had been an asset who led the effort to make his vice presidency a consequential one. "Libby's loss deprived Cheney of his most capable and experienced adviser, his regular stand-in and the overseer of meticulous preparations for nearly everything Cheney did in government."[924] Libby's departure also meant that he lost a chief of staff who was deeply respected by the president's staff. Cheney's influence declined as a result of losing such an instrumental person as Libby.

While Libby was replaced by the very capable David Addington, there were several differences between them that resulted in a void not being filled. While Addington was brilliant about dealing with the bureaucracy and tackling issues from a legal perspective, he lacked Libby's depth of knowledge and especially his management skills.[925] Whereas Libby was outgoing and actively engaged with the president's senior staff, Addington came across as cold and was accused by many of being abrasive.[926] "If a situation could be handled through either conciliation or confrontation, the new chief of staff always seemed to choose the latter."[927]

Complicating matters, Cheney had a friendlier relationship with Libby, considering him a friend, not just a staffer.[928] Addington, however, remained strictly professional with the vice president, even though he had known Cheney for more than twenty years.[929] Libby was more in sync with Cheney's policy positions than Addington, especially regarding the war in Iraq.[930] Addington was not as true a believer in the Iraq War,

166 / Emerging from the Shadows

because he worried that it would be a distraction.[931] Even So, Addington's work with the White House counsel's office and the OLC expanded the president's powers, protected those powers, and served as a strategy for the entire war effort.[932] With Libby gone, a high-ranking administration official remarked, "OVP [Office of Vice President] just doesn't have the room-clearing effect it used to have."[933]

Cheney's office had become less influential, and part of that loss of influence can be explained by Addington's management style and acerbic engagement with Bush's staff.[934] Fractures began to develop between the two staffs. While differences were inevitable, the fractures grew deeper and more problematic. Intense differences developed on policy and the aggressive manner of Cheney's new chief of staff did not help.[935] There were now "Bush people and Cheney people," and the integration of staffs had declined.[936] Addington, who once dominated the White House counsel's office, faced a new counselor who matched his knowledge and background more closely, and thus his influence over legal matters declined.[937] In fact, by the sixth year, two of Cheney's critical staffers, Libby and Matalin, were gone and their replacements did not inherit the title of assistant to the president, significantly altering the arrangement that contributed to Cheney's influence in the first place.

Similarly, Card's departure as chief of staff in the sixth year, and his subsequent replacement by Bolten, would have a detrimental effect on Cheney's influence. Card's management style was less assertive than Bolten's.[938] While Cheney and Card were extremely close, the same could not be said for Cheney and Bolten.[939] "I was sorry when the president replaced him [Card] with Bolten, I didn't have that close relationship with his successor."[940] Bolten was more of an independent figure who chose to align himself with forces other than Cheney and his allies. "Bolten forged alliances with other new faces in high-ranking posts, some of whom brought experience and bureaucratic skill to the jobs that their predecessors had lacked."[941] This meant that Bolten and other administration officials became less reliant on Cheney's office. Bolten's comments were telling about Cheney's diminished role in the White House. He argued,

> The president really took him on as a counselor and not as an alter ego or not even really as a deputy. [The president] takes his advice seriously and says no [but] is more courteous to the vice president than to almost anybody else, but he's not

actually any more deferential. In my six months' experience, it would not fall to the vice president to referee that kind of thing [turf battles between cabinet secretaries]. If it is a presidential decision, the president will make it. If it is not presidential, it is going to be one of the cabinet officers [who] would make it—or me. I think the vice president appreciates that. That his role is in support of the president, not as a second-tier substitute.[942]

Bolten's conception of Cheney's role represented a huge departure from his typical role for most of the administration. In fact, he was chosen to head the Budget Review Board, which made him the referee between the Office of Management and Budget, cabinet secretaries, and the president. However, under Bolten's helm, Cheney's role diminished. Bolten's hands-on approach proved to be an "ominous sign" for Cheney and his influence.[943] Card acknowledged that a change in chief of staff can usher in change for the White House and how it operated.[944] In this case, the change impacted Cheney directly.

Cheney also took less of a role in staffing decisions during the second term. If you recall, he was brought in after a decision was made on replacing Rumsfeld.[945] Bush wanted to make big changes during the second term, and Cheney stated, "I tended to get involved in personnel matters with less frequency than I had at the beginning of our time in office."[946] Bush would make significant changes to the staffing arrangements in the White House that brought in personnel who did not have a close or deferential relationship with the vice president. "In picking [Condi] Rice, [Alberto] Gonzales, and [Margaret] Spellings, Bush was effectively stocking the cabinet with three of his closest advisers, taking firmer hold over the reins of government for the second term."[947] With Cheney's limited role in staffing issues and the president's newfound confidence in handling these decisions, it was inevitable that the administration would have less of his stamp on it.

Beyond the new people who populated the cabinet and the White House staff, many of Cheney's allies were gone. John Yoo at the OLC, Timothy Flanigan at the White House counsel's office, Scooter Libby, Mary Matalin, Andy Card, Paul O'Neill at Treasury, and Donald Rumsfeld and Paul Wolfowitz at Defense had all departed the White House. Cheney understood that this had important ramifications for him and his influence.

He stated, "We changed cabinets, pretty extensive change in the cabinets. Hadley was in as NSC advisor and Condi was over at State by then. So, it was different, and you know, did I have less influence? Probably I had less influence in the second term than I had in the first."[948] As a result of these changes, Cheney would become an isolated voice in the White House and among the senior ranks of the administration.[949]

Rice's elevation to the State Department changed the nature of the relationship between her and Cheney. As national security adviser, Rice had found herself in the center of the disagreements between Powell, on one side, and Cheney and Rumsfeld, on the other.[950] Complicating matters, Cheney had built his own National Security Council staff, which could be a competing entity.[951] Cheney acknowledged that this must have been frustrating for her.[952] Additionally, her role as NSC adviser was as a facilitator and she was not necessarily a peer of the vice president.[953] However, when she became secretary of state, her role changed. She was more forceful in her opinions and no longer felt she was a White House staffer, but instead was at the helm of a large bureaucracy.[954] She stated, "Later, when I became secretary of state, he and I often disagreed and argued vociferously in front of the President. But it was never personal."[955] Rice had a unique relationship with Bush. Everyone in the administration knew that she was the president's closest adviser and truly had the president's ear.[956] She exercised with him, had dinner with the president and first lady in the residence, and spent weekends at Camp David. "He trusted her implicitly, and she made clear she had no agenda other than his."[957] As secretary of state, Rice would rival Cheney.

The institutional changes that occurred had profound consequences for Cheney and his influence. At first, the institutional structures that Cheney had helped construct, worked to his benefit, and provided him with the capacity to exercise unprecedented influence. However, those same institutional structures and arrangements were altered in the lead up to the second term, whereby the vice president watched as many of his allies departed the administration and new people who lacked the same sort of relationship with him took positions. More importantly, he did not have as much a say in personnel matters in the second term and the cabinet became a reflection of Bush, not Cheney. Perhaps, the greatest impact on his influence was the loss of his chief of staff and the replacement of Andy Card by Josh Bolten, both of which would alter his role in the second term, specifically after the sixth-year mark.

Electoral Dynamic

The electoral dynamic represents how the selection of a vice presidential nominee could impact his or her influence and how a reelection campaign or even an election of the vice president to president could impact his or her influence in the White House. Proximity to the president equates with influence so the theory acknowledges that reelection efforts and efforts for a vice president to become president would distance him or her from the day-to-day activities of the White House. In the case of Cheney, the electoral dynamic further enhanced his influence.

First, Cheney was neither selected for political purposes nor for his ability to campaign and raise funds. As Bush made clear, he was looking for a partner to govern.[958] Cheney did not have the same expectations placed on him to engage in electioneering to the extent that other vice presidents had. Sure, the vice president campaigned for their reelection in 2004, but never to the point of being kept out of day-to-day decisions. In the final week of the campaign he visited thirty cities in eight states.[959] The activities that Cheney undertook in the reelection effort reinforced his own portfolio. Terrorism and the fear of another potential attack framed the election, thus providing Cheney with an opportunity to defend the programs, which he had an instrumental part in crafting.[960] Last, governing is what Cheney was selected for, and Cheney continued in that role, despite the looming election. He made sure that he could participate directly in meetings and the governing processes occurring at the White House through SVITS.

Cheney made clear that he did not aspire to be president. This was very freeing for both principals. It allowed Bush to place significant trust and responsibility in his vice president, and it freed Cheney from the demands of a presidential campaign that would have taken him away from the White House, thus diminishing his influence. Unlike his predecessors who faced the constraints imposed by electoral demands, Cheney faced none of them.

Effects on Influence

The four dynamics discussed above demonstrate the fluid nature of influence. In the case of Vice President Cheney, the interpersonal, situational,

170 / Emerging from the Shadows

institutional, and electoral dynamics combined in an unprecedented manner to provide Cheney with a greater capacity to exercise influence than that of any vice president in the modern era. Cheney's relationship with the president was strong and built on trust and admiration. His lack of ambition for the presidency only bolstered that trust. Several people interviewed for this study indeed suggested that this could give a person tremendous influence.[961] "There was a certain at ease [and] lack of suspicion of the calculations being made or the judgements being imposed by the vice president."[962] This provided the foundation for him to exercise influence. Due to the differing strengths of the principals, Cheney took on the unprecedented role of managing the transition and building the administration. As a result, he built the institutional structures and handpicked personnel to fill both the cabinet and subcabinet levels, all with Bush's concurrence. This enabled the vice president to place allies throughout the executive branch, allowing him to reach down through the bureaucracy to engage in policy development. In my interview with Cheney, he recognized the centrality of this for his influence.[963] Furthermore, he organized his vice presidency so that his staff was fully integrated with the president's and several carried the title of assistant to the president or deputy assistant to the president, an unparalleled occurrence for a vice presidential staffer. In many respects, the vice president's staff was treated as if it was the president's staff.[964]

Despite the convergence of the four dynamics in providing Cheney with influence, those same dynamics worked against him during the second term. For one thing, the relationship between Bush and Cheney faced significant strain as a result of Bush's decision not to pardon Libby and the firing of Rumsfeld. Additionally, the president came out in support of a constitutional ban on gay marriage that Cheney deeply opposed. While they remained cordial, their relationship was markedly different. The war on terror also impacted his influence. As casualties mounted in Iraq, approval for the effort began to slip and so did Cheney's. His reluctance to engage with reporters and his penchant for secrecy only contributed to his poor approval. Cheney never assumed responsibility for making himself look good in the public eye.[965] "He never tried to make himself popular, he just didn't care, and in that sense, it eventually came to the point where he really lost some measure of impact because he was perceived so negatively by the public, he became an ineffective messenger for President Bush after a while."[966] As the controversial programs of the war on terror were disclosed, and Cheney's hand in them was apparent, he became even less popular. Moreover, Cheney found himself in the center of controversy with Libby being convicted in the Valerie Plame Wilson scandal, the hunting accident in which he mistakenly shot a fellow hunter, and the failure to disclose the energy task force's documentation to the GAO. The growing list of scandals made Cheney less and less the "go-to-guy." Last, during the second term, he was not as involved in staffing issues and was excluded from the conversation on replacing Rumsfeld. Bush decided to handle his own transition in the second term instead of giving Cheney the responsibility.[967] The loss of his chief of staff, and the replacement of Bush's chief of staff with Josh Bolten, altered his role. No longer did he have a strong personal relationship with Bush's chief of staff, and Bolten's management style was more independent of Cheney, resulting in his loss of influence. The administration looked much different, and the personnel changes affected his influence.[968]

Cheney's influence demonstrates that all vice presidents, no matter how influential they are, will face a similar decline in influence over the course of an administration, sometimes the result of their own efforts, and oftentimes the result of things outside their control. Those in the administration, like Andy Card, and even the vice president himself, recognized Cheney's diminished influence in the second term.[969] Cheney experienced some self-inflicted damage to his influence, but for the most part, the changes to his influence were out of his control. It represented a situation in which a president was becoming more comfortable in his role as president and more fluent in the issues he faced. Bush's improved confidence meant he needed to rely less and less on Cheney, who he leaned on heavily in his first term.[970] Cheney stated, "Over time, I think I was probably more valuable to the president in the early part than the later part. Part of that was a learning process for him. By the time we got down toward the later part of the second term, he was much more—well, he had the experience of having been president for all those years, and he relied less, I think, on staff than had been true earlier."[971] In other words, "George W. Bush was hitting his own stride."[972]

The change in Cheney's influence was apparent for those in the administration. From the six-year mark on, Cheney found himself on the losing side of arguments. He would often start his remarks by stating, "I know I'm going to lose this argument" or "I know I'm alone in this," representing how he was a lonely voice in an administration that changed.[973] This was a significant departure from when he carried the day in convincing Bush on POW status, enhanced interrogation, military

172 / Emerging from the Shadows

commissions, the TSP, and attacking Hussein before the deadline was up. This is not to say that he never lost an argument in the first term. But Cheney's aggressive and more hawkish views on foreign policy were isolated in an administration that became more aligned with diplomatic approaches, which coincided with Rice's elevation as a rival to Cheney's influence when she became secretary of state.[974] Fleischer stated, "He [Bush] would agree with the objectives of the most hawkish members of his administration, but then he would pursue the tactics of the more dovish members of the administration."[975]

Cheney's vice presidency represented unrivaled and unprecedented influence for a vice president. Building off the precedents established by other vice presidents, and incorporating his experience as chief of staff, Cheney built an organizational structure that rivaled the president's, which allowed him to play an influential role. While he would sustain that influence longer than any of his predecessors, he eventually faced the same constraints imposed by the interpersonal, situational, institutional, and electoral dynamics, and his influence waned. The extraordinary run exemplified his understanding of the issues that impact vice presidential influence and his concerted effort to build a vice presidency of consequence. Bush's concurrence with Cheney's role and the fact that Cheney lacked presidential ambition went a long way toward giving him the capacity to exercise influence.[976] Reflecting on his vice presidency, he stated, "I think we demonstrated that it could be a significant post; I think it was for a good part of the time I was there."[977] Without the unique circumstances of the Bush administration, Cheney's vice presidency may have looked much different. Vice presidential influence is much dependent on the president, and in this case, Bush wholeheartedly accepted and endorsed Cheney's conception of a consequential vice presidency.[978]

Chapter 4

Mondale, Bush, Quayle, Gore, and Biden

Tales of Vice Presidential Influence

Walter Mondale's Interpersonal Influence

Walter Mondale, who is credited as being the father of the modern vice presidency, conceptualized a model that many subsequent vice presidents followed.[1] A core feature is a strong personal and professional relationship between the principals with a shared vision for the office that provides for a meaningful role. This model was just as much a credit to President Carter as it was to Mondale, because without Carter's approval, the model would not exist.[2]

When it came to his selection of a vice president, Carter was intent on not repeating the mistakes of the past, particularly Senator George McGovern's selection process in 1972, in which McGovern waited until he clinched the nomination to turn his attention to a running mate.[3] McGovern had his heart set on Senator Edward Kennedy and failed to identify an alternative; so when Kennedy turned him down, McGovern desperately offered it to Senator Thomas Eagleton without fully vetting him.[4] Rumors began to circulate that Eagleton had suffered from mental health issues and received electroshock therapy for treatment.[5] At a time when a stigma was attached to mental illness, McGovern faced pressure for him to resign. After eighteen days, Eagleton resigned from the ticket and was replaced by Sargent Shriver.[6]

Carter was determined to institute a serious process for considering a vice presidential nominee, which started before the convention.[7] As a

173

174 / Emerging from the Shadows

result, "Carter conducted a far more intensive vice presidential selection process than had previously occurred."[8] It was a deliberative process with considerable resources backing it.[9] Carter's selection process would serve as a standard for other presidential candidates to emulate and the result is that the vetting process has produced "more qualified vice presidential candidates."[10]

This provided Carter with ample time to consider the type of role he would want his vice president to play. Hamilton Jordan, an aide of Governor Carter and who would become chief of staff, crafted a memo that "encouraged him to consider elevating the vice presidency and to choose a running mate whom he respected."[11] Most important was that the country would look to the selection process as a reflection of Carter's decision making and that it was important to pick an individual who was qualified to be president.[12] Carter concurred with Jordan's views and thought it "wasteful to underutilize a vice president's talents, an attitude that encouraged him to choose the best person possible."[13] Carter was not threatened by the prospect of having a "well-qualified" vice president; more importantly he thought it would reassure voters who had concerns over his own qualifications, having served as governor for only one term.[14]

Carter decided that his running mate needed to have legislative experience at the national level to counter Carter's deficiency in this area.[15] He sought someone who was compatible, personally and politically.[16] Mondale's personal relationship with Carter was limited; he met Carter only briefly but respected his civil rights work in Georgia.[17] Mondale's interview with Carter increased his prospects of being selected because he thoroughly did his homework—studying the office of the vice president, reviewing Carter's policy positions, and reading Carter's campaign book and speeches.[18] The level of preparation that Mondale undertook impressed Carter. A Carter aide, Greg Schneiders, recalled, "Every question that came up on an issue, Mondale not only could spell out clearly and succinctly his own position, but knew exactly what Carter's position was, and where the two differed."[19] Carter stated, "When Fritz came down to Plains he had really done his homework about me and the campaign. More important, he had excellent ideas about how to make the Vice Presidency a full-time and productive job."[20]

Mondale considered the vice presidency "an arm of the presidency" and was determined to have a substantive role if selected.[21] When Carter asked him about his vision for the office, Mondale responded that he wanted to have an activist role, "enjoying a level of access that few, if any, previous occupants had attained."[22] He was not interested in the ceremonial aspects of the vice presidency or what he called, "the stand-by stuff."[23] Given Carter's lack of national experience, Mondale could be a tremendous asset by helping him "politically and in governing due to his experience and relationships with Jews, labor, liberals, Democrats in Congress, [and] the Washington media."[24] Mondale's more liberal ideology would also enable him to maintain strong connections with the various constituencies of the Democratic Party.[25] Mondale's experience could easily compensate for Carter's weaknesses at the national level.

During the interview in Plains, Georgia, Carter and Mondale hit it off.[26] For one thing, Carter found them compatible both personally and in regard to their vision for the vice presidency. Carter stated, "He was from a small town, as was I, a preacher's son, and shared a lot of my concerns about our nation [and] we were personally compatible."[27] Mondale left the meeting reassured that the position would not be merely ceremonial.[28] While Carter and Mondale had limited prior relations, the meeting in Georgia served as the foundation for a relationship and for a mutually beneficial partnership to exist.

Shortly after Mondale's selection, they decided to coordinate their campaigns and Mondale chose Atlanta, the location of Carter's headquarters, for his vice presidential campaign.[29] This decision helped foster a good relationship and ensured that rival factions did not develop.[30] The campaigns were so intermingled that when they organized a retreat to discuss the campaign, a Carter aide was paired with a Mondale aide for room assignments.[31] This enabled their staffs to get to know each other and build a stronger team that could effectively govern on January 20, 1977.[32] The integration of their staffs "made a big difference," according to Mondale.[33] Carter told his staff, "I want you to treat Mondale's staff as part of our staff and the first time I hear that somebody is mistreating them that will be your last day at the White House."[34] For all intents and purposes Mondale's staff was part of the White House staff.[35]

Carter embraced Mondale as an equal and told him that he wanted his advice on all matters, including the vice presidential role. Moreover, Mondale's staff would offer advice, which the Carter campaign incorporated, even going as far as modeling scheduling after Mondale's own operation.[36] Carter appeared with Mondale at multiple press conferences where the topics included the economy, defense, and foreign policy.[37] In these venues,

176 / Emerging from the Shadows

he frequently turned to Mondale to offer his input and thoughts on the questions and signaled that he was not threatened by his vice presidential running mate, but instead welcomed his full participation.[38]

After winning the election, Carter laid out his intentions to make Mondale a full participant in his administration. Mondale would help Carter interview candidates for positions in the administration, often with Mondale conducting the last interview for the prospective candidates.[39] Not only was he given a voice in appointments, he either convinced or assisted Carter in selecting Joseph Califano as the secretary of health, education, and welfare, Robert Bergland as secretary of agriculture, Cyrus Vance as secretary of state, Werner Blumenthal as secretary of treasury, Neil Goldschmidt as secretary of transportation, and Maurice Landrieu as secretary of housing and urban development.[40] Moreover, many of Mondale's closest aides found jobs in the new administration, thus providing an additional voice for the vice president.[41] Mondale's loyal aides, David Aaron and Bert Carp, were appointed as Carter's deputy national security adviser and domestic policy deputy.[42] These overtures fostered a strong personal and professional relationship with Carter frequently expressing that they had become good friends and promising a greater role for him than other vice presidents.[43]

Mondale's influence with Carter was apparent from the transition onward. Carter, determined to have an equal partner in governing, tasked Mondale with drafting an agenda for the first cabinet meeting in which he laid out priorities and initiatives for the administration's early days in office.[44] "Each member of Carter's new cabinet was given a twenty-nine-page memo of Carter's weekly schedule through the approaching March, prepared by Mondale."[45] Furthermore, Mondale was routinely involved throughout the administration in crafting six-month long agendas laying out presidential and administration activities.[46] Carter was effusive in his praise of Mondale, telling reporters that he would have a large policy portfolio that would provide him with "unprecedented" responsibilities.[47] Carter told his staff that Mondale was their boss.[48] His press secretary, Jody Powell, told reporters that Mondale was the "principal adviser" to Carter and would be "virtually an equal partner."[49]

The Mondale model for the vice presidency was shaped by both Carter and Mondale's shared vision for the office as well as the guidance Vice President Rockefeller provided them during the transition.[50] "They had a broad meeting of the minds. When we had this meeting in the Blair House in December there was almost a perfect coming together of this concept [Mondale Model]."[51] In practice, Carter would ensure that his vice president was part of the "fabric of the White House," by elevating the office from "standby equipment."[52] Mondale laid out his vision, which required access to the president.[53] Rockefeller actually advised Mondale that the single most important "element" in the vice presidency is "a close and intimate working relationship with the president," which Rockefeller argued relied on direct access to president, regular weekly and private meetings, and the president instructing the White House staff to include the vice president and his staff in the process.[54] Both principals agreed that the office had been "a wasted asset" and so Carter was determined to have his vice president fully integrated by including his vice president in congressional relations, reorganization of government, and foreign and domestic policy.[55]

Carter saw an expanded role as a way of relieving him of some of the political, ceremonial, and substantive burdens of the presidency.[56] He provided significant access to Mondale—in the first six months they spent about one-third of their time together.[57] "Carte blanche access" also helped build Mondale's influence with the bureaucracy, Congress, and others who witnessed his day-to-day involvement with Carter.[58] He was convinced that the success of his model depended on a close personal relationship, as attested to by Rockefeller.[59] This would ensure that Carter sought out Mondale's advice and would provide him with substantial duties, particularly reinforcing his advisory role, which was his most important role.[60] "He contributed solid and serious judgment. He was an early warning system for the president and a source of good advice and good judgment regarding options as they were discussed."[61] Mondale concluded that his model, a departure from the past, would include an advisory function on issues of importance and a troubleshooting function where he could bounce ideas off the president, with no operational roles or line assignments.[62] He avoided line assignments because he "didn't want to take any position which would expose him to intense political warfare . . . [and] didn't want to make the time commitment to a continuing line duty. Mondale preferred to stay apart from the mechanics of the policy process, floating in and out of areas as the need arose."[63] Moreover, he did not want to take on "useless responsibilities—if someone is doing it I don't want to do it. I want to be the president's general advisor, troubleshooter," he said.[64]

Mondale understood the importance of laying out the role in advance because the ambiguity of the vice presidential role is what caused most of the problems for his predecessors.[65] He wished to break with the

178 / Emerging from the Shadows

frustration that other vice presidents felt.[66] His model "afforded . . . the chance to get involved in a multitude of activities and has contributed significantly toward enhancing the image of the second office."[67] Both his advisory and troubleshooting roles were dependent on the principals' relationship. That relationship would provide unfettered access and a president who was willing and open to the advice. While the relationship that was forged in their initial meetings and reinforced throughout the campaign and transition was good, it would need to be maintained. The key to that maintenance was access to Carter through regular meetings and open communication, where he could provide "unfiltered, candid views."[68] Witnesses to the relationship viewed it as "unprecedented for the time."[69]

Beyond the relationship, Mondale argued that his advisory function was dependent on access to comprehensive intelligence briefings on par with the president's; an executive branch responsive to requests from the vice president; the ability to participate in advisory groups; inclusion of vice presidential staff on the National Security Council and the Domestic Council; a strong relationship between the vice presidential and presidential staffs; and regular access to the president.[70] Mondale stated, "I knew that if I didn't see everything Carter saw, even the classified material, I could not be an effective adviser."[71] Carter agreed to all.[72] Richard Moe, Mondale's chief of staff, argued, "He established this model and I think it is a lasting model. I think it is probably his most important legacy. He and Carter created something new and lasting."[73] Mondale, reflecting on the model, stated, "The elements of each VP have been very similar to what was written in that memo that Carter agreed [to]," demonstrating the long-lasting legacy of that agreement.[74] He considered it one of his greatest accomplishments—"establishing a model of an engaged VP working effectively to enhance the Carter presidency and with him accomplishing a range of new things that were possible in part because of this new relationship," which has been followed by most of the subsequent vice presidents.[75]

The president's national security adviser, Zbigniew Brzezinski, stated, "Carter was determined to make Fritz a genuinely active Vice President, and it was my task to make certain that Fritz knew what was going on in the national security area."[76] Mondale was included in the weekly Friday breakfasts in which the secretary of state, national security adviser, and the president would discuss foreign policy.[77] The breakfasts provided an opportunity to solve policy disagreements and to discuss broad issues.[78] Carter was also intent on giving Mondale a leading role in presiding over national security. He laid out in a memo his interest in having a meeting set up early in the administration to provide "a recommendation on overall policy and individual cases concerning intelligence and national security," with Mondale presiding over that meeting.[79] This demonstrated early on Carter's intent to include him in all areas of national security.

Carter also agreed to include an office in the West Wing for Mondale, adding the vice president's office on the Oval Office paper flow, establishing weekly private lunches for the principals, the ability to attend any meeting, and an open-door policy to the president, perks previously unheard of.[80] The West Wing office provided Mondale with proximity to Carter, which would grant access and thus provide him with the capacity to exercise influence. He recalled Carter telling him, "I want you to be in the chain of command—a vice president with the power to act in the president's place."[81] The office would keep him in the loop both in terms of paper flow and informal conversations.[82] Last, Carter told his staff that any requests that came from Mondale should be considered as if they came from him personally and that he would not tolerate staff who undercut him.[83] As Carter stated, "We agreed that he would truly be the second in command, involved in every aspect of governing."[84] Carter signed an executive order that placed Mondale as second in command with control over the nuclear arsenal, something that had not existed previously.[85] Up until this time, the National Security Reorganization Act of 1958 named the secretary of state as the deputy commander in chief.[86] Carter and Mondale recognized the importance of Rockefeller's input in developing the role of the vice president. Carter sent Rockefeller a letter thanking him for his suggestions and telling him in a P.S. note, "Your suggestions re: Vice President's role are going to help me & Fritz a lot."[87]

Carter's deliberative selection process, their compatibility, their shared vision for the vice presidency, and Mondale's strengths, which compensated for Carter's weaknesses, went a long way in establishing a strong relationship between the two principals. Furthermore, Carter's effusive praise of Mondale, his willingness to allow Mondale to advise and consult widely on staffing arrangements, which included taking his closest aides into the administration, would ensure that his vice president had a voice. Moreover, Carter's instructions to his staff that Mondale was just as much their boss, further strengthened their relationship and partnership, putting Mondale on equal footing with the president. As Mondale recalled, Carter told his staff, "If you are hearing it from Mondale you are hearing it from me."[88] Carter's offer to include the office of the vice president in the paper flow

180 / Emerging from the Shadows

for the Oval Office, open access to Oval Office meetings, office space in the West Wing, and weekly private lunches provided Mondale with the resources necessary to play a substantially more important and influential role. These gracious overtures built a strong personal relationship that would serve as the foundation for Mondale's influence during the administration and none would be possible without their compatibility.

Carter would frequently praise his vice president, further alluding to his strong relationship with Mondale. And that relationship would only grow and become increasingly close over time.[89] When Carter conducted the swearing-in for the cabinet, he told those assembled that "it would be hard to equal what Fritz Mondale has meant to me, but I believe I will become equally close to the Cabinet members and other leaders that will be sworn in this afternoon."[90] He referred to his "unprecedented . . . superb relationship" with Mondale and that they had a "natural compatibility."[91] Most importantly, Mondale could speak for Carter, something that was becoming more and more widely understood in Washington.[92] Demonstrating how close the two were, Carter stated that there had never been "a President and Vice President who have been bound together more closely with a common philosophical commitment, with a common belief and confidence in the quality of the American people, and a sharing of every possible problem and its potential solution. . . . [Mondale was] in almost every way an equal partner."[93] Their relationship was excellent, which was publicly and privately true and they instinctively knew what "to do and what not to do."[94]

The Mondale model ensured the vice president's influence, but his style and approach to the office also contributed. Eighty percent of the Carter and Mondale aides surveyed stated that "the Vice-President's discretion and low visibility were critical factors in his influence."[95] Mondale preferred to work in the background, rarely took a position in meetings, and reserved his advice for the president in private.[96] His preference was to keep a low-profile, considered "appropriate" for a vice president.[97] One aide stated, "He projected the image of being influential. That was enough for most of us."[98] His influence became a reality shortly after assuming office when Carter sent him on a whirlwind international trip for nine days to visit NATO allies.[99] The importance of the trip was stressed by Jody Powell where he described "Mondale as Carter's 'personal friend as well as a chief policy and political adviser.'"[100] A. Denis Clift, Mondale's national security assistant, stated, "The fact that America's new President had entrusted such prickly summit-level issues to this Vice President was important from the outset in establishing Mondale's role and credibility as international statesman."[101] Carter's advisers recommended that he state, "The Vice President is making this trip at my request, and on my behalf, as a first step toward improving relations with our traditional allies in Western Europe and Japan. . . . I hope this trip will also indicate the important role I intend the Vice President to play, not only as one of my advisers, but also as my personal representative."[102] As one aide put it, "he was liaison to the world."[103] Further demonstrating the importance of the trip, Carter allowed Marine Two to depart from the South Lawn of the White House, something usually reserved for the president only, and the president and first lady attended the departure ceremony.[104] Carter told reporters that Mondale had his "complete confidence" and that he was his "personal representative."[105] After the trip, Carter praised Mondale for "an absolutely super job," stating, he "engaged in the same kind of discussions on the same subjects and with the same depth that I would have if I had gone on the trip myself."[106] Press reports echoed the president's sentiment.[107]

Mondale's influence in foreign policy was widely known. As second in command, he served as a foreign policy spokesman, which required extensive international travel.[108] Often rivaling the secretary of state, Mondale spoke for Carter, and the leaders of the world understood the trust he placed in his vice president.[109] Mondale also filled the lack of Washington experience in the administration by serving as a congressional liaison on several issues, including foreign policy.[110] Given his service in the Senate and his attention to the politics of a policy issue, Mondale was a natural choice. The Panama Canal Treaty represented a success for Mondale in terms of working his extensive relations with Congress.[111] "Mondale was satisfied that by successfully translating his years of service and personal connections in the Senate into votes for the administration, he had helped the president score an impressive legislative victory."[112] He provided a voice to the political aspects of foreign policy decisions, often missing from policy discussions.[113] Bill Kristol, chief of staff to Vice President Quayle, argued that vice presidents have parochial interests that are political and "involve advancing the vice president's fortunes."[114] Due to stagflation, staking out an influential role in domestic policy was not as conceivable as foreign policy.[115] "Mondale, ever the astute politician, was hardly blind to the political advantages to be gained by bolstering his foreign-policy credentials."[116] Mondale brought a political perspective to the foreign policy process that was missing.

Mondale's access to Carter was also unprecedented. They would frequently meet three or four times per day when they were both in town. In fact, Mondale spent approximately 25 percent of his time in

182 / Emerging from the Shadows

office meeting with Carter.[117] Not only did he have access, but he was fully prepared to use the access. The president's chief of staff, Hamilton Jordan, and Walter Mondale were the only two with regular and private access to Carter.[118] This enabled Mondale to offer candid and unvarnished advice, which formed the bedrock of his influence. His meetings were not just limited to the president, he also met extensively with foreign leaders, members of Congress, and administration officials.[119]

In a survey of White House staffers, 80 percent of Carter's staff thought Mondale had influence and 100 percent of Mondale's staff said he had "a great deal of influence."[120] Very little disparity existed between the presidential and vice presidential staffs regarding the perception of Mondale's influence. As a result, many in the White House turned to Mondale to persuade the president.[121] Bert Carp, a domestic affairs adviser to Carter, stated, "His views were important to Carter, so if you were involved in a dispute, you wanted Mondale on your side."[122]

Mondale's uninhibited access meant that he could drop by the Oval Office to see the president at any time. Mondale said, "I'd go in and out of the Oval Office several times a day. Carter had an open-door policy toward me."[123] Mondale's influence was felt early on, when he influenced the administration to change its position on the affirmative action case, *Regents of the University of California v. Bakke,* in which the Justice Department's amicus brief sought restrictions on race-based admissions, which conflicted with Carter's civil rights views.[124] When Mondale found out he immediately went to the president to which Carter ordered a revision to the brief to support affirmative action but not racial quotas.[125] He left it up to Mondale to speak with the attorney general about the brief.[126] Attorney General Griffin Bell stated that the brief was the "first civil rights case in which Mondale made the weight of his office felt."[127]

Mondale also intervened in a foreign policy speech to the United Nations that the secretary of state, Cyrus Vance, was scheduled to deliver.[128] Mondale was unable to convince Vance or the national security adviser, Zbigniew Brzezinski, to soften the tone of the speech, so he called Carter late one night to express his concerns over the speech, even though he had already approved it.[129] Carter reviewed the speech again and decided to side with Mondale's recommendations and the speech was modified.[130] Mondale brought a political perspective to foreign policy that Carter rarely considered.[131] Some argued that Mondale had an "utter infatuation" with the politics of policy.[132] Mondale saw "inadequate strategic political thinking in the development of foreign policy" as a serious drawback to

Carter's foreign policy approach.[133] Mondale stated, "I was coming at foreign policy issues with the politics in mind as well. There's often a disconnect among high officials between policy and whether it will sell. I had to go out of the room and handle the politics and explain the decisions, on the campaign train, on Capitol Hill."[134] Brzezinski referred to Mondale's "political judgment" as his "most important substantive contribution. He was a vital political barometer" for the president.[135] Mondale recalled, "I had hoped I might help Carter navigate these shoals, or at least avoid collisions with our friends."[136]

Mondale was particularly influential in schooling Carter on the ways of Congress and he served as an instrumental link to and for the administration. Carter's legislative adviser, Frank Moore stated, "We needed help. We didn't have a lot of bench strength to draw on. His relationships in the Senate on the liberal side (Republicans and Democrats) [were critical]. We started off with a big advantage given his relationships."[137] Early on the administration's relationship with Congress was not very good.[138] As a result, Carter felt Mondale was indispensable in "introducing" him to the "world of Capitol Hill."[139] "They [members of Congress] appreciated that he could speak to and for Carter. Mondale worked to maintain old, and establish new, relationships on Capitol Hill."[140] More importantly, members of Congress could say things to Mondale that they could never say to the president; for example, they could "gripe about staff and cabinet secretaries."[141] "Members of the Senate would lobby Mondale to carry their water to the president."[142] Mondale stated, "I spent a lot of time up on the Hill with senators and members of the House picking up information that I would bring the president."[143] "He was the person who members of Congress, senators and House members, would pick up the phone and call. He was always available to do that. To some extent it protected Carter from talking to them so much."[144] He became the president's "eyes and ears" and a "good source of fresh information for the president," too.[145] Carter was predisposed to oppose any projects he categorized as "congressional pork," which caused his relations with Congress to suffer.[146] However, Mondale saw it as his duty to bring Carter around. He nudged Carter to approve more spending on social programs and be more understanding of Congress's methods, also instructing him on how to deal with congressional leaders, specifically advising the president to "veto the most egregious pork-barrel items and yield on the others in the interest of party peace."[147] Despite his efforts, he was disenchanted with Carter's propensity to flood Congress with various proposals that went nowhere, which just caused

184 / Emerging from the Shadows

tension with Congress.[148] Mondale became the "chief lobbyist" for the White House.[149] However, his staff was concerned that he was brought in to lobby on insignificant matters and so they recommended to Mondale's chief of staff that when matters rose to the level of the president, Mondale would serve as a surrogate, thus leaving routine and day-to-day lobbying to White House staff.[150] Despite his best efforts, the "consensus" on Capitol Hill was that Carter had good, solid programs, but "they are not fully understood" because lines of communication between the White House and Congress were not ideal.[151] While the criticisms were never leveled at Mondale directly, the overall message was that the administration was "inept in dealing with the Congress."[152]

Mondale's influence was tempered as the administration moved forward and Carter developed confidence in his own ability. Mondale was unable to convince Carter to support a $50 tax rebate, a higher minimum wage, and increased farm supports.[153] He vehemently opposed Carter's cap on the deficit, imposition of a grain embargo on the Soviet Union, and the requirement of a draft registration.[154] Carter thought a draft registration was required to "mobilize more rapidly if the need should arise."[155] However, Mondale and several others thought he was overreacting to the threat imposed by the Soviet Union and it would just hurt their reelection effort.[156] Mondale thought the grain embargo would hurt American farmers more than it would hurt the Soviet Union, which would weaken their support in the farm states.[157] Carter told Mondale that they would do what was necessary to protect American farmers, but he was unconvinced.[158]

Mondale was also frustrated with Carter's approach to the presidency. He felt he spent too much time on foreign policy and on the finer details of domestic policy.[159] One aide argued, "Carter could never see the forest through the trees. Carter would get bogged down in detail. He was not strategically very good. Mondale could get bogged down in detail too, but he was also strategically very good."[160] Mondale also thought the president spent little time on the public presidency, arguing that Carter needed to get out of the White House and build public support.[161] He advised Carter in a 1978 memo that a public relations program would educate the American people and counter suggestions that he was a "weak" and "ineffective president who was overcome with minutiae [and] reclusive, 'preoccupied with foreign affairs,'" and who lacked leadership skills and was merely a manager.[162] Mondale thought the president should "dramatically increase" his public education role, speak more regularly on issues of importance, and travel the country.[163] His concern was that the president did not give sufficient attention to the politics of issues.[164] Brzezinski stated, "Mondale's judgment on foreign policy issues was more and more colored by domestic political interests, and I could sense that he was frequently dismayed by Carter's unwillingness to give a higher priority to electoral concerns than to foreign policy considerations."[165] He was discouraged with Carter's philosophical conviction, or lack thereof.[166] Mondale argued that the president failed to inform the nation on the direction he was taking the country and why.[167]

Last, Carter's "malaise speech" represented a difficult time for the two principals. Mondale strenuously opposed the "malaise speech," in which the president sought to discuss the psychological crisis that permeated the country.[168] Mondale saw the problems as economic, not psychological, and aggressively pressed Carter to reconsider. Mondale stated,

> By late afternoon I was pretty upset, and probably for the only time, I broke with Carter. . . . I said I don't believe this problem is in people's heads. . . . These are real problems. People can't get gas. Their paychecks are getting smaller. They're worrying about their heating bills. . . . You can't blame the American people for the problems they face. We were elected to be a government as good as the people, yet now we're proposing to say that we need people as good as the government. You can't sell that.[169]

Mondale recalling the incident stated, "I probably made an ass of myself. But I was afraid that this would be the end of our administration."[170] "He just thought Carter was way off base there. Carter said things that would destroy the Carter presidency."[171] Carter recalled, "He was distraught. . . . He and I walked around the perimeter fence surrounding Camp David, as I tried to calm him down and persuade him that we were doing the right thing. It is not a way to handle the American people. It was destructive."[172] Although Mondale failed to stop him from giving the speech, his advice toned down the content and removed the word "malaise" from it.[173]

Despite Mondale's dissipating influence, their relationship remained strong, Mondale remained loyal, and Carter appreciated his vice president's role. Carter would comment, "There is not a single aspect of my own responsibilities in which Fritz is not intimately associated. He is the only person that I have with both the substantive knowledge and the

186 / Emerging from the Shadows

political stature to whom I can turn over a major assignment."[174] But Carter acknowledged their differences when he stated, "He has sound judgment and strong beliefs and has never been timid about presenting them forcefully to me. But whenever I made a final decision, even when it was contrary to his own original recommendation, he gave me his full support."[175] At the end of his term, Carter stated, "No president [had a] better Vice President [and he considered them] brothers."[176] He argued that their relationship "constantly improved."[177] Carter effusively praised him, telling Mondale, "I couldn't get along without you. You've made it easier and more enjoyable."[178] Stuart Eizenstat, argued, "No one else had that breadth of relationship with the president."[179]

While Carter may have decided against Mondale's advice in several important cases, he continued to provide him with a voice, and in some instances his advice was influential enough to tone down some of the positions he opposed. The strength of their personal and professional relationship maintained Mondale's access and capacity to exercise influence, even if the advice was not fully taken. Furthermore, their styles were compatible and their vision for the office was completely in sync. Mondale would prevail more often than not. He helped create the Department of Education, was instrumental in the passage of the Panama Canal Treaty, and helped negotiate the Camp David peace accord between Egypt and Israel.[180] In fact, during the lead up to the Middle East summit meeting, Carter relied on Mondale to fill in the void as he attended to the peace process.[181] Carter stated, "Fritz Mondale handled everything possible for me in Washington, and took a helicopter up to Camp David whenever he could get away at night or on weekends. . . . Realizing how busy I was with the peace effort, everyone tried to relieve me of most of the routine administrative duties of the Presidency."[182]

Walter Mondale's Electoral Dynamic

As discussed previously, Mondale goes down in history as the father of the modern vice presidency. Nonetheless, Mondale experienced similar constraints to his influence that all the vice presidents studied have faced. In the case of Walter Mondale, the electoral dynamic negatively impacted his capacity to exert continued influence in the Carter administration.

While Mondale remained influential through most of his tenure, his influence began to diminish as it approached the latter years. Mondale was unable to "escape all the frustrations of the second office."[183] Major disagreements over policy began to develop, specifically over Carter's response to the Soviet Union invading Afghanistan and Carter's policy for combating inflation, which included major cuts to social programs.[184] "When his advice wasn't taken, it damn well got to him. Because he knew in his mind that he was right, and Carter was wrong. And that is hard to live with."[185] However, those disagreements were always discussed with the president in private, usually during their Monday lunches.[186] Nonetheless, Mondale was discouraged by the president's approach to tackling their political problems and argued that Carter needed to ramp up his efforts in reaching out to Congress and the disparate constituency groups.[187] As the disagreements over policy and actions intensified, Mondale grew more and more despondent, choosing to spend less time at the White House starting in 1979.[188] Speculation also ran rampant at this time that the vice president was considering resigning or removing himself from the reelection campaign.[189] William Smith, a Mondale adviser, stated,

> Mondale had a hard time in his relationship with Carter. Mondale agonized a lot particularly in the last couple of years of the Carter presidency about his relationship with Carter as vice president and whether or not he would run again as vice president. He talked a lot about that. He and I would walk all around the White House grounds. He had real qualms and first thoughts about whether he wanted to be vice president again if Carter ran again. It was based on all the criticisms that the Carter administration received.[190]

Given Carter's poor relations with his own party and inability to cogently discuss his philosophy, Mondale was essential to the reelection effort and Carter's "secret weapon," who could "articulate" the Democratic core constituencies' priorities best.[191] Mondale also was best positioned to assume this mantle since the president was reluctant to do it himself, partly because he was not embraced by those elements of the party and partly because he just did not like that sort of thing.[192] Plus, Mondale enjoyed that type of work.[193] "The vice president complained that Carter had failed to tell the nation where he was going and why it should follow. Because the president lacked a compelling political philosophy or well-grounded assumptions to guide his thought, his policies jumped between liberal and conservative."[194] No one knew what the administration stood for.[195]

188 / Emerging from the Shadows

Carter was so focused on managing the presidency that he lost sight of the public aspects of the presidency. Carter dedicated "too much time poring over staff memos [and] not enough time in public giving speeches and appearing with people."[196] Mondale was not the only one voicing these concerns, state governors also felt that the president was not focused enough on politics.[197] As a result, Mondale would need to articulate a vision, defend the administration, and assume responsibility for the public presidency through the reelection effort, something his staff felt was essential if the president was reluctant to do so.[198] Mondale argued, "I think it is important that I devote more time to strengthening our relationship with those constituencies and persuading them that our interests and theirs are inextricably tied together."[199]

However, Mondale was disillusioned over the differences he had with Carter and the difficult task he had trying to keep the traditional constituency of the Democratic Party behind them, which Mondale spent considerable time nurturing. For instance, he routinely engaged with various Democratic constituencies either by attending events or making calls to groups that included labor unions, Hispanics, Catholics, Jewish groups, various ethnic groups, state Democratic conventions, etc.[200] He stated, "I tried to keep our constituency together. . . . It was a tough job for an old progressive like me."[201] He had strong connections to various Democratic constituencies, including: blacks, labor, Jews, and liberals—"He was their interpreter in the West Wing."[202] And he tried to keep Carter out of as much trouble as he could with those groups.[203]

Mondale routinely confided in his staff about his frustrations or what he felt and how he thought things should be changed.[204] This frustration stemmed from a shift in the interpersonal dynamic that resulted in the emergence of philosophical differences between Carter and Mondale. By January 1979, Mondale discussed with his staff the need to revise his approach to the vice presidency, particularly "a new relaxation theory," which would result in a reduced policy-making role in the administration.[205] This represented a shift in his approach to the vice presidency, which was a clear departure from the original interpersonal dynamic that served as the foundation of Mondale's influence. His approach to the office changed. Mondale was so despondent over their differences over policy and strategy that he briefly considered resigning from office, refusing to run for reelection, as mentioned earlier, or accepting but then after the election resigning.[206] Despite his reservations about remaining a member of the administration he stuck it out and put his efforts into the reelection campaign out of a sense of loyalty.[207] Regardless of their disagreements, when the president made a decision, Mondale "got in line," understanding that "his primary goal was to serve the larger goals of the administration."[208] Nonetheless, this put him in a difficult position—having to defend and campaign on policies he did not wholeheartedly embrace, but he did just that, traveling to forty-eight states during his vice presidency as a spokesperson for the administration.[209] "He was a wonderful campaigner."[210] Nonetheless, the electoral dynamic intensified the differences and placed further distance between Carter and his vice president, thus reducing Mondale's influence. And his staff recognized the divide between the administration and their boss, even commenting that he was losing his place as the "progressive conscience of this administration," because of having to defend more conservative policies of the White House.[211]

Given Carter's proclivities to avoid the public presidency, when the reelection campaign began, the president chose a "Rose Garden strategy," which required his vice president to take the predominant role in the election.[212] Carter made the early decision to "stay off the campaign trail" to focus on the most pressing international crisis—the American hostages in Iran.[213] Carter argued that he did not ignore the campaign, however, when the hostages were taken, he "depended on Fritz, Rosalynn, and others to do the campaigning while [he] concentrated on the Iran crisis and [his] other duties."[214] However, Mondale believed there was no substitute for the president in campaigning. Carter noted in his diary, "Fritz thought the American people wanted to see me [more as a candidate, not as a president] actually campaigning and asking for votes. I'll do some of that because we need to raise money, but I think Fritz is wrong on the primary thrust of the campaign effort."[215] Carter continued to disavow campaigning and thus their disagreements from policy began to bleed over to campaign strategy.[216]

The only electoral event Carter agreed to was a three-way debate between him, Ted Kennedy, and Jerry Brown; however, when the Soviets invaded Afghanistan he pulled out of the debate.[217] Carter's refusal to campaign put an immense burden on his vice president, which was intensified by the hostage crisis that seemed to consume the president's focus at the expense of the campaign. As a result, Mondale became the chief surrogate for the reelection effort, which when combined with his reduced policy-making role and the existence of an all-encompassing crisis, the vice president's influence diminished considerably. The vice president spent significant time away from the White House, removed

190 / Emerging from the Shadows

from the day-to-day decision making, while the president remained in Washington to focus on the crisis and managing the presidency. Not only did Mondale distance himself from the policy process in a theoretical sense, he was removed from the policy process in a physical sense because of having to assume major responsibility over the reelection effort, further diminishing his influence in the White House. However, despite the physical distance and the increasing differences over policy and staffing, their personal relationship remained strong. Mondale stated, "We remain very good friends which is kind of a miracle as most presidents and VPs it seems that their relationships seem to become very strained somehow. Sometimes to the point of disruption of having any relationship at all, but Carter and I remain good friends."[218]

George H. W. Bush's Interpersonal Influence

The interpersonal dynamic can also constrain a vice president and marginalize his or her influence. The vice presidency of George H. W. Bush demonstrates the importance of the interpersonal dynamic to vice presidential influence. While Bush maintained a good relationship with President Ronald Reagan, their relationship did not begin on the best footing, and his selection lacked the rigor established by Carter's process. Bush had spent the 1980 Republican primaries challenging Reagan for the nomination, and as a result some animosity was sown.[219] Reagan's first prospect for vice president was former president Gerald Ford, however, after it proved unworkable, Reagan was left with having to make a quick decision regarding his running mate. Reagan would turn to his former rival, George Bush; however, there were doubts about his fit with Reagan, especially among staff and the nominee himself.[220] They questioned whether Bush was committed to Reagan's philosophical ideas.[221] They viewed Bush as moderate, rather than a "movement conservative," and for many he seemed too liberal and out of ideological sync with Reagan.[222] "The Reagans initially didn't want to pick Bush. . . . [However,] the last man standing was Bush and he was big in the polls."[223] Because of having to make a hasty decision, Reagan reluctantly agreed to Bush's selection to unify the party.[224] Max Friedersdorf, Reagan's assistant for legislative affairs, referred to Bush's selection as a "shotgun marriage."[225] Though it did not faze Bush that he was not Reagan's first choice, he was not his second choice either.[226] According to Nancy Reagan, his preferred choice was Senator Paul Laxalt, but his selection would not provide geographic balance to the ticket.[227] James Baker argued, "At that moment, Reagan's preferred candidate for running mate was ABB—Anybody But Bush."[228] Regardless, Bush stated, "What was important, as I saw it, was that six weeks, six months, four years from now, he'd know that however he came to make it, he'd made the right choice."[229]

Despite the ideological differences, a Bush pick had other potential obstacles. For one thing, they did not know each other well. Bush stated, "We'd met several times when I headed the Republican National Committee and he was governor of California, but had never talked at any great length. In 1978, I'd paid a courtesy call at his Los Angeles office to let him know I planned to enter the presidential race; but that, too, was a pro forma meeting—cordial, but arm's length."[230] Bush understood the importance of their relationship, when he stated, "Even when Presidents and Vice Presidents see eye to eye on the issues, their long-term political relationship can only be as strong as their personal relationship."[231]

It would take time to build a strong personal relationship. After all, the primaries pitted Reagan and Bush against each other, highlighting ideological and policy differences. Trust would need to be earned and there were questions on both sides as to whether this political marriage would work. Reagan was concerned about their differences; he was not sure how they could overcome the fact that Bush opposed Reagan's stance on the economy and abortion.[232] Bush was especially "hard hitting" on those issues.[233] Reagan, in discussing the possibility of a Bush pick with his adviser Richard Allen, stated, "I can't take him; that 'voodoo economic policy' charge and his stand on abortion are wrong."[234] However, Reagan was out of options, so when he called Bush to offer him the vice presidency, he stated, "George, is there anything at all . . . about the platform or anything else . . . anything that might make you uncomfortable down the road?"[235] While Bush responded there would be no problems with his support of the platform, the media would question Bush's stand on the key differences highlighted during the primaries.[236] After all, Bush favored the Equal Rights Amendment, was pro-choice, and was not considered a "big tax-cutter."[237] However, Reagan was just the opposite.[238] Bush justified his support for the platform by stating, "My view is that the big issues, the major issues in the fall, will be the questions of unemployment and the economy and there are going to be questions of foreign affairs. I oppose abortion, I favor equal rights for women. I'm not going to say I haven't had differences at some point with Governor Reagan and everybody else,

192 / Emerging from the Shadows

many other people. But what I will be doing is emphasizing common ground. I will be enthusiastically supporting the Republican platform."[239] Bush argued that one of the most important criteria for vice president is supporting his president, and his statement above demonstrated just that, despite their differences.[240]

Bush had aggressively attacked a part of Reagan's economic program as "voodoo economics" and differed with his stance on abortion since he was pro-choice.[241] Bush's public pronouncements regarding "voodoo economics" concerned Reagan's views on lower taxes, increasing defense spending, while raising revenue.[242] He saw it as "economic madness."[243] Bush's image was that of a "younger, centrist, [and] more experienced alternative" to Reagan.[244] The arduous fight that took place during the primaries, especially during the New Hampshire primary left some scars. "Bush insinuated, subtly and not so subtly, that Reagan was too old and too extreme; Reagan argued, subtly and not so subtly, that Bush was too effete and too eastern."[245] Bush would hammer away at his age while Reagan painted Bush as an upper-class elite.[246] The famous New Hampshire debate increased tension between the two men and deepened the scars.

Despite all the personal animosity that formed over the course of the primary, Reagan and Bush put it behind them after Bush agreed to join the ticket. Bush stated, "There was never a hint of negative feeling left over from our fight for the presidential nomination because Reagan's instinct, I learned, is to think the best of the people he works with."[247] Reagan did not hold grudges, and once the election was won he did not hold anything against Bush.[248] "By the end of the first year, I think they had really become close personal friends."[249] Bush was a safe pick who would prove popular with moderates and even some conservatives.[250] Moreover, his credentials helped Reagan's weaknesses, having served in Congress, as ambassador to the UN, CIA director, and chair of the Republican National Committee.[251] "In the campaign months in 1980 a true friendship developed between both couples and especially the two partners, which was not a remarkable thing, actually, given the enormous goodwill and lack of bitterness that characterizes both men."[252] By putting the past behind them, the campaign represented an opportunity for Bush to demonstrate his loyalty, which is a character trait that the Bush family admires and embraces wholeheartedly.[253] He subordinated himself to Reagan and his only constituency was the president.[254] As vice president, the media would argue that "Bush was loyal to a fault."[255] And to critics, his loyalty was overly excessive.[256] *Newsweek* would actually call Bush a wimp, as a result of his unwavering loyalty to Reagan.[257]

Bush's undying loyalty is precisely what he thought a vice president should be. In a letter to Richard Nixon, dated January 12, 1982, Bush stated, "I don't believe a President should have to be looking over his shoulder wondering if the Vice President was out there carving him up or undermining his programs in one way or another."[258] While it would take time to cement their relationship and build trust, Bush was determined to ensure that Reagan had no regrets. Bush was true to his word, he worked tirelessly campaigning for the ticket and told all who asked that he "enthusiastically" supported the platform, and more specifically he would support Reagan's position on abortion.[259] Moreover, the morning after the offer when the Bushes and Reagans met, Barbara Bush confirmed her husband's thinking when she told Reagan, "You're not going to be sorry. We're going to work our tails off for you."[260] Reagan had no regrets, he made the right choice.[261] Bush had ingratiated himself with Reagan as a result of his demeanor during the general election campaign.[262]

Reagan and Bush decided to embrace the model espoused by Carter and Mondale.[263] And Mondale was very helpful in advising Bush during the transition on the specifics of his vice presidency.[264] That decision had important ramifications for the vice presidency, it institutionalized important features that would provide a vice president with the capacity to exercise influence. Bush was included in the paper flow of the White House, given open access to attend meetings of the president, an office in the West Wing, and a weekly private lunch with the president.[265] However, unlike Mondale, Bush chose to operate more often from his office in the Old Executive Office Building, arguing that proximity to the president did not determine influence, but the personal relationship between the principals.[266]

While Bush and Reagan were on a good path to establishing a strong relationship and embracing the tenets of an influential vice presidency espoused by Carter and Mondale, he was not quite trusted by Reagan insiders.[267] "To them, Bush was still the man who dared to contest their chief's claim to the mantle of Republican leadership, who had uttered the phrase 'voodoo economics' . . . and who had gathered under his banner the 'country-club, elitist moderates' who represented what longtime Reagan supporters despised and rejected."[268] "It was really obvious that so many of those Reagan people did not want George Bush on the ticket. They

194 / Emerging from the Shadows

were not happy that Reagan had selected him. They did not want any of us around anymore than we had to be. It was very, very notable."[269]

Despite the presidential staff's misgivings, Reagan brought a Bush insider into his personal orbit by selecting Bush's campaign manager, James Baker, as his chief of staff.[270] Baker argued, "[Reagan was] secure enough in his own skin to ask his chief competitor's staff to be his advisor! I ran two campaigns against Reagan and he nevertheless came to me and asked me to be his White House chief of staff."[271] This personal gesture would go a long way in healing any wounds that remained from the primaries and relay the message that Reagan was beginning to trust Bush and those who were loyal to his vice president. It helped bring the two staffs together, which resulted in close integration and coordination.[272] It also meant that Baker would look out for Bush's interest.[273] Baker stated, "My presence [will] hopefully limit staff conflicts that tend to result in VP being cut out."[274] Baker also saw to it that Bush was not undermined by the president's staff.[275] Baker also tried to facilitate a stronger relationship between the two principals by "supporting the idea that they should have as many opportunities as possible to spend time together."[276] While Baker's appointment helped, the president's staff, particularly those who served with him in Sacramento, were suspicious of him and it would take longer to build the same kind of support Bush had with Reagan with the president's staff.[277] "They saw Baker as a dangerous alien element, if not a wholly subversive force, in the Reagan Revolution."[278] After all, Bush's campaign for president rejected core Reagan policies and James Baker was his campaign manager.

Beyond Reagan's appointment of Baker, Bush was not as successful in staffing the Reagan White House as Mondale was in the Carter White House. Most of the influence Bush had over appointments centered on the Commerce Department, where Malcolm Baldridge was appointed secretary, and who had run Bush's primary campaign in Connecticut.[279] Some of Bush's suggestions fell on deaf ears. He had recommended that an intelligence professional be named CIA director; however, Reagan decided to appoint William Casey, his campaign chair who lacked the necessary background.[280] Bush also cautioned Reagan about appointing Alexander Haig as secretary of state, arguing that problems would develop, but Reagan went with Haig.[281] Ultimately, Bush chose to stay out of staffing and appointment decisions.[282] He did not pressure Reagan to find homes for his people. He was "fully aware that Reagan had won the election and not he."[283] Thus, Bush took a backseat to administration appointments.

Bush's reluctance to exert his influence was also apparent in the case of the firing of Don Regan as Reagan's chief of staff. In her memoirs, Nancy Reagan mentions that not only did she experience tension with Regan, but she was hearing from members of Congress and other government officials that Regan was restricting access to the president and had poor relations with the media and Congress. Furthermore, people began leaving the White House because they could not work for him.[284] Nancy Reagan recalled her conversation with Bush, in which the vice president came to her to express his concern over Regan. She stated,

> Even George Bush came to see me in the residence about Don. As he got off the elevator and we walked into the West Hall, he said, "I didn't want to say this on the phone, but I think Don should resign." "I agree with you," I said, "and I wish you'd tell my husband. I can't be the only one who's saying this to him." "Nancy," he said, "that's not my role." "That's exactly your role," I replied. But as far as I know, George Bush never spoke to Ronnie about Don Regan.[285]

While Bush contends that he did speak to the president about it, Reagan was adamant about Regan staying.[286] However, Bush did not go any further than that, feeling it was not his place to do anything more to convince the president otherwise. In fact, Nancy Reagan wanted Bush to go around her husband's back to pressure Regan to leave and Bush refused.[287] The above exchange further evidences Bush's restrained role in the affairs of the Reagan administration. While the capacity to exercise influence existed, it was tempered by his concerns about overstepping his boundaries, which were self-imposed to a large extent. It meant that his self-interest was put aside for the sake of the president. Bush stated, "A Vice President who puts his own agenda ahead of the President's at the wrong time and place—who places self-interest above all else—wouldn't deserve to be President in any case."[288] The Bush model, as many who worked for him and Reagan referred to it, was seen as the epitome of what a president would want in a vice president, a "model of decorum and loyalty."[289]

Bush's decision to not actively participate in the staffing of the administration is very telling. It foreshadowed the role he would play as vice president. While in theory he accepted the Mondale model, in practice he was much more reserved in its implementation, and this is where the interpersonal dynamic had the greatest impact on the nature

196 / Emerging from the Shadows

of his influence.[290] Reagan and Bush had a rough start to their relationship but both men put the contentious primary battle and any personal slights behind them. Reagan, demonstrating that he wanted to build a strong relationship with his vice president, would name James Baker as his chief of staff. However, resentment continued at the staff level for a short while.[291] Nonetheless, Bush's conception of the vice presidential role was not one of activism but restraint.[292] His main role was to be loyal and take over should anything happen to the president.[293] As a result, when his son was in the White House, he was critical of the role Cheney played as vice president. "Cheney's activist vice presidency had given the administration a harsher image than it might otherwise have had. . . . The vice president at times appeared to have a disproportionate voice in the affairs of the son's administration—and Bush always believed in proportion."[294] He thought a vice president should keep himself in check, and not be heard.[295]

His goal was to win over Reagan's confidence, which he did.[296] Reagan would grow very fond of Bush and valued his input.[297] In winning Reagan's confidence, Bush pledged his unwavering loyalty and support. Bush told him,

> I will never do anything to embarrass you politically. I have strong views on issues and people, but once you decide a matter that's it for me, and you'll see no leaks in Evans and Novak bitching about life—at least you'll see none out of me. . . . Call me if I can lighten the burden. If you need someone to meet people on your behalf, or to turn off overly-eager office seekers, or simply someone to bounce ideas off of—please holler.[298]

The above quote demonstrates that Bush was content waiting in the wings, and if asked, he would get involved. He would not pressure Reagan and would be restrained in his capacity as vice president. And he would do everything to ensure Reagan was "as an effective president as he could [be]."[299]

Bush's chief of staff made clear to the vice president's staff that they would not tolerate staffers who "upstage" the president's staff and that there would be "no surprises and no self-aggrandizement," arguing that it would quickly "alienate" Bush from Reagan.[300] Bush was determined to have his staff demonstrate the same sort of loyalty to Reagan, accepting nothing less.[301] A senior staffer for the vice president recalled,

Bush had a meeting with senior staff in our transition office . . . and it was one of the few times he ever really laid down rules. George Bush is a very gentle and kind and modest person. He said, "I don't want to ever, ever pick up a paper or hear a news report that anyone on my staff is disagreeing with Ronald Reagan or his people. This is the Reagan administration and our job is to make him successful."[302]

Bush's demeanor as vice president was emulated by his staff and helped win Reagan's confidence. "A vice president can be at least the second most trusted person in a president's life if he conducts himself the way President Bush did as vice president because of the extraordinary lengths Bush went to preserve his private role with the president and to never be a divisive factor or an influence for anybody else or any outside position."[303] Frank Carlucci, Reagan's national security adviser, agreed, stating, "Bush conducted himself admirably as vice president. He did not seek the limelight, [and] he did not grandstand."[304] And he expected the same from his staff. In all, Reagan trusted Bush and knew that when he told him something it would remain between the two of them.[305]

Bush would spend most of his vice presidency loyally serving the president and convincing the more conservative parts of Reagan's coalition that he could carry on Reagan's legacy.[306] George W. Bush, recalling his father's vice presidency, stated, "He had been so loyal to President Reagan that he had done almost nothing to promote himself."[307] He saw himself as an adviser but most of all, an absolute loyalist.[308] His unwavering loyalty meant that he lived by three rules: (1) never put distance between you and the president, when a decision becomes unpopular; (2) "don't play the Washington news-leaking game"; and (3) always conduct interviews on record, even if they are friends.[309] These rules adhered to his conception of the vice president—you should be seen but not heard, except for private consultations with the president.[310] This restrained conception of a vice presidential role greatly impacted the degree to which he played an influential role in the Reagan administration and would actually diminish his influence. While they would never be considered equals, Reagan did come to respect and trust Bush's advice.[311] Even when presented with opportunities to exert influence or give the impression of influence, Bush chose to keep himself in check, stand by his president, and loyally serve. And Reagan was not one to seek out advice either. Bush stated, "He's

198 / Emerging from the Shadows

hard to read; he doesn't ask for advice; he doesn't say, 'what do you think about this,' very much—but the other side of that is, I feel uninhibited in bringing things up to him."[312]

Two incidences prove the level of restraint Bush showed as vice president, and both instances would win over not only the president but the suspicious White House staff. Reagan made the decision that Bush would be given the title of "crisis manager," which would invest Bush with some authority in foreign policy and give him the job of coordinating federal response to foreign or domestic emergencies.[313] Reagan wanted his vice president to be more than just "standby equipment."[314] Reagan stated, "I also thought that it was prudent—and important for the country—for the vice-president to play as large a role in the affairs of the administration as possible."[315] As second in command, it was a logical choice to have Bush serve this capacity, but it was seen as a threat to Secretary of State Alexander Haig, even though the position was normally reserved for the national security adviser, not the secretary of state.[316] Haig was furious that Bush would challenge his role as "the vicar of foreign policy" and made his views known to the press.[317] Haig felt like he was being undercut and considered Bush's naming as head of crisis management as limiting his foreign policy role.[318] He also felt that Reagan went back on his promise to make him the "integrator" of foreign policy.[319] Making matters worse, Haig disliked Bush.[320] Bush could have easily capitalized on this event to assert his influence and authority, but he remained quiet and did not boast of his role, which made the vice president more acceptable to the White House staffers and placed Haig as the "odd man out."[321] Bush demonstrated his loyalty to the president by remaining silent. In the end, it reconfirmed Reagan's decision to put Bush in charge. An anonymous White House aide stated, "The President simply feels more comfortable with George because he doesn't let his ego and ambition show and he doesn't come off as strong as Al Haig."[322] Bush's loyal and restrained approach deepened Reagan's trust in his vice president.

The second event that helped foster better relationships with the president and the staff had to do with Reagan's assassination attempt. On March 30, 1981, Bush was traveling in Texas, where he was to speak to the Texas state legislature, when he received word from his press secretary, Pete Teeley, that shots had been fired at the president, but he was unharmed, according to initial reports.[323] However, when the White House received word that Reagan had sustained an injury and that it was serious, Haig contacted Bush on Air Force Two, in which Bush confirmed he was heading back to Washington.[324] Power was never transferred to Bush at the time because Ed Meese, the president's adviser, and James Baker, his chief of staff, thought it was unnecessary.[325] Furthermore, Baker was concerned about the implications of such a move. He stated, "I was sensitive to the fact (and knew George Bush would be, too) that many Reagan loyalists—mindful that we had campaigned against President Reagan in the primaries—still questioned our allegiance to the president. . . . They might view the transfer as something just short of a Bush-Baker *coup d'état*."[326]

Not knowing the extent of the assassination attempt and whether Bush was also a target, his Secret Service detail and staff recommended that he take Marine Two from Andrews Air Force Base and land on the South Lawn of the White House.[327] Bush refused, choosing instead to helicopter to the vice president's residence and then take his motorcade to the White House.[328] Bush argued that only the president lands on the South Lawn of the White House.[329] Bush stated, "Good television, yes—but not the message I thought we needed to send the country and the world."[330] He did not want to come off as trying to "usurp the privileges of the president."[331] This one decision not to upstage the president by demonstrating he was in control and acting as president sent several messages. First, it demonstrated Bush's loyalty to Reagan because he did not jump at the opportunity to step in to fill the president's shoes as his first response. Second, it had a calming effect on the nation.[332] Had the vice president landed on the South Lawn, the optics would express that Reagan's condition was grave, which it was, however, the public was led to believe otherwise. Third, it confirmed Bush's approach to the office, that his role was one of restraint, not activism, which would marginalize his capacity to exercise influence. Fourth, this one simple decision endeared Reagan's staff to the vice president and convinced them that he was truly a loyal second in command. Kathy Osborne, Reagan's secretary, stated, "No one needs to tell George Bush how to behave."[333] "It didn't take very long until the Reagan people realized this guy is going to do what is right. We don't have to worry about him."[334] But there was also a practical reason behind his decision, Nancy Reagan was resting at the White House and he did not want the noise to disrupt her.[335]

The first thing Bush did upon arriving at the White House was to preside over the crisis management meeting in the Situation Room.[336] During the meeting a question arose as to whether to transfer power from the president to Bush. Bush argued it was unnecessary since Reagan's condition was good and he wanted to "make the government function as

200 / Emerging from the Shadows

normally as possible."[337] Bush then provided remarks to the press where he reassured the country and the world that Reagan had come through surgery "with flying colors" and that the government was fully functional.[338] The next day Bush would preside over the cabinet meeting and a bipartisan meeting of congressional leaders, stepping in to ensure the government functioned, but showing great deference to Reagan by sitting in his own chair and conducting some meetings from his own office.[339] While his role was larger than usual, at every opportunity he emphasized that the president was still in control.[340] And he also made sure to clear everything with both Baker and Meese.[341] Bush stated, "The President is still President. . . . He is not incapacitated and I am not going to be a substitute President. I'm here to sit in for him while he recuperates. But he's going to call the shots."[342] In fact, the day after the shooting, Reagan had signed a bill that canceled an increase in price supports for dairy with a tube still in his nose and an IV line still attached to his arm.[343] For all intents and purposes, Bush was acting president, however, to the outside he was just filling in for the president. Bush went out of his way to disclaim any new authority for him, he did not want to upstage the president.[344] "The line we were [taking] on Monday was this: 'do nothing to appear presumptuous, but you don't want to appear in any state of panic either.'"[345] Bush said, "It never occurred to me even for a fleeting moment that I was anything more than a stand-in."[346] David Gergen, a presidential aide stated, "George Bush, given his nature, was very careful in how he handled himself during that time. He didn't want to be seen doing anything that might suggest arrogance or an arrogation of power."[347] William Casey, director of the CIA stated, "When the Vice President did arrive, he quickly made it clear that the only role he wanted to play was to support the President and see that business was carried on, see that the President was fully and properly advised, and protocol obligations met for the President."[348] Michael Deaver, a longtime aide of Reagans, stated, "In truth, the government hardly skipped a beat during the president's recovery, in large part because of the Reagan style. He is a big-picture man who has never enjoyed immersing himself in details. And George Bush was superb at taking over many of the president's obligations, while avoiding the appearance of a man trying on a job for size. This was not, I believe, a political instinct but simply Bush at his considerate best."[349]

This approach was consistent with his views on the vice president's proper role and his own personal style—putting loyalty above all else, including his own political ambition. He deferred to Reagan and was always willing to do whatever it was the president wanted of him.[350] The consequence was that it "excluded [him] from the highest levels of decision making" and placed his political ambitions on hold.[351] Bush stated, "During my first term as Vice President, I was constantly urged by friends to staff my office as if it were a campaign operation, with an eye toward expanding my political base. I went out of the way to do just the opposite, pointing out that the last thing any President needs is a Vice President with his own agenda, grinding his own political ax."[352] Craig Fuller, Bush's chief of staff, stated, "As late as seven years into the presidency, those of us who were working on Vice President Bush's presidential campaign had to literally plead with the vice president to separate himself from the president on some issues and define himself in his own campaign. His basic attitude was that not until he was the nominee of his party in August of 1988 did he want to show any difference on issues with President Reagan."[353] He was so loyal that Ed Meese, Reagan's attorney general, recalled "I remember the vice president giving advice when the president asked about some things, even though it was against his own political interests personally, particularly as he was thinking about running for president."[354] However, it came at a cost. "As the perfect vice president, George had served the Reagan presidency superbly, but at significant cost to his image as a man with his own ideas."[355] Nevertheless, it fostered greater trust with Reagan. "Reagan, already disposed to treat Bush with respect, had all the more reason to believe that his vice president's professions of devotion and duty were genuine."[356] Furthermore, it won over those staffers who were weary of the vice president.[357] "Vice President Bush, too, seems sure to gain in clout because of the calm manner in which he filled in for the President. . . . His demeanor, neither pushy nor retiring, impressed some Reaganites who had considered him a mushy moderate."[358]

This restrained view of the vice presidency even took over when Reagan had bowel surgery in which the president signed over authority to Bush, making him acting president, which had not been done when Reagan was shot.[359] For the eight hours he was acting president, he exercised no constitutional responsibilities but instead spent the time at his official residence talking on the phone, playing tennis, and reading.[360] In fact, he spent the eight hours doing anything but work so as to not be accused of trying to "usurp the president's powers in any way."[361] George Bush's extraordinary restraint helped him win over a suspicious White House staff and further solidify himself as a trusted advisor and friend to the president.[362] Helene von Damm, Reagan's personal secretary stated,

202 / Emerging from the Shadows

"Vice President Bush behaved most admirably during this time. He kept a low profile, wouldn't think of taking [the president's] seat at Cabinet meetings, but maintained a reassuring presence nevertheless. Rumor had it that Mrs. Reagan and Mike Deaver insisted upon it. If true, they need not have worried. George Bush is too much of a gentleman to be reminded of how to behave at a time like that."[363] Kenneth Duberstein, Reagan's chief of staff, stated, "[Reagan] let Bush in. He considered him as a full partner, across the board. He liked Bush."[364] Bush acknowledged that it had a positive effect on his relationship when he stated, "Did it help me with President Reagan? Sure. I think so. He saw—and Nancy saw, I might add—that I'd meant what I'd said all along."[365] More importantly, it relieved Reagan of wondering about his vice president's loyalty. Bush stated, "A president has enough to worry about without having to worry that his vice president is undercutting him, or trying to make himself look good at the president's expense. I'd decided that he deserved my total loyalty, and he got it."[366] However, it had the unintended consequence of marginalizing his influence and forced him to live in the shadow of Ronald Reagan. Craig Fuller, who worked for Bush, stated, "When [Bush] chose to assert influence, the relationship with Ronald Reagan was such that he had considerable influence. He didn't assert that influence that often. He didn't see the office of Vice President as one where he should be shaping policy as much as making sure the President has the information to make decisions."[367] He was very content operating behind the scenes.[368] This meant that the interpersonal dynamic provided him with the capacity to exercise influence, a testament to Bush and Reagan following the Mondale model; however, his influence was tempered by the same interpersonal dynamic, particularly his reserved conception of the role.

George H. W. Bush's Institutional Dynamic

As you recall from the previous discussion of Bush, there was a great degree of suspicion surrounding his vice presidency given that he had challenged Reagan for the nomination in 1980 and because there were various occasions in which the events of the campaign developed animosity between the two. While they would quickly put the contentious campaign behind them and develop a warm and friendly relationship, the same could not be said for the White House staff who were loyal to Reagan. They doubted his loyalty and were suspicious of him.

The suspicions the staff felt toward Bush could have posed significant challenges for him. After all, the institutional dynamic, as we saw in the case of Rockefeller, could have easily proven to be a significant obstacle to the exercising of influence. However, Reagan made an important decision that would relieve Bush of this potential problem. He decided to name a Bush loyalist, James Baker, to be his chief of staff.[369] This important act removed several obstacles for Bush in terms of exercising influence. First, it demonstrated that Reagan had truly put the campaign behind them and that Bush had built enough trust with the president that he would be willing to let a Bush loyalist serve in such an important capacity in his administration, an indication that Reagan was unthreatened by Bush. Second, it sent a strong message to the White House staff that if he was willing to trust Bush and Baker, so should they. While they were not as quick to accept Bush, his actions would result in institutional barriers being lifted. Third, as chief of staff, Baker would be able to ensure that Bush's interest was advanced.[370] Baker stated, "My presence [will] hopefully limit staff conflicts that tend to result in VP being cut out."[371] And he went to great measures to ensure the two principals developed a stronger relationship, providing them with ample opportunity to spend time together.[372]

Baker's presence facilitated an advisory role for Bush that most other vice presidents who were once rivals of their president, such as Lyndon Johnson, would not have had.[373] His careful attention to the principals' relationship and Bush's own interests made all the difference. "[He] kept a sharp eye for decent treatment of the new vice president."[374] As you may recall, a chief of staff can help or hurt a vice president, and in this case, Baker's efforts early on alleviated staff tensions with the vice president and successfully removed some of the institutional obstacles to vice presidential influence. As a result, Bush followed the Mondale model to shape his vice presidency, with one notable exception—he disagreed with Mondale's stance on line assignments. Bush thought the vice president should be a "senior adviser with portfolio."[375] This was "a view consistent with, and perhaps responsive to, Reagan's belief that the vice president, 'like a vice president in a private corporation . . . should be an executive with duties and functions."[376] As a result, Bush embraced the line assignments that Mondale would disavow as vice president.

Bush's influence can be broken down into several categories, to include: line assignments, foreign affairs, ceremonial functions, and Congress. Bush's influence was recognized by many who worked for the administration, as well as those close to Reagan. Reagan's national security

204 / Emerging from the Shadows

adviser, Robert McFarlane, argued that Bush was a "decisive influence" on Reagan.[377] Secretary of State George Shultz, knowing Bush's influence on Reagan, sought out the vice president in meeting with the president to "air complaints about the NSC."[378] And even Nancy Reagan, who was considered a force within the White House, asked Bush to intervene with her husband to help influence his thinking on Soviet/US relations.[379] Reagan's chief of staff, Kenneth Duberstein stated, "[he] let Bush in. He considered him a full partner, across the board [and] he liked Bush."[380] While Bush did not assert his influence very often because of his reserved view of the office, he maintained the capacity.

Despite Bush's restraint he did exert influence in various ways. First, his work heading the Task Force on Regulatory Relief, although considered a line assignment, provided Bush with an opportunity to head up a primary piece of the Reagan Revolution.[381] Deregulation was "one of the president's three or four basic election mandates from 1980," thus it was very important to him.[382] Furthermore, it was a major component of his "economic revitalization program."[383] Reagan was determined to reduce the size of the government and cut unnecessary rules and regulations.[384] "Reagan firmly believed that the heavy hand of regulation was not only stifling the productivity of the economy but [it also] was a freedom issue."[385] Upon taking office, the president ordered a freeze on hiring replacements for those leaving government service, cut government travel costs, put a moratorium on the buying of new equipment, and reduced the number of government contractors.[386] Since this was one of the first actions Reagan undertook, and it was the first assignment Reagan asked of Bush, his acceptance demonstrated that he was willing to do anything the president asked.[387] But Bush staffers also urged him to advise the president of the necessity of creating such a task force. In a memo, the day after the inauguration, Bush staffers recommended to his chief of staff the creation of a committee or task force to undertake a program and policy review to gauge effectiveness of programs and ensure they were in line with Reagan's intent on regulations.[388]

Bush subtly used the task force as a way of healing the wounds from the 1980 primaries, in which conservative Republicans were still fuming over his attack on Reagan's economic program.[389] After all, the purpose of the task force was to review federal regulations and cut as many as possible.[390] Reagan would claim in his State of the Union address, that because of Bush's actions, federal regulations were reduced by 25 percent and the savings amounted to $150 billion over the course of ten years.[391]

Reagan stated, "Under George Bush, we had begun storming the citadel of unnecessary restrictions that obstructed the workings of our economy [and] eliminated thousands of pages from the federal bureaucracy's rules and regulations."[392] According to Boyden Gray, Bush's counsel, "Ronald Reagan delegated a great deal of presidential authority to him, particularly on environmental regulations."[393] However, you would never know this because "it was typical of him to hide in plain sight, exercising a measure of power without being stagey or seeking publicity."[394]

Bush took on an additional assignment in 1982, in which he led the South Florida Task force.[395] The purpose was to provide a federal response to the drug epidemic and for Bush to coordinate the efforts to "choke off the importation of drugs."[396] The cabinet-level task force was merely a coordinating function, which did very little to advance his influence because he lacked authority to force action.[397] The consortium that he coordinated included the attorney general and secretaries of state, defense, and transportation; however, he could not urge them to do anything.[398] Bush asked his chief of staff, a retired four-star admiral, to run the task force and was instrumental in bringing a reluctant Defense Department around, which viewed it as merely a policing effort.[399] Despite his lack of authority, he made the best of the role and the task force was a success in terms of increasing seizures of drugs crossing the border.[400]

One of the last line assignments Bush undertook had to do with combating terrorism.[401] President Reagan established the Task Force on Combatting Terrorism through National Security Directive 179 (NSD 179), in which Bush was given the lead role in ensuring that all resources of the United States were "dedicated" to combating terrorism.[402] NSD 179 required him to assess national priorities in addressing terrorism, assign responsibilities and accountability for "interagency cooperation and coordination before, during, and after a terrorist incident, review existing laws and terrorism related programs, and assess public awareness and evaluate the level of international cooperation that exists to combat terrorism."[403] The task force looked at the following broad areas: policies, resources, organization, diplomatic initiatives, and legal procedures.[404] Bush sought buy-in from members of Congress, the media, airline executives, diplomats, and former cabinet officials.[405] By 1987 the task force presented their findings to the president, in which it concluded that the policy was "sound, effective, and fully in accord with our democratic principles and national ideals," given a thorough review of US policy toward combating terrorism policy.[406] Since the task force found the policy sound, they

206 / Emerging from the Shadows

recommended that the policies and programs in place be followed, citing Iran as an example of failure to follow the policies in place.[407] Bush stated, "Indeed, the mistakes involved in our contacts with Iran resulted from not following the policy."[408] In general, the task force recommended that the State Department take the lead coordinating role and advised that a slight increase in NSC staff dedicated to terrorism be authorized.[409] Furthermore, the task force concluded that an integrated management system needed to be created, a realistic policy framework for decision making enacted, intelligence needed to be more predictive and consolidated, capacity for human intelligence increased, and statutory loopholes needed to be closed to prosecute terrorists effectively.[410] Despite the robust recommendations, many failed to be institutionalized.

Bush's greatest influence was felt in foreign affairs. His staff attended all interagency national security meetings and he joined Reagan for meetings with foreign leaders and members of Congress.[411] He was a regular attendee of all meetings that dealt with global affairs and security issues.[412] He took forty-one trips overseas, often to critical places around the world, such as China, Soviet Union, Europe, and the Middle East.[413] In total, he traveled to seventy-three countries and represented the United States on the world stage.[414] While a lot of trips were ceremonial, attending state funerals, he had a substantive role as well.[415] Aides described Bush as "extraordinarily valuable" to the president—someone who was a "reliable communicator" and "reliable reporter."[416] Foreign leaders understood that when they spoke with Bush it would be reported directly back to the president, thus enhancing his credibility with world leaders.[417] For example, his meetings with Deng Xiaoping, the Chinese leader, helped to secure an agreement governing arms sales to Taiwan.[418] His visit to China in May 1982 was instrumental in the crafting and signing of the third communiqué, which reduced arms sales to Taiwan.[419]

Bush's trip to Western Europe led to NATO deployment of theater-range weapons and included an overture to the Soviet Union to set up a meeting between the Soviet leader, Yuri Andropov, and Reagan to ban intermediate nuclear weapons.[420] During this critical trip, Bush met with the United Nation's Disarmament Committee and with negotiators for the Soviet Union, visited allies, and "spoke publicly to influence public opinion."[421] Western European allies were facing extreme pressure from "nuclear-freeze" proponents, and Bush was tasked with winning over vacillating governments to accept the Pershing and cruise missiles, which would counter Soviet troops who were amassed along the East German border.[422] There was a strong antinuclear posture in Germany, so one of the "chief tasks was to reassure the Germans about the deployment of intermediate range nuclear forces (INF), the Pershing II missiles, in West Germany where they were controversial."[423] The trip was also a public relations counter to the Soviet's call for a summit, which energized those antinuclear elements in Western Europe. And more importantly, it was an opportunity to "defuse Reagan's image as a nuclear cowboy."[424] Bush thought the trip provided a "much better perception of U.S. seriousness and willingness to achieve genuine arms cuts."[425] Daniel Murphy, the vice president's chief of staff, argued that "the goal of the trip was to keep Andropov from 'running away with the ballgame' in the contest for the hearts and minds of Europeans."[426] Bush felt that he reminded those in Europe that Reagan was the one who first called for an informal meeting with the Soviets and that it was the president who talked about summit meetings more than the Soviets.[427] The letter from Reagan that Bush presented to Andropov included the following: "I will drop everything, go anywhere, anytime to sign an agreement."[428] Bush's trip put a "reasonable face on American foreign policy [which] lowered rhetorical tensions."[429] Many regarded the "Euromissile" deployment as the administration's most important foreign policy action, and Bush took the lead on the effort, demonstrating Reagan's confidence and trust in him.[430] He altered public sentiment in Europe, which resulted in the deployment of INF weapons by the US to counter the Soviet threat.[431]

Even when fulfilling ceremonial functions by attending state funerals, he was able to conduct bilateral business on behalf of the administration. His famous quote, "You die, I fly," joked about the preponderance of funerals he attended, especially the funerals of Soviet leaders, three in a period of twenty-eight months.[432] Upon the conclusion of the funeral rites, Bush would be one of the first to meet the new leader of the Soviet Union, in which he would gauge the man and the prospects for improved relations, convey US objectives, and assess the leaders' perception of world affairs.[433] This enabled him to build strong personal relationships with leaders that benefited both President Reagan and later him as president.[434] Bush argued, "But what they overlook is the substance of attending funerals and inaugurations, and the diplomacy that goes with it, the showing of the flag, and the meetings with the Chiefs of State."[435] Bush's meetings with the new Soviet premieres enabled him to take the pulse of each new leader. His memo of his meeting with Chernenko at Yuri Andropov's funeral convinced Reagan to meet the new premiere because he was not

208 / Emerging from the Shadows

as hard-nosed as Andropov.[436] Bush stated, "He [Chernenko] did most of the talking on the Soviet side and what he had to say was, in my view, encouraging. He asked me to tell you that we can have better relations. That he believes it is possible to do so. . . . Chernenko is no pushover but he does seem open and treated us graciously."[437] Also, in meeting Gorbachev, Bush was quick to report back that he was "someone we can work with."[438] He used these ceremonial functions to advance US/Soviet relations, something most people diminished as purely ceremonial with little substance. For Bush, the funerals provided an opportunity to practice "personal diplomacy [which] came naturally to him."[439]

Bush was instrumental in helping the president in congressional relations, too. He spent considerable time on Capitol Hill where he met with members of Congress, including working out with them in the House gym.[440] He would often invite members on Air Force Two or to his home at the Naval Observatory to assess the mood of Congress.[441] He would frequently set up lunches where he could gather "political intelligence" and report back to Reagan.[442] "Bush used his splendid office just off the Senate lobby, his airplanes, his residence, his appearance at fund-raisers, the telephone, the tennis court, and even the steam bath in the House gym to lobby on key votes" for the president.[443] Friedersdorf stated, "We would give him a list of people [in Congress] to call. I don't care how many people you gave him on a list, . . . he called them all and lobbied them."[444] He proved to be a good sounding board for members of Congress who were reluctant to engage in "horse-trading" with the president.[445] Duberstein stated, "Members confided with the Vice President because oftentimes it's easier to tell a Vice President something. . . . You tell the vice president, 'It would really help me if you'd look at X,' Bush was terrific at being the train conductor on stuff like that."[446] His efforts in Congress helped Reagan pursue his legislative agenda.[447]

While Bush was nowhere near as influential as some other vice presidents, particularly Mondale, Gore, or Cheney, he was far more influential than people initially thought, given that Reagan and Bush were once rivals. The key to Bush's influence was winning over Reagan and the White House staff. He did this by demonstrating his loyalty to Reagan at every chance he got. However, Bush's influence was made possible by Reagan's hiring of James Baker as chief of staff, which set the tone for the rest of the administration. In that capacity, Baker reduced institutional obstacles he faced by looking out for his interests and helping to build rapport between the two principals, which demonstrates the importance of the institutional dynamic to vice presidential influence. "Over time however, Bush built a strong personal relationship with Reagan, established himself as a loyal soldier, and the president came to appreciate him," which further solidified his influence.[448] Despite the importance of the institutional dynamic to his influence, it was tempered by the interpersonal dynamic, specifically his approach to the office and what he saw as the proper role of a vice president. It was one of restraint that reduced the degree of influence exerted, even if the capacity was there.

Dan Quayle's Institutional Dynamic

As seen with both Rockefeller and Cheney, a vice president's influence can be negatively impacted by the institutional dynamic. While Vice President Dan Quayle's influence worked on the margins, his influence was especially affected by the institutional dynamic, particularly the decision-making apparatus in the White House. While critics of Quayle often derided his lack of influence, the record illustrates a much more nuanced view, one in which Quayle exerted influence, especially regarding political matters and congressional relations. "Quayle functioned as an important and effective presidential adviser and troubleshooter with the resources of his immediate predecessors. Quayle was very much engaged in the George H. W. Bush administration, and his tenure consolidated developments that Mondale had begun and Bush continued."[449] According to David Beckwith, Quayle's press secretary, "When we moved in, there was a certain inherent inertia in the office, whereas every vice president wants to make sure that he is at least as important as the previous one was."[450] Beckwith argued that Quayle had more responsibilities than Bush as vice president.[451] Despite this, Quayle faced institutional obstacles that marginalized his influence in key areas of the administration.

Quayle had hoped when he became vice president that he would be able to make significant contributions to foreign policy in the Bush administration. After all, he had served on the Senate Armed Services Committee and routinely engaged in foreign policy and defense issues. However, this would not be the case. Even though he had experience in this realm, Bush's strength was foreign affairs; thus Quayle was "careful not to upstage or challenge the president in anyway."[452] Quayle's selection, unlike many of the vice presidents in the modern era, was chosen for political reasons, not for the sake of governing.[453] His selection did

210 / Emerging from the Shadows

not offer significant balance for Bush, except for in the areas of politics and congressional relations. While Quayle had all the same access that Mondale and Bush enjoyed as vice president, including to the President's Daily Brief, national security meetings, paper flow, and intelligence, his influence in national security and foreign policy was tempered by the institutional obstacles imposed by the decision-making apparatus.[454] He was exposed to and involved in daily "discussion and decisions on vital national and international issues."[455] But this involvement was mostly to keep him informed, not to influence the nature of decision making. Bush valued his input, but it did not necessarily move the needle.[456] Quayle would offer "political advice" in meetings of the National Security Council, which proved helpful, but his substantive policy contributions were limited because of institutional obstacles.[457] Some of Quayle's own advisers questioned his influence within the administration, arguing, "I don't know how important he was to the decision-making process. There were times I felt that he lost the arguments as far as we could tell. You can argue whether he was very important to the administration in regard to decision making."[458] And in the case of foreign policy, this seemed to be the reality given the nature of the process and the actors involved in decision making.

Quayle's diminished influence in foreign policy and national security was less a reflection on him and more a reflection of the institutional structures established for decision making in the White House. After all, his experience on the Senate Armed Services committee provided him with expertise on arms control, foreign policy, and military affairs.[459] The foreign policy team consisted of the "Big Eight," which included Bush, Quayle, James Baker (secretary of state), Dick Cheney (secretary of defense), Brent Scowcroft (national security adviser), Robert Gates (deputy national security adviser), Colin Powell (chair of the Joint Chiefs), and John Sununu (chief of staff).[460] Many argued Quayle was a second-tier player who was not situated within that "inner-inner circle" within the Big Eight.[461] The inner circle was dominated by Bush, Scowcroft, Cheney, and Baker.[462] Given the nature of Bush's own experience and the impressive résumés of the other members of the inner circle, it was difficult for him to compete for influence. Quayle argued, "I can bring certain facts and things to the table that are important to [Bush], . . . but he has so many resources on foreign policy and he is so steeped in foreign policy himself."[463] Bill Kristol, Quayle's chief of staff, noted, "Between Bush, Baker, and Scowcroft there wasn't that much room for him to maneuver. They didn't need a lot of expertise."[464] Colin Powell echoed this sentiment when he stated, "He was somewhat youthful, and he was dealing with very powerful cabinet officers in the form of Jim Baker, Dick Cheney, and Brent Scowcroft and people like that so he did not get deeply immersed in the day-in and day-out of foreign policy and national security affairs."[465] The inner circle within the "Big Eight" was so influential that Scowcroft almost always had the last word before a decision was made when it came to national security matters.[466] Joseph DeSutter, the vice president's national security adviser, argued, "George Bush could have had [Henry] Kissinger or Benjamin Franklin at his side [as vice president] and would have still kept his own brief on foreign policy with his portfolio. He didn't rely on Quayle in that area as much."[467] Regardless of who his vice president was, Bush did not need his help in foreign policy and instead "reserved that area for himself."[468] Thus, Quayle's contribution would be tempered by the reality of the institutional framework he found himself operating within in foreign policy. "The policy planning process and the strategic planning process were opaque, at least in the beginning" of the term, further solidifying the inner circle and alienating those outside the circle, including Quayle.[469] Scowcroft argued, "There was frustration on the [vice president's] staff with me because I did not let them participate as much as they felt they should, but I never had a particular issue with Quayle."[470]

Further complicating matters for Quayle in foreign policy was State Department obstructionism.[471] "While Quayle played the role of loyal servant to the president, the advice he offered within NSC and cabinet settings led to occasional clashes of opinions with others in the structure."[472] Tension between Baker and Quayle existed, particularly since they both had different worldviews and different ideological beliefs.[473] For one thing, Quayle tended to be more suspicious of Gorbachev and was rather more hawkish than Baker.[474] Kristol stated, "You know, there were lots of instances where we would sort of pull at the margins of policy and I think Baker didn't like that much. . . . There was a certain amount of tension; they didn't quite regard us as trustworthy from their point of view at the State Department."[475] A tense relationship existed between Quayle and Baker going back to his selection and rollout as vice president and that carried over into the administration.[476] This was especially problematic since Baker was part of that "inner-inner circle" and Quayle was not, further alienating himself from the decision-making apparatus on foreign policy. He was considered the "odd man out."[477] Bush even recognized this when he stated that Quayle and Sununu were "two

212 / Emerging from the Shadows

important individuals, though involved mainly in domestic policy [who] contributed to our foreign policy team."[478]

Quayle's role would be routinely marginalized due to the role of the State Department. State blocked him from traveling to Moscow, the Middle East, and Eastern Europe, which complicated his role in foreign policy.[479] Quayle's staff tried to advocate for him to take trips to these key areas of the world to demonstrate his "heavyweight diplomacy," but their efforts were repudiated by the State Department.[480] It appears that Baker did play an obstructionist role regarding some of Quayle's activities in foreign policy. While he did travel extensively overseas, nineteen trips to forty-two countries, these were mostly ceremonial and rarely involved travel to areas where "sensitive diplomacy" was required or where Baker was focused.[481] For instance, Quayle's proposed trip to Germany during unification negotiations was recommended against by Baker, arguing that "the vice president did not belong in the middle of the sensitive talks."[482] Baker would win these battles at the expense of Quayle. "It was made clear by a number of sources that the secretary of state does not want Quayle to be a major player in the formulation or implementation of foreign policy."[483] Carnes Lord, Quayle's national security adviser, stated, "He was kept away from Europe by Baker because he didn't want Quayle mucking around with the important capitals of the world."[484] Thus, he found himself visiting mostly Latin American and Asian countries, however, still under the purview of Baker.[485]

Further complicating matters for Quayle was the White House staff's lack of trust in him and his staff.[486] "The working relationship between the Quayle White House team and the Bush White House team wasn't that great. They became competitive. As a consequence, the White House staff had a tendency to respond as White House staffs normally would in those circumstances and that is simply do their own thing and not involve the vice president's staff any more than they would have to."[487] Frustration loomed large on the president's staff regarding the activities of Quayle's chief of staff, Bill Kristol.[488] He was "frequently at odds with the presidential staff on substantive issues, including the end game in the Persian Gulf War."[489] Moreover, many on the president's staff viewed Kristol as the source of administration leaks and were wary about including Kristol in the administration's inner circle, thus effectively diminishing a voice for the vice president.[490] Kristol was aggressive in his role as chief of staff and was a strong policy person.[491] He had even been turned down by Sununu for a White House staff position prior to signing on with

Quayle—apparently, Sununu did not want him in the White House.[492] Beckwith stated, "[Kristol] enjoyed back-grounding the press and that is where we got in trouble because there was a feeling in the Bush White House that informed criticism of the process and decisions coming out and it did not go unnoticed that Kristol's friends in the press were making those criticisms."[493] The personalities within the institutions amplified the institutional obstacles Quayle faced in exercising influence. Clayton Yeutter, an assistant to Bush for economic and domestic policy stated,

> Sununu was a bit of a lightning rod with a lot of people. To some degree that may have provided some of the conflict with the vice-presidential office. And also Dick Darman was there as head of OMB and Darman was a bit of a lightning rod too, who was a tremendously talented individual but with not great human relations skills. And Sununu did not have great human relations skills. And you had Kristol over in Dan Quayle's shop who didn't have great human relations skills. There was an awful lot of opportunity for conflict.[494]

However, according to Quayle, the conflict mostly was between Bush's chiefs of staff and his staff.[495] "I think that the most important thing was to make sure you're not cut out at the staff level. I knew I wouldn't be cut out at my level with my relationship with the president. But the staff, that's where the wars are fought, and you've got to have your people there to fight those wars."[496] While Quayle's relationship with the president may have been strong, the staff wars had the inadvertent effect of limiting Quayle's influence because of the suspiciousness by which his staff was viewed.[497] Moreover, Sununu ran the White House as a "pretty closed ship," further contributing to staff conflict and skepticism toward the vice presidential staff.[498] Ultimately, some on Quayle's staff, such as Kristol, made it harder for him. Sununu stated, "The biggest problem that we had was that the vice president's staff was not loyal to the vice president. Quayle's staff was stabbing Quayle in the back."[499] This alludes to the fact that many of the administration's leaks were blamed on the vice president's office, particularly Kristol, thus causing unnecessary problems for Quayle with the president's staff.

Furthermore, "Bush himself was occasionally put out by what he found to be Quayle's reflexive conservatism and by the Quayle staff's eagerness to position their principal as the most reliably right-wing

214 / Emerging from the Shadows

voice in the White House."[500] "[Quayle] saw himself as a leader in the conservative movement and so he would be more expressive on those issues than probably President Bush would have been," and it came off as more "polarizing than President Bush."[501] Bush would tell Quayle, "You've got to realize this party is broader than just the conservatives. Don't get carried away."[502] The president's staff "distrusted Quayle as a kind of conservative beachhead. They knew he had hired conservatives on his staff, and they didn't want him exercising influence in the White House."[503] They obviously leaned much further right than the president's staff.[504] And even when there was speculation of Bush dumping Quayle in the reelection bid, Quayle's staff leaked a story to the *Washington Post* to "cut off debate over the vice president's future" by reporting that Bush informed Quayle that he would remain, even though the conversation did not take place.[505] Quayle recognized the constraints imposed on him, acknowledging he had greater independence as a member of the Senate. He stated, "[it] is a 'much more confining job. You don't have your own agenda. . . . Wherever I might go, somebody has primary jurisdiction, and that's one of the problems with being vice president.'"[506] And this was the case regarding his involvement in foreign policy.

The confluence of the foreign policy heavyweights who dominated the Bush administration and the institutional obstacles he faced from the State Department, as well as the lack of trust emplaced in him and his staff, resulted in a diminished role for Quayle with limited influence in foreign policy. Scowcroft and Baker were distrustful of Quayle and his conservative staff and clearly maneuvered to "ignore" him and his staff as much as possible in foreign affairs.[507] Quayle also willingly or unwillingly contributed to his lack of influence in foreign policy by accepting, without opposition, the packing of his schedule with photo opportunities and other ceremonial duties, which were purposely added by a suspicious State Department that took a lead role in decision making.

Further exacerbating the situation, Quayle assumed a similar vice presidential posture as Bush, concerned about perception and loyalty. He recognized that his number-one constituency was Bush, and he was most interested in protecting the relationship.[508] He adopted a "cautious" and "low-key" strategy.[509] Bush as a former vice president also expected three qualities from his vice president: "subordination, loyalty and total confidentiality."[510] As a result, Quayle would be unwilling to rock the boat by challenging the institutional obstacles he faced. And he perfectly fulfilled Bush's conditions. Quayle characterized his role with Bush as a "confidant."[511] He stated, "When he told me things he knew they wouldn't go anywhere else not even revealed to my staff. We had an understanding. It was just a total mutual trust and he was loyal to me and I was loyal to him and that was never questioned between the two of us either way."[512]

Bush recognized Quayle's loyalty and demonstrated his own by refusing to drop him from the ticket, despite prodding from his sons, James Baker, and even former president Ford.[513] The argument was that you had to make a change in your vice president to reinvigorate the reelection.[514] Baker argued, "It was a different situation in '92. Bush was way behind, and we had been there for twelve years. When we went to run for reelection, we had a bad economy and people wanted change. We also had [Ross] Perot taking one of every two votes from us running as an independent. One good move we might have made was to run a new vice president in '92."[515] Additionally, "We had a hell of a time trying to portray ourselves as agents of change through eighteen years. One of the ways to do that would have been to change the vice president."[516] Yet, Bush remained loyal to Quayle and valued his loyalty.[517] He stated in an interview with CBS's *Sunday Morning*, "Some things are more important than winning, and one of them is loyalty. . . . I don't believe in cutting and running."[518] From his perspective, Quayle deserved his loyalty because he "never tried to better his own nest and so forth, which is always the fear that presidents have about their vice presidents."[519] Moreover, he "didn't have it in him, he didn't like to fire people. He knew that Quayle did everything he was asked to do and did it. He is a genuine, humane and caring person, which is pretty rare at that level."[520] Bush also did not want to face any "humiliation" that would be inflicted by removing him from the ticket.[521]

Dan Quayle's Electoral Dynamic

Dan Quayle's selection positioned him to play an influential role in the workings of the Bush administration, particularly regarding domestic policy, congressional relations, and political affairs. While he encountered institutional obstacles in his attempt to exert influence in foreign policy, his experience was a major asset in other issue areas. "The senior George Bush's choice of the youthful Quayle was widely regarded as a blatantly political one."[522] His selection, in comparison to other modern vice presidents, balanced the ticket more effectively for electoral purposes.

216 / Emerging from the Shadows

Quayle's selection helped Bush on several fronts. "George Bush selected me, I think, for three major reasons. The first reason was generational: I belonged to the 'baby boomer' generation, an enormous segment of our voting population. The second reason was ideological: I came more from the conservative wing of the party, as did Ronald Reagan. And the third reason was geographical: I was from the Midwest, and that region was going to be a battleground in the election campaign."[523] Bush's selection of Quayle, who was considerably more conservative, was meant to reassure conservatives and helped him tap into elements of the party that remained suspicious.[524] He wanted to convince these groups that he was the "inheritor of the Reagan conservative movement."[525] And Quayle's selection was a potential bridge to the movement, especially given that he was being challenged for the nomination by a "supply side/traditional values conservative" like Jack Kemp.[526] Moreover, Quayle was highly thought of in the conservative movement. He was young, energetic, and won his reelection effort by a significant margin, demonstrating his electoral prowess.[527] He was "good-looking, conservative, and, at forty-one, a generation younger than the sixty-four-year-old presidential nominee—a real advantage, some of us thought."[528] His youthful appearance, according to Roger Ailes, could be an asset. He stated, "Bush had been seen for so long as the junior guy to Reagan that it made sense for Bush's own VP to appear clearly junior."[529] Beckwith argued, "They weren't equals. In fact, that is one of the reasons I suspect is why Quayle was picked. They didn't want someone that would be seen as overshadowing Bush who had a somewhat weak image."[530] Bush also sought loyalty. "Bush wanted his own Bush as vice president. That is, perhaps he wanted a totally loyal and uncomplaining Republican who would happily serve in the shadow of the president as Bush had done as Reagan's standby for eight years."[531] "He was seeking a vice president who would be to him what he was to Reagan and I think he got that in Quayle in so far as loyalty is concerned."[532] Quayle actively campaigned for the number-two spot but made sure to stress his willingness to be a loyal soldier.[533] He told a national audience, "Whoever Bush picked for his running mate, Quayle said, would realize that 'the themes, the issues, the articulation on the campaign will be George Bush's."[534] And as a vice presidential candidate he understood that he took his direction from "the top man on the ticket."[535] His deferential treatment of Bush characterized his vice presidency and in many ways, he argued, his vice presidency was very similar to Bush's.[536]

Quayle is very skilled when it comes to politics, and he made every effort to position himself as a potential choice for Bush.[537] In the lead up to the decision, he became more active. He gave more speeches, wrote increasingly more op-eds, and spoke up more aggressively in closed meetings.[538] Furthermore, he became a much more frequent visitor to Bush's Capitol office, often meeting with key campaign aides of Bush—Roger Ailes and Robert Teeter—both of whom had worked for Quayle in his Senate campaign.[539] Quayle would spend approximately six-months courting Bush and getting on his radar.[540] Quayle stated, "[Bush] certainly noticed what we were doing and paid attention . . . all along."[541] Quayle's efforts underscored his political acumen and most likely convinced Bush of the electoral balance he could provide.

Quayle's influence mainly fell within three broad categories: domestic policy, congressional relations, and political affairs. Quayle was able to liaison with core constituencies of this group to advance the domestic policy of the administration, by fostering relations on Capitol Hill and attending to the political affairs of the administration through fundraising and campaigning. His influence was also recognized by many in the White House. In advance of his weekly lunches with Bush, it was not unusual for him to get calls from others in the administration to pass along messages to him, understanding that he had the president's ear during those private lunches.[542]

In terms of domestic policy, one line assignment dominated his activities: the President's Council on Competitiveness.[543] The Council was a sequel to the task force that Bush ran as vice president.[544] However, the council went a bit further than Bush's work on deregulation because, according to Quayle, they "really reviewed all these regulations and the economic impact studies."[545] The council was created at the suggestion of Sununu, Bush's chief of staff, who argued it would provide a mechanism to "maintain and improve our international competitiveness," which would be possible through "the full development of our human resource potential; the promotion of scientific and technological progress; removal of barriers to innovation; careful assessment of any governmentally-imposed burdens on the free enterprise system; and removal of domestic barriers to the flow of goods and services."[546] The council provided a couple of advantages for the Bush administration. First, it provided another link to the Reagan coalition by demonstrating the importance placed on deregulation.[547] Second, it gave Quayle significant responsibility over an issue area that he himself

218 / Emerging from the Shadows

embraced his entire career.[548] Quayle was a "self-proclaimed 'zealot when it comes to deregulation.'"[549] He used the council as an opportunity to insert him and his staff into "unpublicized controversies over important federal regulations," resulting in an expansive reach to include: commercial transportation, housing and property, biotechnology, telecommunications, bank loans, disability accessibility, prescription drug approvals, civil justice reform, manufacturing, pensions, real estate, child care, and environmental issues.[550] The council tried to resolve "regulatory conflicts" before they worked their way up to the top echelons of government.[551]

Quayle's work on the council represented his most substantial role as vice president, in which Bush granted him broad authority to ensure that "regulatory creep" was curbed.[552] The council's regulatory review was to ensure any rules that existed "maximized benefits and minimized costs, based on sound analysis," thus agencies were required to provide cost/benefit data regarding rules.[553] The council consisted of seven members, including: the vice president, chief of staff, attorney general, director of OMB, chair of the Council of Economic Advisers, secretary of treasury, and secretary of commerce.[554] However, most of the work was personally done by Quayle and his staff.[555] The work of the council was an important initiative of the Bush administration given his work on the topic as vice president and the need to buttress his administration's conservative credentials. Quayle's leading role over the council's jurisdiction demonstrated his influence with those in the administration. The council became a "power center."[556] Recalling the council, Quayle argued it was the "most potent council in an administration."[557] Members of Congress were referring to it as a "shadow government."[558] Bush made clear to his cabinet that Quayle had his full support and authority to make binding decisions. "The council's power is enhanced by what several officials described as an unwritten administration rule that no Cabinet official will appeal its actions to Bush."[559] Quayle contended, "The cabinet always knew they could take it to the president over my objections," but they never did.[560] As a result, none of Quayle's decisions were appealed or overturned by the president, further evidencing his influence.[561]

Quayle's influence within the administration was also palpable in the business community. "Dan Quayle [was] the man to see in the Bush administration for business people across the country and their Washington lobbyists."[562] Further enhancing his influence, Congress had failed to confirm the assistant director for regulatory affairs in OMB, which resulted in those responsibilities falling to him and his staff.[563] Quayle stated, "That Democratic Congress did me a real favor, because I had fought my entire political life against excessive government regulation and the overzealous impulses of the federal bureaucracy."[564] He argued, "We had a lot more power than the eye could see."[565] The council provided him influence with both the cabinet and Bush.[566] Due to Quayle's efforts, it was estimated that the annual cost savings from the actions announced would be $15 to 20 billion.[567] Quayle's focus on federal regulations during his career in Congress, combined with the electoral dynamic that led to his selection and the need to affirm Bush's conservative credentials, enabled him to play an influential role in the Bush administration. And Bush was pleased with "the outstanding job" he did in the administration on the Competitiveness Council.[568]

Due to his connections on Capitol Hill, he was the natural choice for reaching out to members in the more conservative wing of the Republican Party, those in the Senate, and those who were disillusioned with Bush.[569] His insight into how Congress operated benefited the administration.[570] More so than Bush, "he was in touch with sentiment on the Hill."[571] Quayle stated, "In my case, I had a huge assignment on Capitol Hill because I had come from the House and the Senate and he had a House background and never did understand the Senate. I had a major responsibility there."[572] Conservative's viewed Quayle as "their man" in the White House.[573] For instance, when Sununu declined to discuss the tax increase situation with congressional Republicans, it was Quayle who took their concerns to Bush to diffuse the situation.[574] He was affectionately referred to as Bush's "legislative counselor," demonstrating his importance and influence.[575] Understanding the importance of his legislative liaison role, he typically spent two afternoons per week working in his Capitol Hill office.[576]

Quayle's influence on congressional matters was apparent on Capitol Hill and in the White House.[577] According to three dozen members of Congress surveyed, Quayle was viewed as a direct link to the White House and many argued he was more influential and active with congressional relations than Bush was as vice president.[578] "He lobbied each side of the aisle on nearly every major issue."[579] Newt Gingrich, the assistant minority leader in the House stated, "He's attuned to the mood and rhythm of this institution more than anyone down there."[580] Sununu argued, "When we lay out a legislative strategy, almost automatically, he's a key part of the discussions."[581] Cheney, who at the time was defense secretary, noted, "[Quayle] probably has better ties at any given moment, or a better read

220 / Emerging from the Shadows

on . . . the mood of the Senate Republicans—and the Senate generally—than just about anybody else."[582] Whenever the White House staff found themselves in a bind with Congress, they looked to him to lobby members to secure votes.[583] His instincts with Congress usually proved accurate.[584] He is credited with having won over key House votes in opposition to a Democratic measure on childcare and an attempt to override the president's veto of a civil rights bill.[585]

Quayle took the lead in lobbying Congress on most efforts. For instance, when Bush had first nominated John Tower as defense secretary, Quayle's "vote-count estimates" were on point in explaining that the effort would be unsuccessful.[586] When the administration nominated Clarence Thomas to the Supreme Court, he was the first administration official to reach out to Senators John Danforth (R-MO) and Sam Nunn (D-GA) to press for their support.[587] He also successfully "headed off" a conservative filibuster of the White House's 1989 minimum wage bill.[588] Demonstrating the importance of his outreach to conservatives, he lobbied hard to secure passage of the president's tax bill that would overturn Bush's "read my lips" campaign pledge, despite his own opposition to the measure.[589] Quayle stated, "I am sure that all my lobbying and arm-twisting made a difference on the vote, but not as much as I had hoped."[590] While the effort was successful, it did create bad blood between conservatives and the White House, who were angered for the compromise.[591] Newt Gingrich stated, "There was a period where we were not talking with [budget director Richard G.] Darman and Sununu. For three or four days, Quayle was the primary source of information between the most active wing of the House Republican Party and the White House. . . . And he did so without breaking his ties in either direction."[592] His efforts were successful in diffusing the situation and reducing the fall. Quayle noted, "I had to work hard to retain the loyalty of the movement conservatives."[593]

While Quayle experienced obstruction in a foreign policy role, he was able to engage in it by serving as a liaison to Congress over the Gulf War.[594] Kristol stated, "Quayle did firm up our Hill relations during the Gulf War, especially since he was the only ex-senator in the senior reaches of the administration."[595] He worked on moderate Democrats like Joe Lieberman and Chuck Robb and the administration easily carried the day.[596] He was influential in pushing the president to get a congressional authorization on the war effort and building support on Capitol Hill.[597] Furthermore, after the war commenced, he became a vocal critic of members of Congress that failed to support the effort, especially liberal Democrats who he "perceived [as] weak on using military force in the Gulf."[598] His political instincts were important to the foreign policy debate, in which he would raise political implications of foreign policy decisions and then serve as a liaison in Congress to lobby for the administration's position.[599]

The last role that demonstrates Quayle's influence is his involvement in political affairs. Quayle served as a political surrogate for Bush by meeting with conservative activists and undertaking political campaigning.[600] Quayle was a natural choice for this assignment because he "has a very good political mind and had an ability to frame issues politically."[601] Overall, "his political judgment was excellent."[602] "As political surrogate, Quayle visited all fifty states, often handling invitations that merited attention but that Bush could not accept."[603] Quayle argued, "The burden of political campaigning falls to the vice president the majority of the time."[604] This fell in his wheelhouse even more so, given his connection with the conservative wing of the Republican Party and Bush's determination to avoid dealing with politics.[605] His efforts raised more than fifteen million dollars for Republican candidates in the 1990 midterm elections.[606] His political travel was accelerated toward the end of the administration's first year. Several memos originating with his office pushed in the early part of the administration to ramp up his political travel, partly to deal with the limited funds his office had for official travel, and partly because Quayle was an effective political surrogate for Bush.[607]

Bush's aversion to politics, despite his staff's prodding him to get more involved, meant that Quayle would pick up the slack. Quayle stated, "When invitations came to the White House, John Sununu brought the stack into our morning meeting with the president. 'They really want you in Illinois,' Sununu said to the president. Then there was a pause. And Sununu handed the invitation to me. 'They really want you in Colorado,' he said. Silence again. So Sununu handed me that invitation. And so it went until the stack was gone."[608] In truth, Quayle excelled in small groups where he could work a crowd and where he demonstrated his adeptness at fundraising. He was in constant demand.[609] Rank-and-file Republicans flocked to his events.[610] Quayle noted, "[Bush] was not a 'movement conservative' as I was. Clearly, I was the logical person to work with this faction, and I had some very tough discussions with my friends about the political philosophy of the Bush presidency."[611] As a result, he spent a lot of time on the road. He would usually take one to two political trips per week, and over the course of the term, he traveled to more than 200 cities and raised more than $20 million for the Republican Party.[612] In 1992 alone,

222 / Emerging from the Shadows

he took a total of 219 official, political, or official/political mixed trips.[613] It was being reported that he was "The Quayle Cash Machine" because of his remarkable fundraising ability.[614] His main objective was to "touch the dozens of reelection bases that Bush [did] not have time to visit."[615] Even if he was not traveling, his days almost always included fundraising events and other politicking efforts.[616] The goal was to make sure Bush's right flank was protected by putting Quayle before as many conservative audiences as possible.[617] According to Roger Stone, a Republican political consultant, "No one has worked the Republican Party circuit more than Quayle has."[618]

The electoral dynamic sheds light on the nature of Vice President Quayle's influence in the Bush administration. The nature of his selection and the ideological balance he brought to the ticket helped ease suspicions from the more conservative wing of the party. As a result, Quayle became a conservative voice within the administration as well as a liaison to those groups who questioned Bush's conservative credentials. He used that position to champion traditional conservative principles through his position as chair of the Competitiveness Council, which not only provided influence but was also recognized as a "power center." And his connections with the conservative wing of the party enabled him to be the go-to-guy on congressional relations and political affairs, all of which was made possible by the electoral dynamic, increasing his stature and influence both in the White House and beyond.

Al Gore's Situational Dynamic

The selection of Al Gore as vice president in 1992 demonstrates the importance of the situational dynamic to vice presidential influence. Gore's selection went against the norms established in the premodern era in which running mates balanced the ticket for electoral purposes (geographic, age, etc.). Instead, the Gore selection represented very little in terms of demographic balancing; he was a contemporary of Bill Clinton, both were Southern Baptists, hailed from the same region of the country, and were ideologically similar as well.[619] In fact, Gore was precisely selected because of his similarities to Clinton.[620] In selecting Gore, "Clinton was attempting to accentuate rather than offset his own characteristics."[621] Clinton stated, "It would present America with a new generation of leadership and prove I was serious about taking the party and the country in a different direction."[622] Gore's selection would contribute to Clinton's efforts to redefine the Democratic Party.[623] "Clinton decided to double himself. He put all his chips on one square."[624] "He just decided he was going to double down on what he thought was working about his candidacy."[625]

But Gore did balance Clinton in more important ways, particularly regarding his résumé. Gore had served in Congress since winning his first congressional seat in 1976, and then ran and won a Senate seat in 1984, providing him with extensive Washington experience that Clinton lacked.[626] "He boasted a whiz-kid mastery of the technical details of opaque policy issues such as arms control."[627] Gore had extensive experience in foreign policy, the environment, and technological issues and having run for president in 1988, he was considered prepared to assume the presidency should anything happen to Clinton.[628] Last, Gore's family man persona deflected from Clinton's personal scandals of infidelity.[629] Although Clinton and Gore did not know each other well, their two-hour meeting during the veepstakes, demonstrated their compatibility and was one of the most important deciding factors for Clinton in his selection.[630] Not only were they compatible on the issues but personally as well.[631] Clinton was surprised that they had such a good rapport during the meeting.[632] He came away from the meeting feeling that Gore could be a trusted ally. Dee Dee Myers, Clinton's press secretary, stated, "Clinton felt like he and Gore had a lot of the same goals and shared a lot of the same theories and ideas about what government's role should be and what it could do and how it should operate and what sort of an ambitious, centrist Democratic presidency could accomplish."[633] "In many respects, Gore reminded him of his one invaluable political ally through the years, his wife, Hillary. With Hillary, he had an implicit trust that whatever he asked her to do would be done right, and he sensed the same would be true of Gore."[634] When pressed as to why he was selecting Gore he stated, "I could die, that's why."[635]

While they lacked a strong relationship prior to Gore being tapped, mutual admiration and respect grew between them and they had a great rapport that matured into a true partnership.[636] During the campaign, "Often the two candidates would sit together on the lead bus, talking away for long periods as the reporters cooled their heels outside. Once, the pair sat gabbing so long that the press corps en masse started to rock the bus until they sheepishly emerged."[637] The campaign not only brought the two closer, they became fast friends, as a result of the bus tour.[638] Hillary Clinton stated, "Traveling on the buses gave us all a chance to get to know one another better. Bill, Al, Tipper and I spent hours

224 / Emerging from the Shadows

talking, eating, waving out the window and stopping the bus convoy to conduct impromptu rallies."[639] It became more than just business; it was a true friendship. "They seemed to me very friendly, very at home with one another."[640] "It was an easy relationship. I never felt like I was straddling any type of bridge with the two of them."[641] They also joked around considerably and, in many ways, demonstrated a sibling rivalry.[642] They got along so well that they eschewed previous campaign strategies that split the presidential and vice presidential nominees up to campaign and cover more ground; instead they campaigned together quite often.[643] "The interpersonal relationship, at least as I saw, was one of interactive engagement, listening, really listening. The same for Vice President Gore to President Clinton. They each learned from each other. It made them better as a team."[644]

Gore's vice presidency started off on a high note. He had established a rapport with Clinton during the campaign based on mutual admiration and strong compatibility, which enabled them to become close friends and partners in governing.[645] The goal was to integrate the vice president and his staff into the administration.[646] John Podesta, Clinton's chief of staff, remarked, "His [Gore's] senior White House staff—his chief of staff, his chief policy advisor—were actively integrated into my daily operations."[647] "He would never stop scrapping for power, for a place at the table, but he would do it without seeming disrespectful or publicly embarrassing himself or Clinton."[648] He worked tirelessly to build rapport with the White House staff, mindful that "fissures . . . could develop between a vice president and the White House staff."[649] Starting during the campaign, he was disciplined in meeting with anyone who "might be relevant" to shore up support for himself, which helped him exercise influence.[650] However, George Stephanopoulos, the White House communications director and senior policy adviser, interpreted Gore's overtures as a threat. He stated, "But Gore's kind words also carried an implicit threat—'Don't even think about trying to shut me out; if it comes down to you or me, I'll cut your nuts off.'"[651] The two never had a strong or close relationship because they were both trying to position themselves in proximity to the president and Stephanopoulos worked to undercut Gore.[652] "In the White House proper I think that Gore initially had a stronger relationship with Clinton than Clinton's people wanted him to have because Gore was bringing controversial ideas up like a carbon tax, environmental issues that the George Stephanopouloses of the world didn't want to deal with."[653] However, Gore's influence was strengthened by the situational dynamic, he complimented Clinton's weaknesses.

Gore's extensive Washington experience and credentials filled the voids in Clinton's résumé, thus providing the opportunity for Gore to exercise greater influence as vice president.[654] "Al Gore is a perfectionist. He knew how Washington worked. He knew how the process worked."[655] In just their first week in office, a retreat was scheduled at Camp David that brought together the cabinet, consultants, staff, the Clintons, and the Gores to set priorities and build relations.[656] The weekend retreat was "Gore's baby," and he was instrumental in setting it up.[657] His early influence was a testament to the fact that both Clinton and Gore embraced the Mondale model for the vice presidency, which called for a consequential role within the administration.[658] A two-page document was crafted that outlined Gore's role.[659] "He didn't want to simply become a token figure in the Clinton administration, but he was assured by Clinton that that wouldn't be the case."[660] The situational dynamic, in which Gore found himself, made the exercising of influence possible. Clinton needed him to help him navigate Washington. "The result was the most active vice presidency in the twentieth century."[661]

Gore would become the "across-the-board presidential adviser," assuming responsibility for key policy areas and given operational roles as well.[662] His role differed from the Mondale model in one respect—he embraced some line assignments, choosing to work in fields where he had an interest (arms control, the environment, and technology issues, science, and telecommunications).[663] "The president ceded to Vice President Gore an enormous amount of responsibility in [these] key areas."[664] However, he undertook fewer line assignments than Bush and Quayle.[665] Gore's activist role and influence was shaped by the interpersonal dynamic and furthered by the situational dynamic, namely, the political conditions they encountered and the issues they dealt with. And Clinton was true to his word of allowing Gore to be a "full partner" in the White House, where he was involved in all aspects of the administration.[666]

Clinton came to office with a weak grasp of foreign policy and a weak reputation.[667] "He [Gore] has been very active and influential in foreign policy, due in large part to the unique circumstances he finds himself."[668] Not only was there a poor impression of Clinton's capabilities in this area, but he also was very unpopular in the first couple of years of his administration, which resulted in the Democratic Party losing control of the House and Senate in 1994, the first time in nearly fifty years.[669] In fact, not one Republican incumbent lost a congressional or gubernatorial reelection bid during the midterms.[670] Gore's strength where Clinton was weak, as well as Clinton's unpopularity, bolstered his influence in the

226 / Emerging from the Shadows

administration. It was palpable to outside observers who argued Gore was a "presidential vice president" as the Economist described in September 1994, implying that Gore was more presidential than Clinton.[671]

The foreign policy apparatus at the White House enabled Gore to take a leading role. "The president early on established that he wished to know the vice president's opinion on matters pending in international affairs and trade."[672] That meant that "the vice president was one of the last people to meet with the president before any decision was made."[673] Secretary of State Warren Christopher was rather passive and was willing to defer to Gore, and to some extent this continued under his successor, Madeleine Albright, which further solidified Gore's role in foreign affairs.[674] A partial explanation is that Gore had a hand in Albright's selection.[675]

Early on in the administration a "foreign policy leadership vacuum" existed, which was complicated by Clinton's unwillingness to engage in foreign policy.[676] He was continually criticized for his lack of leadership, his inability to manage the policy process, and the chaotic nature of decision making.[677] His chair of the Joint Chiefs, Colin Powell, argued that the NSC system was chaotic and that the atmosphere was like that found in a "coffeehouse" and foreign policy was in "bureaucratic disarray."[678] Gore would easily step into the policy vacuum and assert order and push Clinton to pay greater attention to foreign policy, with Gore, in many cases, taking the lead.[679] Clinton sought Gore to take on a more public role in foreign policy and Christopher encouraged this, in many ways, reducing his own influence over foreign policy.[680]

> Taking a cue from Secretary of State Dean Acheson, Christopher soon learned the fine art of delegation. A beneficiary of that delegation was the vice president, who received an enhanced foreign-policy role in large part due to the behest of Christopher, who urged Clinton after a series of foreign-policy setbacks in the fall of 1993 to give Gore a more active role. "I can only be in one place at a time," Christopher explained. "No Secretary of State can do it all. It would be foolish if he thought he could. One reason I'm so confident is that the vice president is thoroughly reliable."[681]

Gore performed the tasks normally associated with the secretary of state, national security adviser, and even the president, since foreign policy was Clinton's weak area.[682]

Gore chaired three foreign policy commissions outside the White House.[683] This demonstrated that he was one of, if not the sole, foreign policy spokesman and someone who was widely respected internationally. The three commissions included: The Gore-Chernomyrdin Commission, the Gore-Mubarak Commission, and the Gore-Mbecki Commission.[684] The commission work enabled Gore to raise his public profile in the international community and serve as a representative of the president who was authorized to make deals. Gore's work involved implementation on broad policies, which was very important to bilateral relations.[685] The work of the commissions, in many respects, became the central focus of the administration's relations with those countries due to Gore's relationship with Clinton.[686] And the Gore-Chernomyrdin Commission spawned the other bilateral commissions because foreign leaders were contacting the administration asking if a similar arrangement could be made for them.[687]

Gore's most successful work centered on the Gore-Chernomyrdin Commission, in which he was considered "the main channel" between the Russian prime minister, Viktor Chernomyrdin, and the White House.[688] This commission operated outside of normal diplomatic channels, demonstrating that Gore in many instances, superseded the State Department as the chief spokesperson.[689] The commission attempted to "institutionalize" US and Russian relations.[690] In this capacity, Gore signed numerous agreements with Russia that facilitated cooperation over space, trade and business development, defense conversion, science and technology, energy, nuclear safety, and the environment.[691] The consequences of the commission work were significant. Gore signed a pact with Chernomyrdin that established the US and Russia as partners in the international space station, which would result in a Russian astronaut joining American astronauts on the space shuttle Discovery.[692] The agreements, which numbered seventeen, established joint projects in economic development, technological ventures, environmental issues, and "oil and gas exploration."[693] Most importantly, Gore's efforts resulted in Russia agreeing to phase out their plutonium-producing nuclear reactors, which were used to produce nuclear weapons.[694]

Gore's influence in foreign policy was such that when Christopher had difficulty getting on Clinton's calendar, he met with Gore instead.[695] With no regularly scheduled meetings between Christopher and Clinton, he established a weekly Friday meeting with Gore.[696] Christopher stated, "I know he'll be a very influential figure if we talk something through. . . . [Gore] is relied on more heavily than any vice president has ever been in the past. Not just in foreign policy, but as far as I can tell,

228 / Emerging from the Shadows

across the board."[697] Not only did Christopher suggest an increased role in foreign policy, but he turned to him for advice, thus supplanting his own influence and bolstering Gore's. The foreign policy leadership vacuum combined with Clinton's indecisiveness, gave him a significant role.[698]

Gore's influence was also transferred to his staff. Leon Fuerth, his national security adviser, attended Oval Office meetings and meetings of other foreign policy advisers, including sitting in on Deputies Committee meetings, where policy proposals are discussed and assessed.[699] Joseph DeSutter, an adviser who served both Quayle and Gore, argued that Leon Fuerth was a "determinate voice" in decisions of the NSC.[700] Fuerth was just as influential as Gore because the White House knew he spoke for Gore. "In fact . . . if the president's NSA, Anthony Lake, advised something to Clinton that Fuerth disagreed with, 'it would be a significant event. It would not be inconsequential.'"[701] DeSutter stated, "All of sudden, NSC counterparts who I had to maneuver to get their attention [when I worked for Quayle] were lined up outside my door because they didn't want to find out six months from now that Leon [Fuerth] didn't like [something]."[702] As a result, Fuerth was a "co-equal" of Clinton's national security advisers.[703] He had an arrangement with Tony Lake and Sandy Berger, that he and the vice president "would be kept rigorously informed of what was happening in real time," which further positioned Gore and Fuerth as equals to the president and his staff.[704]

Gore took a consequential role in building support for the North American Free Trade Agreement (NAFTA), going as far as debating Ross Perot on *Larry King Live*, which many argued was one of his finest moments.[705] "The highly effective debate propelled . . . Gore into domestic and international credibility and played a key role pushing him into more of a foreign-policy role within the Clinton administration."[706] Gore committed to the CNN debate with Perot, despite objections from Clinton's staff, particularly George Stephanopoulos, and "Clinton had no choice but to buy in [to the CNN debate]."[707] Stephanopoulos admitted he "misjudged how crushingly effective Gore would be."[708] The debate performance combined with his efforts in Congress proved instrumental to NAFTA's bipartisan passage.[709]

Regarding the crises in Bosnia and Haiti, Gore was involved in the day-to-day policy formulation and convinced Clinton to intervene in Bosnia.[710] During the debate on whether to intervene, Gore framed the argument in terms of a humanitarian crisis, since Serbians were using UN peacekeepers as human shields during bombing campaigns, which helped convince Clinton to accept his position.[711] He spent considerable time during his career on nonproliferation issues and as a result, Clinton turned over the arms-control portfolio to the vice president.[712] Consequently, he worked tirelessly to try and extend the Nuclear Nonproliferation Treaty by working through the UN.[713]

Gore's role in staffing the White House was not limited to just Albright in her post as secretary of state. Instead, during the transition, Gore and his aide, Roy Neel, met with Clinton, Vernon Jordan, and Warren Christopher to consider appointments to the administration, specifically the cabinet.[714] Gore was instrumental in placing key associates in positions at the EPA, Department of State, and the Council on Environmental Quality.[715] Clinton sought his input on every appointment and gave him the authority to fill positions at the EPA, the Federal Communications Commission, and the Civil Division at the Justice Department.[716] His influence was so great that when he voiced opposition to Larry Summers's appointment as chair of the Council of Economic Advisers, Clinton pursued an alternative.[717] And his role in staffing grew after their reelection in 1996. He often interviewed prospective cabinet nominees with Clinton often holding off on making decisions until he conferred with Gore.[718] He also helped place William Cohen at Defense, William Daley at Commerce, Andrew Cuomo at Housing and Urban Development, and orchestrated the move of Federico Pena from Transportation to Energy.[719] He even persuaded Clinton to replace his childhood friend, Mack McLarty as chief of staff.[720] His influence over the makeup of the administration had a similar effect, as was seen during Cheney's vice presidency. Folks who attributed their appointment to Gore were placed in strategic positions in the executive branch, specifically in issue areas that he took an interest in, thus giving him greater capacity to exercise influence.

Gore's role was expansive. "Within the White House it became understood that Gore was essentially president of the subjects within his spheres of interest."[721] Kay Casstevens, Gore's assistant in legislative affairs, stated, "We worked closely with the president's staff but on Gore things we never had to seek approval or anything."[722] He particularly had the lead role on any policies dealing with the environment or science.[723] He referred to himself as a "general-adviser," who counseled the president on all major issues.[724] "There were three independent power centers: Clinton, Hillary, and Gore."[725] Gergen argued that the "three-headed system . . . caused untold delays, confusions, and divided loyalties. A member of the cabinet or staff might think that the President had decided something on Tuesday

230 / Emerging from the Shadows

only to find that he was in a different place on Wednesday because he had since talked to his wife or the Vice President."[726] This meant that if an administration official thought Clinton would be opposed to an idea he or she would lobby his wife or Gore to win their support, which in turn could influence the president's decision in their favor.[727] This also extended to Congress. Members of Congress knew that if they could convince Gore they might have a good shot at convincing Clinton.[728] "Al has never been a backslapping buddy in the Senate cloakroom but a lot of people, especially on the environmental issues, would view Gore as their man in the White House and so they would go to Gore quite a bit."[729] "It was very clear that Clinton listened carefully to Gore. He didn't always agree but he considered Gore a vital sounding board for his own work as president."[730]

Gore's only rival for influence proved to be the first lady. Theirs was a strained relationship, partly because they were so alike in their approach to policy and partly because they both were vying to be the president's political partner.[731] And it got worse over time.[732] Gore wanted to be Clinton's right-hand man, but it was complicated by Hillary, who some aides thought resented "Gore's role and his face time with her husband."[733] The tension was further confounded when Clinton tasked his wife with comprehensive health-care reform, which you usually "give your vice president something of that level."[734] Nonetheless, Gore was part of the inner circle and Clinton felt strongly about him and his counsel.[735] Stephanopoulos argued, "[a] president has no real peers but Gore was getting close."[736] He was the "first advisor in chief across all domestic, budgetary and foreign policy matters," according to John Podesta.[737] In many ways, he was a "co-president" on a lot of issues.[738]

His influence was palpable among the White House staff because everyone saw Gore as an instrumental ally who they should try to win over.[739] "I think from a staff level there was a sense that vice president Gore could be strategically deployed in a lot of areas to not tell the president what to do but to get the president to focus and bring a decision to its conclusion. . . . It often fell to the vice president to help get a decision made."[740] Perhaps this was because Gore was the one person in the administration who could speak candidly with the president, produce order, deliver results, and relay a message to the president.[741] "He would often tease the president to make a decision and [would say], 'we [can] talk about this for another couple of days or we can make a decision.'"[742] He could "deliver a message" to the president unlike anyone else.[743] In fact, in one incident, Clinton was complaining to aides about recent events and inquired as to what could be done, to which Gore stated, "You can get with the goddamn program," something no one would dare say to a president.[744] This spoke of Gore's personal influence with Clinton and his lack of inhibitions, even in meetings with others present.[745]

Gore's general adviser role enabled him to get involved in a host of domestic policy issues. He was involved in Clinton's two Supreme Court nominations, pressured Clinton to support a balanced budget proposal, convinced him to stay firm in budget negotiations with Republicans in 1995 (which resulted in a government shutdown), and provided counsel on the environment, telecommunications, and reinventing government, which Clinton followed.[746] Regarding telecommunications policy, David Beier, Gore's domestic policy adviser recalled,

> The president's chief of staff called me up and said, "David, I want you to come over and we are going to have a meeting with the CEO of this telecommunications firm. But I want you to come five minutes early and tell me what the issues are and what our position is." I went in and briefed the president's chief of staff—there was no paper, no memo. He was a very quick study. He said, "Okay, I get it." The CEO came in and he said, "I'm sure you know David, he speaks for the president."[747]

This spoke to the level of influence Gore and his staff carried in the White House, specifically regarding policy that Gore had "de facto authority" over.[748] The Telecommunications Act turned out to be "Gore's baby."[749] Gore also chaired the White House Commission on Aviation Safety and Security, which merged his interests of defense, technology, and intelligence.[750] He had served on the intelligence committee when he was a member of the House and he had a "wonkish" fascination with the issues.[751] As a result, he was a great help to the director of the CIA. Tenet stated, "He asked a lot of questions about the impact on national security of water shortages, disease, and environmental concerns. 'Bugs and bunnies,' some people called it. But I learned a lot from him on these matters. . . . Those kinds of issues can have a profound effect on population flow, migration, civil wars, ethnic strife, and the like."[752] More importantly, he was an "avid" consumer of intelligence and helped the CIA acquire additional resources.[753]

One of Gore's most remembered roles, a line assignment, was his leadership of the National Partnership for Reinventing Government

232 / Emerging from the Shadows

(REGO).[754] Gore, who was initially reluctant to take on line assignments, agreed to REGO because Hillary Clinton had been named to lead the health-care reform task force when Gore turned down the role, believing it would occupy too much of his time.[755] However, Gore did want to take on an important assignment to dispel the perception that his role was diminishing, thus accepting the tasking.[756] "REGO was to Gore what health care was to Hillary—a worthy goal that grew out of control, another White House within a White House."[757] It would require a thorough review of everything the government did.[758] He exercised significant independence in his leadership of REGO.[759] His actions would result in him appropriating 250 civil servants to conduct an extensive review of executive department performance.[760] Clinton stated, "Al took to the job like a duck to water, bringing in outside experts and consulting widely with government employees."[761] After six months, the report was released on September 7, 1993, and consisted of 384 recommendations, which sought to eliminate 252,000 government jobs and save the government $108 billion.[762] Clinton would enact, through executive order, many of those recommendations.[763] By February 1995, Gore's recommendations cut the federal workforce by 100,000 and saved $63 billion, and by 1996 the savings would amount to $118 billion.[764] In total, sixteen thousand pages were cut from the Federal Register and ten thousand pages from federal employee manuals and the size of the federal government was "smaller than it had been since the Kennedy Administration."[765] Clinton, recalling Gore's efforts, stated, "Al Gore's highly successful initiative confounded our adversaries, elated our allies, and escaped the notice of most of the public because it was neither sensational nor controversial."[766] Gore reveled in these technical policy-oriented issues the most.

His involvement in the environment and technological issues was also extensive.[767] He helped save the Kyoto negotiations on climate change, which resulted in him meeting with representatives from key countries to help push through the Kyoto Protocol, even though it had little chance of getting through the Senate.[768] Gore also cochaired the United States-China Policy Forum on Environment and Development, which promoted sustainable development.[769] And he was instrumental in pushing Clinton to support a new energy tax or BTU tax over the opposition of White House staffers, although it would eventually be dropped due to concerns over the impact on the middle class and its inability to get through Congress.[770] And his work on REGO helped establish a regulatory reform group to institute environmental protection efforts by providing incentives to the private sector.[771]

The influence of Gore's staff, as seen in foreign policy, bled over into domestic policy as well. The vice president's chief of staff and chief policy adviser were included in a working group that included the treasury secretary and his deputy, the OMB director and his deputy, and three "policy council chairs," who met to discuss and "hammer" out the budget and pending legislation, and to make decisions on what to veto and what to sign into law.[772] The group "effectively teed up the decision for the president to make about mostly domestic policy."[773]

Overall, Gore's across-the-board advisory role was possible because of the situational dynamic and particularly the conditions the two principals found themselves in given their respective strengths and weaknesses. Clinton stated, "Al Gore helped me a lot in the early days, encouraging me to keep making hard decisions and put them behind me, and giving me a continuing crash course in how Washington works."[774] Clinton needed Gore to help him navigate Washington and to attend to policies in which he was considered an expert.[775] And as the administration progressed, Gore's influence and role strengthened. When Clinton was facing the Whitewater allegations, Gore was instrumental in helping him weather the storm. Clinton stated, "The cabinet and staff seemed to understand and tolerate my occasional flare-ups, and Al Gore helped me get through them."[776] Their personal relationship was strengthened because of the adversity they faced, which solidified his standing in Clinton's inner circle. Gore's influence was felt on a host of programs from reinventing government and balancing the budget to technological innovations such as the v-chip and connecting schools with the "information superhighway" to foreign policy commissions, staffing decisions, and environmental policy.[777] His advisory role was far reaching and reflected the times in which they governed. In particular, "it was made possible by the fact that Clinton chose a running mate who matched the right criteria."[778] He brought strength in the areas in which Clinton was weak, and it so happened to coincide with the issues the administration faced, thus evidencing the impact of the situational dynamic on Gore's influence.

The situational dynamic also negatively impacted Gore's influence in the Clinton White House. As he approached the latter part of his time in office, the administration faced several scandals that altered his involvement and influence in the day-to-day activities. Gore himself was

234 / Emerging from the Shadows

implicated in a fundraising scandal in 1997, just as he was beginning to put together his presidential campaign.[779] The accusations of campaign finance irregularities stemmed from the Clinton/Gore reelection and Republicans in Congress undertook investigations focused on Gore and his activities.[780] The allegations included fundraising at a Buddhist temple in California, fundraising phone calls, and "dark accusations of a stealthy plot by China to buy the American presidency."[781] Fueling the accusations was a story in the *Washington Post* by Bob Woodward, in which questions were raised about Gore's fundraising activities.[782] While Gore was cleared of any wrongdoing in the investigations conducted by the FBI, the existence of a perceived scandal "rattled" him.[783] "What embarrassed him most, according to friends, was that his judgment and character were being called into question by the Washington elite."[784] The campaign finance scandal also questioned his integrity and thus he felt "tainted by the charges."[785]

While Gore's involvement in the fundraising scandal did not cause the White House to put distance between Clinton and Gore, it proved to be a distraction that took his attention away from policy. The investigation, at that time, represented the "single largest investigation in U.S. history."[786] As one might expect, Gore and his staff found themselves defending him against the accusations, which when combined with the task of building a presidential campaign organization for the 2000 bid, left him very little time to engage in policy discussions and the day-to-day activities of the administration. Those in the White House viewed the scandal as an attempt to derail his presidential prospects and thus did not give it much credence.[787] Gore's diminished influence was brought on by the scandal but not because of a response by the White House to that scandal.

The second scandal that further diminished Gore's influence pertained to the president's affair with a White House intern, Monica Lewinsky. While the scandal emanated with the president, it had significant implications for Gore and his influence in the White House. "[It] had changed the dynamics quite a bit."[788] This scandal would not only lead to Clinton's impeachment, but it would cause Clinton's and Gore's relationship to suffer greatly.

Clinton had reassured Gore that there was no truth to the allegations. "Gore was near the doorway of the Oval Office when Clinton told him that he did not have sex with Monica Lewinsky. As soon as Clinton turned around, a look of disbelief crossed the vice president's face."[789] Regardless of whether Gore believed him or not, he tried to support Clinton and worked to "keep the White House together."[790] Nonetheless,

Mondale, Bush, Quale, Gore, and Biden / 235

he felt betrayed when the truth emerged that Clinton did indeed have inappropriate relations with Lewinsky.[791] "It impacted his life more than it did Clinton's in the political future."[792] He had a hard time accepting his behavior.[793] After all, he had defended him by saying, "The president has denied the charges, and I believe him."[794] Gore put his own integrity on the line, and he was not alone in his feelings; many in the White House felt a sense of betrayal.[795] According to Hillary Clinton, "Al and Tipper were as shocked and hurt as everybody else in August when Bill admitted his wrongdoing, but both were supportive throughout the ordeal, personally and politically."[796]

As the scandal unfolded, Gore remained supportive of Clinton as he weathered the impeachment, however, their relationship was estranged and became more complicated as he began to gear up for his own presidential bid.[797] He found himself defending a president, who being linked to, could taint his image with the voters he would have to appeal to if he wanted to win in 2000. For his part, he remained loyal by stating that it was "time to take what he said to heart and move on to the people's business" and urged the Democratic congressional leaders and members of the cabinet to support the president.[798] However, Gore could not help but distance himself from Clinton if he were to have any chance at the presidency. "Vice President Gore was thinking more about his campaign and had less time to think about [day-to-day activities in the White House]. I think he moved away on his own."[799] The scandal made Gore's job as a candidate much more challenging.[800] "As Clinton's personal misdeeds drew more menacing to his presidency with each new disclosure, Gore's own role in the inner circle inevitably diminished."[801] He became more and more concerned about the secondary effects—the effect on his campaign and the effect on policy.[802] Privately he wondered how he could break away from Clinton without coming across as disloyal.[803] However, he was quick to admonish Clinton in interviews for his "inexcusable" behavior.[804]

Gore found himself struggling more and more with how to deal with Clinton.

> Vice President Gore's world changed when he stopped being so much the vice president and really was the frontrunner for the Democratic presidential nomination in 2000. And that did change the relationship because all of sudden the vice president wasn't serving the role as the number two, he was out with a different set of priorities. And the relationship was not in

236 / Emerging from the Shadows

the last two years, was not as close I think professionally or personally.[805]

He initially thought that once the scandal ended the political environment would return to normal and he could run for president without the burdens of the scandal looming over his bid.[806] At times he thought he might become president sooner than expected, because the prospect of Clinton resigning existed, while at other times he felt that this might derail his efforts altogether.[807] Sometimes he defended Clinton, sometimes he expressed "disappointment," and sometimes he embraced the administration and its successes.[808] His response was all over the place because he struggled with how to handle the situation against the backdrop of a presidential campaign. Gore was preoccupied with how the voters would view him given the scandal. "Gore worried that voters concerned above all about personal moral qualities might not choose him because of his association with Clinton."[809] As these questions surrounded him, he retreated more and more from Clinton's inner circle and became determined to show that he was his own man. Most vice presidents who run for president choose to distinguish themselves from their president but the scandal complicated things.[810] He had to create his own identity, separate from Clinton.[811] Clinton understood Gore's need to distance himself. He stated, "The biggest challenge Al faced was how to show independence while still getting the benefit of our record. He had already said he disagreed with my personal misconduct but was proud of what we had accomplished for the American people."[812]

In the aftermath of the scandal, Clinton's approval ratings rose while Gore's fell by four percentage points.[813] People were clearly separating Gore from the president in more ways than he had hoped. "In a sense he was running a campaign that was taking the best from Clinton but also repudiating the worst of Clinton in his mind."[814] In distancing himself from the president personally, he also distanced himself from the administration's successes. However, Gore believed in the "Clinton fatigue" theory, which argued that voters were "exhausted" by the scandals surrounding the president and they would reject him, and anyone associated with him.[815] He felt no other alternative than to continue distancing himself. To demonstrate that distance, he moved his headquarters to Nashville (in which he failed to discuss it with Clinton in advance), and in his campaign announcement he tried to diminish his role in the Clinton administration and did not ask the president to play any role in the campaign.[816]

Clinton wanted to help his vice president desperately, but his counsel and assistance were not sought.[817] Clinton stated, "All vice presidents who run for President have two problems: most people don't know what they've done and don't give them credit for the accomplishments of the administration, and they tend to get typecast as number-two men. I had done everything I could to help Al avoid those problems by giving him many high-profile assignments and making sure he received public recognition for his invaluable contribution to our successes."[818] Clinton was willing to hang in the shadows if that helped Gore win the election.[819] However, the only advice Clinton could provide was through a circuitous route.[820] "After eight years together, here is the state of the relationship between President Clinton and Vice President Al Gore: Mr. Gore won't pick up the phone. He doesn't call, and Mr. Clinton doesn't know why. . . . Mr. Clinton is both hurt by the personal rebuff and bewildered as to why his political heir won't come to him for the advice he is itching to give."[821] When asked what help he was receiving from Clinton, Gore stated, "This is a campaign that I am running on my own."[822] "Clinton is a political animal. He wanted to run for president for Gore. And for a lot of good reasons, Gore did not want him to do that. So, in that case you had a vice president actively resisting a president for wanting to be involved rather than the other way around. Al didn't want to be responsible for Clinton; he wanted to be responsible for Al."[823]

While their professional relationship remained, their personal relationship was damaged by the scandal, the election, and Gore's distancing.[824] "To be sure, the last year or so of their joint service witnessed a deterioration of the relationship."[825] As a result, Gore's influence suffered. Myers argued, "If the vice president is interested in running then your priorities start to diverge. Once he starts running for office and he's pursuing his own interests, of course the president is going to cut him out more."[826] His influence suffered from a confluence of several dynamics—interpersonal, situational, and electoral. The presence of scandal (situational dynamic) forced Gore to distance himself from the president, which was magnified by the presence of his campaign for the presidency (electoral dynamic), which then resulted in a deterioration in their personal relationship (interpersonal dynamic). While the scandal was not self-inflicted, the distancing from the scandal for electoral reasons greatly impacted their relationship and as a direct result diminished his influence. The election basically took Gore out of the day-to-day activities, which curbed his influence, but it was exacerbated by the fact that Gore distanced himself even more from

238 / Emerging from the Shadows

Clinton because of the scandal. "Gore stepped back from a place in that top box on the management chart."[827] Ultimately, "the relationship clearly was not as warm unfortunately when they ended as when they began."[828]

Joe Biden

An analysis of Joe Biden's influence as vice president is explained by both the interpersonal and institutional dynamic. Joe Biden, as in many of his predecessors in the modern era, was selected for his ability to compensate for the weaknesses at the top of the ticket and to assist in governing. According to David Plouffe, Barack Obama's campaign manager, "We knew Biden could be somewhat long-winded and had a history of coloring outside the lines a bit, but honestly, that was very appealing to Obama, because he wanted someone to give him the unvarnished truth. What do you need in a vice president? He knows and understands Congress, has great foreign policy and domestic experience. He had the whole package from a VP standpoint."[829] In comparison to Obama, he had a "wealth of experience" that would serve the president well in the White House, having served in Congress for thirty-five years.[830] Nonetheless, Biden's and Obama's relationship as running mates started out on fragile ground. First, Biden and Obama were challenging each other for the Democratic nomination for president in 2008. Second, Biden who is known for his gaffes, stated on the day he announced running for president, "[Obama was] the first mainstream African-American who is articulate and bright and clean and a nice-looking guy."[831] Their relationship in the Senate, while cordial, was never close.[832] "He'd [Biden] started out, like all the veterans in the field, thinking Obama was too big for his britches, not ready to be president."[833] In the Senate, Biden's attitude toward Obama was "condescending and patronizing to the point where it rankled [Obama]."[834] "As senators, Barack Obama and Joe Biden were far from close. Obama served on the Foreign Relations Committee, which Biden led; and Biden, who felt that he had earned his stars the old-fashioned way, bristled at Obama's status as an instant superstar. . . . Before Biden dropped out of the [2008] race he criticized Obama as a foreign-policy neophyte who was copying his ideas."[835]

Despite the tenuous start to their relationship, the two men warmed to each other. Biden's attitude toward Obama was changed by the race speech he gave in Philadelphia in March 2008.[836] Biden told his aides, "It was the best oration he had heard since Dr. King."[837] For his part, Obama was able to transcend the "condescending and patronizing" way Biden came across and began to appreciate him.[838] He valued his experience, ability to relate to certain core constituencies of the Democratic Party, and his approach to campaigning.[839]

While the interpersonal dynamic demonstrated a shaky foundation early on, it would develop and come to explain Biden's ability to exercise influence. The Obama and Biden relationship would mature into one of deep admiration and true friendship. So much so, that over the course of their time in office, the media reports frequently alluded to a "bromance," even noting that the two had matching "friendship bracelets."[840] As their relationship improved, Biden became an irreplaceable "counselor in chief."[841] He advised on all important decisions from foreign and domestic policy to congressional relations, judicial appointments, and legislative strategy.[842] Obama ensured that Biden was included on "every critical decision."[843] Like previous vice presidents, Biden positioned himself as a senior adviser to the president.[844] He spent nearly six hours per day with the president, with Obama always seeking out his advice.[845] Biden stated, "I literally get to be the last guy in the room with the president."[846] Further demonstrating the importance of the interpersonal dynamic to Biden's influence was the fact that both principals were on the same page when it came to the role the vice president would play, which was an activist role. This enabled Biden to take on important responsibilities.

Biden, like some of his predecessors, chose a reduced role when it came to line assignments. He did not want to undertake specific duties or "cut as wide a swatch as Vice President Cheney."[847] "[Biden] has a fairly clear sense in his own mind . . . that he didn't want to be the guy in charge of x portfolio."[848] He did not want to be burdened with administrative or departmental-level responsibilities.[849] Despite this, Biden played an instrumental role during the transition in chairing economic meetings to assist in developing a comprehensive economic recovery package, which became an important agenda for the incoming Obama administration as a result of the economic crisis.[850] As vice president, he would lead the charge to sell the package to Congress and the public.[851] He would serve as the primary contact for state governors and mayors in tracking the progress of the economic recovery across the country.[852] He also took on a line assignment that involved chairing the White House Task Force on Working Families, which nestled nicely with his work on the economy.[853] He led the fiscal cliff battles the country faced as well as gun control initiatives in response to various shooting incidents.[854]

240 / Emerging from the Shadows

In congressional relations, Biden used his relations on Capitol Hill and his workouts in the Senate gym to help pass the economic recovery plan, convince Republican Senator Arlen Specter to run for reelection as a Democrat, get the Senate to ratify the START Treaty, negotiate repeal of "Don't Ask, Don't Tell" policy, work with the Senate Republican leader to craft a tax bill to extend Bush-era tax cuts, worked to raise the debt ceiling and set spending limits, and was instrumental in budget talk negotiations in 2011, 2012, and early 2013.[855] Many in the Senate viewed him as a reliable partner. Senator Lindsey Graham (R-S.C.) stated, "I feel like if there's something really important I needed to deliver, he'd be the guy to call."[856]

Biden was an outspoken participant in foreign policy and especially in meetings regarding strategy in Iraq and Afghanistan. He viewed "himself as the one who asked the unpleasant and searching questions."[857] He was rather blunt with his advice and outspoken in any meetings he participated.[858] He was critical of the surge in Afghanistan and instead sought the administration to follow a plan he termed "counterinsurgency plus," which would require fewer troops on the ground and would reduce America's footprint in the region.[859] While the president sought a troop surge instead, he did appreciate Biden's role in the discussions. He wanted Biden to be blunt, ask tough questions, and provoke debate to ensure that all sides of the argument were addressed, which is what the vice president did during these discussions.[860] Biden asked questions that gave the president "decision-making space" in order to "stir up a vigorous debate."[861] While Biden did not necessarily win the debate on Afghanistan, he influenced the president to develop a "compromise plan for managing the remaining troops in Afghanistan."[862] Many saw Biden as being on the losing side of the issue, however, Obama felt otherwise. He stated, "I don't think anyone who was party to the very, very exhaustive discussions we had would say that. Joe was enormously helpful in guiding those discussions. The decision that ultimately emerged was a synthesis of some of the advice he gave me, along with the advice of the generals."[863] After all, the president would withdraw 30,000 troops by summer of 2012, which was in-line with Biden's advice.[864]

In terms of Iraq, Biden routinely challenged the military's advice and any attempts to follow the status quo and thus, became the point person for the withdrawal from Iraq.[865] The military had a less than pleasant view of Biden's role in discussions of Iraq and Afghanistan, with criticism being leveled by Generals David Petraeus and Stanley McCrystal.[866] Furthermore, Secretary of Defense Robert Gates, who often disagreed with Biden, accused him, of "poisoning the well" against military leaders who supported a surge.[867] He often was on the losing side of the argument juxtaposed against other senior administration officials such as Hillary Clinton, Leon Panetta, and Robert Gates.[868] He opposed intervention into Libya and warned against the Osama bin Laden raid as well.[869] His cautious approach fit with Obama's foreign policy philosophy of avoiding "errors," though.[870]

An initial assessment of Biden's influence demonstrates that the apex of his influence occurred during the first term and early part of the second term. During this time, his "indispensability and influence" were evident.[871] As mentioned earlier, he negotiated for the extension of the Bush tax cuts and witnessed the passage of the START Treaty, all during a lame-duck session of Congress.[872] He also took a leading role in the fiscal cliff negotiations, which had him in direct negotiations with the Senate minority leader, Mitch McConnell to forestall the impending crisis.[873] He was viewed as the "Democrats' deal-maker-in-chief."[874] While Biden was instrumental in negotiating deals with Senator McConnell in 2011 and 2013, his influence waned.[875] As the government shutdowns commenced in October 2013, Biden was sidelined from the negotiations, partially because the previous deals he brokered did not "age well" with the Democratic Caucus.[876] His previous negotiations with McConnell produced an agreement that only forestalled sequestration-style cuts for two months and yielded on tax rates for Americans earning up to $450,000 per year.[877] This infuriated the Democratic Caucus and so Senator Harry Reid (D-N.V.), the Senate majority leader, requested that Biden not be involved in any of the negotiations taking place during the government shutdown in 2013.[878] "Reid doesn't want Biden swooping in and negotiating another 11th-hour deal with Republicans."[879] He felt that Biden failed to drive a hard enough bargain in the negotiations.[880] The administration, to smooth things over with members of its own party, capitulated to Reid's demands and as such Biden was left out of the picture.[881] There was little protest from Obama.[882] Biden's absence was noticeable though. Senator John McCain argued that "his old friend had been placed in 'the witness protection program.'"[883]

Interestingly, the height of Biden's influence coincided with Rahm Emanuel's departure as chief of staff, who was particularly domineering in his approach and a powerful force in the White House.[884] "With [his] departure . . . and Mr. Obama's need to negotiate with Congressional

242 / Emerging from the Shadows

Republicans if he is to advance his agenda, the president is increasingly using Mr. Biden as a multipurpose emissary while continuing to seek his counsel behind the scenes."[885] Reporters noticed his indispensability as well, stating "The success of Obama's presidency hinges more and more on the negotiating skills and political instincts of his No. 2."[886] Biden's influence was helped by the departure of Emanuel, which Biden stepped in to fill the void, demonstrating the consequences of institutional changes on vice presidential influence.[887] Initially, the institutional dynamic, represented by Rahm Emanuel's tenure as chief of staff, seemed to curb some of Biden's influence; however, once Emanuel left that post, he seemed to play a more pivotal role. Helping matters, Biden followed Cheney's lead in staffing his office with individuals in the key policy areas (economic, foreign, and diplomatic) who were on par with those on the president's staff and were integrated within the White House.[888]

While the interpersonal and the changing institutional dynamics allowed Biden to play an influential role in the first term, by the second term he became "less central to Obama's decision making."[889] Though he had become a less visible player, he remained personally close with Obama.[890] While still engaged in foreign policy, his focus had shifted to areas of the world that are of secondary importance to the United States.[891] The shift was noticeable, with some close to the administration noticing his less active role in foreign affairs, arguing that he "kind of disappeared behind the foreign-policy curtain."[892] He also became less outspoken in the principal's meetings of the National Security Council.[893] As the institutional dynamics changed, the electoral dynamic began to alter the nature of his influence. Biden's standing within the administration came into question when reports began to surface that members of the administration were considering dropping Biden from the reelection ticket in 2012 in favor of Hillary Clinton.[894] As speculation mounted, his influence took another hit when Robert Gates released his memoirs in which he was critical of Biden's positions on foreign policy and national security. Gates argued that Biden had been "wrong on nearly every major foreign policy and national security issue over the past four decades."[895]

In terms of the institutional dynamic, Biden's gut-driven approach to politics often conflicted with the White House staff's reliance on "Big Data, metrics-driven game," thus never allowing him to fully break into the inner circle.[896] He would often become annoyed with the young White House staff.[897] However, his approach also conflicted with Obama's, which was much more in line with his young staff's.[898] While relations between

Obama and Biden remained good, tension existed between the staff and the vice president. When Biden attempted to replace his own chief of staff, his first choice was vetoed by Plouffe and others on Obama's staff.[899] Eventually, he would prevail with his second choice, despite opposition from the same folks, but only after appealing to Obama directly and giving him his assurances on the soundness of the pick.[900] His influence was remarkably different in the second term because of the changing institutional dynamic and the staff turnover. "The chemistry of the White House had changed . . . By the summer of 2014, Biden's associates Tom Donilon, Bill Daley, and Jay Carney had left the White House, and Obama's inner ring of advisers—including his chief of staff, Denis McDonough, and Valerie Jarrett, Benjamin Rhodes, and Susan Rice—was no longer stocked with veterans of Bidenworld."[901]

Biden's proclivity for gaffes also complicated his relationship with staff, which marginalized his influence. Obama's campaign team referred to Biden's gaffes as "Joe Bombs."[902] During the 2012 campaign, Biden gave an interview in which he declared his "off-message support for gay marriage," which forced Obama's hand on the issue.[903] "Obama's team didn't buy Biden's explanation that the gay marriage endorsement was accidental—and, until recently, Obama's team blocked Biden from doing much national media to keep him from shredding the talking points. The freeze-out was not subtle: The vice president was personally excluded from planning meetings he had been invited to attend four years earlier, and his people were treated with open contempt in the weeks following."[904]

In terms of the electoral dynamic, during the buildup to the 2012 elections, Biden sought to expand his political future but all attempts to "expand his political team" ended up being blocked by "Obama's sharp-elbowed protectors."[905] For instance, when Biden's political adviser added some additional fundraising stops to a previously scheduled visit to the West Coast, David Plouffe (Obama's senior adviser) and Jim Messina (Obama's campaign manager) stopped it.[906] Biden was attempting to meet with potential "2016 donors."[907] "Plouffe was tasked with laying out the ground rules and told Biden that everything he said or did needed to be cleared with the Chicago campaign headquarters first. 'We can't have people going off doing things on their own. . . . Everything has to be part of the larger plan.'"[908] After these attempts to meet with 2016 donors, the vice president was excluded from campaign related strategy meetings.[909]

As the end of the second term loomed and the 2016 presidential election cycle approached, further strains were placed on Biden's influ-

244 / Emerging from the Shadows

ence because of the electoral dynamic. Despite telling Obama during the 2008 presidential campaign that he would not be a candidate for president, speculation began to grow and the efforts he tried to undertake to expand his political team during the 2012 presidential campaign began to reemerge.[910] Back in 2008, Biden told Obama, "The good news is, I'm sixty-five and you're not going to have to worry about my positioning myself to be president."[911] Despite the assurances, Biden began taking steps to explore a potential run. As early as 2011, the vice president was hosting strategy sessions with key family members and longtime loyalists for the purposes of entertaining a presidential run.[912] "Officials working on the Obama-Biden campaign . . . were struck by how the vice president always seemed to have one eye on a run, including aggressively courting the president's donors."[913] These actions built tension within the administration toward Biden, and whether intentionally or unintentionally marginalized his influence. "With Biden in the midst of a metamorphosis from also-ran to possible 2016 contender, his relationship with the West Wing [was] becoming more complicated."[914]

Conclusion

The vice presidencies of Walter Mondale, George H. W. Bush, Dan Quayle, Al Gore, and Joe Biden demonstrate the importance of the interpersonal, situational, institutional, and electoral dynamics to vice presidential influence. What is clear from the analysis is that all vice presidents, regardless of what position they start in or how influential they are in comparison to others, will experience a marginalization of their influence during their time in office. Furthermore, the general trend for vice presidential influence is diminishment over time. Due to the intervention of the four dynamics, influence wanes over the course of an administration, mostly out of the vice president's personal control. Even those vice presidents who are the most influential also experience a similar phenomenon to their influence.

In the case of Walter Mondale, his influential role at the start of the Carter administration was predicated on the compatibility of his and Carter's conception of the vice presidency as well as the strength of their personal and professional relationship. Because both principals were on the same page regarding their vision of the office, there was no uncertainty as to the proper role Mondale should or could play in the White House. Carter provided Mondale with the resources necessary to be an influential vice president, mainly office space in the West Wing and unlimited access to the president, paper flow, and information. Carter's confidence in Mondale and his willingness to integrate their staffs, even before they entered the White House, further buttressed his influence. As a result, he would serve as a chief adviser to the president across all issue areas, with a focus on foreign affairs, congressional affairs, and political matters. Mondale successfully took part in negotiations for the Panama Canal Treaty, the Camp David Accords, and helped create the Department of Education during his tenure.

Despite the precedent setting nature of Mondale's vice presidency and the conception of a sustained model that most subsequent vice presidents followed, his influence became marginalized toward the end of the administration because of the electoral dynamic. The effect was further impacted by the growing differences between the president and vice president over policy and strategy. Mondale found himself at frequent odds with Carter on laying out a vision for America that others would be willing to follow, the need to engage in more of the public presidency aspects of the office, and differences in opinion on dealing with tax issues, domestic spending, and the threat posed by the Soviet Union. Mondale was particularly incensed by Carter's approach to the "malaise" speech and his willingness to paint the issue as psychological rather than economic. As Mondale became more frustrated with his inability to influence Carter, he turned further and further away from policy and became more focused on the public presidency that Carter was unwilling to engage. He told his staff that he would approach the vice presidency through a "new relaxation theory," which provided a revised conceptualization of his advisory role. Mondale made a concerted effort to spend less time at the White House and instead picked up the slack posed by Carter's "Rose Garden strategy" to the election. While Carter remained at the White House, it fell to him and other presidential surrogates to campaign for reelection, thus reducing his influence on the day-to-day activities and decisions over policy in the White House.

While the electoral dynamic provides a direct explanation of Mondale's marginalized influence toward the end of the term, it did not occur in a vacuum. Instead, his influence was impacted by the confluence of both the electoral and interpersonal dynamics. More specifically, the interpersonal dynamic, which was alluded to in the earlier description of Mondale's influence, shifted toward the end of the term that resulted in philosophical differences emerging between the president and vice president. As a

246 / Emerging from the Shadows

result of this shift, Mondale reconceptualized his role based on his "new relaxation theory," which only further marginalized his influence. Many of the dynamics that help explain vice presidential influence work in conjunction with each other in providing a full conceptualization of said influence. These dynamics may not always be completely distinct, as was the case with Mondale. Instead, they tend to overlap and bleed into each other, which is clear from many of the case studies discussed.

George H. W. Bush followed the Mondale model and relied on his advice in approaching the office, however, he did not disavow line assignments in the same way that Mondale did. Bush's capacity to exercise influence was greatly helped by having Jim Baker, his close ally and friend, serve as Reagan's first chief of staff. The institutional dynamic, specifically Baker's role as chief of staff, helped reduce institutional obstacles to Bush's influence. This was all the more significant because Reagan and Bush had been political rivals in 1980. Reaganites in the administration were skeptical of Bush and his support of Reagan's philosophical views on taxes and abortion. Given the skepticism, had Baker not been present to protect Bush's interests, or at the very least ensure that he was treated fairly by the president's staff, Bush's vice presidency would have looked differently. The normal battles between presidential and vice presidential staffs would have made a Bush vice presidency look eerily similar to Rockefeller's. As a result of Baker's position, he took every effort to protect the president's and vice president's relationship and ensured they met frequently. Furthermore, he was constantly on the lookout for any potential obstacles imposed by Reagan staff who were skeptical of Bush and his loyalty.

The institutional obstacles were also reduced by Bush's approach to the office. His number-one goal was to serve his constituency of one— Ronald Reagan. He was also committed to demonstrating at every possible opportunity his undying loyalty to the president. Bush's actions after the controversy over his naming as crisis manager, the assassination attempt on the president, and Reagan's bowel surgery helped convince the reluctant White House staff that Bush could be trusted. This provided Bush with the capacity to exercise greater influence that would normally not be accorded to a one-time rival of the president. As a result, he became an important envoy for the president in international relations, successfully negotiating the placement of weapons in Western Europe to counter the threat posed by the Soviet Union. He also used ceremonial travel and the frequent funerals of Soviet leaders to advance diplomacy, size up the new leader, and determine how receptive they would be to the US. In domestic policy, Bush took the lead in one of the most important initiatives of the Reagan initiative—regulatory reform. This was not only a major component of Reagan's economic policy and a campaign promise, but it also helped Bush ingratiate himself with Reagan supporters who were skeptical of Bush's conservative credentials. He also headed task forces on drug interdiction in South Florida as well as a terrorism task force, both of which were hot-button issues at the time.

Despite Bush's capacity for exercising influence through the institutional dynamic, his influence was tempered by the interpersonal dynamic, specifically his restrained conception of the office and his role. Bush's loyalty and determination not to cross a line meant that he would operate in the background and exert influence on a limited basis. He refused to press for friends or political allies to receive appointments in the administration, stressing that the prerogative belonged to Reagan. He cautioned his staff that they would only give interviews on the record, and he never wanted to hear or read about disagreements with Reagan or the president's staff. Last, Bush did everything to avoid any political gain at the expense of the president, even going so far as to offer advice that he knew could hurt him politically in his attempt to run for office in 1988. In fact, it took significant pressure for Bush to finally relent and politically campaign for the presidency by distancing himself from Reagan, choosing to do so only after he secured the Republican nomination. While the capacity to exercise influence existed in Bush's vice presidency, the interpersonal dynamic constrained his ability to exercise influence because of his restrained conception of the office.

Dan Quayle's vice presidency, not surprisingly, followed Bush's model of a restrained role. Despite this, Quayle's influence was made possible due to the electoral dynamic and given the nature of his selection as vice president. Rather than picking a running mate who could help Bush govern, he was more concerned about balancing the ticket electorally. He sought a vice president who could help him with the conservative wing of the Republican Party that was still skeptical of Bush's conservatism. Quayle was instrumental in serving as a political surrogate for Bush by attending a host of political activities, party building efforts, and campaign events. Quayle raised a considerable amount of money for the Republican Party and drew large crowds at these political events. He was influential in keeping Bush and the administration linked with the core constituencies who they would need for reelection.

Quayle's activities also involved serving as a liaison with Congress. Members of Congress, specifically those in the more conservative wing

248 / Emerging from the Shadows

of the Republican Party, were convinced that Quayle was their man in the administration. Many in the administration recognized how much of an asset he was in terms of congressional relations and reading the political tea leaves on Capitol Hill. He was always involved in discussions of a political nature and his political judgment and insight were usually on point. He lobbied members of Congress to support the president's appointment of Clarence Thomas to the Supreme Court, convinced Bush of the need to receive a congressional authorization for the Gulf War and successfully worked Capitol Hill to gain its passage, and helped smooth over relations with Congress over Bush's reversal on his "no new taxes" campaign pledge, despite his opposition. Last, his work heading up the Competitiveness Council was instrumental in helping foster Bush's political relations, especially since the work of the council fit with political philosophy of the conservatives. His influence was apparent to those inside and outside the administration. The council was considered a "power center" and provided Quayle with a resource by which to exercise influence.

While Quayle was influential when it came to politics, campaigning, and congressional relations, his influence was negatively impacted by the institutional dynamic, especially regarding foreign policy. Despite Quayle's background in defense and foreign policy issues, he was unable to compete with the other heavyweights who made up Bush's inner circle in the "Big Eight." Specifically, he was unable to compete with Baker, Cheney, or Scowcroft, all of whom had terrific résumés. Furthermore, Bush did not need to rely on many for advice when it came to foreign policy, given his own depth of knowledge on the issues. While Quayle was kept informed, his input was not usually sought, and his influence was not palpable. Baker and Scowcroft were suspicious of Quayle and obstructed his full participation. They were required to sign off on any vice presidential trips before they would even make it to the president for a decision. Baker opposed Quayle's visits to the important capitals of the world, which relegated him to Asian and Latin American countries. Even Quayle recognized the difficulties imposed by the decision-making structures in the White House and his inability to compete.

Quayle's influence was further marginalized by the staffing arrangements. The president's staff was suspicious of him and his staff. Quayle's staff was considerably more conservative than Bush and even the president felt they pushed too far to advocate for more conservative positions. Quayle admitted that his staff was aggressive, thus contributing to potential conflict. The difficulties surrounded Bill Kristol, Quayle's chief of staff, who the White House staff viewed as the person responsible for being the administration's leak. The level of suspicion resting with Quayle's staff, and Kristol more specifically, had the unintended consequence of bleeding over onto the vice president, which not only affected his influence but marginalized his voice as a result of his staff being locked out of discussions.

Al Gore's selection as vice president was exceptional because his candidacy reinforced Clinton's own candidacy, rather than providing any sort of electoral balance. However, Gore's selection was primarily focused on governing. Clinton understood the handicaps he had in relation to policy and Washington experience and looked to select a running mate who he could rely on and help him govern. The situational dynamic, specifically the strengths and weaknesses of the two principals, elevated Gore's stature in the administration and provided him with significant influence over policy and strategy. In many respects, Gore was viewed as a peer of the president and as such was very frank in his discussions with Clinton, including in open meetings with others present. His experience on Capitol Hill, in foreign affairs, and policies such as technology, telecommunications, the environment, and a host of other issues, enabled him to be the point person on all those matters. He was provided with significant autonomy and discretion in carrying out line assignments in which he had experience or an interest in. Many, both inside and outside the White House, understood the level of influence Gore carried with the president, and so they lobbied him in hopes of swaying Clinton. Members of Congress and those in the White House knew that if you could get Gore on board it was just as good as getting the president on board. The situational dynamic allowed Gore to head the Reinventing Government initiative and bilateral commissions on foreign affairs. He was instrumental in the passage of NAFTA, convincing the president on a consumption tax, and pressuring Clinton to act in Bosnia. Gore's penchant for being a policy wonk had him deeply involved in environmental, science and technology issues, and national security affairs. In fact, he was considered such a strategic force in the White House that his influence transferred to his staff in those key policy areas as well.

While Gore maintained good personal relations with Clinton through most of his term in office, the relationship became strained because of the situational dynamic and the presence of scandal. The scandal, particularly the Monica Lewinsky incident, amplified the impact of the situational dynamic on Gore's influence. It was further complicated by Gore's own bid for the presidency in 2000. He felt betrayed by Clinton's behavior and was

250 / Emerging from the Shadows

determined to distance himself from the president. Complicating matters was that he was running for president in his own right and had the difficult balancing act of distancing himself from Clinton and his scandal, while simultaneously taking credit for the successes of the Clinton presidency. At times he struggled with how to effectively do this. Ultimately, he chose to take himself out of Clinton's inner orbit by spending most of his time on the campaign trail, moving his campaign headquarters to Nashville (without consulting with Clinton), and refusing Clinton's help on the campaign trail. He was a proponent of the "Clinton fatigue theory," and as a result, he looked for ways to distance himself from his president. Clinton wanted nothing more than to help him win but was disillusioned by Gore's unwillingness to take his support. The same situational dynamic that fostered Gore's influence during the administration undermined and marginalized that influence by the end of the term. Gore was so preoccupied with his own election he was no longer acting as a vice president, but rather a candidate. As a result, he was not involved in the day-to-day activities and decision making in the White House. By the end of the term, the two principals were barely speaking, and their relationship was never as sound as it once was. In fact, any advice Clinton provided Gore was given through an intermediary on the campaign.

Biden's influence seems to have followed a similar trajectory to that of other vice presidents in the modern era. In the initial stages of the administration, Biden's influence was fostered by the close interpersonal relationship that developed between the two principals as well as their compatible vision for the office. It was also furthered by the institutional dynamic, as many Biden loyalists found themselves in key positions in the administration and Rahm Emanuel departed the White House, which provided an opportunity for Biden to be one of the chief negotiators for the administration. During this time, Biden witnessed a great degree of success in helping the president push through his agenda. Despite the successes, the institutional dynamic was altered once again with the departure of many "Bidenworld" associates, as well as the uncertainty surrounding a potential Biden run in 2016. Biden's actions of trying to meet with donors and not completely standing behind his original campaign assurances placed great stress on his relations in the White House, thus marginalizing his influence even further.

The interpersonal, situational, institutional, and electoral dynamics provide a mechanism by which to understand vice presidential influence and identify those factors that may increase or marginalize said influence.

Vice presidential influence, regardless of the vice president, is malleable and subject to change, given the evolving interpersonal, situational, institutional, and electoral dynamics. As an administration matures, these changes in dynamics may work to advance or marginalize influence. One thing is certain, all vice presidents in the modern era, regardless of their level of influence, will encounter diminishing influence over the course of their vice presidency, either self-inflicted or due to no action of their own.

Conclusion

As a constitutional officer, the vice president occupies a unique position as a nationally elected officeholder to assist the president with his or her duties. However, studies of the presidency inadequately address the nature of vice presidential influence and the instrumental role it plays in presidential administrations. Up until recently the vice presidency failed to capture the attention of most students of the presidency. Many scholars viewed the office as unimportant, and throughout history the vice presidency has been ridiculed for its lackluster stature. For instance, Daniel Webster, a prominent nineteenth-century senator, declined the nomination as vice president by arguing, "I do not propose to be buried until I am really dead."[1]

Much an afterthought by the founding fathers, the vice presidency perhaps suffers greatly from institutional vagueness, more so than the presidency itself. Thus, it is "symptomatic of the problems of neglect and obscurity" that affect those entrusted with the office.[2] As Michael Turner states, the vice presidency is "an office historically and constitutionally weak and devoid of power."[3] The speculation that the vice presidency is merely an afterthought and thus often ridiculed is reinforced by its brief discussion in the Constitution. Joel Goldstein states, "The American vice presidency has been the target of more derision than any other national office."[4] Nonetheless, Jules Witcover argues that the founding fathers intended the vice presidency, "if there had to be one, as a position to be filled by a man of experience and renown second only to the president's."[5] This is evident from the manner in which the vice president was originally selected. The candidate who received the second most votes would occupy the office.

254 / Emerging from the Shadows

The derogatory way the vice presidency has been viewed for most of its history has only been flamed by those who have occupied the office. John Adams, the nation's first vice president, eloquently expressed his frustration with the office. "My country in its wisdom contrived for me the most insignificant office that ever the invention of man contrived or his imagination conceived."[6] Rather candidly, yet less eloquently than John Adams, John Nance Garner, Franklin Roosevelt's first vice president, discussed his antipathy toward the office when he stated, "the vice presidency isn't worth a pitcher of warm piss." Further elaborating on the worthlessness of the office as he saw it, Garner argued, "[vice presidents are] the spare tire on the automobile of government."[7] President Woodrow Wilson's vice president, Thomas Marshall, concluded that the vice president had only one job, "to ring the White House bell every morning and ask what is the state of the health of the president?"[8] Other vice presidents, from the likes of Theodore Roosevelt and Calvin Coolidge, articulated similar frustrations with the office.

While critics of the office remain, presidents and vice presidents, over the course of forty years have invigorated the vice presidency with greater purpose and influence, thus quelling some of the critics. Facing the increasing burdens of the office, presidents sought relief by delegating some of their presidential functions.[9] President Woodrow Wilson described the position of president prior to taking office as "the most heavily burdened officer in the world."[10] Likewise, Truman, contemplating his tenure of office as president stated, "I think no absolute monarch ever had such decisions to make or the responsibility that the President of the United States has. . . . No one man can really fill the Presidency. The Presidency has too many and too great responsibilities. All a man can do is try to meet them. He must be able to judge men, delegate responsibility and back up those he trusts."[11] As a result of such burdensome tasks, it is no wonder that the vice presidency can no longer be characterized as insignificant. Presidents have the authority to delegate powers in the exercise of their responsibilities, and the Supreme Court has ruled that this power is implied "and acts performed by such officials, if pursuant to law, will be presumed to be the President's acts."[12] Vice presidents, and willing presidents, stretched the boundaries of the vice presidency by instilling it with more authority, stature, and influence. Due to the responsibilities given to the presidency in domestic and foreign policy, the vice president began to play a more active role by chairing committees for specific programs, acting as a liaison between the White House and Congress, attending cabinet meetings, traveling to foreign countries as "surrogate head of state," serving as a spokesperson for the administration, and being actively involved in party politics.[13]

As argued by Richard Neustadt, presidents must utilize informal powers to be effective. Presidents rely on their vice presidents in both formal and informal manners and subsequently transcend the obstacles they encounter. As a result, a greater opportunity for the exercise of vice presidential influence exists now more so than at any other time in history. If we apply the fundamentals of Neustadt's argument to the vice presidency several things become clear. First, like the president, the vice president encounters a constrained office that is quite limited in terms of constitutional responsibilities. Second, some vice presidents are more effective than others, providing evidence that informal powers, informal institutional arrangements, and the politics in which they govern can, and often do, offer vice presidents greater influence.

Perhaps one of the greatest roles characteristic of the modern vice presidency is the role of adviser to the president. With ever increasing demands on the office, the president must surround him- or herself with capable advisers who have the necessary skills and experience to assist the president in executing his or her constitutional duties. As the presidency has grown, so too has the vice presidency. With the increase in staff, budget, and responsibilities, as well as the proximity of the vice president to the president (office now located in the West Wing), vice presidents in the modern era are important advisers to the president.[14] Because influence depends on access, this role enables them to wield significantly more influence than the vice presidents of yesteryear. In other words, proximity breeds influence and the nature of the modern vice presidency is predicated on an assumption that the position carries influence.

This study focused on explaining variation in vice presidential influence over time, between vice presidents, and within individual vice presidencies by analyzing the office from a constitutional, behavioral, contextual, and institutional perspective. The research undertaken distinguishes itself from the scholarship of others by conceptualizing how the informal roles of the vice president provide an outlet for exercising influence within an administration, the dynamics that affect the capacity for and exercise of vice presidential influence, and the fairly predictable phenomenon of diminishing influence over the course of an administration.

256 / Emerging from the Shadows

In order to showcase vice presidential influence and fully understand its origins, I analyzed the impact of vice presidential selection, electoral incentives, institutional arrangements, and the personal/professional relationship between the president and vice president on influence, and the political time in which these dynamics played out. Furthermore, a framework was developed to shed light on the different dynamics that impact the capacity of a vice president to exercise influence. This provides the reader with an appreciation for the unique nature of vice presidential influence and the ways in which it may be enhanced or marginalized from vice president to vice president or even within vice presidencies. Vice presidential influence seems to follow a certain trajectory with the same outcome for all vice presidents—diminishing influence. While no two vice presidents are carbon copies, regardless of the level and capacity for influence, one thing is certain—the vice president will become marginalized and influence will diminish. This predicament can be attributed to personal, political, and professional decisions of the two principals (president and vice president), their surrogates, or circumstances in which they find themselves governing within.

Conceptualizing and understanding influence is an age-old puzzle that has baffled scholars for decades, and by no means does this study present itself as the panacea to understanding the elusive nature of influence. Instead, this research provides a new perspective by which to understand influence within the context of the vice presidency, while distinguishing influence from what many mistakenly regard as power. A clear distinction exists between influence and power. Vice presidential influence is very difficult to ascertain because of the intangible nature of influence. It is often assumed that power begets influence and vice versa.[15] While the two concepts of power and influence seem to be very similar there are significant differences. Power can be conceived as a consequence of "positive or negative sanctions."[16] Similarly, power involves the exertion of "force, coercion and sanctions."[17] Power is usually conferred by a position, authority, office, or some other structural arrangement that provides the ability to exert some sort of sanction to achieve a specific outcome. In the case of the vice presidency, there is little that the vice president can do to exert a positive or negative sanction based on his or her position, statutory role, or constitutional powers.

On the other hand, influence occurs through persuasion or the provision of information or advice.[18] It does not require the exertion of sanctions as found in the concept of power.[19] Instead "influence derives from expectations that group members have for each other's competence."[20] With regard to the vice presidency, this seems to be the case. While vice presidents might lack the ability to exert positive or negative sanctions because of their limited powers as outlined in the Constitution, they do rely heavily on the expectations of others in influencing the president. Influence manifests itself through the exercise of informal powers of the vice president, particularly the advisory role. In fact, every vice president since Walter Mondale viewed their chief responsibility to serve as a senior adviser to the president of the United States and their influence was derived from this role.[21] Because vice presidential influence is highly dependent on the adviser role, the ability to observe influence may be "covertly suppressed" or "insensible or invisible . . . without the employment of material force . . . [or] formally or overtly expressed."[22] Therefore, in order to have influence you must have access to assert it in the first place. Influence is a more indirect function than the exercise of power and as such it is more nuanced and harder to conceptualize.

This study is most interested in identifying the conditions that foster or marginalize vice presidential influence. The capacity to exercise influence is more important than the actual exercising of influence by the vice president. The capacity for influence brings with it certain expectations of access, which contributes to the power and influence of the vice president. If a vice president is seen as having access to the president, then other political players will seek out the vice president as a conduit to the president for the sake of influencing, as was seen in the case of Al Gore and Dan Quayle. This provides the vice president with a personal cache of political power. This does not mean that a vice president can go rogue. All vice presidents since Walter Mondale have cautiously balanced these expectations with the actual access they have been given. In other words, vice presidents are very cognizant that the capacity for influence is tenuous and can shift in undesirable ways due to some events that might be out of their control (e.g., a strong chief of staff, electoral pressures, etc.). As a result, they cautiously safeguard their relationship with the president to maintain access and the capacity to exercise influence.

Given the state of the literature on influence and power, and for the sake of this research, influence is considered a distinct concept from power. Although I do not refute the notion that some interconnectedness exists, this study asserts that the presence of one does not automatically evidence the existence of the other. The exertion of influence does not have to be dependent on one's position, but instead could be understood

258 / Emerging from the Shadows

according to informal resources available and the interpersonal, situational, institutional, and electoral dynamics.

The research demonstrates that the capacity to exert vice presidential influence has increased during the modern era. Several reasons exist for the more influential role: the make-up of the president's and vice president's staff, the personal and professional relationship between the principals, the management style of the chief of staff, the selection of vice presidents based on their capacity to govern, the politics in which they govern, and the institutionalization of the advisory role of the vice president. Just as much as these factors enhance vice presidential influence, the presence of scandal, tensions between presidential/vice presidential staffs, an assertive chief of staff, and electoral incentives can have a dramatic impact on the nature of vice presidential influence. Regardless, one thing is certain, influence will diminish over the term of the administration, creating potential difficulties for the vice president.

I assert that vice presidential influence is better understood as contingent influence—one that is dependent on several intervening elements that may or may not be in the vice president's complete control—and represents the potential influence of the vice president. Contingent influence in the vice presidency is shaped by the four dynamics that serve as the theoretical foundation of this study, which includes an examination of the interpersonal, situational, institutional, and electoral dynamics on the capacity of a vice president to exercise influence. Any changes in these conditions or dynamics can usher in a corresponding change to vice presidential influence, which could very well result in influence diminishing or becoming marginalized. What distinguishes one vice presidency from another is the interplay of the four dynamics mentioned above and its effect on vice presidential influence. This research demonstrates that within a vice presidency these four dynamics can shift, resulting in a change in the capacity for a vice president to exercise influence. As demonstrated in all the case studies examined, many of the dynamics that help explain vice presidential influence work in conjunction with each other in providing a full conceptualization of said influence. In fact, these dynamics may not always be completely distinct; instead, they tend to overlap and bleed over into each other. As a result, the confluence of various dynamics provides a more vivid picture of a vice president's capacity for exercising influence.

The interpersonal dynamic is the bedrock for vice presidential influence. It consists of the most important factors in determining vice presidential influence. These include the presidential/vice presidential relationship (including pre-presidency), the principals' perspectives on the role of the vice presidency, the president's and vice president's style, the president's and vice president's respective personalities, and the respective capacity and skills of the president and vice president.[23] As stated earlier, the personal and professional relationship between the president and vice president is a precursor to the establishment of vice presidential influence.

The situational dynamic forms the backdrop of the environment in which the vice president acts. This includes national and international events and political conditions. In some cases, political conditions will affect vice presidential influence significantly, in both positive and negative ways. The reality of political conditions may force a reluctant president to take certain actions that might curb the vice president's influence or in some cases enable said influence. Political conditions include the shifting alliances presidents need in order to govern successfully, the state of the congressional/presidential relations, political timing, and the presence of both presidential and/or vice presidential scandal.

The institutional dynamic within the White House will shape vice presidential influence and can either make it much easier for a vice president to exercise influence within the administration or not. Institutional dynamics include such factors as: input on and changes in staffing (presidential and vice presidential), and the chief of staff and his management style, and the office of the vice presidency's institutional resources (budget, vice presidential staffers, office space, etc.).

The last dynamic is electoral, which is closely linked with vice presidential selection. As mentioned before, vice presidential selection transformed in the modern era from a condition based solely on electoral benefit or balancing the ticket electorally to one of balancing the ticket for governing purposes. Subsequently, the likelihood of witnessing influential vice presidents has become more prevalent.

While these considerations generally increase the likelihood of vice presidents playing a greater and more influential role in their respective administrations once elected, electoral considerations can also marginalize vice presidential influence once the president seeks reelection or the vice president considers running for president in his or her own right. Unlike the president, vice presidents do not have the benefit of traveling with the White House. In other words, if a vice president is removed from the White House for extended periods of time, he or she has less proximity to the president, and this is important because the president is the center of decision making. Thus, the vice president can be quickly sidelined due to the realities of running for office. Sitting presidents running for reelection generally use their vice presidents to do extensively more electioneering and travel to help secure reelection. Furthermore, vice presidents are routinely used as the president's attack dog to enable the president to remain above the fray. Vice presidents are uniquely positioned to sing the praises of the administration. "Presidential candidates cannot sing their own praises publicly to the extent they might like. Their running mates need show no such inhibitions. They can be the unabashed champions of the presidential candidates, lavishing them with praise or defending them from attack."[24] These realities make it highly likely that the vice president will spend more time on electioneering rather than on governing, which will as expected marginalize his or her influence since he or she will be so separated from the day-to-day decision-making process.

A similar reality affects vice presidents who are seeking election to the presidency but with an additional difficulty—they must demonstrate how they are different from the president and are their own person. Not only do the electioneering activities take the vice president away from the White House for extended periods of time, as is the case of reelection efforts, but a campaign for president alienates the vice president from the president on a personal level. In many ways, the concerted efforts of the vice president to distance him- or herself from the administration creates the appearance of disloyalty. However, aligning oneself too closely to a president runs the risk of creating the image that the president is due all the credit, not the vice president.[25] A case in point is the 2000 presidential election when Al Gore was running against George W. Bush. "His [Al Gore's] biggest difficulty probably lay in successfully defining himself in relation to the president."[26] Gore had to walk a tightrope that enabled him to take credit for the successes of the administration while simultaneously distancing himself from the various scandals and policies of Clinton so he could be seen as his own man. This is very difficult for any vice president to manage and ultimately it strains the relationship of the principals. Thus, vice presidents who are running for president face a double blow to their influence—personal as well as professional.

This study analyzed the vice presidencies of Nelson Rockefeller, Walter Mondale, George H. W. Bush, Dan Quayle, Al Gore, Dick Cheney, and Joe Biden. These vice presidents were selected because they represent the modern vice presidency, which is the focus of the study. Particular emphasis was centered on the vice presidencies of Rockefeller and Cheney, because Rockefeller's vice presidency ushered in the possibility for an influential vice presidency to exist and is the start of the modern vice presidency, as I define it, and Cheney epitomizes the apex of vice presidential influence. The one thing that all scholars agree on is that Cheney transformed the office of vice president and demonstrated significant influence as a result.[27] These two vice presidencies allow for a greater understanding of vice presidential influence and its fleeting nature because even though Rockefeller laid the foundation to exercise influence he still encountered obstacles to exercising that influence, and while Cheney is considered the most influential vice president in history, he too faced similar constraints that marginalized his influence. The applicability of the theory to vice presidential influence is further evidenced by examining the vice presidencies of Mondale, Bush, Quayle, Gore, and Biden.

In order to get at the heart of vice presidential influence, archival research was conducted at the Ford, Carter, Reagan, and George H. W. Bush presidential libraries. In addition, the papers of Walter Mondale and Nelson Rockefeller were examined at the Minnesota State Historical Society and the Rockefeller Archive Center, respectively. The archival research provided insight into the day-to-day activities of the vice presidents under study and was useful in examining any institutional changes to the office across vice presidencies in terms of organization and responsibilities. The research offered a picture of the contextual environment that each vice president governed within. Extensive in-depth interviews were also conducted with individuals from each presidential administration. The interviews helped clarify some of the information gathered from the archival research and assisted in framing the working relationship between each president and vice president and the changes in influence over time. Over seventy interviews were conducted with vice presidents, cabinet secretaries, press secretaries, chiefs of staff, national security advisers, and other presidential/vice presidential advisers. This study represents the first major effort utilizing both in-depth interviews with political practitioners and extensive archival research to examine changes in vice presidential influence and the evolution of the office in the modern era. Furthermore, it is the first of its kind to ascertain the true nature of vice presidential influence and how that influence diminishes over time.

Nelson Rockefeller

Rockefeller's vice presidency started on a very high note, which created the expectation that he would indeed be an influential vice president, and

262 / Emerging from the Shadows

for a short time he was in fact influential. Rockefeller won key battles against the president's chief of staff, Don Rumsfeld, in regard to personnel actions and operation of the Domestic Council, the redesign of the vice presidential seal, the recommendations on a scientific adviser, and even his CIA recommendations. Despite these early successes, Rockefeller's attempts faced the obstruction of a White House institutional structure that was resistant to his efforts, recommendations, and change. While Rockefeller was able to circumvent the structure to receive the president's support and approvals, those actions would still need to be carried out by the White House staff, which limited Rockefeller's effectiveness and influence, as was seen with his EIA proposal.

An evolution took place regarding his influence that was palpable to Rockefeller. He stated, "Now, his [Ford's] concept was way beyond that and it started out on a very high plane and then gradually jealousies developed which slowly made it more and more difficult without fighting."[28] He continued, "And, at least, during the first two-thirds, three-quarters of the time I was Vice President I had never been busier heading commissions, undertaking special projects for the President and traveling both at home and abroad."[29] Furthermore, he felt his vice presidency was unique in that he did not "think there is any Vice-President in the history of the United States who has been given as many responsibilities and as great a latitude as I have."[30]

Nonetheless, an evolution to his role took place—one that all vice president's face at some point during their terms of office, one that results in diminished influence. Rockefeller's role changed because of interpersonal, situational, institutional, and electoral dynamics that made it increasingly difficult for him to exercise sustained influence. Some of it was self-inflicted. Rockefeller resigned his supervisory authority over the Domestic Council, which was supposed to be the main source of his influence, due to its inability to meet the intent established by him and the president because of institutional obstacles such as turf battles between Rockefeller and the White House staff and a strong chief of staff. The institutional dynamic is only part of the story.

In terms of the interpersonal dynamic, Ford and Rockefeller's relationship remained excellent throughout his tenure and beyond. However, Ford's management style enabled the White House staff to obstruct the vice president and perpetuate the conflicts that led to Rockefeller's diminished influenced. While he was influential enough to get the president to support his position or take a position advocated by him, "his problem was he [Ford] wouldn't tell people what to do."[31] Rockefeller continued, "He [Ford] was so used to this congressional business of trying to get a consensus that he couldn't get used to the fact that he was President . . . on a direct confrontation he did not like to tell people that this is what we are going to do."[32] Rumsfeld argues that the decisions Ford made early on in his presidency, like giving the vice president authority over domestic policy, were decisions of a legislator not an executive; however, as time went on Ford became a very good executive.[33] And as the administration evolved so too did Rockefeller's role. Others, like Melvin Laird, also noticed Ford's hesitancy. Laird stated, "I wish Jerry had some of the same drive and ambition. You have to kick Jerry in the ass usually to get him to do anything. Even in the House you had to keep prodding him."[34] This nonconfrontational management style allowed problems to persist and allowed the White House staff to dictate the proper role for the vice president, even if it was contrary to what had been agreed on between the two principals.

Ultimately, Rockefeller's conclusions about Ford encapsulate his predicament as vice president: "He [Ford] was given to imprecision and could not always be relied upon to support his own previous decisions."[35] Rockefeller tried to protect himself from these "shifts in presidential positions or challenges to vice presidential actions from senior White House staff members" by ensuring that he always sought Ford's approval by signature for every action he carried out.[36] However, even that was not enough to overcome the situational, institutional, and electoral dynamics that imperiled his vice presidency and influence.

The situational dynamic also impacted Rockefeller's influence. Prior to his selection, the political conditions and situation welcomed a figure like Rockefeller to the vice presidency. He had national name recognition and could appeal to some Democrats and to the more liberal wing of the Republican Party. Furthermore, his experience as a fixer was a positive, since Ford sought to "fix" the country and restore public confidence in government after Watergate. He was adept at proposing large and costly government programs to help solve problems. However, his style of governing would suffer a setback when conditions quickly changed. The country faced a declining economy and the president instituted a policy of "no new starts." Rockefeller would be adversely affected due to his role as head of the Domestic Council. The "no new starts" policy basically took the wind out of his sails. The Domestic Council was the vehicle by which he could develop proposals to address the nation's problems, which tended to be

264 / Emerging from the Shadows

both grand and expensive in scope. Thus, the new landscape made these proposals even more difficult to gain traction, and political support both within the administration and beyond became more and more difficult to count on. And even when they did gain support by the president, as was the case of EIA, they failed to become law because White House staff was reluctant to fight for it and Congress lacked the political will to move forward on Ford's proposal due to the timing of the initiative—a looming presidential election.

The electoral dynamic also acted as a blow to Rockefeller's influence. The political reasons for his selection and approval in Congress for vice president, which was advantageous, would become a political liability to Ford and his election effort in 1976. Ford faced a strong opponent in Ronald Reagan for the Republican nomination; as a result, Rockefeller's more liberal policy positions and record were significant obstacles for him. Many of Ford's advisers, including his chiefs of staff (Rumsfeld and Cheney) and his campaign manager, lobbied for Rockefeller's replacement to win in the Deep South, which was Reagan territory.[37] Cheney stated, "If we didn't replace Rockefeller on the ticket, we were going to have real trouble winning the nomination in Kansas City. He would be a rallying point for all the conservatives who would like to go with Reagan anyway."[38] Once he was dropped from the ticket, the campaign and White House staff further distanced themselves from him as they looked forward to the future and focused on Ford's election efforts.

As demonstrated, all four dynamics adversely affected Rockefeller's vice presidency and ability to continue to exercise influence in the manner in which his vice presidency began. The evolution to his influence began approximately six to eight months after his confirmation and precipitously declined. While witnessing the jealousies and turf battles that existed in his administration, Ford failed to diffuse the situation by strongly asserting his will and directing the White House to support his agreement with his vice president, thus further alienating Rockefeller and diminishing his influence. Despite the eventual decline in vice presidential influence, some argue that the Mondale vice presidency, which scholars believe is beginning of the modern vice presidency, was "largely formed by the Ford-Rockefeller relationship."[39] As James Cannon stated, "Up 'til that point he was as influential, probably more influential in his personal conversations with the president. . . . Ford liked to have Rocky there and get his advice and views. Looking back, Rocky was the most influential vice president up until that time."[40]

Dick Cheney

In the case of Vice President Cheney, the interpersonal, situational, institutional, and electoral dynamics combined in an unprecedented manner to provide him with the greatest capacity to exercise influence than that of any vice president in the modern era. His relationship with Bush was strong and built on trust and admiration. His lack of ambition for the presidency only bolstered that trust, which could give a person tremendous influence.[41] "There was a certain at ease [and] lack of suspicion of the calculations being made or the judgments being imposed by the vice president."[42] This provided the foundation for him to exercise influence.

Due to the differing strengths of the principals, Cheney took on the unprecedented role of managing the transition and building the administration. He built the institutional structures and handpicked personnel to fill both the cabinet and subcabinet levels, all with Bush's concurrence. This enabled him to place allies throughout the executive branch, allowing him to reach down through the bureaucracy to engage in policy development. In my interview with Cheney, he recognized the centrality of this for his influence.[43] Furthermore, he organized his vice presidency so that his staff was fully integrated with the president's and several carried the title of assistant to the president or deputy assistant to the president, an unparalleled occurrence for a vice presidential staffer. In many respects, the vice president's staff members were treated as if they were the president's staff.[44] The organization and staffing of his office mirrored that of the president's, thereby providing him with the resources required to exert significant influence. Then as the administration faced the attacks on 9/11, Cheney's expertise and experience became indispensable. Cheney recognized, "In the aftermath of 9/11, it would be hard to find anyone who had that combination of experiences" to take a lead role.[45] The situation created an opportunity to exercise unprecedented influence in crafting a response to the attacks, remaking the intelligence community, creating the office of homeland security, and devising the controversial programs that became a hallmark of the war on terror.

Despite the convergence of the four dynamics in providing Cheney with influence, those same dynamics worked against him during the second term. For one, the relationship between Bush and Cheney faced significant strain because of Bush's decision not to pardon Libby and the firing of Rumsfeld. Additionally, the president came out in support of a constitutional ban on gay marriage that Cheney deeply opposed.

266 / Emerging from the Shadows

While they remained cordial, their relationship was markedly different. The situation the administration found itself in during the war on terror also impacted his influence. As casualties mounted in Iraq, approval for the effort began to slip and so did Cheney's. His reluctance to engage with reporters and his penchant for secrecy only contributed to his poor approval. "He never tried to make himself popular, he just didn't care, and in that sense, it eventually came to the point where he really lost some measure of impact because he was perceived so negatively by the public, he became an ineffective messenger for President Bush after a while."[46] As the controversial programs of the war on terror were disclosed, and Cheney's hand in them was apparent, he became even less popular and many placed the blame on him. Moreover, he found himself in the center of controversy with Libby being convicted in the Valerie Plame Wilson scandal, the hunting accident in which he mistakenly shot a fellow hunter, and the failure to disclose the energy task force's documentation to the GAO. The growing list of scandals made him less and less the "go-to-guy" in the administration. Last, during the second term, he was not as involved in personnel and staffing issues and was excluded from the conversation on replacing Rumsfeld. Bush decided to handle his own transition in the second term instead of giving Cheney the responsibility.[47] The loss of his chief of staff and the replacement of Bush's chief of staff with Josh Bolten, altered his role. No longer did he have a strong personal relationship with the president's chief of staff, and Bolten's management style was more independent of the vice president, resulting in a loss of influence for him. The administration looked much different and the personnel changes impacted his influence.[48] Many of his key allies were gone and their replacements were not as deferential to the vice president, many of whom lacked a relationship with him. Ultimately, Cheney found himself isolated in his views among the administration's senior staff.

Cheney's influence demonstrates that all vice presidents, no matter how influential they are, will face a similar decline in influence over the course of an administration, sometimes the result of their own efforts, and oftentimes the result of factors outside their control. Those in the administration, like Andy Card, and even the vice president himself, recognized his diminished influence in the second term.[49] Cheney experienced some self-inflicted damage to his influence, but mostly the changes to his influence were out of his control. It represented a situation in which a president was becoming more comfortable in his role as president and more fluent in the issues he faced. It also demonstrated a building confidence in the

Conclusion / 267

president's own abilities and as a result, less and less of a need to rely on Cheney, who he leaned on heavily in his first term.[50] Cheney stated, "Over time, I think I was probably more valuable to the president in the early part than the later part. Part of that was a learning process for him. By the time we got down toward the later part of the second term, he was much more—well, he had the experience of having been president for all those years, and he relied less, I think, on staff than had been true earlier."[51] In other words, "George W. Bush was hitting his own stride."[52]

The change in Cheney's influence was apparent for those in the administration. After the reelection, and specifically from the six-year mark on, Cheney found himself on the losing side of arguments. He would often start his remarks by stating, "I know I'm going to lose this argument" or "I know I'm alone in this," representing how he was a lonely voice in an administration that had changed.[53] This was a significant departure from early on in the administration, in which he carried the day when he convinced the president about POW status, enhanced interrogation, military commissions, the TSP, and attacking Hussein before the deadline was up. This is not to say that he never lost an argument in the first term. He had lost several arguments over skipping the UN resolution process for Iraq, but losing an argument was less likely in the first term. As the administration matured, he was on the losing side more and more often. For instance, when Israel invaded Lebanon due to terrorist attacks emanating from Lebanon, Cheney argued that they should allow the war to continue and let it run its course, however, Bush decided to seek a ceasefire.[54] Cheney argued that they should not seek a ceasefire resolution, but instead should "let the Israelis finish the job.[55] In another instance, when the administration was attempting to negotiate with North Korea over their nuclear weapons program, Cheney unsuccessfully lobbied the president not to remove North Korea from the list of countries who sponsored terrorism.[56] He even voiced his concerns to Hadley, the president's national security adviser but was unsuccessful in lobbying Bush.[57] When North Korea helped build a nuclear reactor in Syria, Cheney unsuccessfully tried to convince Bush to take unilateral action and take out the facility.[58] Bush decided against that course of action and instead, Israel took it out, which Cheney was thankful for.[59] Cheney's aggressive and more hawkish views on foreign policy were isolated in an administration that became more aligned with diplomatic approaches, which coincided with Rice's elevation as a rival to Cheney's influence when she became secretary of state.[60] Fleischer stated, "He [Bush] would agree with the objectives of the

268 / Emerging from the Shadows

most hawkish members of his administration, but then he would pursue the tactics of the more dovish members of the administration."[61]

Cheney's vice presidency represented unrivaled and unprecedented influence for a vice president in the modern era. He would sustain influence longer than any of his predecessors, but he eventually faced the same constraints imposed by the interpersonal, situational, institutional, and electoral dynamics and his influence waned. The extraordinary run he had exemplified his understanding of the issues that impact vice presidential influence and his concerted effort to build a vice presidency that would be consequential. Bush's concurrence with Cheney's role and the fact that Cheney lacked presidential ambition went a long way toward giving him the capacity to exercise influence.[62] Reflecting on his vice presidency, he stated, "I think we demonstrated that it could be a significant post; I think it was for a good part of the time I was there."[63]

Walter Mondale, George H. W. Bush, Dan Quayle, Al Gore, and Joe Biden

The vice presidencies of Walter Mondale, George H. W. Bush, Dan Quayle, Al Gore, and Joe Biden demonstrate the importance of the interpersonal, situational, institutional, and electoral dynamics to vice presidential influence as well. What is clear from the analysis is that all vice presidents, regardless of what position they start in or how influential they are in comparison to others, will experience a marginalization of their influence during their time in office. Even those vice presidents who are the most influential in modern history, such as Mondale, Gore, and Cheney, experience a similar phenomenon regarding their influence.

In the case of Walter Mondale, his influential role at the start of the Carter administration was predicated on the compatibility of his and Carter's conception of the vice presidential role as well as the strength of their personal and professional relationship, thus the interpersonal dynamic. Because both principals were on the same page regarding their vision of the office, there was no uncertainty as to the proper role Mondale should or could play in the White House. Carter provided Mondale with the resources necessary to be an influential vice president, mainly office space in the West Wing and unlimited access to the president, paper flow, and information. Carter's confidence in Mondale and his willingness to integrate their staffs, even before they entered the White House, fur-

Conclusion / 269

ther buttressed Mondale's standing and influence. As a result, Mondale would serve as a chief adviser to the president across all issue areas, with particular attention focused on foreign affairs, congressional affairs, and political matters. Mondale successfully took part in negotiations for the Panama Canal Treaty, the Camp David Accords, and helped create the Department of Education during his tenure.

Despite the precedent-setting nature of Mondale's vice presidency and the conception of a sustained model for the vice presidency that most subsequent vice presidents followed, his influence was marginalized toward the end of the administration as a result of the electoral dynamic. The effect of the electoral dynamic on Mondale's influence was further impacted by the growing differences between the president and vice president over policy and strategy. Mondale found himself at frequent odds with Carter on laying out a vision for America that others would be willing to follow, the need to engage in more of the public presidency aspects of the office, and differences in opinion on dealing with tax issues, domestic spending, and the threat posed by the Soviet Union. Mondale was particularly incensed by Carter's approach to the "malaise" speech and his willingness to paint the issue as psychological rather than economic. As Mondale became more frustrated with his inability to influence Carter, he turned away from policy and became more focused on the public aspects of the presidency that Carter was unwilling to engage. He told his staff that he would approach the vice presidency differently. He made a concerted effort to spend less time at the White House and instead picked up the slack posed by Carter's reelection strategy. While Carter remained at the White House, it fell to Mondale and other presidential surrogates to campaign for reelection, thus reducing Mondale's influence on the day-to-day activities and decisions about policy in the White House.

George H. W. Bush followed the Mondale model and relied on his advice in approaching the office, however, he did not disavow line assignments in the same way that Mondale did. Bush's capacity to exercise influence was greatly helped by having Jim Baker, his close ally and friend, serve as Reagan's first chief of staff. The institutional dynamic, specifically Baker's role as chief of staff, helped reduce institutional obstacles to Bush's influence. This was all the more significant because Reagan and Bush had been political rivals vying for the Republican nomination in 1980. Reaganites in the administration were skeptical of Bush and his support of Reagan's philosophical views on taxes and abortion. Given the skepticism, had Baker not been present to protect Bush's interests, or at the very least

270 / Emerging from the Shadows

ensure that Bush was treated fairly by the president's staff, Bush's vice presidency would have looked much different. The normal internecine battles between presidential and vice presidential staffs would have made a Bush vice presidency look eerily similar to Rockefeller's. Baker made every effort to protect the president's and vice president's relationship and ensured that they met frequently. Furthermore, he was constantly on the lookout for any potential obstacles imposed by Reagan staff who were skeptical of Bush and his loyalty.

The institutional obstacles that might have existed from a skeptical White House staff were also reduced by Bush's approach to the office. His number-one goal was to serve his constituency of one—Ronald Reagan. He was also committed to demonstrating at every possible opportunity his undying loyalty to the president. Bush's actions after the controversy over being named crisis manager, the assassination attempt on the president, and Reagan's bowel surgery, helped convince the reluctant White House staff that Bush could be trusted. This provided Bush with the capacity to exercise greater influence that would normally not be accorded to a one-time rival of the president. Bush became an important envoy for Reagan in international relations, successfully negotiating the placement of weapons in Western Europe to counter the threat posed by the Soviet Union. He also used ceremonial travel and the frequent funerals of Soviet leaders to advance diplomacy, size up the new leader, and determine how receptive they would be to the US. In regard to domestic policy, Bush took the lead in one of the most important Reagan initiatives—regulatory reform. This was not only a major component of Reagan's economic policy and a campaign promise, but it also helped Bush ingratiate himself with Reagan supporters who were skeptical of Bush's conservative credentials. In addition, he headed task forces on drug interdiction in South Florida, as well as a terrorism task force, both of which were hot-button issues at the time.

Even though Bush's capacity for exercising influence was fostered by the institutional dynamic, his influence was tempered by the interpersonal dynamic, specifically his restrained conception of the office and his role. Bush's loyalty and determination not to cross a line meant that he would operate in the background and exert influence on a limited basis. He refused to press for friends or political allies to receive appointments in the administration, stressing that the prerogative belonged to Reagan. He cautioned his staff that they would only give interviews on the record, and he never wanted to hear or read about disagreements with Reagan or his staff. Last, Bush did everything to avoid any political gain at the expense

Conclusion / 271

of the president, even going so far as to offer advice that he knew could hurt him politically in his attempt to run for office in 1988. In fact, it took significant pressure for Bush to finally relent and politically campaign for the presidency by distancing himself from Reagan, choosing to do so only after he secured the Republican nomination. While the capacity to exercise influence existed, the interpersonal dynamic constrained his ability to exercise influence as a result of his restrained conception of the office.

Dan Quayle's vice presidency, not surprisingly, followed Bush's model of a restrained role. Despite this, Quayle's influence was made possible due to the electoral dynamic and given the nature of his selection as vice president. Rather than picking a running mate who could help Bush govern, the president was more concerned about balancing the ticket electorally. More specifically, he was looking for someone who could help him with the conservative wing of the Republican Party, which was still skeptical of Bush's conservatism. Quayle was instrumental in serving as a political surrogate for Bush by attending a host of political activities, party-building efforts, and campaign events. He raised a considerable amount of money for the party and drew large crowds at these political events. He was influential in keeping Bush and the administration linked with the core constituencies who they would need to seek reelection.

Quayle's activities also involved serving as a liaison with Congress. Members of Congress, specifically those in the more conservative wing of the party, were convinced that Quayle was their man in the administration. Many in the administration recognized how much of an asset he was in terms of congressional relations and reading the political tea leaves on Capitol Hill. He was always involved in discussions of a political nature and his political judgments and insights were usually on point. He lobbied members of Congress to support the president's appointment of Clarence Thomas to the Supreme Court, convinced Bush of the need to seek a congressional authorization for the Gulf War and successfully worked Capitol Hill to gain its passage, and helped smooth over relations with Congress over Bush's reversal on his "no new taxes" campaign pledge, despite his opposition. Last, his work heading up the Competitiveness Council was instrumental in helping foster Bush's political relations, especially since the work of the council fit with political philosophy of the conservative wing of the party. His influence was apparent to those inside and outside the administration. The council was considered a locus of power and provided Quayle with an opportunity to take on a task that was not only important to conservatives but important to him as well.

272 / Emerging from the Shadows

While Quayle was influential when it came to politics, campaigning, and congressional relations, his influence was negatively impacted by the institutional dynamic, especially in regard to foreign policy. Despite Quayle's background in defense and foreign policy issues, he was unable to compete with the other heavyweights who made up Bush's inner circle. Specifically, he was unable to compete with Jim Baker, Dick Cheney, or Brent Scowcroft, all of whom had terrific résumés in foreign affairs. Furthermore, Bush did not need to rely on many for advice when it came to foreign policy, given his own depth of knowledge on the issues. While Quayle was kept informed, his input was not usually sought, and his influence was not palpable. Baker and Scowcroft were suspicious of the vice president and obstructed his full participation. They were required to sign off on any vice presidential trips before they would even make it to the president for a decision, and Baker opposed Quayle's visits to the important capitals of the world, which relegated him to Asian and Latin American countries. Quayle recognized the difficulties imposed by the decision-making structures in the White House and his inability to compete.

Quayle's influence was further marginalized by the staffing arrangements within the White House. Many on the president's staff were suspicious of the vice president and his staff. Quayle's staff was considerably more conservative than Bush, and even the president felt they pushed too far to advocate for a more conservative position. Quayle admitted that his staff was pretty aggressive, thus contributing to potential conflict. He was quick to point out that the problems never existed between him and the president or even the chiefs of staff and himself. The difficulties surrounded Bill Kristol, Quayle's chief of staff, who the White House staff viewed as the person responsible for the administration's leak. The level of suspicion resting with Quayle's staff, and Kristol more specifically, had the unintended consequence of bleeding over onto the vice president, which not only affected his influence but marginalized his voice as a result of his staff being locked out of discussions.

Al Gore's selection as vice president was exceptional in respect to the way his candidacy reinforced Clinton's own candidacy, rather than providing any sort of electoral balance. His selection was primarily focused on governing. President Clinton understood the handicaps he had in relation to policy and Washington experience and looked to select a running mate who he could rely on and who could help him govern. The situational dynamic, specifically the strengths and weaknesses of the two principals, elevated Gore's stature in the administration and provided

Conclusion / 273

him with significant influence over policy and strategy. In many respects, Gore was viewed as a peer of the president and as such was very frank in his discussions with Clinton, including in open meetings with others present. His experience on Capitol Hill, in foreign affairs, and policies such as technology, telecommunications, the environment, plus a host of other issues, enabled him to be the point person on all those matters. He was provided with significant autonomy and discretion in carrying out line assignments related to those policies or any he had an interest in. Many, both inside and outside the White House, understood the level of influence Gore carried with Clinton and so they lobbied him in hopes of swaying the president. Members of Congress and those in the White House knew that if you could get Gore on board it was just as good as getting the president on board. The situational dynamic allowed Gore to head the Reinventing Government initiative and bilateral commissions on foreign affairs. He also was instrumental in the passage of NAFTA, convincing the president on a consumption tax, and pressuring the president to act in Bosnia. He was considered such a strategic force in the White House that his influence transferred to his staff in those key policy areas as well.

While Gore maintained good personal relations with the president through most of his term in office, the relationship became strained because of the situational dynamic and the presence of scandal. The scandal, particularly the Monica Lewinsky incident, amplified the impact of the situational dynamic on Gore's influence. It was further complicated by Gore's own bid for the presidency in 2000. He felt betrayed by Clinton's behavior during the scandal and was determined to distance himself from the president. Complicating matters was that he was running for president and had the difficult balancing act of distancing himself from Clinton and his scandal while simultaneously taking credit for the successes of the Clinton presidency. At times, he struggled with how to effectively do this. Ultimately, he chose to take himself out of Clinton's inner orbit by spending most of his time on the campaign trail, moving his campaign headquarters to Nashville, and refusing Clinton's help on the campaign trail. He looked for ways to distance himself from his president. Clinton wanted nothing more than to help Gore win the presidency but was disillusioned by his vice president's unwillingness to accept his support. The same situational dynamic that fostered his influence during the administration undermined and marginalized that influence by the end of the term. He was so preoccupied with his own election that he was no longer acting as a vice president but rather as a candidate. As a result, he was not involved in

274 / Emerging from the Shadows

the day-to-day decision making in the White House. By the end of the term, the two principals were barely speaking, and their relationship was never as sound as it once was. In fact, any advice Clinton provided Gore was given through an intermediary on the campaign.

Joe Biden's influence seems to have followed a similar trajectory to that of other vice presidents in the modern era. In the initial stages of the administration, Biden's influence was fostered by the close interpersonal relationship that developed between the two principals, as well as their compatible vision for the office. It was also furthered by the institutional dynamic as many Biden loyalists found themselves in key positions in the administration. Rahm Emanuel's departure as chief of staff provided an opportunity for Biden to be one of the chief negotiators for the administration. During this time, he witnessed a great degree of success in helping the president push through his agenda to extend the Bush tax cuts, repeal Don't Ask, Don't Tell, negotiate budget numbers with Republicans, and a host of other issues. Despite the successes, the institutional dynamic was altered once again by the departure of many loyal Biden associates as well as the uncertainty surrounding a potential Biden run in 2016. Biden's actions of trying to meet with donors and not completely standing behind his original campaign assurances placed great stress on his relations in the White House, thus marginalizing his influence even further.

This study is the first of its kind to grapple with, in a more systematic way, the rather ambiguous subject of vice presidential influence. The interpersonal, situational, institutional, and electoral dynamics provide a mechanism by which to understand vice presidential influence and identify those factors that may increase or marginalize said influence. The research demonstrates that vice presidential influence, regardless of the vice president, is malleable and subject to change, given the evolving interpersonal, situational, institutional, and electoral dynamics. As an administration matures, these changes in dynamics may work to advance or marginalize influence, as has been the case of all vice presidents during the modern era.

The vice presidency, unlike any other time in history, has played a central role in the decision-making and policy-making apparatus of the country. Presidents and vice presidents have willingly invested the office with a greater capacity to exercise influence. Rockefeller's vice presidency created the environment from which the Mondale vice presidential model would emerge, serving as the benchmark for all future vice presidents. The careful attention to the selection process, and the compatible vision for the office, enabled Walter Mondale to enjoy unprecedented access and create precedents that enabled influence to be exercised. While the vice presidencies of George H. W. Bush and Dan Quayle did not distinguish themselves as groundbreaking in the sense of expanding vice presidential influence, no regression occurred under their watch, as they followed the precedents established by Mondale. They still exercised influence, however, in a more understated fashion, which was compatible with their respective visions of the office. Al Gore, Dick Cheney, and Joe Biden, the most recent vice presidents, continued to follow the Mondale model, with changes that both followed their visions for the office and the agreements established with their respective presidents. In all instances, the vice presidency was transformed in ways that provided them with unparalleled access, staff integration, and influence. Vice President Cheney's tenure witnessed remarkable influence, which produced an arrangement some scholars arguably referred to as a copresidency. The vice presidency of the modern era represents a break from the vice presidency of the past that once would have been unimaginable. It is no longer the same office that was described in unflattering terms by many of its historic occupants. Having emerged from the shadows, the vice presidency is now an influential and instrumental cog within the machinations of government.

Appendixes

Appendix A: Interviews Conducted

Name	Administration	Position	Date Conducted
Richard Allen	Reagan	National Security Adviser	7-22-2008
Richard Allison	Ford	Assistant to the Vice President	6-17-2008
James Baker	Reagan/H. W. Bush	Chief of Staff/Sec. of Treasury/Sec. of State	6-25-2008
Dan Bartlett	W. Bush	Communications Director	6-24-2010
David Beckwith	H. W. Bush	VP Press Secretary	7-13-2008
David Beier	Clinton	VP Domestic Policy Adviser	4-22-2009
Michael Berman	Carter	VP Legal Counsel and Deputy Chief of Staff	5-14-2008
Paul Brountas	N/A	Dukakis Campaign Chair	4-6-2009
Zbigniew Brzezinski	Carter	National Security Adviser	11-24-2008
Nicholas Calio	H. W. Bush/ W. Bush	Legislative Affairs	8-20-2008
James Cannon	Ford	Domestic Affairs	5-12-2008
Andy Card	W. Bush	Chief of Staff	10-1-2010
Frank Carlucci	Reagan	National Security Adviser	6-5-2008

continued on next page

278 / Emerging from the Shadows

Name	Administration	Position	Date Conducted
Kay Casstevens	Clinton	VP Director of Legislative Affairs	10-8-2008
Dick Cheney	Ford/H. W. Bush/W. Bush	Chief of Staff/Sec. Def./Vice President	12-1-2011
T. Kenneth Cribb	Reagan	Domestic Affairs	6-16-2008
R. Joseph DeSutter	H. W. Bush	VP National Security Adviser	9-19-2008
Robert Douglass	Ford	VP Counsel	6-25-2008
Michael Dukakis	N/A	1988 Presidential Candidate	3-19-2008; 12-3-2008
Al Eisele	Carter	VP Press Secretary	2-20-2008
Geraldine Ferraro	N/A	1984 Vice Presidential Candidate	5-5-2008
Marlin Fitzwater	Reagan/H. W. Bush	Press Secretary	6-2-2008
Ari Fleischer	W. Bush	Press Secretary	5-15-2009
Max Friedersdorf	Ford/Reagan	Legislative Affairs	5-9-2008
Leon Fuerth	Clinton	VP National Security Adviser	4-20-2009
Craig Fuller	Reagan	VP Chief of Staff	4-28-2009
Donald Gips	Clinton	VP Domestic Policy Adviser	No Date
Donald Gregg	Reagan	Deputy Asst to VP for National Security	6-6-2008
Shirley Moore Green	Reagan	VP Acting Chief of Staff	7-2-2008
William J. Gribbin	H. W. Bush	VP Legislative Affairs	No Date
Robert Guttman	H. W. Bush	VP Chief of Staff	9-15-2008
Lawrence Haas	Clinton	VP Director of Communications	12-29-2008
Stephen Hadley	W. Bush	National Security Adviser	11-1-2010
Roger Hooker	Ford	Asst to VP, Congress	5-14-2008

Appendixes / 279

Appendix B: Interviews Cited by Chapter

Interviews Cited in the Introduction

Interview with Dick Cheney. 2011. Conducted by Richard M. Yon. December 1.
Interview with Walter Mondale. 2008. Conducted by Richard M. Yon. February 11.
Interview with Dan Quayle. 2008. Conducted by Richard M. Yon. November 5.

Interviews Cited in Chapter 1

Interview with Dick Cheney. 2011. Conducted by Richard M. Yon. December 1.
Interview with Mack McLarty. 2010. Conducted by Richard M. Yon. May 19
    and June 4.
Interview with Walter Mondale. 2008. Conducted by Richard M. Yon. February 11.
Interview with Dan Quayle. 2008. Conducted by Richard M. Yon. November 5.

Interviews Cited in Chapter 2

Interview with Richard Allison. 2008. Conducted by Richard M. Yon. June 17.
Interview with James Cannon. 2008. Conducted by Richard M. Yon. May 12.
Interview with Dick Cheney. 2011. Conducted by Richard M. Yon. December 1.
Interview with Roger Hooker. 2008. Conducted by Richard M. Yon. May 14.
Interview with Ronald Nessen. 2008. Conducted by Richard M. Yon. May 6.
Interview with Donald Rumsfeld. 2010. Conducted by Richard M. Yon. June 14.
Interview with Brent Scowcroft. 2008. Conducted by Richard M. Yon. May 15.

Interviews Cited in Chapter 3

Interview with Dan Bartlett. 2010. Conducted by Richard M. Yon. June 24.
Interview with Nicholas Calio. 2008. Conducted by Richard M. Yon. August 20.
Interview with Andy Card. 2010. Conducted by Richard M. Yon. October 1.
Interview with Dick Cheney. 2011. Conducted by Richard M. Yon. December 1.
Interview with Dick Cheney. 2012. Conducted by Richard M. Yon. November 2.
Interview with Ari Fleischer. 2009. Conducted by Richard M. Yon. May 15.
Interview with Stephen Hadley. 2010. Conducted by Richard M. Yon. November 1.
Interview with Dana Perino. 2009. Conducted by Richard M. Yon. April 22.
Interview with Colin Powell. 2008. Conducted by Richard M. Yon. June 16.
Interview with Condoleezza Rice. 2010. Conducted by Richard M. Yon. September 21.
Interview with Karl Rove. 2011. Conducted by Richard M. Yon. December 23.
Interview with Donald Rumsfeld. 2010. Conducted by Richard M. Yon. June 14.
Interview with Brent Scowcroft. 2008. Conducted by Richard M. Yon. May 15.

280 / Emerging from the Shadows

INTERVIEWS CITED IN CHAPTER 4

Interview with Richard Allen. 2008. Conducted by Richard M. Yon. July 22.
Interview with James Baker. 2008. Conducted by Richard M. Yon. June 25.
Interview with David Beckwith. 2008. Conducted by Richard M. Yon. July 13.
Interview with David Beier. 2009. Conducted by Richard M. Yon. April 22.
Interview with Zbigniew Brzezinski. 2008. Conducted by Richard M. Yon.
    November 24.
Interview with Nicholas Calio. 2008. Conducted by Richard M. Yon. August 20.
Interview with Frank Carlucci. 2008. Conducted by Richard M. Yon. June 5.
Interview with Kay Casstevens. 2008. Conducted by Richard M. Yon. October 8.
Interview with Dick Cheney. 2011. Conducted by Richard M. Yon. December 1.
Interview with T. Kenneth Cribb, Jr. 2008. Conducted by Richard M. Yon. June 16.
Interview with Joseph DeSutter. 2008. Conducted by Richard M. Yon. September 19.
Interview with Al Eisele. 2008. Conducted by Richard M. Yon. February 20.
Interview with Marlin Fitzwater. 2008. Conducted by Richard M. Yon. June 2.
Interview with Max Friedersdorf. 2008. Conducted by Richard M. Yon. May 9.
Interview with Leon Fuerth. 2009. Conducted by Richard M. Yon. April 20.
Interview with Craig Fuller. 2009. Conducted by Richard M. Yon. April 28.
Interview with Shirley Moore Green. 2008. Conducted by Richard M. Yon. July 2.
Interview with Donald Gregg. 2008. Conducted by Richard M. Yon. June 6.
Interview with Lawrence Haas. 2008. Conducted by Richard M. Yon. December 29.
Interview with Anthony Lake. 2009. Conducted by Richard M. Yon. May 18.
Interview with Joseph Lockhart. 2009. Conducted by Richard M. Yon. May 8.
Interview with Carnes Lord. 2008. Conducted by Richard M. Yon. July 16.
Interview with Mike McCurry. 2009. Conducted by Richard M. Yon. June 8.
Interview with Mack McLarty. 2010. Conducted by Richard M. Yon. May 19
    and June 4.
Interview with Ed Meese. 2008. Conducted by Richard M. Yon. June 17.
Interview with Richard Moe. 2008. Conducted by Richard M. Yon. April 25.
Interview with Walter Mondale. 2008. Conducted by Richard M. Yon. February 11.
Interview with Frank Moore. 2008. Conducted by Richard M. Yon. April 2.
Interview with Dee Dee Myers. 2010. Conducted by Richard M. Yon. February 17.
Interview with Roy Neel. 2008. Conducted by Richard M. Yon. May 6.
Interview with Colin Powell. 2008. Conducted by Richard M. Yon. June 16.
Interview with Dan Quayle. 2008. Conducted by Richard M. Yon. November 5.
Interview with Carol Rasco. 2009. Conducted by Richard M. Yon. June 5.
Interview with Brent Scowcroft. 2008. Conducted by Richard M. Yon. May 15.
Interview with Greg Simon. 2009. Conducted by Richard M. Yon. February 4.
Interview with Sam Skinner. 2008. Conducted by Richard M. Yon. August 13.
Interview with William Smith. 2008. Conducted by Richard M. Yon. April 26.
Interview with John Sununu. 2008. Conducted by Richard M. Yon. October 20.

Interview with Peter Teeley. 2008. Conducted by Richard M. Yon. October 22.
Interview with Chase Untermeyer. 2010. Conducted by Richard M. Yon. July 26.
Interview with Clayton Yeutter. 2008. Conducted by Richard M. Yon. October 1.

INTERVIEWS CITED IN THE CONCLUSION

Interview with Dan Bartlett. 2010. Conducted by Richard M. Yon. June 24.
Interview with James Cannon. 2008. Conducted by Richard M. Yon. May 12.
Interview with Andy Card. 2010. Conducted by Richard M. Yon. October 1.
Interview with Dick Cheney. 2011. Conducted by Richard M. Yon. December 1.
Interview with Ari Fleischer. 2009. Conducted by Richard M. Yon. May 15.
Interview with Stephen Hadley. 2010. Conducted by Richard M. Yon. November 1.
Interview with Roger Hooker. 2008. Conducted by Richard M. Yon. May 14.
Interview with Walter Mondale. 2008. Conducted by Richard M. Yon. February 11.
Interview with Dana Perino. 2009. Conducted by Richard M. Yon. April 22.
Interview with Dan Quayle. 2008. Conducted by Richard M. Yon. November 5.
Interview with Condoleezza Rice. 2010. Conducted by Richard M. Yon. September 21.
Interview with Karl Rove. 2011. Conducted by Richard M. Yon. December 23.
Interview with Donald Rumsfeld. 2010. Conducted by Richard M. Yon. June 14.

Notes

Introduction

1. Michael Nelson, *A Heartbeat Away: Report of the Twentieth Century Fund Task Force on the Vice Presidency* (New York: Priority Press), 4; Elliot A. Rosen, "'Not Worth a Pitcher of Warm Piss': John Nance Garner as Vice President," in *At the President's Side: The Vice Presidency in the Twentieth Century*, ed. Timothy Walch (Columbia: University of Missouri Press, 1997), 45.

2. Rosen, "'Not Worth a Pitcher,'" 53.

3. Joel K. Goldstein, *The Modern American Vice Presidency: The Transformation of a Political Institution* (Princeton, NJ: Princeton University Press, 1982), 306.

4. Eli E. Nobleman, "The Delegation of Presidential Functions: Constitutional and Legal Aspects," *Annals of the American Academy of Political and Social Sciences* 307 (September 1956): 135.

5. Nobleman, "Delegation of Presidential Functions," 135–36.

6. Nobleman, "Delegation of Presidential Functions," 142.

7. Richard E. Neustadt, "Vice Presidents as National Leaders: Reflections Past, Present, and Future," in *At the President's Side: The Vice Presidency in the Twentieth Century*, ed. Timothy Walch (Columbia: University of Missouri Press, 1997), 186; Goldstein, *Modern American Vice Presidency*, 174.

8. Goldstein, *Modern American Vice Presidency*, 151, 301.

9. Memo from Nicholas deB. Katzenbach, "Participation by the Vice President in the Affairs of the Executive Branch" (Washington, DC: Office of Legal Counsel, 1961), 1.

10. Goldstein, *Modern American Vice Presidency*, 140–41, 184; Irving G. Williams, *The American Vice-Presidency: New Look* (Garden City, NY: Doubleday, 1954), 69.

11. Williams, *American Vice-Presidency*, 69; Goldstein, *Modern American Vice Presidency*, 167; Memo from Nicholas deB. Katzenbach, "Participation by the Vice President" (Washington, DC: Office of Legal Counsel, 1961), 7.

12. Goldstein, *Modern American Vice Presidency*, 172–73.

284 / Notes to Chapter 1

13. Paul C. Light, *Vice-Presidential Power: Advice and Influence in the White House* (Baltimore, MD: Johns Hopkins University Press, 1984).

14. Light, *Vice-Presidential Power*.

15. Jody C. Baumgartner, *The American Vice Presidency Reconsidered* (Westport, CT: Praeger, 2006), 109–11.

16. Richard Yon, "The Biden Vice Presidency: Perpetuating Influence or Restoring Historical Insignificance?," in *The Obama Presidency*, eds. Robert P. Watson, Jack Covarrubias, Tom Lansford, and Douglas M. Brattebo (New York: SUNY Press, 2012).

17. Yon, "Biden Vice Presidency."

18. Yon, "The Biden Vice Presidency"; Nelson, *A Heartbeat Away*.

19. Yon, "The Biden Vice Presidency: Perpetuating Influence or Restoring Historical Insignificance?"

20. Yon, "The Biden Vice Presidency."

21. George C. Edwards, "Presidential Influence in Congress: If We Ask the Wrong Questions, We Get the Wrong Answers," *American Journal of Political Science* 35 (1991): 724–29.

22. E. E. Schattschneider, *The Semisovereign People* (New York: Holt, Rinehart & Winston, 1960).

23. Michael Turner, *The Vice President as Policy Maker: Rockefeller in the Ford White House* (Westport, CT: Greenwood Press, 1982).

24. See Appendix A.

25. David McCullough, *Truman* (New York: Simon & Schuster, 1992).

26. Bradley H. Patterson Jr., *The White House Staff: Inside the West Wing and Beyond* (Washington, DC: Brookings Institution Press, 2000).

Chapter 1

1. David Willer, Michael J. Lovaglia, and Barry Markovsky, "Power and Influence: A Theoretical Bridge," *Social Forces* 76 (1997): 571.

2. Andreas Dur and Dirk De Bievre, "The Question of Interest Group Influence," *Journal of Public Policy* 27 (2007): 2.

3. Willer, Lovaglia, and Markovsky, "Power and Influence: A Theoretical Bridge," 571.

4. Willer, Lovaglia, and Markovsky, "Power and Influence," 572.

5. Willer, Lovaglia, and Markovsky, "Power and Influence," 573, 592.

6. Dennis H. Wrong, *Power: Its Forms, Bases, and Uses* (New Brunswick, NJ: Transaction Publishers, 1980).

7. Wrong, *Power: Its Forms, Bases, and Uses*; Phillip G. Zimbardo and Michael R. Leippe, *The Psychology of Attitude Change and Social Influence* (New York: McGraw-Hill, 1991), 2.

Notes to Chapter 1 / 285

8. Robert Bierstedt, "An Analysis of Social Power," *American Sociological Review* 15 (1950): 161–84.

9. Talcott Parsons, "On the Concept of Political Power," *Proceedings of the American Philosophical Society* 107 (1963): 338.

10. Robert J. Mokken and Frans N. Stokman, "Power and Influence and Political Phenomena" in *Power and Political Theory: Some European Perspectives*, ed. Brian Barry (Somerset, NJ: John Wiley, 1976), 37.

11. Charles Lemert, *Social Theory: The Multicultural and Classic Readings* (Boulder, CO: Westview Press, 2004).

12. Donald E. Comstock, "Dimensions of Influence in Organizations," *Pacific Sociological Review* 23 (1980): 68; Robb Willer, Lisa Troyer, and Michael J. Lovaglia, "Influence over Observers of Structural Power: An Experimental Investigation," *Sociological Quarterly* 46 (2005): 264.

13. Comstock, "Dimensions of Influence in Organizations," 70.

14. Comstock, "Dimensions of Influence in Organizations," 68.

15. Christopher Kenny and Eric Jenner, "Direction versus Proximity in the Social Influence Process," *Political Behavior* 30 (2008): 74.

16. Robert Huckfeldt and John Sprague, "Discussant Effects on Vote Choice: Intimacy, Structure, and Interdependence," *Journal of Politics* 53 (1991): 125.

17. Kenny and Jenner, "Direction versus Proximity," 76.

18. Virginia W. Smith, "How Interest Groups Influence Legislators, *Social Work* 24 (1979): 236.

19. Comstock, "Dimensions of Influence in Organizations," 70.

20. Dur and De Bievre, "The Question of Interest Group Influence," 5.

21. Kimberly H. Conger, "A Matter of Context: Christian Right Influence in U.S. State Republican Politics," *State Politics & Policy Quarterly* 10 (2010): 254.

22. Michael Nelson, *A Heartbeat Away: Report of the Twentieth Century Fund Task Force on the Vice Presidency* (Washington, DC: CQ Press, 1988); Paul C. Light, *Vice-Presidential Power: Advice and Influence in the White House* (Baltimore, MD: Johns Hopkins University Press, 1984); Joel K. Goldstein, *The Modern American Vice Presidency: The Transformation of a Political Institution* (Princeton, NJ: Princeton University Press, 1982); Jody C. Baumgartner, *The American Vice Presidency Reconsidered* (Westport, CT: Praeger, 2006); Walter Mondale, in conversation with the author, February 2008; Cheney, in conversation with the author; Dan Quayle, in conversation with the author, November 2008.

23. Mokken and Stokman, "Power and Influence and Political Phenomena."

24. Willer, Lovaglia, and Markovsky, "Power and Influence: A Theoretical Bridge," 573.

25. Willer, Lovaglia, and Markovsky, "Power and Influence: A Theoretical Bridge," 572.

26. Kenny and Jenner, "Direction versus Proximity," 74.

286 / Notes to Chapter 1

27. Willer, Troyer, and Lovaglia, "Influence over Observers of Structural Power," 264.

28. Stephen Skowronek, *The Politics Presidents Make: Leadership from John Adams to George Bush* (Cambridge, MA: Harvard University Press, 1993).

29. Skowronek, *The Politics Presidents Make*, 30.

30. Kenny and Jenner, "Direction versus Proximity," 76.

31. Dennis W. Gleiber and Steven A. Shull, "Presidential Influence in the Policymaking Process," *Western Political Quarterly* 45 (1992): 459.

32. Alexander Baturo and Johan A. Elkink, "Office or Officeholder? Regime Deinstitutionalization and Sources of Individual Political Influence," *Journal of Politics* 76 (2014): 859.

33. Dur and De Bievre, "The Question of Interest Group Influence," 6.

34. James David Barber, *The Presidential Character: Predicting Performance in the White House* (Hoboken, NJ: Prentice Hall, 1992).

35. Barber, *The Presidential Character*.

36. Barber, *The Presidential Character*.

37. Barber, *The Presidential Character*, 4.

38. Stephen F. Hayes, *Cheney: The Untold Story of America's Most Powerful and Controversial Vice President* (New York: HarperCollins, 2007); Joel K. Goldstein, "The Contemporary Presidency: Cheney, Vice Presidential Power, and the War on Terror," *Presidential Studies Quarterly* 40 (2010): 102–39.

39. Conger, "A Matter of Context," 250.

40. E. E. Schattschneider, *The Semisovereign People* (New York: Holt, Rinehart & Winston, 1960), 68.

41. Kimberly Maslin-Wicks, "Two Types of Presidential Influence in Congress," *Presidential Studies Quarterly* 28 (1998): 108.

42. Maslin-Wicks, "Two Types of Presidential Influence," 115.

43. William H. Riker, *The Art of Political Manipulation* (New Haven, CT: Yale University Press, 1986), ix.

44. Goldstein, "The Contemporary Presidency," 109.

45. Goldstein, "The Contemporary Presidency," 109.

46. Joel K. Goldstein, "The Rising Power of the Modern Vice Presidency," *Presidential Studies Quarterly* 38 (2008): 374–89.

47. Joel K. Goldstein, *The White House Vice Presidency: The Path to Significance, Mondale to Biden* (Lawrence: University Press of Kansas, 2016).

48. Jules Witcover, *Crapshoot: Rolling the Dice on the Vice Presidency* (New York: Crown, 1992).

49. Light, *Vice-Presidential Power*.

50. Robert Caro, *The Passage of Power: The Years of Lyndon Johnson* (New York: Knopf, 2013).

51. Danny M. Adkinson, "The Electoral Significance of the Vice Presidency," *Presidential Studies Quarterly* 12, no. 3 (1982): 331.

Notes to Chapter 1 / 287

52. Nelson W. Polsby and Aaron B. Wildavsky, *Presidential Elections: Strategies of American Electoral Politics* (New York: Charles Scribner's, 1968).

53. Ed Hornick and Josh Levs, "What Obama Promised Biden," CNN, December 11, 2008, http://www.cnn.com/2008/POLITICS/12/21/transition.wrap/index.html?eref=ib_to. Date Accessed 12/10/10.

54. Hornick and Josh Levs, "What Obama Promised Biden."

55. Witcover, *Crapshoot: Rolling the Dice*, 196–97.

56. Witcover, *Crapshoot: Rolling the Dice; Alexander Haig, Caveat: Realism, Reagan, and Foreign Policy* (New York: Macmillan, 1984).

57. Yon, "The Biden Vice Presidency."

58. Yon, "The Biden Vice Presidency."

59. Cheney, in conversation with the author.

60. Walter Mondale, in conversation with the author, February 2008.

61. Mack McLarty, in conversation with the author, May and June 2010.

62. Barton Gellman, *Angler: The Cheney Vice Presidency* (New York: Penguin, 2008).

63. Cheney, in conversation with the author.

64. Cheney, in conversation with the author.

65. James P. Pfiffner, "The President's Chief of Staff: Lessons Learned," *Presidential Studies Quarterly* 23, no. 1 (1993): 77–102; Samuel Kernell and Samuel L. Popkin, *Chief of Staff: Twenty-five Years of Managing the Presidency* (Los Angeles, CA: University of California Press, 1986).

66. David B. Cohen, "From the Fabulous Baker Boys to the Master of Disaster: The White House Chief of Staff in the Reagan and G. H. W. Bush Administrations," *Presidential Studies Quarterly* 32, no. 3 (2002): 463–83.

67. Charles E. Walcott, Shirley Anne Warshaw, and Stephen J. Wayne, "The Chief of Staff," *Presidential Studies Quarterly* 31, no. 3 (2001): 464–89.

68. Kernell and Popkin, *Chief of Staff: Twenty-five Years of Managing the Presidency*, 174–75.

69. Kernell and Popkin, *Chief of Staff*, 175.

70. Ronald Reagan, *Ronald Reagan: An American Life* (New York: Simon and Schuster, 1990).

71. Pfiffner, "The President's Chief of Staff: Lessons Learned."

72. Cohen, "From the Fabulous Baker Boys to the Master of Disaster: The White House Chief of Staff in the Reagan and G. H. W. Bush Administrations."

73. John P. Burke, *The Institutional Presidency: Organizing and Managing the White House From FDR to Clinton* (Baltimore, MD: Johns Hopkins University Press, 2000).

74. Reagan, *Ronald Reagan: An American Life*, 537.

75. Bob Woodward, *Obama's Wars* (New York: Simon & Schuster, 2010).

76. Richard Yon, "The Biden Vice Presidency: Perpetuating Influence or Restoring Historical Insignificance?," in *The Obama Presidency*, eds. Robert P.

288 / Notes to Chapter 1

Watson, Jack Covarrubias, Tom Lansford, and Douglas M. Brattebo (Albany: SUNY Press, 2012).

77. Cheney, in conversation with the author.

78. John P. Burke, *Honest Broker? The National Security Advisor and Presidential Decision Making* (College Station, TX: Texas A&M University Press, 2009), 5; Cohen, "From the Fabulous Baker Boys to the Master of Disaster: The White House Chief of Staff in the Reagan and G. H. W. Bush Administrations."

79. Pfiffner, "The President's Chief of Staff: Lessons Learned," 86.

80. David Gergen, *Eyewitness to Power: The Essence of Leadership* (New York: Simon & Schuster, 2000), 180.

81. Pfiffner, "The President's Chief of Staff: Lessons Learned."

82. David B. Cohen and Charles E. Walcott, "Serving Our Country in Historic Times: The Chiefs of Staff in the George W. Bush White House" (paper presented at the Annual Meeting of the American Political Science Association, Washington DC, September 2–5, 2010), 3.

83. David B. Cohen and George A. Krause, "Presidents, Chiefs of Staff, and White House Organizational Behavior: Survey Evidence from the Reagan and Bush Administrations," *Presidential Studies Quarterly* 30, no. 3 (2000): 421–42.

84. David B. Cohen and Charles E. Walcott, "Serving Our Country in Historic Times: The Chiefs of Staff in the George W. Bush White House" (paper presented at the Annual Meeting of the American Political Science Association, Washington DC, September 2–5, 2010).

85. Cheney, in conversation with the author.

86. Burke, *Institutional Presidency: Organizing and Managing the White House From FDR to Clinton.*

87. Stephen Hess, *Organizing the Presidency* (Washington DC: Brookings Institution Press, 2002).

88. Bradley H. Patterson, *White House Staff: Inside the West Wing and Beyond* (Washington, DC: Brookings Institution Press, 2000), 301.

89. Burke, *Institutional Presidency*, 23; Patterson, *White House Staff*, 134).

90. Patterson, *White House Staff*, 301; Light, *Vice-Presidential Power: Advice and Influence in the White House.*

91. "Fiscal Year 2020 Congressional Budget Submission," 116th Congress, *Congressional Record* (2020).

92. Light, *Vice-Presidential Power.*

93. Irving G. Williams, *The American Vice-Presidency: New Look* (Garden City, NY: Doubleday, 1976), 179.

94. Goldstein, *The Modern American Vice Presidency: The Transformation of a Political Institution*, 68.

95. Polsby and Wildavsky, *Presidential Elections: Strategies of American Electoral Politics.*

96. Baumgartner, *American Vice Presidency Reconsidered*, 56.

Notes to Chapter 2 / 289

97. Walter Mondale, in conversation with the author, February 2008.

98. Jimmy Carter, *Keeping Faith: Memoirs of a President* (New York: Bantam Books, 1982).

99. Goldstein, *Modern American Vice Presidency*, 100.

100. Baumgartner, *American Vice Presidency Reconsidered*, 142.

101. *American Vice Presidency Reconsidered*, 142.

Chapter 2

1. Paul C. Light, *Vice-Presidential Power: Advice and Influence in the White House* (Baltimore, MD: Johns Hopkins University Press, 1984).

2. Dick Cheney, in conversation with the author, December 2011.

3. Joseph E. Persico, *The Imperial Rockefeller* (New York: Simon and Schuster, 1982).

4. Persico, *Imperial Rockefeller*.

5. Persico, *Imperial Rockefeller*.

6. Persico, *Imperial Rockefeller*.

7. Gerald Ford, in discussion with Trevor Armbrister, 1977; Nelson Rockefeller, in discussion with Bob Hartmann, December 1977.

8. Nelson Rockefeller, in discussion with Bob Hartmann, December 1977.

9. Rockefeller, in discussion with Bob Hartmann.

10. Persico, *The Imperial Rockefeller*.

11. Rockefeller, in discussion with Bob Hartmann.

12. Rumsfeld, in conversation with the author.

13. Jules Witcover, *Very Strange Bedfellows: The Short and Unhappy Marriage of Richard Nixon and Spiro Agnew* (New York: Public Affairs, 2007).

14. Gerald Ford, *A Time to Heal: The Autobiography of Gerald R. Ford* (New York: Harper and Row, 1979).

15. John R. Alford, "We're All in This Together: The Decline of Trust in Government, 1958–1996," in *What Is It about Government that American's Dislike?*, eds. John R. Hibbing and Elizabeth Theiss-Morse (New York: Cambridge University Press, 2001).

16. Rockefeller, in discussion with Bob Hartmann.

17. Rockefeller, in discussion with Bob Hartmann.

18. Persico, *The Imperial Rockefeller*.

19. Persico, *Imperial Rockefeller*.

20. Rockefeller, in discussion with Bob Hartmann.

21. Rockefeller, in discussion with Bob Hartmann.

22. Jerald F. terHorst, *Gerald Ford and the Future of the Presidency* (New York: Harper Collins, 1974).

23. Ford, in discussion with Trevor Armbrister.

290 / Notes to Chapter 2

24. Roger Hooker, in discussion with the author, May 2008.

25. Rockefeller, in discussion with Bob Hartmann.

26. Persico, *Imperial Rockefeller*.

27. James Cannon, "Gerald R. Ford and Nelson A. Rockefeller," in *At the President's Side: The Vice Presidency in the Twentieth Century*, eds. Timothy Walch (Columbia: University of Missouri Press, 1997).

28. Jody C. Baumgartner, *The American Vice Presidency Reconsidered* (Westport, CT: Praeger, 2006).

29. Persico, *Imperial Rockefeller*.

30. Persico, *Imperial Rockefeller*.

31. Ford, in discussion with Trevor Armbrister.

32. James Cannon, *Time and Chance: Gerald Ford's Appointment with History* (Ann Arbor: University of Michigan Press, 1994), 367.

33. Remarks of the President, "Remarks of the President upon His Announcing Nelson Rockefeller as Vice President-Designate," dated August 20, 1974, Box 2689, WHCF, Gerald R. Ford Library; *Cannon, Time and Chance: Gerald Ford's Appointment with History*, 367; Dick Cheney, *In My Time: A Personal and Political Memoir* (New York: Threshold), 68; Ford, *A Time to Heal*, 142–43; Gerald R. Ford, in discussion with Hugh Morrow, 1979.

34. Ford, *A Time to Heal*, 142.

35. Tabulations and Summaries for VP, "Vice Presidential Vacancy, 1974 Tabulations and Summaries for Suggestions (1)," dated 1974, Box 21, Robert T. Hartmann Files, 1974–1977, Gerald R. Ford Library.

36. Tabulations and Summaries for VP.

37. Ford, in discussion with Trevor Armbrister.

38. Cannon, *Time and Chance*, 367.

39. Cannon, "Gerald R. Ford and Nelson A. Rockefeller," 138.

40. Ford, in discussion with Trevor Armbrister.

41. Cheney, *In My Time*, 68.

42. Ford, *A Time to Heal*, 143.

43. Cannon, *Time and Chance*, 423.

44. Michael Turner, *The Vice President as Policy Maker: Rockefeller in the Ford White House* (Westport, CT: Greenwood Press, 1982), xv.

45. Cheney, *In My Time* (New York: Threshold Editions, 2011), 68.

46. Richard Allison, in discussion with the author, June 2008.

47. Ronald Nessen, in discussion with the author, May 2008; Cheney, in conversation with the author.

48. Gerald R. Ford, in discussion with Hugh Morrow, 1979.

49. Ford, in discussion with Hugh Morrow.

50. Ford, *A Time to Heal*, 144.

51. Cannon, *Time and Chance*, 367.

52. Richard Reeves, *A Ford, Not a Lincoln* (New York: Harcourt Brace Jovanovich, 1975), 149.

Notes to Chapter 2 / 291

53. Ford, *A Time to Heal*, 143.

54. Ford, in discussion with Trevor Armbrister.

55. Nelson Rockefeller, in discussion with Bob Hartmann, December 1977.

56. Ford, in discussion with Hugh Morrow.

57. Lou Cannon, "Rockefeller Aiming at Major Role in Administration," *Washington Post*, February 2, 1975.

58. Rockefeller, in discussion with Mike Turner.

59. Ford, in discussion with Trevor Armbrister.

60. Reeves, *A Ford, Not a Lincoln*, 149.

61. Ford, *A Time to Heal*.

62. Reeves, *A Ford, Not a Lincoln*, 149); Cannon, *Time and Chance*, 367; Ford, in discussion with Trevor Armbrister.

63. Ford, *A Time to Heal*.

64. Persico, *Imperial Rockefeller*.

65. Turner, *Vice President as Policy Maker*.

66. Rockefeller, in discussion with Bob Hartmann.

67. Ford, *A Time to Heal*.

68. Turner, *Vice President as Policy Maker*, 45.

69. Turner, *The Vice President as Policy Maker*, 45.

70. Ford, in discussion with Trevor Armbrister; Ford, *A Time to Heal*.

71. Cannon, "Rockefeller Aiming at Major Role."

72. Cannon, "Rockefeller Aiming at Major Role."

73. Rockefeller, in discussion with Mike Turner.

74. Richard Allison, in discussion with the author, June 2008.

75. Remarks of Press Secretary Ronald H. Nessen, "Rockefeller Role in the Ford Administration," dated December 27, 1974, Box 2, James Cannon Paper (Domestic Council), Gerald R. Ford Library.

76. Cannon, "Rockefeller Aiming at Major Role in Administration."

77. Rockefeller, in discussion with Bob Hartmann, December 1977.

78. Cannon, "Rockefeller Aiming at Major Role in Administration."

79. Rockefeller, in discussion with Bob Hartmann, December 1977.

80. Nessen, "Rockefeller Role in the Ford Administration"; Cannon, "Rockefeller Aiming at Major Role."

81. Baumgartner, *American Vice Presidency Reconsidered*.

82. Rockefeller, in discussion with Mike Turner.

83. Ford, in discussion with Trevor Armbrister.

84. Rockefeller, in discussion with Trevor Armbrister.

85. Cheney, *In My Time*, 80.

86. Rockefeller, in discussion with Trevor Armbrister.

87. Jules Witcover, "Rocky to Speak Out if He Disagrees with Ford," *Washington Post*, December 1974.

88. Witcover, "Rocky to Speak Out."

89. Cheney, *In My Time*; Cheney, in conversation with the author.

292 / Notes to Chapter 2

90. Cannon, "Rockefeller Aiming at Major Role"; Gerald R. Ford Library, "Executive Order 11828," dated January 4, 1975, folder "Rockefeller Role in the Ford Administration," Box 2, James Cannon Papers (Domestic Council), Gerald R. Ford Library.

91. Turner, *Vice President as Policy Maker*, 148.

92. Turner, *Vice President as Policy Maker*.

93. Ford, *A Time to Heal*, 229.

94. Ford, *A Time to Heal*, 229.

95. Ford, *A Time to Heal*, 230.

96. Ford, *A Time to Heal*, 230.

97. Gerald R. Ford Library, "Nelson Rockefeller to Gerald Ford," dated June 19, 1975, folder "Vice President's Memos for the President (1)," Box 6, Dorothy E. Downton Files, 1974–1977, at Gerald R. Ford Library.

98. Gerald R. Ford Library, "Nelson Rockefeller to Gerald Ford."

99. Gerald R. Ford Library, "Nelson Rockefeller to Gerald Ford."

100. Rockefeller, in discussion with Bob Hartmann.

101. Rockefeller, in discussion with Hugh Morrow.

102. Rockefeller, in discussion with Bob Hartmann; Rockefeller, in discussion with Mike Turner.

103. Rockefeller, in discussion with Mike Turner.

104. Turner, *The Vice President as Policy Maker*, 147.

105. Turner, *The Vice President as Policy Maker*, 147.

106. Ford, *A Time to Heal*, 325.

107. Ford, in discussion with Hugh Morrow.

108. Turner, *Vice President as Policy Maker*, 148.

109. Turner, *Vice President as Policy Maker*, 148.

110. Turner, *Vice President as Policy Maker*, 148.

111. Turner, *Vice President as Policy Maker*, 148–49.

112. Rockefeller Archive Center, "Report, Murphy Commission," dated January 5, 1977, Rockefeller Family Collection, Record Group 26, Series 19, Box 6, Folder 120, Rockefeller Archive Center.

113. Rockefeller Archive Center, "Report, Murphy Commission."

114. Rockefeller Archive Center, "Report, Murphy Commission."

115. Rockefeller Archive Center, "Report, Murphy Commission."

116. Commission on the Organization of the Government for the Conduct of Foreign Policy, n.d.

117. Commission on the Organization of the Government.

118. Commission on the Organization of the Government.

119. Commission on the Organization of the Government.

120. Commission on the Organization of the Government.

121. Commission on the Organization of the Government for the Conduct of Foreign Policy.

Notes to Chapter 2 / 293

122. Commission on the Organization of the Government.

123. Commission on the Organization of the Government for the Conduct of Foreign Policy.

124. Commission on the Organization of the Government.

125. Commission on the Organization of the Government.

126. Cannon, "Rockefeller Aiming at Major Role."

127. Gerald R. Ford Library, "Press Conference with Nelson Rockefeller," dated November 6, 1975, folder "VP 10/75–11/75," Box 12, James Cannon Papers (Domestic Council), at Gerald R. Ford Library.

128. Ford, in discussion with Trevor Armbrister.

129. Rockefeller Archive Center, "Agenda Meetings," dated December 27, 1974 to September 10, 1975, Rockefeller Family Collection, Record Group 26, Series 18, Volume 27: Meetings with the President December 27, 1974 to September 10, 1975, at Rockefeller Archive Center; Gerald R. Ford Library, "Agenda Meetings," dated June 19, 1975 to January 21, 1976, folders "Vice President's Memos for the President (1) and Vice President's Memos for the President (4)," Box 6, Dorothy E. Downton Files, 1974–1977, at Gerald R. Ford Library.

130. Dom Bonafede, "White House Report/Rockefeller's Role Fails to Match Ford Promise," *National Journal*, August 23, 1975.

131. Ford, *A Time to Heal*.

132. Persico, *Imperial Rockefeller*.

133. Gerald R. Ford Library, "Weekly Briefing/Report for the Vice President," dated August 9, 1974 to March 31, 1975, filed "MC 4-9 Weekly Briefing/Report for the Vice President 8/9/74–3/31/75," Box 21, WHCF, Subject File, MC: Meetings-Conferences, at Gerald R. Ford Library.

134. Gerald R. Ford Library, "Presidential Meetings with House Members" dated January 31, 1975 to August 4, 1976, folder "Howe, Jon," Box 1515, WHCF, Name File, Howe, Jon, Gerald R. Ford Library, folders "Presidential Meetings with House Members, January 1975; February 1975; March 1975; April 1975; June 1975; July 1975; April–June 1976; July 1976–January 1977," Box 6, Max L. Friedersdorf Files, 1974–1977, Gerald R. Ford Library; Gerald R. Ford Library, "Presidential Meetings with Senate" dated January 27, 1975 to September 6, 1976, folders "Presidential Meetings with Senate Members, January 1975; February 1975; September 1975; March–December 1976," Box 7, Max L. Friedersdorf Files, 1974–1977, at Gerald R. Ford Library; Gerald R. Ford Library, "Republican Leadership Meetings" dated January 14, 1975 to August 5, 1976, folders "Republican Leadership Meetings, January–March 1975; April–August 1975; September–December 1975; January–April 1976; May–December 1976," Box 8, Max L. Friedersdorf Files, at Gerald R. Ford Library.

135. Rockefeller Archive Center, "Meetings with Congressional Leaders," dated January 1975 to September 1975; October 1976 to June 1976, folders 290: "Meetings with Congressional Leaders, January–September 1975 and 290.1: Meet-

294 / Notes to Chapter 2

ings with Congressional Leaders, October–June 1976," Box 11, Rockefeller Family Collection, Record Group 26, Series 19, Rockefeller Archive Center.

136. Gerald R. Ford Library, "Memo, Jeanne W. Davis to Jon Howe," dated January 16, 1976, folder "Howe, Jon," Box 1515, WHCF, Name File, Howe, Jon, Gerald R. Ford Library.

137. Gerald R. Ford Library, "Memo, James Cannon to Nelson Rockefeller," dated March 5, 1975, folder "Vice Presidential Memoranda, March 5–20, 1975," Box 86, James Cannon Files, at Gerald R. Ford Library.

138. Gerald R. Ford Library, "Memo, James Cannon to Nelson Rockefeller," dated April 14, 1975, folder "Vice Presidential Memoranda, April 1–21, 1975," Box 86, James Cannon Files, at Gerald R. Ford Library.

139. Gerald R. Ford Library, "Memo, James Cannon to Nelson Rockefeller," dated April 23, 1975, folder "Vice Presidential Memoranda, April 22–30, 1975," Box 86, James Cannon Files, at Gerald R. Ford Library.

140. Gerald R. Ford Library, "Memo, Spofford Canfield to Nelson Rockefeller through Jon Howe," dated February 4, 1976, folder "Howe, Jon," Box 1515, WHCF, Name File, Howe, Jon, at Gerald R. Ford Library.

141. Gerald R. Ford Library, "Memo, Spofford Canfield to Nelson Rockefeller."

142. Gerald R. Ford Library, "Memo, Spofford Canfield to Nelson Rockefeller."

143. Gerald R. Ford Library, "Memo, Jeanne W. Davis to Jon Howe," dated August 8, 1975, folder "Howe, Jon," Box 1515, WHCF, Name File, Howe, Jon, at Gerald R. Ford Library.

144. Gerald R. Ford Library, "Memo, Tom Cantrell to Nelson Rockefeller," dated January 8, 1975, folder "Rockefeller Role in the Ford Admin.," Box 2, James Cannon Papers (Domestic Council), at Gerald R. Ford Library.

145. Ford, *A Time to Heal*, 228–29.

146. Ford, *A Time to Heal*, 228–29.

147. Turner, *Vice President as Policy Maker*.

148. Turner, *Vice President as Policy Maker*.

149. Turner, *Vice President as Policy Maker*, 87.

150. Turner, *Vice President as Policy Maker*, 87.

151. Turner, *Vice President as Policy Maker*, 87.

152. Turner, *Vice President as Policy Maker*, 87.

153. Turner, *Vice President as Policy Maker*, 87.

154. Rockefeller, in discussion with Mike Turner 1977.

155. Turner, *Vice President as Policy Maker*, 94.

156. Turner, *Vice President as Policy Maker*, 94.

157. Turner, *Vice President as Policy Maker*, 94.

158. Turner, *Vice President as Policy Maker*, 94.

159. Turner, *Vice President as Policy Maker*, 94.

160. Turner, *Vice President as Policy Maker*, 97.

161. Rockefeller, in discussion with Trevor Armbrister.

162. Rockefeller, in discussion with Trevor Armbrister.
163. Rockefeller, in discussion with Trevor Armbrister.
164. Turner, *Vice President as Policy Maker*, 115–17.
165. Ford, A Time to Heal.
166. Turner, *Vice President as Policy Maker*, 115–17.
167. Turner, *Vice President as Policy Maker*, 115–17.
168. Turner, *Vice President as Policy Maker*, 115–17.
169. Turner, *Vice President as Policy Maker*, 117.
170. Turner, *Vice President as Policy Maker*, 117.
171. Donald Rumsfeld n.d., in discussion with Trevor Armbrister.
172. Donald Rumsfeld, in conversation with the author, June 2010.
173. Gerald Ford, in discussion with Trevor Armbrister.
174. Gerald Ford, in discussion with Trevor Armbrister.
175. Rockefeller, in discussion with Trevor Armbrister.
176. Donald Rumsfeld, in conversation with the author.
177. Ford, in discussion with Hugh Morrow.
178. Ford, in discussion with Trevor Armbrister.
179. Rockefeller, in discussion with Mike Turner.
180. Turner, *Vice President as Policy Maker*.
181. Cannon, "Gerald R. Ford and Nelson A. Rockefeller," 141.
182. Turner, *The Vice President as Policy Maker*, 169.
183. Turner, *The Vice President as Policy Maker*, 118.
184. Turner, *The Vice President as Policy Maker*, 121.
185. Turner, *The Vice President as Policy Maker*, 121.
186. Turner, *The Vice President as Policy Maker*, 121.
187. Turner, *The Vice President as Policy Maker*, 121.
188. Turner, *The Vice President as Policy Maker*, 121.
189. Turner, *The Vice President as Policy Maker*, 122.
190. Turner, *The Vice President as Policy Maker*, 157.
191. Turner, *The Vice President as Policy Maker*, 165.
192. Rumsfeld, in conversation with the author.
193. Gellman, *Duty: Memoirs of a Secretary at War*.
194. Gellman, *Duty: Memoirs of a Secretary at War*.
195. Gellman, *Duty: Memoirs of a Secretary at War*.
196. Gellman, *Duty: Memoirs of a Secretary at War*.
197. Cheney, in conversation with the author.
198. Cheney, in conversation with the author.
199. Turner, *Vice President as Policy Maker*.
200. Turner, *Vice President as Policy Maker*, 48.
201. Turner, *Vice President as Policy Maker*.
202. Turner, *Vice President as Policy Maker*, 46–47.
203. Rockefeller, in discussion with Bob Hartmann 1977.

196 / Notes to Chapter 2

204. Turner, *Vice President as Policy Maker*, 47.

205. Turner, *Vice President as Policy Maker*, 47.

206. Turner, *Vice President as Policy Maker*, 47.

207. Cannon, "Rockefeller Aiming at Major Role."

208. Rockefeller, in discussion with Trevor Armbrister; Ford, *A Time to Heal*.

209. Ford, 234–35.

210. Turner, *Vice President as Policy Maker*.

211. Gerald R. Ford Library, "Memo, Jack Veneman to Jim Cannon," dated January 20, 1975, folder "Domestic Council—Vice President's Role, 1/75–12/75," Box 3, Richard Cheney Files, 1974–77, at Gerald R. Ford Library.

212. Rockefeller, in discussion with Bob Hartmann; Ford, *A Time to Heal*.

213. Ford, *A Time to Heal*, 234–35.

214. Rumsfeld, n.d., in discussion with Trevor Armbrister.

215. Rockefeller, in discussion with Bob Hartmann.

216. Rockefeller, in discussion with Bob Hartmann.

217. Rockefeller, in discussion with Bob Hartmann.

218. Ford, *A Time to Heal*, 234–35.

219. Ford, *A Time to Heal*, 234–35.

220. Rumsfeld, in conversation with the author.

221. Brent Scowcroft, in discussion with the author, May 2012.

222. Ford, *A Time to Heal*.

223. Gerald R. Ford Library, "Memo, Jack Veneman to Jim Cannon," dated April 18, 1975, folder "VP 3/75–5/75," Box 11, James Cannon Papers (Domestic Council), at Gerald R. Ford Library; Gerald R. Ford Library, "Memo, Nelson Rockefeller to Gerald R. Ford," dated January 8, 1975a, folder "Rockefeller, Nelson—General (1)," Box 60, Philip Buchen Files, 1974–77, Gerald R. Ford Library.

224. Rockefeller, in discussion with Bob Hartmann.

225. Rockefeller, in discussion with Bob Hartmann; Rockefeller, in discussion with Mike Turner.

226. Rockefeller, in discussion with Bob Hartmann; Rockefeller, in discussion with Mike Turner.

227. Ford, *A Time to Heal*, 235; Ford, in discussion with Trevor Armbrister.

228. Turner, *The Vice President as Policy Maker*, 1977.

229. Ford, *A Time to Heal*.

230. Cannon, "Gerald R. Ford and Nelson A. Rockefeller."

231. Cannon, "Gerald R. Ford and Nelson A. Rockefeller."

232. Rockefeller, in discussion with Bob Hartmann.

233. Rockefeller, in discussion with Bob Hartmann.

234. Rockefeller, in discussion with Bob Hartmann.

235. Rockefeller, in discussion with Bob Hartmann.

236. Rockefeller, in discussion with Bob Hartmann.

237. Rockefeller, in discussion with Bob Hartmann; Gerald R. Ford Library, "Memo, Jack Veneman to Jim Cannon" dated April 18, 1975, folder "VP 3/75–5/75,"

Box 11, James Cannon Papers (Domestic Council), at Gerald R. Ford Library; Rockefeller, in discussion with Mike Turner.

238. Ford, in discussion with Hugh Morrow.

239. Ford, in discussion with Trevor Armbrister.

240. Turner, *Vice President as Policy Maker*.

241. Cannon, "Gerald R. Ford and Nelson A. Rockefeller."

242. Rockefeller, in discussion with Bob Hartmann.

243. Rockefeller, in discussion with Bob Hartmann.

244. Gerald R. Ford Library, "Memo, Roy Ash to Gerald Ford," dated January 13, 1975a, folder "Domestic Council—Vice President's Role, 1/75–12/75," Box 3, Richard Cheney Files, 1974–77, Gerald R. Ford Library.

245. Rockefeller, in discussion with Trevor Armbrister.

246. Rockefeller, in discussion with Bob Hartmann.

247. Rockefeller, in discussion with Trevor Armbrister.

248. Rockefeller, in discussion with Bob Hartmann.

249. Rockefeller, in discussion with Mike Turner; Nelson Rockefeller, in discussion with Bob Hartmann.

250. Rockefeller, in discussion with Bob Hartmann.

251. Rockefeller, in discussion with Bob Hartmann.

252. Rockefeller, in discussion with Bob Hartmann.

253. Turner, *The Vice President as Policy Maker*.

254. Rockefeller, in discussion with Mike Turner.

255. Turner, *Vice President as Policy Maker*; Gerald R. Ford Library, "Letter, Nelson Rockefeller to Gerald R. Ford," dated December 16, 1975, folder "Domestic Council—Vice President's Role, 1/75–12/75," Box 3, Richard Cheney Files, 1974–77, at Gerald R. Ford Library.

256. Rockefeller, in discussion with Hugh Morrow.

257. Cannon, "Gerald R. Ford and Nelson A. Rockefeller."

258. Cannon, in discussion with the author.

259. Rumsfeld, in conversation with the author.

260. Gerald R. Ford Library, "Letter, Nelson Rockefeller to Gerald R. Ford," dated December 16, 1975, folder "Domestic Council—Vice President's Role, 1/75–12/75," Box 3, Richard Cheney Files, 1974–77, at Gerald R. Ford Library.

261. Rockefeller Archive Center, "Memo, Nelson Rockefeller to Gerald Ford," dated December 16, 1975, Rockefeller Family Collection, Record Group 26, Series 18, Volume 9, 166–69, at Rockefeller Archive Center.

262. Rockefeller Archive Center, "Memo, Nelson Rockefeller to Gerald Ford.

263. Rockefeller Archive Center, "Memo, Nelson Rockefeller to Gerald Ford.

264. Gerald R. Ford Library, "Memo, Nelson Rockefeller to Gerald Ford," dated December 16, 1975a, folder "Domestic Council—Vice President's Role, 1/75–12/75," Box 3, Richard Cheney Files, 1974–77, Gerald R. Ford Library.

265. Gerald R. Ford Library, "Memo, Nelson Rockefeller to Gerald Ford.

266. Cannon, "Gerald R. Ford and Nelson A. Rockefeller."

298 / Notes to Chapter 2

267. Cannon, "Rockefeller Aiming at Major Role."

268. Ford, in discussion with Trevor Armbrister.

269. Ford, in discussion with Trevor Armbrister; Cannon, in discussion with the author.

270. Ford, in discussion with Trevor Armbrister; Ford, *A Time to Heal*.

271. Rockefeller, in discussion with Trevor Armbrister.

272. Rockefeller, in discussion with Trevor Armbrister.

273. Rockefeller, in discussion with Trevor Armbrister.

274. Rockefeller, in discussion with Trevor Armbrister.

275. Ford, in discussion with Trevor Armbrister.

276. Rockefeller, in discussion with Hugh Morrow.

277. Rockefeller, in discussion with Hugh Morrow.

278. Rockefeller, in discussion with Hugh Morrow.

279. Rockefeller, in discussion with Trevor Armbrister.

280. Rockefeller, in discussion with Trevor Armbrister.

281. Cheney, *In My Time*, 80.

282. Ford, in discussion with Trevor Armbrister.

283. Ford, in discussion with Hugh Morrow.

284. Dom Bonafede, "The Forgotten Man," *National Journal*, February 14, 1976.

285. Gerald R. Ford Library, "Handwritten Note, Nelson Rockefeller to Gerald R. Ford, n.d.," folder "FG Vice President (1)," Box 16, Presidential Handwriting File, Gerald R. Ford Library; Gerald R. Ford Library, "Letter, Gerald R. Ford to Nelson Rockefeller," dated January 27, 1976, folder "Domestic Council—Vice President's Role, 1/75–12/75," Box 3, Richard Cheney Files, 1974–77, at Gerald R. Ford Library.

286. Rockefeller, in discussion with Bob Hartmann.

287. Ford, in discussion with Trevor Armbrister.

288. Memo March 7, 1975a; Remarks of the President, "Remarks of Ford at the Salute to the Vice President Dinner at the Waldorf Astoria," dated February 13, 1975, Rockefeller Family Collection, Record Group 26, Series 13: Press Releases, Box 13, File folder 713, Rockefeller Archive Center.

289. Remarks of the President, "Remarks of."

290. Rockefeller, in discussion with Hugh Morrow.

291. Turner, *Vice President as Policy Maker*, 1982.

292. Ford, in discussion with Trevor Armbrister.

293. Bonafede, "The Forgotten Man."

294. Cannon, "Gerald R. Ford and Nelson A. Rockefeller."

295. Cannon, "Gerald R. Ford and Nelson A. Rockefeller."

296. Turner, *Vice President as Policy Maker*, 173.

297. Cannon, "Gerald R. Ford and Nelson A. Rockefeller," 141.

298. Cheney, *In My Time*.

299. Cheney, *In My Time*, 79–80.

300. Cheney, *In My Time*, 79–80.

301. Cheney, *In My Time*, 80.

302. Cannon, in discussion with the author.

303. Allison, in discussion with the author.

304. *Vice President as Policy Maker*, 173; Cheney, *In My Time*.

305. Cheney, *In My Time*, 80.

306. Turner, *Vice President as Policy Maker*.

307. Nessen, in discussion with the author, May 2008.

308. Ford, *A Time to Heal*.

309. Nessen, in discussion with the author.

310. Turner, *Vice President as Policy Maker*.

311. Turner, *Vice President as Policy Maker*, 177.

312. Turner, *Vice President as Policy Maker*, 177.

313. Turner, *Vice President as Policy Maker*, 177.

314. Light, *Vice-Presidential Power*.

315. Baumgartner, *American Vice Presidency Reconsidered*.

316. Light, *Vice-Presidential Power*, 65–67.

317. Cannon, "Rockefeller Aiming at Major Role."

318. Rockefeller Archive Center, "Vice Presidential Organizational Chart," dated November 11, 1976, Rockefeller Family Collection, Record Group 26, Series 18, Volume 39, 6–10, at Rockefeller Archive Center.

319. Cannon, "Rockefeller Aiming at Major Role."

320. Cannon, "Rockefeller Aiming at Major Role."

321. Allison, in discussion with the author.

322. Turner, *Vice President as Policy Maker*.

323. Light, *Vice-Presidential Power*.

324. Rockefeller Archive Center, "Vice Presidential Staff Descriptions, n.d.," Rockefeller Family Collection, Record Group 25, Series 18, Volume 39, 11–34, Rockefeller Archive Center; Rockefeller Archive Center, "Memo, John Howe to Nelson Rockefeller," dated March 22, 1975, Rockefeller Family Collection, Record Group 26, Series 19, Box 11, Folder 299, Rockefeller Archive Center.

325. Gerald R. Ford Library, "Memo, Jack Marsh to Gerald R. Ford," dated December 20, 1974, folder "Rockefeller, Nelson—Role as V.P.," Box 10, Richard Cheney Files, 1974–1977, at Gerald R. Ford Library.

326. Gerald R. Ford Library, "Memo, Jack Marsh to Gerald R. Ford."

327. Gerald R. Ford Library, "Memo, Jack Marsh to Gerald R. Ford."

328. Gerald R. Ford Library, "Memo, Jack Marsh to Gerald R. Ford."

329. Gerald R. Ford Library, "Memo, Jack Marsh to Gerald R. Ford."

330. Nelson Rockefeller, in discussion with Hugh Sidey and Bonnie Angelo, January 1975.

331. Rockefeller, in discussion with Hugh Sidey and Bonnie Angelo.

300 / Notes to Chapter 2

332. Press Conference with Nelson Rockefeller July 9, 1975.

333. Cannon, "Rockefeller Aiming at Major"; Rockefeller, in discussion with Trevor Armbrister.

334. Terry M. Moe, "Vested Interests and Political Institutions," *Political Science Quarterly* 130 (2015): 277–318.

335. Turner, *Vice President as Policy Maker*.

336. Rockefeller, in discussion with Hugh Morrow.

337. Rockefeller, in discussion with Hugh Morrow.

338. Ford, in discussion with Hugh Morrow; Rockefeller, in discussion with Hugh Morrow.

339. Rockefeller, in discussion with Hugh Morrow.

340. Rockefeller, in discussion with Hugh Morrow.

341. Rockefeller, in discussion with Hugh Morrow.

342. Turner, *Vice President as Policy Maker*, 172.

343. David B. Cohen and Charles E. Walcott, "Serving Our Country in Historic Times: The Chiefs of Staff in the George W. Bush White House" (paper presented at the Annual Meeting of the American Political Science Association, Washington, DC, September 2–5, 2010).

344. Cheney, in conversation with the author.

345. Allison, in discussion with the author.

346. Rumsfeld, in conversation with the author.

347. Rumsfeld, in conversation with the author.

348. Ford, in discussion with Hugh Morrow.

349. Rockefeller, in discussion with Hugh Morrow.

350. Rumsfeld, n.d., in discussion with Trevor Armbrister.

351. Rumsfeld, n.d., in discussion with Trevor Armbrister.

352. Rockefeller, in discussion with Hugh Morrow; Rockefeller, in discussion with Bob Hartmann.

353. Rockefeller, in discussion with Hugh Morrow.

354. Rockefeller, in discussion with Hugh Morrow.

355. Rockefeller, in discussion with Hugh Morrow.

356. Cheney, in conversation with the author.

357. Bonafede, "The Forgotten Man."

358. Bonafede, "The Forgotten Man."

359. Turner, *Vice President as Policy Maker*, 172.

360. Turner, *Vice President as Policy Maker*.

361. Rockefeller, in discussion with Mike Turner.

362. Rockefeller, in discussion with Trevor Armbrister.

363. Rockefeller, in discussion with Bob Hartmann,

364. Rockefeller, in discussion with Trevor Armbrister.

365. Rockefeller, in discussion with Mike Turner.

366. Rockefeller, in discussion with Mike Turner.

Notes to Chapter 2 / 301

367. Rockefeller, in discussion with Hugh Morrow.

368. Rockefeller, in discussion with Hugh Morrow.

369. Ford, in discussion with Trevor Armbrister.

370. Ford, in discussion with Trevor Armbrister.

371. Persico, *Imperial Rockefeller*, 261.

372. Ford, *A Time to Heal*.

373. Rockefeller, in discussion with Kershaw.

374. Ford, *A Time to Heal*; Jim Squires, "Rocky Hopes for Last Laugh," *Chicago Tribune*, February 5, 1976.

375. Rowland Evans and Robert Novak, "Deepening the Rocky Dilemma," *Washington Post*, July 28, 1975; Gerald R. Ford, in discussion with Hugh Morrow, 1979; Gerald Ford, in discussion with Trevor Armbrister, 1977.

376. Ford, *A Time to Heal*, 279.

377. Rowland Evans and Robert Novak, "Deepening the Rocky Dilemma."

378. Nelson Rockefeller, in discussion with Trevor Armbrister, October 1977.

379. Richard Allison, in discussion with the author, June 2008.

380. Fred Barnes, "Is Divorce the Next Step for Ford and Rockefeller?," *Washington Star*, July 25, 1975.

381. Ford, in discussion with Hugh Morrow.

382. Ford, *A Time to Heal*.

383. Ford, in discussion with Hugh Morrow.

384. Louis Harris, "Rockefeller Opposed for No. 2 Spot," *Washington Post*, September 11, 1975; Ford, *A Time to Heal*; Harris Poll, September 11, 1975.

385. DeFrank, Thomas M. *Write It When I'm Gone: Remarkable Off-the-Record Conversations with Gerald R. Ford* (New York: G. P. Putnam's Sons, 2007), 93.

386. Rockefeller, in discussion with Hugh Morrow.

387. Gerald R. Ford Library, "Memo, Nelson Rockefeller to Gerald R. Ford," dated May 8, 1975, folder "Rockefeller, Nelson," Box 19, Richard Cheney Files, 1974–1977, at Gerald R. Ford Library.

388. Rockefeller Archive Center, "Stu Spencer to Nancy Towell," dated September 1, 1976, Rockefeller Family Collection, Record Group 26, Series 18, Volume 31, 16–24, Rockefeller Archive Center.

389. Rockefeller Archive Center, "Stu Spencer to Nancy Towell."

390. Allison, in discussion with the author.

391. Rockefeller, in discussion with Trevor Armbrister.

392. Rockefeller, in discussion with Trevor Armbrister.

393. Cheney, *In My Time*, 80–81.

394. Ford, in discussion with Hugh Morrow.

395. Rockefeller, in discussion with Bob Hartmann.

396. Dick Cheney, in conversation with the author, December 2011.

397. Rockefeller, in discussion with Bob Hartmann.

398. DeFrank, *Write It When I'm Gone*, 93.

302 / Notes to Chapter 3

399. DeFrank, *Write It When I'm Gone*, 93.

400. Gerald R. Ford Library, "Letter, Nelson Rockefeller to Gerald R. Ford," dated November 3, 1975, folder "VP 10/75–11/75," Box 12, James Cannon Papers (Domestic Council), at Gerald R. Ford Library.

401. Ford, in discussion with Trevor Armbrister.

402. Turner, *Vice President as Policy Maker*, 175.

403. Turner, *Vice President as Policy Maker*, 175.

404. Rockefeller, in discussion with Hugh Morrow.

405. Persico, *Imperial Rockefeller*, 277.

406. Rockefeller, in discussion with Hugh Morrow.

407. Rockefeller, in discussion with Hugh Morrow.

408. Laird, n.d., in discussion with Trevor Armbrister.

409. Cheney, in conversation with the author.

410. Cheney, in conversation with the author.

411. Hooker, in discussion with the author.

412. Cannon, in discussion with the author.

Chapter 3

1. Dick Cheney, in conversation with the author, December 2011.

2. James Rosen, *Cheney One on One: A Candid Conversation with America's Most Controversial Statesman* (Washington, DC: Regnery), 117.

3. Rosen, *Cheney One on One*, 117.

4. Stephen F. Hayes, *Cheney: The Untold Story of America's Most Powerful and Controversial Vice President* (New York: Harper Collins, 2007), 2.

5. Jody C. Baumgartner, *The American Vice Presidency Reconsidered* (Westport, CT: Praeger, 2006).

6. Shirley Ann Warshaw, *The Co-Presidency of Bush and Cheney* (Stanford, CA: Stanford University Press, 2009).

7. Bob Woodward, *Plan of Attack* (New York: Simon & Schuster, 2004).

8. Warshaw, *Co-Presidency of Bush and Cheney*.

9. Karl Rove, *Courage and Consequence: My Life as a Conservative in the Fight* (New York: Threshold Editions, 2010); Karen Hughes, *Ten Minutes from Normal* (New York: Viking Penguin, 2004); Jon Meacham, *Destiny and Power: The American Odyssey of George Herbert Walker Bush* (New York: Random House, 2015); George W. Bush, *Decision Points* (New York: Crown Publishers, 2010); Warshaw, *Co-Presidency of Bush and Cheney*; Cheney, *In My Time*; Baker, *Days of Fire*; *Cheney: Untold Story*; Baumgartner, *American Vice Presidency Reconsidered*.

10. Bush, *Decision Points*; Warshaw, *Co-Presidency of Bush and Cheney*; Baumgartner, *American Vice Presidency Reconsidered*; Cheney, *In My Time*; Rove, *Courage and Consequence*; Baker, *Days of Fire*; Hughes, *Ten Minutes from Normal*.

Notes to Chapter 3 / 303

11. Baker, *Days of Fire*, 55.

12. Warshaw, *Co-Presidency of Bush and Cheney*, 24.

13. James Mann, *Rise of the Vulcans: The History of Bush's War Cabinet* (New York: Penguin, 2004); Ari Fleischer, in conversation with the author, May 2009.

14. Rove, *Courage and Consequence*, 167.

15. Lou Dubose and Jake Bernstein, *Vice: Dick Cheney and the Hijacking of the American Presidency* (London: Pimlico, 2006).

16. Dubose and Bernstein, *Vice: Dick Cheney and the Hijacking*, 139.

17. Cheney, *In My Time*, 255.

18. Joel K. Goldstein, "The Rising Power of the Modern Vice Presidency," *Presidential Studies Quarterly* 38 (2008): 374–89; Rove, *Courage and Consequence*; Cheney, *In My Time*; Baumgartner, *American Vice Presidency Reconsidered*; Baker, *Days of Fire: Bush and Cheney*; Barton Gellman, *Angler: The Cheney Vice Presidency* (New York: Penguin, 2008).

19. Gellman, *Angler: Cheney Vice Presidency*.

20. Fleischer, in conversation with the author.

21. Gellman, *Angler: Cheney Vice Presidency*, 3–4.

22. Baumgartner, *American Vice Presidency Reconsidered*; Baker, *Days of Fire*.

23. Baumgartner, *American Vice Presidency Reconsidered*.

24. Rove, *Courage and Consequence*, 171.

25. Bush, *Decision Points*.

26. Bush, *Decision Points*, 65.

27. Bush, *Decision Points*, 65.

28. Cheney, *In My Time* 266–67.

29. Rove, *Courage and Consequence*.

30. Rove, *Courage and Consequence*.

31. Dubose and Bernstein, *Vice: Dick Cheney and the Hijacking*, 138–39.

32. Dubose and Bernstein, *Vice: Dick Cheney and the Hijacking*, 138–39.

33. Dubose and Bernstein, *Vice: Dick Cheney and the Hijacking*, 139.

34. Cheney, *In My Time*.

35. Rosen, *Cheney One on One*, 89.

36. Jody C. Baumgartner, with Thomas F. Crumblin, *The American Vice Presidency: From the Shadow to the Spotlight* (New York: Rowman & Littlefield, 2015), 158.

37. Cheney, in conversation with the author.

38. Rosen, *Cheney One on One*.

39. Rosen, *Cheney One on One*, 104–5.

40. The shortlist by early summer included Governors Lamar Alexander, Tom Ridge, Frank Keating, and John Engler as well as Senators Jack Danforth, Jon Kyle, Chuck Hagel, Bill Frist, and Fred Thompson. Bush, George W. *Decision Points* (New York: Crown, 2010).

41. Bush, *Decision Points*.

304 / Notes to Chapter 3

42. Hughes, *Ten Minutes from Normal.*
43. Meacham, *Destiny and Power.*
44. Cheney, in conversation with the author.
45. Baker, *Days of Fire*, 57.
46. Baker, *Days of Fire*, 60.
47. Baker, *Days of Fire*, 60.
48. Woodward, *Plan of Attack.*
49. Baker, *Days of Fire.*
50. Baker, *Days of Fire*, 15–16.
51. Baker, *Days of Fire*, 61.
52. Cheney, in conversation with the author.
53. Cheney, in conversation with the author.
54. Hayes, *Cheney: Untold Story*, 278.
55. Gellman, *Angler: Cheney Vice Presidency*, 15.
56. Hayes, *Cheney: Untold Story*, 281.
57. Hayes, *Cheney: Untold Story*, 281–82.
58. Meacham, *Destiny and Power.*
59. Bush, *Decision Points.*
60. Woodward, *Plan of Attack*, 27.
61. Woodward, *Plan of Attack*, 27.
62. Woodward, *Plan of Attack*, 27.
63. Woodward, *Plan of Attack*, 27.
64. Laura Bush, *Spoke from the Heart* (New York: Scribner, 2010), 157–58.
65. Hughes, *Ten Minutes from Normal*, 142.
66. Mann, *Rise of the Vulcans*, 252.
67. Warshaw, *Co-Presidency of Bush and Cheney*, 28.
68. Warshaw, *Co-Presidency of Bush and Cheney*, 28.
69. Hayes, *Cheney: The Untold Story.*
70. Warshaw, *Co-Presidency of Bush and Cheney.*
71. Cheney, *In My Time*; Hayes, *Cheney: The Untold Story.*
72. Cheney, *In My Time.*
73. Warshaw, *Co-Presidency of Bush and Cheney*, 28.
74. Warshaw, *Co-Presidency of Bush and Cheney*, 28.
75. Warshaw, *Co-Presidency of Bush and Cheney*, 3.
76. Rove, *Courage and Consequence*; Gellman, *Angler: Cheney Vice Presidency.*
77. Rove, *Courage and Consequence*, 168.
78. Rove, *Courage and Consequence*, 168.
79. Hayes, *Cheney: The Untold Story.*
80. Baumgartner, with Crumblin, *American Vice Presidency.*
81. Hayes, *Cheney: The Untold Story*, 274.
82. Hayes, *Cheney: The Untold Story*, 274.
83. Cheney, *In My Time*, 252.

Notes to Chapter 3 / 305

84. Baumgartner, with Crumblin, *American Vice Presidency*.

85. Baumgartner, with Crumblin, *American Vice Presidency*, 158.

86. Cheney, *In My Time*, 252.

87. Mann, *Rise of the Vulcans*; Hayes, *Cheney: The Untold Story*; Rove, *Courage and Consequence*.

88. Baker, *Days of Fire*, 58.

89. Hayes, *Cheney: The Untold Story*, 277.

90. Goldstein, "Rising Power," 385.

91. Bush, *Decision Points*, 68.

92. Bush, *Decision Points*, 69.

93. Hughes, *Ten Minutes from Normal*.

94. Hughes, *Ten Minutes from Normal*.

95. Cheney, *In My Time*.

96. Cheney, *In My Time*, 262–63.

97. Cheney, *In My Time*, 262–63.

98. Cheney, *In My Time*, 262–63.

99. Baker, *Days of Fire*; Cheney, *In My Time*.

100. Cheney, *In My Time*.

101. Cheney, *In My Time*, 263.

102. Cheney, *In My* Time, 263.

103. Cheney, *In My Time*, 263–64.

104. Rove, *Courage and Consequence*; Warshaw, *Co-Presidency of Bush and Cheney*.

105. Cheney, *In My Time*, 264.

106. Cheney, *In My Time*, 264.

107. Hayes, *Cheney: The Untold Story*, 282.

108. Rove, *Courage and Consequence*, 169.

109. Rove, *Courage and Consequence*, 169.

110. Rove, *Courage and Consequence*, 169.

111. Rove, *Courage and Consequence*, 169.

112. Rove, *Courage and Consequence*, 169.

113. Rove, *Courage and Consequence*, 170.

114. Rove, *Courage and Consequence*, 170.

115. Rove, *Courage and Consequence*, 170.

116. Bush, *Decision Points*, 69–70.

117. Rove, *Courage and Consequence*, 172.

118. Baumgartner, with Crumblin, *The American Vice Presidency*.

119. Rove, *Courage and Consequence*, 172.

120. Baker, *Days of Fire: Bush and Cheney*, 58.

121. Woodward, *Plan of Attack*, 27–28.

122. Bush, *Decision Points*; Hughes, *Ten Minutes from Normal*.

123. Warshaw, *Co-Presidency of Bush and Cheney*, 29.

306 / Notes to Chapter 3

124. Cheney, *In My Time.*

125. Baker, *Days of Fire: Bush and Cheney*, 60; Hayes, *Cheney: The Untold Story*, 284.

126. Baumgartner, *American Vice Presidency Reconsidered*, 79.

127. Baumgartner, with Crumblin, *American Vice Presidency*, 159.

128. Donald Rumsfeld, *Known and Unknown* (New York: Sentinel, 2011), 273.

129. Warshaw, *Co-Presidency of Bush and Cheney*, 23.

130. Warshaw, *Co-Presidency of Bush and Cheney*, 24.

131. Warshaw, *Co-Presidency of Bush and Cheney*, 24.

132. Baker, *Days of Fire: Bush and Cheney*, 58.

133. Hayes, *Cheney: The Untold Story*, 285.

134. Hayes, *Cheney: The Untold Story*, 286–87.

135. Hayes, *Cheney: The Untold Story*, 286–87.

136. Baumgartner, with Crumblin, *American Vice Presidency*.

137. Hayes, *Cheney: The Untold Story*, 277.

138. Bob Woodward, *State of Denial* (New York: Simon & Schuster, 2006).

139. Bush, *Decision Points*, 68.

140. Bush, *Decision Points*, 68.

141. Warshaw, *Co-Presidency of Bush and Cheney*, 2.

142. Warshaw, *Co-Presidency of Bush and Cheney*, 3.

143. Mann, *Rise of the Vulcans*; 252–53.

144. Bush, *Decision Points.*

145. Warshaw, *Co-Presidency of Bush and Cheney.*

146. Warshaw, *Co-Presidency of Bush and Cheney.*

147. Warshaw, *Co-Presidency of Bush and Cheney.*

148. Warshaw, *Co-Presidency of Bush and Cheney.*

149. Baumgartner, with Crumblin, *American Vice Presidency.*

150. Warshaw, *Co-Presidency of Bush and Cheney.*

151. Baker, *Days of Fire: Bush and Cheney.*

152. Baker, *Days of Fire: Bush and Cheney*, 58.

153. Meacham, *Destiny and Power*; Baker, *Days of Fire: Bush and Cheney.*

154. Gellman, *Angler: The Cheney Vice Presidency*, 35.

155. Gellman, *Angler: The Cheney Vice Presidency*, 35.

156. Warshaw, *Co-Presidency of Bush and Cheney.*

157. Bob Woodward, *The War Within* (New York: Simon & Schuster, 2008).

158. Mann, *Rise of the Vulcans*, 370.

159. Warshaw, *Co-Presidency of Bush and Cheney*, 57.

160. Hayes, *Cheney: The Untold Story.*

161. Meacham, *Destiny and Power*, 590.

162. Baker, *Days of Fire*; Rumsfeld, *Known and Unknown.*

163. Baker, *Days of Fire.*

164. Rumsfeld, *Known and Unknown.*

Notes to Chapter 3 / 307

165. Rumsfeld, *Known and Unknown*, 285.

166. Baker, *Days of Fire: Bush and Cheney*, 81.

167. Hayes, *Cheney: The Untold Story*, 307.

168. Hayes, *Cheney: The Untold Story*, 307.

169. Hayes, *Cheney: The Untold Story*, 307.

170. Hayes, *Cheney: The Untold Story*, 307.

171. Cheney, in conversation with the author.

172. Hayes, *Cheney: The Untold Story*; Cheney, in conversation with the author.

173. Hayes, *Cheney: The Untold Story*, 288.

174. Hayes, *Cheney: The Untold Story*, 505–6.

175. David Frum, *The Right Man: The Surprise Presidency of George W. Bush* (New York: Random House, 2003), 61–62.

176. Baker, *Days of Fire: Bush and Cheney*; Goldstein, *White House Vice Presidency*, 131.

177. Baker, *Days of Fire: Bush and Cheney*; Goldstein, *White House Vice Presidency, Mondale to Biden*.

178. Warshaw, *Co-Presidency of Bush and Cheney*.

179. Jules Witcover, *The American Vice Presidency: From Irrelevance to Power* (Washington, DC: Smithsonian Books, 2014); Warshaw, *Co-Presidency of Bush and Cheney*.

180. Witcover, *American Vice Presidency*.

181. Joel K. Goldstein, *The White House Vice Presidency: The Path to Significance, Mondale to Biden* (Lawrence: University Press of Kansas, 2016), 131.

182. Goldstein, *White House Vice Presidency*.

183. Gellman, *Angler: The Cheney Vice Presidency*, 51.

184. Gellman, *Angler: The Cheney Vice Presidency*, 51.

185. Gellman, *Angler: The Cheney Vice Presidency*, 51.

186. Gellman, *Angler: The Cheney Vice Presidency*, 51.

187. Gellman, *Angler: The Cheney Vice Presidency* 57–58.

188. Gellman, *Angler: The Cheney Vice Presidency*, 58.

189. Baker, *Days of Fire: Bush and Cheney*, 88.

190. Gellman, *Angler: The Cheney Vice Presidency*; Baumgartner, with Crumblin, *American Vice Presidency*.

191. Gellman, *Angler: The Cheney Vice Presidency*, 58.

192. Baumgartner, with Crumblin, *The American Vice Presidency*, 168.

193. Hayes, *Cheney: The Untold Story*, 307.

194. Hayes, *Cheney: The Untold Story*, 305.

195. Cheney, *In My Time*.

196. Gellman, *Angler: The Cheney Vice Presidency*, 87.

197. Cheney, *In My Time*, 305.

198. Cheney, *In My Time*, 305.

308 / Notes to Chapter 3

199. Robert M. Gates, *Duty: Memoirs of a Secretary at War* (New York: Alfred A. Knopf, 2014), 7–8.

200. Meacham, *Destiny and Power*, 587–88.

201. Meacham, *Destiny and Power*, 590.

202. Bush, *Decision Points*, 86.

203. Hayes, *Cheney: The Untold Story*.

204. Condoleezza Rice, in conversation with the author, September 2010.

205. Baker, *Days of Fire: Bush and Cheney*.

206. Baker, *Days of Fire: Bush and Cheney*, 92.

207. Baker, *Days of Fire: Bush and Cheney*, 92.

208. Baker, *Days of Fire: Bush and Cheney*, 92.

209. Baker, *Days of Fire: Bush and Cheney*, 86.

210. Fleischer, in conversation with the author.

211. Baker, *Days of Fire: Bush and Cheney*, 229.

212. Hayes, *Cheney: The Untold Story*, 307.

213. Dana Perino, in conversation with the author, April 2009.

214. Nicholas Calio, in conversation with the author, August 2008.

215. Rumsfeld, *Known and Unknown*, 320; Dan Bartlett, in conversation with the author, June 2010.

216. Goldstein, *White House Vice Presidency*.

217. Calio, in conversation with the author.

218. Hayes, *Cheney: The Untold Story*.

219. Mann, *Rise of the Vulcans*; Cheney, *In My Time*; Stephen Hadley, in discussion with the author, November 2010.

220. Cheney, *In My Time*, 337.

221. Mann, *Rise of the Vulcans*, 297.

222. Scott McClellan, *What Happened: Inside the Bush White House and Washington's Culture of Deception* (Philadelphia, PA: Public Affairs, 2008), 85.

223. Hayes, *Cheney: The Untold Story*.

224. Gellman, *Angler: The Cheney Vice Presidency*.

225. Gellman, *Angler: The Cheney Vice Presidency; John P. Burke, Honest Broker? The National Security Advisor and Presidential Decision Making* (College Station: Texas A&M University Press, 2009).

226. George Tenet, *At the Center of the Storm: My Years at the CIA* (New York: HarperCollins Publishers, 2007).

227. Goldstein, *White House Vice Presidency*.

228. Goldstein, *White House Vice Presidency* Gellman, *Angler: The Cheney Vice Presidency*.

229. Cheney, *In My Time*.

230. Cheney, *In My Time*; Cheney, in conversation with the author.

231. Gellman, *Angler: The Cheney Vice Presidency*.

232. Gellman, *Angler: The Cheney Vice Presidency*, 70.

Notes to Chapter 3 / 309

233. Baumgartner, with Crumblin, *The American Vice Presidency*.

234. Gellman, *Angler: The Cheney Vice Presidency*.

235. Gellman, *Angler: The Cheney Vice Presidency*, 196.

236. Gellman, *Angler: The Cheney Vice Presidency*, 196.

237. Gellman, *Angler: The Cheney Vice Presidency*, 196.

238. Gellman, *Angler: The Cheney Vice Presidency*, 169.

239. Baker, *Days of Fire*; Goldstein, *The White House Vice Presidency*.

240. Baker, *Days of Fire: Bush and Cheney*, 386.

241. Baumgartner, with Crumblin, *American Vice Presidency*.

242. Woodward, *Plan of Attack*; Goldstein, *White House Vice Presidency*.

243. Baumgartner, with Crumblin, *American Vice Presidency*; Bush, *Decision Points*.

244. Baker, *Days of Fire*, 97.

245. Johnathan Masters, "The U.S. Vice President and Foreign Policy," *Council on Foreign Relations* (June 2016), http://www.cfr.org/united-states/us-vice-president-foreign-policy/p38104 (accessed June 30, 2016).

246. Baker, *Days of Fire: Bush and Cheney*, 110.

247. Baker, *Days of Fire: Bush and Cheney*, 216.

248. Baumgartner, with Crumblin, *American Vice Presidency*; Fleischer, in conversation with the author.

249. Baumgartner, with Crumblin, *American Vice Presidency*, 165.

250. Baumgartner, with Crumblin, *American Vice Presidency*, 168.

251. Baumgartner, with Crumblin, *American Vice Presidency*, 168.

252. Rosen, *Cheney One on One*, 2.

253. Rosen, *Cheney One on One*, 2.

254. Gellman, *Angler: The Cheney Vice Presidency*.

255. Cheney, *In My Time*.

256. Cheney, *In My Time*, 314.

257. Hayes, *Cheney: The Untold Story*, 328.

258. Tenet, *At the Center of the Storm*, 137.

259. Rosen, *Cheney One on One*.

260. Rosen, *Cheney One on One*, 2.

261. Gellman, Angler: The Cheney Vice Presidency, 244.

262. Gellman, Angler: The Cheney Vice Presidency, 244.

263. Gellman, Angler: The Cheney Vice Presidency, 244.

264. Gellman, Angler: The Cheney Vice Presidency, 244.

265. Warshaw, *Co-Presidency of Bush and Cheney*; Cheney, *In My Time*; Hayes, *Cheney: The Untold Story*; Gellman, *Angler: The Cheney Vice Presidency*; Baker, *Days of Fire*.

266. Warshaw, *Co-Presidency of Bush and Cheney*, 6.

267. Rumsfeld, *Known and Unknown*, 604.

268. Gellman, *Angler: The Cheney Vice Presidency*.

310 / Notes to Chapter 3

269. Gellman, *Angler: The Cheney Vice Presidency*, 82.

270. Woodward, *War Within*, 418–19.

271. Hayes, *Cheney: The Untold Story*.

272. Woodward, *War Within*, 417–18.

273. Woodward, *War Within*, 417–18.

274. Warshaw, *Co-Presidency of Bush and Cheney*.

275. Warshaw, *Co-Presidency of Bush and Cheney*, 4.

276. Gellman, *Angler: The Cheney Vice Presidency*.

277. Gellman, *Angler: The Cheney Vice Presidency*, 68–69.

278. Condoleezza Rice, *No Higher Honor* (New York: Crown, 2011).

279. Gellman, *Angler: The Cheney Vice Presidency*.

280. Rice, *No Higher Honor*.

281. Gellman, *Angler: The Cheney Vice Presidency*, 259–60.

282. Gellman, *Angler: The Cheney Vice Presidency*, 259–60.

283. Gellman, *Angler: The Cheney Vice Presidency*, 260.

284. Gellman, *Angler: The Cheney Vice Presidency*, 260.

285. Hayes, *Cheney: The Untold Story*.

286. Hayes, *Cheney: The Untold Story*.

287. Witcover, *American Vice Presidency*, 491.

288. Gellman, *Angler: The Cheney Vice Presidency*, 52–53.

289. Baker, *Days of Fire: Bush and Cheney*, 110.

290. Warshaw, *Co-Presidency of Bush and Cheney*.

291. Baker, *Days of Fire: Bush and Cheney*; Hayes, *Cheney: The Untold Story*; Gellman, *Angler: The Cheney Vice Presidency*.

292. Cheney, *In My Time*.

293. Cheney, *In My Time*, 35.

294. Warshaw, *Co-Presidency of Bush and Cheney*, 305.

295. Warshaw, *Co-Presidency of Bush and Cheney*, 305.

296. Hayes, *Cheney: The Untold Story*, 305.

297. Hayes, *Cheney: The Untold Story*, 305.

298. Hayes, *Cheney: The Untold Story*, 305.

299. Hayes, *Cheney: The Untold Story*, 305.

300. Hayes, *Cheney: The Untold Story*, 305.

301. Bush, *Decision Points*, 86–87.

302. Perino, in conversation with the author.

303. Gellman, *Angler: The Cheney Vice Presidency*.

304. Baumgartner, with Crumblin, *American Vice Presidency*.

305. Cheney, *In My Time*.

306. Hayes, *Cheney: The Untold Story*; Baumgartner, with Crumblin, *American Vice Presidency*; McClellan, *What Happened: Inside the Bush White House*.

307. Hayes, *Cheney: The Untold Story*.

308. Cheney, *In My Time*, 295.

309. Warshaw, *Co-Presidency of Bush and Cheney*; Baker, *Days of Fire: Bush and Cheney*.

310. Ari Fleischer, *Taking Heat: The President, the Press, and My Years in the White House* (New York: William Morrow, 2005), 9.

311. Terry Sullivan, *The Nerve Center: Lessons in Governing from the White House Chiefs of Staff* (College Station, Texas A&M University Press, 2004); Fleischer, *Taking Heat: The President, the Press*; Clay Johnson III, "The 2000–2001 Presidential Transition: Planning, Goals, and Reality," in *The White House World: Transitions, Organization, and Office Operations*, eds. Martha Joynt Kumar and Terry Sullivan (New York: Columbia University Press, 2003).

312. Johnson, "The 2000–2001 Presidential Transition."

313. John P. Burke, "The Bush 2000 Transition: The Historical Context," in *The White House World: Transitions, Organizations, and Office Operations*, eds. Martha Joynt Kumar and Terry Sullivan (College Station: Texas A&M University Press, 2009).

314. Burke, "The Bush 2000 Transition," 320.

315. Burke, "The Bush 2000 Transition," 320.

316. Warshaw, *Co-Presidency of Bush and Cheney*.

317. Warshaw, *Co-Presidency of Bush and Cheney*.

318. Warshaw, *Co-Presidency of Bush and Cheney*.

319. Warshaw, *Co-Presidency of Bush and Cheney*, 51.

320. Warshaw, *Co-Presidency of Bush and Cheney*, 51.

321. Baumgartner, with Crumblin, *The American Vice Presidency*, 127.

322. Warshaw, *Co-Presidency of Bush and Cheney*.

323. Warshaw, *Co-Presidency of Bush and Cheney*; Witcover, *American Vice Presidency*.

324. Johnathan Masters, "The U.S. Vice President and Foreign Policy," *Council on Foreign Relations* (June 2016), http://www.cfr.org/united-states/us-vice-president-foreign-policy/p38104 (accessed June 30, 2016); Goldstein, *The White House Vice Presidency*; Hayes, *Cheney: The Untold Story*; Warshaw, *Co-Presidency of Bush and Cheney*.

325. Warshaw, *Co-Presidency of Bush and Cheney*, 40.

326. Warshaw, *Co-Presidency of Bush and Cheney*, 40.

327. Hayes, *Cheney: The Untold Story*.

328. Witcover, *American Vice Presidency*.

329. Hayes, *Cheney: The Untold Story*.

330. Hayes, *Cheney: The Untold Story*.

331. Warshaw, *Co-Presidency of Bush and Cheney*, 1.

332. Warshaw, *Co-Presidency of Bush and Cheney*, 37.

333. Warshaw, *Co-Presidency of Bush and Cheney*; Witcover, *American Vice Presidency*.

334. Goldstein, *White House Vice Presidency*, 130.

312 / Notes to Chapter 3

335. Goldstein, *White House Vice Presidency*; Gellman, *Angler: The Cheney Vice Presidency*.

336. Cheney, *In My Time*, 300.

337. Johnson, "2000–2001 Presidential Transition."

338. Cheney, *In My Time*.

339. Warshaw, *Co-Presidency of Bush and Cheney*.

340. Warshaw, *Co-Presidency of Bush and Cheney*.

341. Warshaw, *Co-Presidency of Bush and Cheney*.

342. Gellman, *Angler: The Cheney Vice Presidency*.

343. Gellman, *Angler: The Cheney Vice Presidency*, 39.

344. Cheney, in conversation with the author.

345. Hayes, *Cheney: The Untold Story*.

346. Hayes, *Cheney: The Untold Story*, 309–10.

347. Hayes, *Cheney: The Untold Story*, 309–10.

348. Hayes, *Cheney: The Untold Story*, 309–10.

349. Cheney, in conversation with the author.

350. Hayes, *Cheney: The Untold Story*, 310.

351. Cheney, in conversation with the author.

352. Hayes, *Cheney: The Untold Story*.

353. Hayes, *Cheney: The Untold Story*; Baumgartner, with Crumblin, *The American Vice Presidency*; McClellan, *What Happened*.

354. Hayes, *Cheney: The Untold Story*.

355. Hayes, *Cheney: The Untold Story*, 313.

356. Hayes, *Cheney: The Untold Story*, 313.

357. Hayes, *Cheney: The Untold Story*, 313.

358. Hayes, *Cheney: The Untold Story*, 313.

359. Hayes 2007.

360. Hayes, *Cheney: The Untold Story*, 313.

361. Hayes, *Cheney: The Untold Story*, 313–14.

362. McClellan, *What Happened: Inside the Bush White House*, 96.

363. Hayes, *Cheney: The Untold Story*.

364. Hayes, *Cheney: The Untold Story*.

365. Hayes, *Cheney: The Untold Story*.

366. Witcover, *American Vice Presidency*.

367. Hayes, *Cheney: The Untold Story*.

368. Hayes, *Cheney: The Untold Story*, 315.

369. Cheney, *In My Time*, 315–16.

370. Hayes, *Cheney: The Untold Story*, 315.

371. Baumgartner, with Crumblin, *American Vice Presidency*.

372. Baker, *Days of Fire: Bush and Cheney*, 95.

373. Witcover, *The American Vice Presidency*, 486.

374. Gellman, *Angler: The Cheney Vice Presidency*, 84.

Notes to Chapter 3 / 313

375. Baumgartner, with Crumblin, *American Vice Presidency*.
376. Hayes, *Cheney: The Untold Story*.
377. Hayes, *Cheney: The Untold Story*.
378. Goldstein, *White House Vice Presidency*.
379. Hayes, *Cheney: The Untold Story*, 360.
380. Hayes, *Cheney: The Untold Story*.
381. Witcover, *The American Vice Presidency*, 486–87.
382. Hayes, *Cheney: The Untold Story*.
383. Hayes, *Cheney: The Untold Story*, 323.
384. Baker, *Days of Fire: Bush and Cheney*.
385. Hayes, *Cheney: The Untold Story*.
386. Baker, *Days of Fire: Bush and Cheney*, 102.
387. Cheney, *In My Time*, 317–18.
388. Cheney, *In My Time*, 317.
389. Hayes, *Cheney: The Untold Story*, 324.
390. Witcover, *The American Vice Presidency*.
391. Hayes, *Cheney: The Untold Story*, 324.
392. Witcover, *The American Vice Presidency*; Cheney, *In My Time*.
393. Cheney, *In My Time*.
394. Baker, *Days of Fire: Bush and Cheney*, 95.
395. Baker, *Days of Fire: Bush and Cheney*, 95.
396. Baker, *Days of Fire: Bush and Cheney*, 95.
397. Baker, *Days of Fire: Bush and Cheney*, 95.
398. Baker, *Days of Fire: Bush and Cheney*, 95.
399. Baker, *Days of Fire: Bush and Cheney*, 95.
400. Baker, *Days of Fire: Bush and Cheney*, 95.
401. Rosen, *Cheney One on One*.
402. Baker, *Days of Fire: Bush and Cheney*.
403. Baker, *Days of Fire: Bush and Cheney*.
404. Baker, *Days of Fire: Bush and Cheney*, 96.
405. Gellman, *Angler: The Cheney Vice Presidency*, 90.
406. Baker, *Days of Fire: Bush and Cheney*, 97.
407. Cheney, *In My Time*.
408. Cheney, *In My Time*.
409. Gellman, *Angler: The Cheney Vice Presidency*, 57.
410. Gellman, *Angler: The Cheney Vice Presidency*, 73–74.
411. Gellman, *Angler: The Cheney Vice Presidency*, 73–74.
412. Gellman, *Angler: The Cheney Vice Presidency*, 73–74.
413. Baker, *Days of Fire: Bush and Cheney*, 100.
414. Hayes, *Cheney: The Untold Story*.
415. Hayes, *Cheney: The Untold Story*, 382.
416. Hayes, *Cheney: The Untold Story*, 382.

314 / Notes to Chapter 3

417. Hayes, *Cheney: The Untold Story*, 382.
418. Hayes, *Cheney: The Untold Story*, 382.
419. Hayes, *Cheney: The Untold Story*, 382.
420. Hayes, *Cheney: The Untold Story*, 382.
421. Hayes, *Cheney: The Untold Story*, 382.
422. Woodward, *Plan of Attack*.
423. Woodward, *Plan of Attack*, 168.
424. Woodward, *Plan of Attack*, 169.
425. Woodward, *Plan of Attack*, 190.
426. Woodward, *Plan of Attack*, 169.
427. Gellman, *Angler: The Cheney Vice Presidency*.
428. Gellman, *Angler: The Cheney Vice Presidency*, 215.
429. Gellman, *Angler: The Cheney Vice Presidency*, 215.
430. Gellman, *Angler: The Cheney Vice Presidency*, 217.
431. Gellman, *Angler: The Cheney Vice Presidency*, 217.
432. Gellman, *Angler: The Cheney Vice Presidency*, 249.
433. Hayes, *Cheney: The Untold Story*, 384.
434. Hayes, *Cheney: The Untold Story*, 384.
435. Cheney, *In My Time: A Personal and Political Memoir*.
436. Hayes, *Cheney: The Untold Story*, 481.
437. Hayes, *Cheney: The Untold Story*, 481.
438. Hayes, *Cheney: The Untold Story*, 481.
439. Goldstein, *White House Vice Presidency*.
440. Hayes, *Cheney: The Untold Story*, 481.
441. Cheney, *In My Time*.
442. Cheney, in conversation with the author.
443. Baker, *Days of Fire: Bush and Cheney*.
444. Baker, *Days of Fire: Bush and Cheney*, 426.
445. Baker, *Days of Fire: Bush and Cheney*, 426.
446. Hayes, *Cheney: The Untold Story*.
447. Cheney, in conversation with the author.
448. Cheney, in conversation with the author.
449. Cheney, *In My Time*.
450. Cheney, *In My Time*; Baker, *Days of Fire: Bush and Cheney*.
451. Cheney, *In My Time*, 344.
452. Cheney, *In My Time*, 344.
453. Tenet, *At the Center of the Storm*.
454. Cheney, *In My Time*; Baker, *Days of Fire: Bush and Cheney*.
455. Baker, *Days of Fire: Bush and Cheney*, 163.
456. Baker, *Days of Fire: Bush and Cheney*, 163.
457. Tenet, *At the Center of the Storm*.
458. Rosen, *Cheney One on One*; Cheney, in conversation with the author.

Notes to Chapter 3 / 315

459. Tenet, *At the Center of the Storm*.

460. Baker, *Days of Fire: Bush and Cheney*.

461. Baumgartner, with Crumblin, *The American Vice Presidency*.

462. Witcover, *The American Vice Presidency*; Baker, *Days of Fire: Bush and Cheney*.

463. Cheney, *In My Time*.

464. Witcover, *The American Vice Presidency*; Cheney, *In My Time*.

465. Cheney, *In My Time*, 348–49.

466. Cheney, *In My Time*, 348–49.

467. Goldstein, *White House Vice Presidency*.

468. Cheney, *In My Time*, 349.

469. Cheney, *In My Time*, 350.

470. Baker, *Days of Fire*, 164–65.

471. Baker, *Days of Fire*, 164–65.

472. Rosen, *Cheney One on One*.

473. Baker, *Days of Fire: Bush and Cheney*; Rosen, *Cheney One on One*.

474. Baker, *Days of Fire: Bush and Cheney*, 165.

475. Hayes, *Cheney: The Untold Story*.

476. Rosen, *Cheney One on One*.

477. McClellan, *What Happened: Inside the Bush White House*.

478. Goldstein, *The White House Vice Presidency*.

479. Woodward, *Plan of Attack*.

480. Cheney, *In My Time:*.

481. Woodward, *Plan of Attack*.

482. Woodward, *Plan of Attack*.

483. Cheney, *In My Time*.

484. Woodward, *Plan of Attack*.

485. Woodward, *Plan of Attack*.

486. Gellman, *Angler: The Cheney Vice Presidency*.

487. Cheney, *In My Time*.

488. Cheney, *In My Time*.

489. Cheney, *In My Time*.

490. Hayes, *Cheney: The Untold Story*, 401–2.

491. Cheney, in conversation with the author.

492. Cheney, in conversation with the author.

493. Cheney, *In My Time*.

494. Hayes, *Cheney: The Untold Story*; Cheney, *In My Time*.

495. Hayes, *Cheney: The Untold Story*, 402–3.

496. Hayes, *Cheney: The Untold Story*, 402–3.

497. Hayes, *Cheney: The Untold Story*, 402–3.

498. Hayes, *Cheney: The Untold Story*; Cheney, *In My Time*; Cheney, in conversation with the author.

316 / Notes to Chapter 3

499. Cheney, *In My Time*.

500. Hayes, *Cheney: The Untold Story*, 404–5.

501. Cheney, *In My Time*.

502. Hayes, *Cheney: The Untold Story*.

503. Hayes, *Cheney: The Untold Story*, 405.

504. Gellman, *Angler: The Cheney Vice Presidency*.

505. Cheney, *In My Time*, 313.

506. Cheney, in conversation with the author.

507. Hayes, *Cheney: The Untold Story*.

508. Baumgartner, with Crumblin, *American Vice Presidency*.

509. Cheney, *In My Time*, 306–7.

510. Gellman, *Angler: The Cheney Vice Presidency*; Baker, *Days of Fire: Bush and Cheney*.

511. Gellman, *Angler: The Cheney Vice Presidency*.

512. Cheney, *In My Time*; Goldstein, *White House Vice Presidency*.

513. Hayes, *Cheney: The Untold Story*.

514. Hayes, *Cheney: The Untold Story*.

515. Hayes, *Cheney: The Untold Story*, 401.

516. Cheney, *In My Time*.

517. Cheney, *In My Time*; Baker, *Days of Fire: Bush and Cheney*.

518. Cheney, *In My Time*, 307.

519. Gellman, *Angler: The Cheney Vice Presidency*.

520. Mann, *Rise of the Vulcans: The History of Bush's War Cabinet*.

521. Hayes, *Cheney: The Untold Story*.

522. Cheney, *In My Time*, 320.

523. Cheney, *In My Time*; Cheney, in conversation with the author.

524. Cheney, *In My Time*.

525. Cheney, *In My Time*, 321.

526. Cheney, in conversation with the author.

527. Cheney, *In My Time*; Rosen, *Cheney One on One*.

528. Cheney, *In My Time*; Rosen, *Cheney One on One*.

529. Rosen, *Cheney One on One*, 105–6.

530. Hayes, *Cheney: The Untold Story*, 368.

531. Hayes, *Cheney: The Untold Story*, 368.

532. Cheney, *In My Time*.

533. Cheney, *In My Time*.

534. Hayes, *Cheney: The Untold Story*, 288.

535. Woodward, *Plan of Attack*.

536. Gellman, *Angler: The Cheney Vice Presidency*, 160; Hayes, *Cheney: The Untold Story*, 479–80.

537. Gellman, *Angler: The Cheney Vice Presidency*.

538. Gellman, *Angler: The Cheney Vice Presidency*, 161.

539. Gellman, *Angler: The Cheney Vice Presidency*, 161.

540. Cheney, *In My Time*; Baumgartner, with Crumblin, *The American Vice Presidency*; Woodward, *Plan of Attack*.

541. Rosen, *Cheney One on One*.

542. Woodward, *Plan of Attack*.

543. Hayes, *Cheney: The Untold Story*, 319–20.

544. Hayes, *Cheney: The Untold Story*, 319–20.

545. Hayes, *Cheney: The Untold Story*, 319–20.

546. Hayes, *Cheney: The Untold Story*; Witcover, *The American Vice Presidency*; Gellman, *Angler: The Cheney Vice Presidency*.

547. Hayes, *Cheney: The Untold Story*.

548. Cheney, *In My Time*, 318.

549. Hayes, *Cheney: The Untold Story*.

550. Hayes, *Cheney: The Untold Story*, 319–20.

551. Hayes, *Cheney: The Untold Story*, 319–20.

552. Rice, *No Higher Honor*.

553. Rice, *No Higher Honor*.

554. Rosen, *Cheney One on One*.

555. Mann, *Rise of the Vulcans*.

556. Cheney, *In My Time*.

557. Cheney, *In My Time*.

558. Goldstein, *White House Vice Presidency*.

559. Cheney, *In My Time*, 319.

560. Baumgartner, with Crumblin, *The American Vice Presidency*; Cheney, *In My Time*.

561. Baker, *Days of Fire*; Hayes, *Cheney: The Untold Story*.

562. Hayes, *Cheney: The Untold Story*.

563. Hayes, *Cheney: The Untold Story*; Mann, *Rise of the Vulcans*; Baker, *Days of Fire: Bush and Cheney*.

564. Hayes, *Cheney: The Untold Story*.

565. Baker, *Days of Fire: Bush and Cheney*, 121.

566. Hayes, *Cheney: The Untold Story*.

567. Hayes, *Cheney: The Untold Story*.

568. Gellman, *Angler: The Cheney Vice Presidency*; Baker, *Days of Fire: Bush and Cheney*.

569. Hayes, *Cheney: The Untold Story*.

570. Baker, *Days of Fire: Bush and Cheney*; Hayes, *Cheney: The Untold Story*.

571. Gellman, *Angler: The Cheney Vice Presidency*; Baker, *Days of Fire: Bush and Cheney*.

572. McClellan, *What Happened: Inside the Bush White*.

573. Rove, *Courage and Consequence*, 251.

574. Baker, *Days of Fire: Bush and Cheney*; Hayes, *Cheney: The Untold Story*; Mann, *Rise of the Vulcans*.

575. Gellman, *Angler: The Cheney Vice Presidency*, 114.

318 / Notes to Chapter 3

576. Hayes, *Cheney: The Untold Story*.

577. Hayes, *Cheney: The Untold Story*, 332.

578. Baker, *Days of Fire: Bush and Cheney*; Hayes, *Cheney: The Untold Story*; Mann, *Rise of the Vulcans*; Gellman, *Angler: The Cheney Vice Presidency*.

579. Gellman, *Angler: The Cheney Vice Presidency*, 115.

580. Gellman, *Angler: The Cheney Vice Presidency*, 115.

581. Gellman, *Angler: The Cheney Vice Presidency*; Baker, *Days of Fire: Bush and Cheney*; Mann, *Rise of the Vulcans*.

582. Hayes, *Cheney: The Untold Story*.

583. Baker, *Days of Fire: Bush and Cheney*.

584. Hayes, *Cheney: The Untold Story*.

585. Hayes, *Cheney: The Untold Story*.

586. Mann, *Rise of the Vulcans*; Rosen, *Cheney One on One*; Gellman, *Angler: The Cheney Vice Presidency*.

587. Hayes, *Cheney: The Untold Story*; Mann, *Rise of the Vulcans*; Baker, *Days of Fire: Bush and Cheney*.

588. Mann, *Rise of the Vulcans*, 295.

589. Fleischer, *Taking Heat: The President, the Press*; Gellman, *Angler: The Cheney Vice Presidency*.

590. Bush, *Decision Points*, 129.

591. Hayes, *Cheney: The Untold Story*; Rosen, *Cheney One on One*.

592. Hayes, *Cheney: The Untold Story*, 336.

593. Gellman, *Angler: The Cheney Vice Presidency*.

594. Gellman, *Angler: The Cheney Vice Presidency*, 117.

595. Hayes, *Cheney: The Untold Story*; Mann, *Rise of the Vulcans*; Rove, *Courage and Consequence*; Baker, *Days of Fire: Bush and Cheney in the White House*.

596. Hayes, *Cheney: The Untold Story*.

597. Mann, *Rise of the Vulcans*296.

598. Hughes, *Ten Minutes from Normal*, 241.

599. Rosen, *Cheney One on One*.

600. Rosen, *Cheney One on One*, 210.

601. Gellman, *Angler: The Cheney Vice Presidency*, 118.

602. Hayes, *Cheney: The Untold Story*.

603. Cheney, in conversation with the author.

604. Cheney, in conversation with the author.

605. Cheney, in conversation with the author.

606. Hayes, *Cheney: The Untold Story*; Baker, *Days of Fire*.

607. Hayes, *Cheney: The Untold Story*; Hughes, *Ten Minutes from Normal*.

608. Hayes, *Cheney: The Untold Story*; Baker, *Days of Fire*.

609. Hayes, *Cheney: The Untold Story*.

610. Hayes, *Cheney: The Untold Story*, 338.

611. Hayes, *Cheney: The Untold Story*, 338.

612. Rove, *Courage and Consequence*, 253.

613. Rove, *Courage and Consequence*, 253.

614. Rove, *Courage and Consequence*, 253.

615. Rove, *Courage and Consequence*, 253.

616. Bush, *Decision Points*, 129.

617. Bush, *Decision Points*, 129.

618. Rice, *No Higher Honor*, 73–74.

619. Witcover, *The American Vice Presidency*.

620. Witcover, *The American Vice Presidency*, 479–80.

621. Goldstein, *White House Vice Presidency*.

622. Baker, *Days of Fire*, 124–25.

623. Goldstein, *White House Vice Presidency*.

624. Witcover, *American Vice Presidency*, 479–80.

625. Goldstein, *White House Vice Presidency*, 137.

626. Hayes, *Cheney: The Untold Story*.

627. Gellman, *Angler: The Cheney Vice Presidency*, 119; Baker, *Days of Fire*, 125.

628. Baker, *Days of Fire: Bush and Cheney*; Hayes, *Cheney: The Untold Story*.

629. Baker, *Days of Fire: Bush and Cheney*; Hayes, *Cheney: The Untold Story*.

630. Hayes, *Cheney: The Untold Story*.

631. Baker, *Days of Fire: Bush and Cheney*, 125.

632. Hayes, *Cheney: The Untold Story*, 339.

633. Gellman, *Angler: The Cheney Vice Presidency*, 119–20.

634. Baker, *Days of Fire*.

635. Hayes, *Cheney: The Untold Story*.

636. Hayes, *Cheney: The Untold Story*, 339.

637. Hayes, *Cheney: The Untold Story*, 339.

638. Bush, *Decision Points*, 131.

639. Andy Card, in conversation with the author, October 2010.

640. Card, in conversation with the author.

641. Hayes, *Cheney: The Untold Story*.

642. Hayes, *Cheney: The Untold Story*, 345.

643. Hayes, *Cheney: The Untold Story*, 345.

644. Hayes, *Cheney: The Untold Story*, 345.

645. Hughes, *Ten Minutes from Normal*, 271.

646. Woodward, *Plan of Attack*, 30.

647. Hayes, *Cheney: The Untold Story*.

648. Hayes, *Cheney: The Untold Story*.

649. Hayes, *Cheney: The Untold Story*.

650. Hayes, *Cheney: The Untold Story*.

651. Baker, *Days of Fire: Bush and Cheney*.

652. Hayes, *Cheney: The Untold Story*.

320 / Notes to Chapter 3

653. Hayes, *Cheney: The Untold Story*.
654. Hayes, *Cheney: The Untold Story*.
655. Hayes, *Cheney: The Untold Story*, 354–45.
656. Hayes, *Cheney: The Untold Story*, 355.
657. Hayes, *Cheney: The Untold Story*.
658. Hayes, *Cheney: The Untold Story*.
659. Hayes, *Cheney: The Untold Story*.
660. Hayes, *Cheney: The Untold Story*.
661. Hayes, *Cheney: The Untold Story*.
662. Hayes, *Cheney: The Untold Story*.
663. Burke, *Honest Broker? The National Security Advisor*, 248.
664. Hayes, *Cheney: The Untold Story*.
665. Hayes, *Cheney: The Untold Story*, 352.
666. Hayes, *Cheney: The Untold Story*, 352.
667. Hayes, *Cheney: The Untold Story*, 367.
668. Baker, *Days of Fire: Bush and Cheney*.
669. Mann, *Rise of the Vulcans*.
670. Hayes, *Cheney: The Untold Story*.
671. Hayes, *Cheney: The Untold Story*, 372.
672. McClellan, *What Happened: Inside the Bush White House*, 136–37.
673. Hayes, *Cheney: The Untold Story*.
674. Hayes, *Cheney: The Untold Story*, 317–18.
675. Hayes, *Cheney: The Untold Story*, 319.
676. Perino, in conversation with the author.
677. Hayes, *Cheney: The Untold Story*.
678. Mann, *Rise of the Vulcans*.
679. Hayes, *Cheney: The Untold Story*.
680. Hayes, *Cheney: The Untold Story*, 378.
681. Tenet, *At the Center of the Storm*, 343.
682. Perino, in conversation with the author.
683. Tenet, *At the Center of the Storm*, 343–44.
684. Baker, *Days of Fire*.
685. Mann, *Rise of the Vulcans*.
686. Hayes, *Cheney: The Untold Story*.
687. Hayes, *Cheney: The Untold Story*.
688. Thomas E. Ricks, *Fiasco: The American Military Adventure in Iraq* (New York: Penguin, 2006), 49.
689. Ricks, *Fiasco: American Military Adventure in Iraq*.
690. Hayes, *Cheney: The Untold Story*.
691. McClellan, *What Happened: Inside the Bush White House*, 137.
692. Rice, in conversation with the author.
693. Hayes, *Cheney: The Untold Story*.

694. Fleischer, *Taking Heat: The President, the Press.*

695. Hayes, *Cheney: The Untold Story of America's Most Powerful and Controversial Vice President*, 380–81.

696. McClellan, *What Happened: Inside the Bush White House*, 138.

697. McClellan, *What Happened: Inside the Bush White House*, 138.

698. Hayes, *Cheney: The Untold Story*, 380–81.

699. Tenet, *At the Center of the Storm.*

700. Tenet, *At the Center of the Storm.*

701. Bush, *Decision Points*, 91.

702. Hayes, *Cheney: The Untold Story*, 381–82.

703. Hayes, *Cheney: The Untold Story*, 381–82.

704. Bush, *Decision Points*, 91.

705. Tenet, *At the Center of the Storm*; McClellan, *What Happened: Inside the Bush White House.*

706. Burke, *Honest Broker? National Security Advisor.*

707. Rice, *No Higher Honor*, 180.

708. Hayes, *Cheney: The Untold Story*; Baker, *Days of Fire: Bush and Cheney.*

709. Bush, *Decision Points*, 237–38.

710. Hayes, *Cheney: The Untold Story.*

711. Hayes, *Cheney: The Untold Story.*

712. Hayes, *Cheney: The Untold Story.*

713. Hayes, *Cheney: The Untold Story.*

714. Hayes, *Cheney: The Untold Story.*

715. Hayes, *Cheney: The Untold Story*, 388.

716. Hayes, *Cheney: The Untold Story*, 387.

717. Hayes, *Cheney: The Untold Story*, 387.

718. Hayes, *Cheney: The Untold Story*, 387.

719. Hayes, *Cheney: The Untold Story*, 389–90.

720. Hayes, *Cheney: The Untold Story*, 389–90.

721. Rice, *No Higher Honor.*

722. Hayes, *Cheney: The Untold Story.*

723. Hayes, *Cheney: The Untold Story*, 397.

724. Baker, *Days of Fire: Bush and Cheney.*

725. Baker, *Days of Fire: Bush and Cheney.*

726. Hayes, *Cheney: The Untold Story*; Baker, *Days of Fire: Bush and Cheney.*

727. Hayes, *Cheney: The Untold Story.*

728. Hayes, *Cheney: The Untold Story.*

729. Hayes, *Cheney: The Untold Story*; Rice, *No Higher Honor.*

730. Woodward, *Plan of Attack.*

731. Woodward, *Plan of Attack*; Baker, *Days of Fire: Bush and Cheney.*

732. Woodward, *Plan of Attack.*

733. Cheney, *In My Time*, 398.

322 / Notes to Chapter 3

734. Cheney, *In My Time*, 398.
735. Hayes, *Cheney: The Untold Story*.
736. Hayes, *Cheney: The Untold Story*.
737. Hayes, *Cheney: The Untold Story*, 391.
738. Hayes, *Cheney: The Untold Story*, 391.
739. Hayes, *Cheney: The Untold Story*, 391–92.
740. Baker, *Days of Fire: Bush and Cheney*260.
741. Hayes, *Cheney: The Untold Story*.
742. Hayes, *Cheney: The Untold Story*.
743. Hayes, *Cheney: The Untold Story*, 393.
744. Rumsfeld, *Known and Unknown*.
745. Hayes, *Cheney: The Untold Story*.
746. Hayes, *Cheney: The Untold Story*.
747. Hayes, *Cheney: The Untold Story*, 479.
748. Hayes, *Cheney: The Untold Story*; McClellan, *What Happened: Inside the Bush White House*.
749. Rice, *No Higher Honor*, 104–5.
750. Hayes, *Cheney: The Untold Story*.
751. Baker, *Days of Fire: Bush and Cheney*, 354–5.
752. Cheney, *In My Time*.
753. Baker, *Days of Fire: Bush and Cheney*, 194.
754. Baker, *Days of Fire: Bush and Cheney*, 194.
755. Cheney, in conversation with the author.
756. Rice, *No Higher Honor*.
757. Goldstein, *White House Vice Presidency*.
758. Rosen, *Cheney One on One*.
759. Rosen, *Cheney One on One*.
760. Cheney, *In My Time: A Personal and Political Memoir*.
761. Johnathan Masters, "The U.S. Vice President and Foreign Policy," *Council on Foreign Relations* (June 2016), http://www.cfr.org/united-states/us-vice-president-foreign-policy/p38104 (accessed June 30, 2016).
762. Masters, "The U.S. Vice President."
763. Gellman, *Angler: The Cheney Vice Presidency*.
764. Gellman, *Angler: The Cheney Vice Presidency*, 132–33.
765. Cheney, in conversation with the author.
766. Baker, *Days of Fire: Bush and Cheney*; Fleischer, in conversation with the author.
767. Bartlett, in conversation with the author.
768. Fleischer, in conversation with the author.
769. Baker, *Days of Fire: Bush and Cheney*, 5.
770. Baker, *Days of Fire: Bush and Cheney*, 5.
771. Baker, *Days of Fire: Bush and Cheney*, 5.

Notes to Chapter 3 / 323

772. Baker, *Days of Fire: Bush and Cheney*, 5.
773. Baker, *Days of Fire: Bush and Cheney*, 5.
774. Hayes, *Cheney: The Untold Story*.
775. Hayes, *Cheney: The Untold Story*, 3–4.
776. Hayes, *Cheney: The Untold Story*, 3–4.
777. Hayes, *Cheney: The Untold Story*, 3.
778. Hayes, *Cheney: The Untold Story*, 281.
779. Bush, *Decision Points*, 87.
780. McClellan, *What Happened: Inside the Bush White House*, 85.
781. Rove, in conversation with the author.
782. Rice, in conversation with the author.
783. Meacham, *Destiny and Power*.
784. Baker, *Days of Fire: Bush and Cheney*, 325.
785. Baker, *Days of Fire: Bush and Cheney*, 325.
786. Cheney, *In My Time*.
787. Witcover, *The American Vice Presidency*.
788. Cheney, in conversation with the author.
789. Cheney, in conversation with the author.
790. Baumgartner, with Crumblin, *The American Vice Presidency*.
791. Hayes, *Cheney: The Untold Story*.
792. Hayes, *Cheney: The Untold Story*.
793. Bush, *Decision Points*.
794. Bush, *Decision Points*.
795. Bush, *Decision Points*, 87.
796. Baker, *Days of Fire: Bush and Cheney*.
797. Baker, *Days of Fire: Bush and Cheney*, 305.
798. Cheney, *In My Time*; Perino, in conversation with the author.
799. Baker, *Days of Fire: Bush and Cheney*.
800. Baker, *Days of Fire: Bush and Cheney*.
801. Baker, *Days of Fire: Bush and Cheney*, 311–12.
802. Baker, *Days of Fire: Bush and Cheney*, 311–12.
803. Hayes, *Cheney: The Untold Story*, 461.
804. Baker, *Days of Fire: Bush and Cheney*.
805. Rosen, *Cheney One on One*.
806. Hayes, *Cheney: The Untold Story*.
807. Hayes, *Cheney: The Untold Story*.
808. Baker, *Days of Fire: Bush and Cheney*.
809. Baker, *Days of Fire: Bush and Cheney*.
810. Baumgartner, with Crumblin, *American Vice Presidency:*.
811. Witcover, *American Vice Presidency*, 492.
812. Bush, *Decision Points*, 105.
813. Bush, *Decision Points*, 105.

324 / Notes to Chapter 3

814. Witcover, *The American Vice Presidency*, 492.

815. Perino, in conversation with the author,; Bartlett, in conversation with the author.

816. Bush, *Decision Points*, 105.

817. Bush, *Decision Points*, 105.

818. Baker, *Days of Fire: Bush and Cheney*, 651–52.

819. Woodward, *State of Denial*.

820. Cheney, in conversation with the author.

821. Baker, *Days of Fire: Bush and Cheney*507.

822. Rosen, *Cheney One on One*, 131.

823. Cheney, in conversation with the author.

824. Rosen, *Cheney One on One*.

825. Rosen, *Cheney One on One*, 142.

826. Cheney, in conversation with the author.

827. Mann, *Rise of the Vulcans*.

828. Baker, *Days of Fire: Bush and Cheney*, 305.

829. Richard Morin, "18%?," *Washington Post*, March 5, 2006, http://www.washingtonpost.com/wpdyn/content/article/2006/03/03/AR2006030302045.html (accessed June 30, 2016).

830. Morin, "18%?"

831. Hayes, *Cheney: The Untold Story*.

832. Baker, *Days of Fire: Bush and Cheney*.

833. Hayes, *Cheney: The Untold Story*.

834. Cheney, in conversation with the author,.

835. Baker, *Days of Fire: Bush and Cheney*.

836. Cheney, *In My Time*.

837. Cheney, *In My Time*.

838. Cheney, *In My Time*.

839. Cheney, *In My Time*.

840. Baker, *Days of Fire: Bush and Cheney*.

841. Woodward, *State of Denial*, 456–47.

842. Woodward, *State of Denial*, 456–47.

843. Baker, Days of Fire: Bush and Cheney.

844. Baker, Days of Fire: Bush and Cheney, 441.

845. Baker, Days of Fire: Bush and Cheney, 441.

846. Baker, Days of Fire: Bush and Cheney, 441.

847. Baker, Days of Fire: Bush and Cheney, 441.

848. Baker, Days of Fire: Bush and Cheney, 441.

849. Baker, Days of Fire: Bush and Cheney, 443.

850. Baker, Days of Fire: Bush and Cheney, 443.

851. Baker, Days of Fire: Bush and Cheney, 443.

852. Baker 2013, 443–34.

853. Baker, *Days of Fire: Bush and Cheney*, 441.

854. Baker, *Days of Fire: Bush and Cheney*, 444.

855. Baker, *Days of Fire: Bush and Cheney*, 444.

856. Baker, *Days of Fire: Bush and Cheney*, 444.

857. Baker, *Days of Fire: Bush and Cheney*, 444.

858. Baker, *Days of Fire: Bush and Cheney*, 446.

859. Baker, *Days of Fire: Bush and Cheney*, 446.

860. Baker, *Days of Fire: Bush and Cheney*, 446.

861. Cheney, in conversation with the author.

862. Burke, "The Bush 2000 Transition."

863. Burke, "The Bush 2000 Transition."

864. Gellman, *Angler: The Cheney Vice Presidency.*

865. Gellman, *Angler: The Cheney Vice Presidency.*

866. Card, in conversation with the author.

867. Goldstein, *White House Vice Presidency.*

868. Gellman, *Angler: The Cheney Vice Presidency*, 35.

869. Rosen, *Cheney One on One.*

870. Rosen, *Cheney One on One.*

871. Meacham, *Destiny and Power.*

872. Baumgartner, with Crumblin, *American Vice Presidency.*

873. Rice, *No Higher Honor*, 17.

874. Hayes, *Cheney: The Untold Story*, 521.

875. Cheney, in conversation with the author.

876. Cheney, in conversation with the author.

877. Baker, *Days of Fire: Bush and Cheney*, 451.

878. Baumgartner, with Crumblin, *American Vice Presidency*, 168.

879. Baker, *Days of Fire: Bush and Cheney*, 451.

880. Rosen, *Cheney One on One.*

881. Dick Cheney, in conversation with the author, December 2011.

882. Cheney, in conversation with the author.

883. Baker, *Days of Fire: Bush and Cheney*, 229.

884. Perino, in conversation with the author; Fleischer, in conversation with the author.

885. Hughes, *Ten Minutes from Normal*, 204.

886. Warshaw, *The Co-Presidency of Bush and Cheney.*

887. Warshaw, *The Co-Presidency of Bush and Cheney.*

888. Warshaw, *The Co-Presidency of Bush and Cheney*, 60.

889. Warshaw, *The Co-Presidency of Bush and Cheney*, 60.

890. Gellman, *Angler: The Cheney Vice Presidency.*

891. Scowcroft, in conversation with the author.

326 / Notes to Chapter 3

892. Warshaw, *Co-Presidency of Bush and Cheney*; Woodward, *Plan of Attack*.

893. Warshaw, *Co-Presidency of Bush and Cheney*.

894. McClellan, *What Happened: Inside the Bush White House*.

895. Calio, in conversation with the author.

896. Cheney, *In My Time*; Cheney, in conversation with the author.

897. Warshaw, *Co-Presidency of Bush and Cheney*.

898. Gellman, *Angler: The Cheney Vice Presidency*.

899. Woodward, *Plan of Attack*, 48.

900. Gellman, *Angler: The Cheney Vice Presidency*, 44.

901. Warshaw, *Co-Presidency of Bush and Cheney*; Cheney, *In My Time: A Personal and Political Memoir*.

902. Cheney, in conversation with the author.

903. Gellman, *Angler: The Cheney Vice Presidency*.

904. Rosen, *Cheney One on One*; Gellman, *Angler: The Cheney Vice Presidency*; Cheney, *In My Time*; Baker, *Days of Fire: Bush and Cheney*.

905. Rosen, *Cheney One on One*, 106.

906. Rosen, *Cheney One on One*, 106.

907. Gellman, *Angler: The Cheney Vice Presidency*.

908. Gellman, *Angler: The Cheney Vice Presidency*, 49.

909. Gellman, *Angler: The Cheney Vice Presidency*, 50.

910. Hayes, *Cheney: The Untold Story*.

911. Hayes, *Cheney: The Untold Story*.

912. Hayes, *Cheney: The Untold Story*; Witcover, *The American Vice Presidency*; Powell, in conversation with the author.

913. Meacham, *Destiny and Power*, 588.

914. Meacham, *Destiny and Power*, 589.

915. Warshaw, *Co-Presidency of Bush and Cheney*.

916. Meacham, *Destiny and Power*, 590.

917. Warshaw, *Co-Presidency of Bush and Cheney*.

918. Warshaw, *Co-Presidency of Bush and Cheney*; Cheney, in conversation with the author.

919. Warshaw, *Co-Presidency of Bush and Cheney*, 58.

920. Warshaw, *Co-Presidency of Bush and Cheney*, 4.

921. Warshaw, *Co-Presidency of Bush and Cheney*, 4.

922. Cheney, in conversation with the author.

923. Warshaw, *Co-Presidency of Bush and Cheney*.

924. Gellman, *Angler: The Cheney Vice Presidency*, 364.

925. Gellman, *Angler: The Cheney Vice Presidency*, 364.

926. Hayes, *Cheney: The Untold Story*.

927. Hayes, *Cheney: The Untold Story*, 478.

928. Hayes, *Cheney: The Untold Story*, 478.

Notes to Chapter 3 / 327

929. Hayes, *Cheney: The Untold Story*, 478.
930. Hayes, Cheney: The Untold Story.
931. Hayes, *Cheney: The Untold Story*.
932. Hayes, *Cheney: The Untold Story*.
933. Gellman, *Angler: The Cheney Vice Presidency*, 364.
934. Gellman, *Angler: The Cheney Vice Presidency*, 364.
935. Baker, *Days of Fire: Bush and Cheney*; Gellman, *Angler: The Cheney Vice Presidency*; Hayes, *Cheney: The Untold Story*.
936. Baker, *Days of Fire: Bush and Cheney*, 229.
937. Gellman, *Angler: The Cheney Vice Presidency*.
938. Gellman, *Angler: The Cheney Vice Presidency*; Baker, *Days of Fire: Bush and Cheney*.
939. Rosen, *Cheney One on One*.
940. Cheney, in conversation with the author.
941. Gellman, *Angler: The Cheney Vice Presidency*, 364.
942. Gellman, *Angler: The Cheney Vice Presidency*, 365.
943. Baker, *Days of Fire: Bush and Cheney*.
944. Card, in conversation with the author.
945. Cheney, *In My Time*.
946. Cheney, *In My Time*, 425.
947. Baker, *Days of Fire: Bush and Cheney*, 365.
948. Rosen, *Cheney One on One*, 1240.
949. Gates, *Duty: Memoirs of a Secretary at War*.
950. Gellman, *Angler: The Cheney Vice Presidency*.
951. Rosen, *Cheney One on One*.
952. Rosen, *Cheney One on One*.
953. Baker, *Days of Fire: Bush and Cheney*.
954. Baker, *Days of Fire: Bush and Cheney*.
955. Rice, *No Higher Honor*, 17.
956. Baker, *Days of Fire: Bush and Cheney*.
957. Baker, *Days of Fire: Bush and Cheney*, 362.
958. Bush, *Decision Points*, 2010.
959. Baumgartner, with Crumblin, *American Vice Presidency*.
960. Woodward, *State of Denial*.
961. Rumsfeld, in discussion with the author; Rove, in conversation with the author; Rice, in conversation with the author.
962. Bartlett, in conversation with the author.
963. Cheney, in conversation with the author.
964. Card, in conversation with the author.
965. Rumsfeld, in discussion with the author.
966. Ari Fleischer, in conversation with the author.

328 / Notes to Chapter 4

967. Baker, *Days of Fire: Bush and Cheney*.

968. Hadley, in discussion with the author; Cheney, in conversation with the author.

969. Card, in conversation with the author; Cheney, in conversation with the author.

970. Perino, in conversation with the author; Bartlett, in conversation with the author; Hadley, in discussion with the author.

971. Baker, *Days of Fire: Bush and Cheney*, 640.

972. Card, in conversation with the author.

973. Gates, *Duty: Memoirs of a Secretary at War*, 97–98.

974. Baker, *Days of Fire: Bush and Cheney*.

975. Fleischer, in conversation with the author.

976. Rove, in conversation with the author.

977. Cheney, in conversation with the author.

978. Cheney, in conversation with the author.

Chapter 4

1. Joel K. Goldstein, *The White House Vice Presidency: The Path to Significance, Mondale to Biden* (Lawrence: University Press of Kansas, 2016); Jules Witcover, *The American Vice Presidency: From Irrelevance to Power* (Washington, DC: Smithsonian Books, 2014); Jody C. Baumgartner, *The American Vice Presidency Reconsidered* (Westport, CT,: Praeger 2006).

2. Goldstein, *White House Vice Presidency*.

3. Witcover, *American Vice Presidency*.

4. Adam Clymer, "Thomas F. Eagleton, 77, a Running Mate for 18 Days, Dies," *New York Times*, March 5, 2007.

5. Clymer, "Thomas F. Eagleton," 77."

6. Clymer, "Thomas F. Eagleton," 77.

7. Witcover, *American Vice Presidency*.

8. Goldstein, *White House Vice Presidency*, 37.

9. Witcover, *American Vice Presidency*.

10. Jody C. Baumgartner, with Thomas F. Crumblin, *The American Vice Presidency: From the Shadow to the Spotlight* (New York: Rowman & Littlefield, 2015), 90.

11. Goldstein, *White House Vice Presidency*, 38.

12. Goldstein, *White House Vice Presidency*, 38.

13. Goldstein, *White House Vice Presidency*, 38.

14. Steven M. Gillon, "A New Framework: Walter Mondale as Vice President," in *At the President's Side: The Vice Presidency in the Twentieth Century*, ed. Timothy Walch (Columbia: University of Missouri Press, 1997).

Notes to Chapter 4 / 329

15. Witcover, *The American Vice Presidency.*

16. Betty Glad, *Jimmy Carter: In Search of the Great White House* (New York: W. W. Norton, 1980).

17. Goldstein, *White House Vice Presidency.*

18. Witcover, *e American Vice Presidency.*

19. Witcover, *American Vice Presidency*, 431.

20. Jimmy Carter, *Keeping Faith: Memoirs of a President* (New York: Bantam Books, 1982), 37.

21. Goldstein, *White House Vice Presidency*, 41.

22. Paul Kengor, *Wreath Layer or Policy Player?* (New York: Lexington Books, 2000), 85.

23. Walter Mondale, in conversation with the author, February 2008.

24. Goldstein, *White House Vice Presidency*, 41.

25. Goldstein, *White House Vice Presidency*, 41.

26. Goldstein, *White House Vice Presidency*, 41.

27. Carter, *Keeping Faith: Memoirs of a President*, 7.

28. Goldstein, *White House Vice Presidency.*

29. Paul C. Light, *Vice-Presidential Power: Advice and Influence in the White House* (Baltimore, MD: Johns Hopkins University Press, 1984); Walter Mondale, in conversation with the author, February 2008.

30. Baumgartner, with Crumblin, *American Vice Presidency.*

31. Goldstein, *White House Vice Presidency.*

32. Walter Mondale, in conversation with the author, February 2008.

33. Mondale, in conversation with the author.

34. Mondale, in conversation with the author.

35. Al Eisele, in conversation with the author, February 2008.

36. Goldstein, *White House Vice Presidency.*

37. Goldstein, *White House Vice Presidency.*

38. Goldstein, *White House Vice Presidency.*

39. Jules Witcover, *Crapshoot: Rolling the Dice on the Vice Presidency* (New York: Crown, 1992).

40. Light, *Vice-Presidential Power*; Carter, *Keeping Faith: Memoirs of a President.*

41. Goldstein, *White House Vice Presidency.*

42. Paul Kengor, "The Vice President, Secretary of State, and Foreign Policy, *Political Science Quarterly* 115 (2): 2000; Paul Kengor, *Wreath Layer or Policy Player? The Vice President's Role in Foreign Policy*, 2002; Gillon, "A New Framework: Walter Mondale."

43. Zbigniew Brzezinski, in conversation with the author, November 2008; Goldstein, *White House Vice Presidency.*

44. Minnesota Historical Society Library, "Walter Mondale to Jimmy Carter," dated April 1, 1977, Box 1, Locator 154.J.8.6F, Minnesota Historical Society Library.

330 / Notes to Chapter 4

45. Witcover, *American Vice Presidency*.

46. Jimmy Carter Library, "Cabinet Meeting Minutes—10/3/77–2/27/78," dated April 4, 1977, Box 7, Vertical File, WHCF, Jimmy Carter Library.

47. Goldstein, *White House Vice Presidency*, 50.

48. Light, *Vice-Presidential Power*.

49. Goldstein, *White House Vice Presidency*, 50–51.

50. Memo November 5, 1976; Rockefeller Archive Center, "Nelson Rockefeller to Walter Mondale," dated November 5, 1976, Group 26, Series 18, Vol. 38, 217–24.

51. Richard Moe, in conversation with the author, April 2008.

52. Goldstein, *White House Vice Presidency*, 52.

53. Goldstein, *White House Vice Presidency*, 53; Minnesota Historical Society Library, "Walter Mondale to Jimmy Carter," dated December 9, 1976, Box 2, Locator 154.J.8.7B, Minnesota Historical Society Library.

54. Memo November 5, 1976; Rockefeller Archive Center, "Nelson Rockefeller to Walter Mondale," dated November 5, 1976, Group 26, Series 18, Vol. 38, 217–24.

55. Goldstein, *White House Vice Presidency*.

56. Goldstein, *White House Vice Presidency*.

57. Minnesota Historical Society Library, "Mike Berman to Denis Clift, Al Eisele, Jim Johnson, Bill Smith, and Gail Harrison," dated July 25, 1977, Box 2, Locator 154.J.8.7B, Minnesota Historical Society Library.

58. Eisele, in conversation with the author.

59. Rockefeller Archive Center, "Nelson Rockefeller to Walter Mondale," dated November 5, 1976, Group 26, Series 18, Volume 38, 217–24, Rockefeller Archive Center.

60. Goldstein, *White House Vice Presidency*.

61. Zbigniew Brzezinski, in conversation with the author, November 2008.

62. Light, *Vice-Presidential Power*; Goldstein, *White House Vice Presidency*; Baumgartner, with Crumblin, *American Vice Presidency*; Mondale, in conversation with the author.

63. Light, *Vice-Presidential Power*, 207.

64. Mondale, in conversation with the author.

65. Gillon, "A New Framework."

66. Gillon, "A New Framework."

67. Marie D. Natoli, "The Vice Presidency: Gerald Ford as Healer?" *Presidential Studies Quarterly* 10, no. 4 (1980): 664.

68. Goldstein, *White House Vice Presidency*, 55.

69. Eisele, in conversation with the author.

70. Witcover, *American Vice Presidency*; Goldstein, *White House Vice Presidency*; Light, *Vice-Presidential Power*.

71. Walter F. Mondale, *The Good Fight: A Life in Liberal Politics* (New York: Scribner, 2010).

72. Carter, *Keeping Faith: Memoirs of a President*.

73. Moe, in conversation with the author.

74. Mondale, in conversation with the author.

75. Mondale, in conversation with the author; Eisele, in conversation with the author.

76. Zbigniew Brzezinski, *Power and Principle: Memoirs of the National Security Advisor 1977–1981* (New York: Farrar, Straus and Giroux, 1983), 33.

77. A. Denis Clift, *With Presidents to the Summit* (Fairfax, VA: George Mason University Press, 1993); Carter, *Keeping Faith: Memoirs of a President*; Jimmy Carter Library, "Al Moses to Walter Mondale," dated August, 21, 1980, Box 1, Collection #133, Jimmy Carter Library.

78. John P. Burke, *Honest Broker? The National Security Advisor and Presidential Decision Making* (College Station: Texas A&M University Press, 2009).

79. Jimmy Carter Library, "Jimmy Carter to Walter Mondale, Cyrus Vance, Griffin Bell, Zbigniew Brzezinski, Stansfield Turner, and Robert Lipshutz," Box 226, Office of Staff Secretary, Jimmy Carter Library.

80. Witcover, *American Vice Presidency*; Goldstein, *White House Vice Presidency; Moore*, in conversation with the author.

81. Mondale, *The Good Fight*, 172.

82. Light, *Vice-Presidential Power; Moore*, in conversation with the author.

83. Light, *Vice-Presidential Power*.

84. Carter, *Keeping Faith: Memoirs of a President*, 39.

85. Kengor, *Wreath Layer or Policy Player?*

86. Kengor, *Wreath Layer or Policy Player?*

87. Rockefeller Archive Center, "Jimmy Carter to Nelson Rockefeller," dated November 9, 1976, Record Group 26, Series 18, vol. 38, 217–24, Rockefeller Archive Center.

88. Mondale, in conversation with the author.

89. Moe, in conversation with the author.

90. Brzezinski, *Power and Principle*, 17.

91. Goldstein, *White House Vice Presidency*, 68.

92. Goldstein, *White House Vice* Presidency, 68.

93. Goldstein, *White House Vice Presidency*, 68–69.

94. William Smith, in conversation with the author, April 2008.

95. Light, *Vice-Presidential Power*, 212.

96. Light, *Vice-Presidential Power*, 212.

97. Jimmy Carter Library, "Walter Mondale to Jimmy Carter," dated February 16, 1977, Box 7, Gerald Rafshoon Subject Files, Jimmy Carter Library; Minnesota Historical Society Library, "Mike Berman to Denis Clift, Al Eisele, Jim Johnson, Bill Smith, and Gail Harrison," dated July 25, 1977, Box 2, Locator 154.J.8.7B, Minnesota Historical Society Library.

332 / Notes to Chapter 4

98. Light, *Vice-Presidential Power*, 213.

99. Clift, *With Presidents to the Summit*; Eisele, in conversation with the author.

100. Goldstein, *White House Vice Presidency*, 67.

101. Clift, *With Presidents to the Summit*, 138.

102. Jimmy Carter Library, "Jim Fallows through Jody Powell to Jimmy Carter," dated January 22, 1977, Box FG-157, Federal Government–Organizations, Jimmy Carter Library.

103. Smith, in conversation with the author.

104. Goldstein, *The White House Vice Presidency*; Jimmy Carter Library, "Jim Fallows through Jody Powell."

105. Goldstein, *White House Vice Presidency*, 67.

106. Goldstein, *White House Vice Presidency*, 67.

107. Jimmy Carter Library, "Walter Mondale to Jimmy Carter."

108. Paul Kengor, *Wreath Layer or Policy Player?*

109. Moore, in conversation with the author.

110. Paul Kengor, *Wreath Layer or Policy Player? The Vice President's Role in Foreign Policy*.

111. Jimmy Carter Library, "Walter Mondale, Stu Eizenstat, and Executive Committee to President," dated August 15, 1979, Box 109, Lisa Bourdeaux Files, Jimmy Carter Library; Jimmy Carter Library, "Cabinet Meeting Minutes—10/3/77–2/27/78," dated January 9, 1978, Box 7, Vertical File, WHCF, Jimmy Carter Library; Jimmy Carter Library, "Cabinet Meeting Minutes—10/3/77–2/27/78," dated February 16, 1978, Box 7, Vertical File, WHCF, Jimmy Carter Library.

112. Kengor, *Wreath Layer or Policy Player?*, 97.

113. Kengor, *Wreath Layer or Policy Player?*, 97.

114. Kengor, *Wreath Layer or Policy Player?*, 97.

115. Kengor, *Wreath Layer or Policy Player?*, 97.

116. Steven M. Gillon, *The Democrats' Dilemma: Walter F. Mondale and the Liberal Legacy* (New York: Columbia University Press, 1992), 180, 228.

117. Goldstein, *White House Vice Presidency*.

118. Goldstein, *White House Vice Presidency*.

119. Goldstein, *White House Vice Presidency*.

120. Light, *Vice-Presidential Power*, 177.

121. Goldstein, *White House Vice Presidency*, 70.

122. Goldstein, *White House Vice Presidency*, 70.

123. Goldstein, *White House Vice Presidency*, 73.

124. Witcover, *American Vice Presidency*.

125. Witcover, *American Vice Presidency*.

126. Light, *Vice-Presidential Power*.

127. Goldstein, *White House Vice Presidency*, 73.

128. Goldstein, *White House Vice Presidency*, 73.

129. Goldstein, *White House Vice Presidency*, 73.

130. Goldstein, *White House Vice Presidency*, 73.

131. Brzezinski, *Power and Principle*.

132. Kengor, *Wreath Layer or Policy Player?*, 84.

133. Goldstein, *White House Vice Presidency*, 78.

134. Goldstein, *White House Vice Presidency*, 75.

135. Brzezinski, *Power and Principle*, 34–35.

136. Mondale, *The Good Fight*, 186–87.

137. Moore, in conversation with the author.

138. Eisele, in conversation with the author.

139. Carter, *Keeping Faith: Memoirs of a President*, 67.

140. Goldstein, *White House Vice Presidency*, 79.

141. Moore, in conversation with the author.

142. Moore, in conversation with the author.

143. Mondale, *The Good Fight*, 186–87.

144. Smith, in conversation with the author.

145. Mondale, in conversation with the author 2008.

146. Goldstein, *White House Vice Presidency*, 71.

147. Witcover, *American Vice Presidency*, 436.

148. Witcover, *Crapshoot: Rolling the Dice*.

149. Smith, in conversation with the author.

150. Minnesota Historical Society Library, "Bill Smith to Dick Moe," dated November 13, 1977, Box 2, Locator 154.J.8.7B, Walter F. Mondale Papers, Minnesota Historical Society Library; Minnesota Historical Society Library, "Mike Berman to Denis Clift, Al Eisele, Jim Johnson, Bill Smith, and Gail Harrison," dated July 25, 1977, Box 2, Locator 154.J.8.7B, Minnesota Historical Society Library.

151. Memo November 3, 1977; "Zbigniew Brzezinski to Jimmy Carter," Jimmy Carter Library, dated November 3, 1977, File 3, Box 4, Brzezinski Material: President's Daily Report File.

152. Jimmy Carter Library, "Walter Mondale to Jimmy Carter," dated February 16, 1977, Box 7, Gerald Rafshoon Subject Files, Jimmy Carter Library.

153. Goldstein, *The White House Vice Presidency*.

154. Brzezinski, *Power and Principle*; Carter, *Keeping Faith: Memoirs of a President*.

155. Carter, *Keeping Faith: Memoirs of a President*, 482.

156. Carter, *Keeping Faith: Memoirs of a President*, 482.

157. Mondale, *The Good Fight*; Witcover, *The American Vice Presidency*; Brzezinski, *Power and Principle*; Mondale, in conversation with the author.

158. Carter, *Keeping Faith: Memoirs of a President*.

159. Goldstein, *White House Vice Presidency*.

160. Smith, in conversation with the author.

161. Goldstein, *White House Vice Presidency*.

334 / Notes to Chapter 4

162. Goldstein, *White House Vice Presidency*, 77.

163. Jimmy Carter Library, "Walter Mondale to Jimmy Carter," dated April 19, 1978, Box 205, Papers of Walter F. Mondale, Donated Material, Collection #133, Jimmy Carter Library.

164. Brzezinski, *Power and Principle*.

165. Brzezinski, *Power and Principle*, 437.

166. Gillon, "A New Framework: Walter Mondale."

167. Gillon, "A New Framework: Walter Mondale."

168. Witcover, *American Vice Presidency*.

169. Mondale, *The Good Fight*, 236.

170. Mondale, *The Good Fight*, 236.

171. Smith, in conversation with the author.

172. Carter, *Keeping Faith: Memoirs of a President*, 115–16.

173. Light, *Vice-Presidential Power*.

174. Kengor, *Wreath Layer or Policy Player?*, 88.

175. Carter, *Keeping Faith: Memoirs of a President*, 39.

176. Goldstein, *White House Vice Presidency*, 91.

177. Goldstein, *White House Vice Presidency*, 91.

178. Jimmy Carter Library, "Jimmy Carter to Nelson Rockefeller," dated December 22, 1978, Box FG-161, Federal Government-Organizations, Jimmy Carter Library.

179. Kengor, *Wreath Layer or Policy Player?*, 88.

180. Witcover, *American Vice Presidency*; Brzezinski, *Power and Principle*; Light, *Vice-Presidential Power*; Clift, *With Presidents to the Summit*; Glad, *Jimmy Carter*; Carter, *Keeping Faith: Memoirs of a President*; Frank Moore, in conversation with the author, April 2008.

181. Carter, *Keeping Faith: Memoirs of a President*.

182. Carter, *Keeping Faith: Memoirs of a President*, 370.

183. Goldstein, *White House Vice Presidency*, 89.

184. Mondale, in conversation with the author; Witcover, *The American Vice Presidency*; Jimmy Carter, *White House Diary* (New York: Farrar, Straus and Giroux, 2010); Goldstein, *White House Vice Presidency*; Jimmy Carter Library, "Walter Mondale to Charlie Schultze," dated May 17, 1978, Box 55, Staff Office–CEA (Council on Economic Advisers), Jimmy Carter Library; Jimmy Carter Library, "Walter Mondale to Charlie Schultze," dated April 11, 1977, Box 55, Staff Office–CEA (Council of Economic Advisers), Jimmy Carter Library.

185. Smith, in conversation with the author.

186. Moe, in conversation with the author; Moore, in conversation with the author; Mondale, in conversation with the author; Eisele, in conversation with the author.

187. Goldstein, *White House Vice Presidency*; Eisele, in conversation with the author.

Notes to Chapter 4 / 335

188. Goldstein, *White House Vice Presidency*.

189. Gillon, *Democrats' Dilemma: Walter F. Mondale*, 251–66.

190. Smith, in conversation with the author.

191. Goldstein, *White House Vice Presidency*, 91.

192. Baumgartner, with Crumblin, *American Vice Presidency*; Carter, *White House Diary*.

193. Carter, *White House Diary*.

194. Gillon, "A New Framework: Walter Mondale," 149.

195. Minnesota Historical Society Library, "Bill Smith to Walter Mondale," dated February 1, 1979, Box 2, Locator 154.J.8.7B, Administrative Assistant to President of the Senate, Minnesota Historical Society Library.

196. Gillon, "A New Framework: Walter Mondale," 149.

197. Jimmy Carter Library, "Jack Watson and Larry Gilson to Walter Mondale," dated January 15, 1978, Box 21, Jack Watson Files 1/77–1/81, Jimmy Carter Library.

198. Minnesota Historical Society Library, "Bill Smith to Walter Mondale," dated February 1, 1979, Box 2, Locator 154.J.8.7B, Administrative Assistant to President of the Senate, Minnesota Historical Society Library.

199. Witcover, *American Vice Presidency*, 438.

200. Jimmy Carter Library, "Jack Watson and Landon Butler to Walter Mondale," dated September 4, 1980, Box 21, Jack Watson Files January 1977–January 1981, Jimmy Carter Library; Jimmy Carter Library, "Landon Butler to Walter Mondale," dated May 25, 1979, Box 141, Landon Butler Files, Jimmy Carter Library; Witcover, *The American Vice Presidency*; Memo n.d., "Senior Staff to Walter Mondale," folder "V.P. Yearly Assessment," Box 2, Locator 153.J.8.7B, Administrative Assistant to President of the Senate, Vice Presidential Files, Walter F. Mondale Papers, Minnesota Historical Society Library; Jimmy Carter Library, "Walter Mondale with Jewish Leaders," dated October 27, 1978, Box FG-161, Federal Government-Organizations, Jimmy Carter Library.

201. Witcover, *The American Vice Presidency*, 438.

202. Light, *Vice-Presidential Power*, 216.

203. Smith, in conversation with the author.

204. Smith, in conversation with the author; Mondale, in conversation with the author.

205. Gillon, "A New Framework: Walter Mondale"; Minnesota Historical Society Library, "Richard Moe to Walter Mondale," dated January 29, 1976, Box 3, Locator 154.J.9.6F, Chief of Staff Richard Moe Files, Minnesota Historical Society Library.

206. Gillon, "A New Framework: Walter Mondale."

207. Gillon, "A New Framework: Walter Mondale"; Smith, in conversation with the author.

208. Moe, in conversation with the author.

336 / Notes to Chapter 4

209. Baumgartner, with Crumblin, *The American Vice Presidency*; Smith, in conversation with the author.

210. Moore, in conversation with the author.

211. Minnesota Historical Society Library, "Al Eisele to Dick Moe, Mike Berman, Jim Johnson, Denis Clift, Gail Harrison, and Bill Smith, dated February 6, 1976, Box 2, Locator: 154.J.8.7B, Administrative Assistant to President of the Senate, Minnesota Historical Society Library.

212. Witcover, *The American Vice Presidency*.

213. Witcover, *The American Vice Presidency*, 440–41.

214. Carter, *Keeping Faith: Memoirs of a President*, 464.

215. Carter, *Keeping Faith: Memoirs of a President*, 555.

216. Carter, *White House Diary*.

217. Witcover, *American Vice Presidency*.

218. Mondale, in conversation with the author.

219. Baumgartner, with Crumblin, *American Vice Presidency*.

220. Chase Untermeyer, "Looking Forward: George Bush," in *At the President's Side*, ed. Timothy Walch (Columbia: University of Missouri Press, 1997).

221. Chase Untermeyer, in conversation with the author, July 2010.

222. Untermeyer, "Looking Forward: George Bush," 1997.

223. James Baker, in conversation with the author, June 2008.

224. Untermeyer, "Looking Forward: George Bush as Vice President"; James Baker, in conversation with the author, June 2008.

225. Max Friedersdorf, in conversation with the author, May 2008.

226. George Bush, *Looking Forward: An Autobiography* (New York: Doubleday, 1987).

227. Nancy Reagan, *My Turn: The Memoirs of Nancy Reagan* (New York: Random House, 1989).

228. James A. Baker III, "*Work Hard, Study . . . And Keep Out of Politics!*," New York: G. P. Putnam's, 2006), 98.

229. Bush, *Looking Forward: An Autobiography*, 16.

230. Bush, *Looking Forward: An Autobiography*, 9.

231. Bush, *Looking Forward: An Autobiography*, 16.

232. Richard Allen, in conversation with the author, July 2008.

233. T. Kenneth Cribb Jr., in conversation with the author, June 2008.

234. Jon Meacham, *Destiny and Power* (New York: Random House, 2015), 251.

235. Bush, *Looking Forward: An Autobiography*, 15.

236. Bush, *Looking Forward: An Autobiography* 15.

237. Meacham, *Destiny and Power*, 229.

238. Meacham, *Destiny and Power*, 229.

239. Meacham, *Destiny and Power*, 255.

240. Meacham, *Destiny and Power*, 225.

Notes to Chapter 4 / 337

241. Bush, *Looking Forward: An Autobiography*; Baumgartner, with Crumblin, *American Vice Presidency*; Cribb, in conversation with the author.

242. Witcover, *American Vice Presidency*; James A. Baker III, *"Work Hard, Study."*

243. Meacham, *Destiny and Power*, 235.

244. Untermeyer, "Looking Forward: George Bush," 158.

245. Meacham, *Destiny and Power*, 227.

246. Meacham, *Destiny and Power*, 227.

247. Bush, *Looking Forward: An Autobiography*.

248. Friedersdorf, in conversation with the author.

249. Marlin Fitzwater, in conversation with the author, June 2008.

250. Meacham, *Destiny and Power*.

251. Michael K. Deaver, *Behind the Scenes* (New York: William Morrow, 1987).

252. Untermeyer, "Looking Forward," 158.

253. Shirley Anne Warshaw, *Co-Presidency of Bush and Cheney* (Stanford, CA: Stanford University Press, 2008).

254. George H. W. Bush Library, "National Public Radio Commentary on Bush, n.d.," Office of Policy, OA/ID 41202, Office of Vice President George Bush, George H. W. Bush Library.

255. Marlin Fitzwater, *Call the Briefing!* (New York: Times Books, 1995), 75.

256. George H. W. Bush Library, "National Public Radio Commentary on Bush, n.d."

257. Fitzwater, in conversation with the author.

258. George Bush, *All the Best, George Bush: My Life in Letters and Other Writings* (New York: Lisa Drew/Scribner, 1999), 315–16.

259. Meacham, *Destiny and Power*; Baker, in conversation with the author.

260. Meacham, *Destiny and Power*, 254.

261. Baker, in conversation with the author.

262. Allen, in conversation with the author.

263. Untermeyer, "Looking Forward: George Bush."

264. Barbara Bush, *Barbara Bush: A Memoir* (New York: Charles Scribner's, 1994).

265. Untermeyer, "Looking Forward: George Bush"; Bush, *All the Best, George Bush*.

266. Untermeyer, "Looking Forward: George Bush."

267. Baumgartner, with Crumblin, *American Vice Presidency*.

268. Untermeyer, "Looking Forward: George Bush," 159–60.

269. Shirley Moore Green, in conversation with the author, July 2008.

270. Untermeyer, "Looking Forward: George Bush."

271. Baker, in conversation with the author.

272. Ed Meese, in conversation with the author, June 2008.

338 / Notes to Chapter 4

273. Witcover, *American Vice Presidency*.

274. Meacham, *Destiny and Power*, 261.

275. Baker, in conversation with the author.

276. Baker, "*Work Hard, Study*," 157.

277. Fitzwater, in conversation with the author; Green, in conversation with the author.

278. Untermeyer, "Looking Forward: George Bush," 160.

279. Untermeyer, "Looking Forward: George Bush Goldstein, *White House Vice Presidency*; Lou Cannon, *President Reagan: The Role of a Lifetime* (New York: Public Affairs, 1991).

280. Bush, *All the Best, George Bush*; Goldstein, *White House Vice Presidency*.

281. Goldstein, *White House Vice Presidency*.

282. Goldstein, *White House Vice Presidency*.

283. Untermeyer, "Looking Forward: George Bush," 160.

284. Reagan, *My Turn: The Memoirs of Nancy Reagan*.

285. Reagan, *My Turn: The Memoirs of Nancy Reagan*, 315.

286. Meacham, *Destiny and Power*; Douglas Brinkley, *The Reagan Diaries* (New York: HarperCollins, 2007).

287. Meacham, *Destiny and Power*.

288. Bush, *Looking Forward: An Autobiography*, 245.

289. Scowcroft, in conversation with the author; Cribb., in conversation with the author.

290. Fitzwater, in conversation with the author.

291. Fitzwater, in conversation with the author.

292. Meacham, *Destiny and Power*.

293. Goldstein, *White House Vice Presidency*.

294. Meacham, *Destiny and Power*, 587–58.

295. Meacham, *Destiny and Power*, 587–58.

296. Meacham, *Destiny and Power*, 587–58.

297. Baker, "*Work Hard, Study*"; Baker, in conversation with the author.

298. Meacham, *Destiny and Power*, 261.

299. Donald Gregg, in conversation with the author, June 2008.

300. Meacham, *Destiny and Power*, 262.

301. Allen, in conversation with the author.

302. Green, in conversation with the author.

303. Fitzwater, in conversation with the author.

304. Carlucci, in conversation with the author.

305. Peter Teeley, in conversation with the author, October 2008; Green, in conversation with the author.

306. Meacham, *Destiny and Power*; Witcover, *American Vice Presidency*.

307. George W. Bush, *Decision Points* (New York: Crown, 2010), 42.

308. Meacham, *Destiny and Power*; Scowcroft, in conversation with the author.

Notes to Chapter 4 / 339

309. Bush, *Looking Forward: An Autobiography*, 227–30.

310. Meacham, *Destiny and Power*.

311. Meacham, *Destiny and Power*.

312. Meacham, *Destiny and Power*, 262.

313. Herbert L. Abrams, *"The President Has Been Shot"*: *Confusion, Disability, and the 25th Amendment in the Aftermath of the Attempted Assassination of Ronald Reagan* (New York: W. W. Norton, 1992); Goldstein, *White House Vice Presidency*; Baker, in conversation with the author.

314. Ronald Reagan, *Ronald Reagan: An American Life* (New York: Simon and Schuster, 1990), 225.

315. Reagan, *Ronald Reagan: An American Life*, 255.

316. Untermeyer, "Looking Forward: George Bush"; Brinkley, *The Reagan Diaries*; Reagan, *Ronald Reagan: An American Life*.

317. Untermeyer, "Looking Forward: George Bush."

318. Burke, *Honest Broker? The National Security Advisor*; Reagan, *Ronald Reagan: An American Life*; Meacham, *Destiny and Power*.

319. Cannon, *President Reagan: The Role of a Lifetime*.

320. Allen, in conversation with the author.

321. Untermeyer, "Looking Forward: George Bush," 161.

322. Meacham, *Destiny and Power*, 267.

323. Abrams, *"The President Has Been Shot."*

324. Abrams, *"The President Has Been Shot."*

325. Baker, "Work Hard, Study.

326. Baker, "Work Hard, Study," 145–46.

327. Meacham, *Destiny and Power*.

328. Baumgartner, with Crumblin, *The American Vice Presidency*; Baker, in conversation with the author.

329. Untermeyer, "Looking Forward: George Bush."

330. Bush, *Looking Forward: An Autobiography*, 224.

331. Meacham, *Destiny and Power*, 276.

332. Donald T. Regan, *For the Record* (Orlando, FL: Harcourt Brace Jovanovich, 1988).

333. Green, in conversation with the author.

334. Green, in conversation with the author.

335. Untermeyer, "Looking Forward: George Bush."

336. Abrams, *"The President Has Been Shot."*

337. Abrams, *"The President Has Been Shot,"* 99.

338. Abrams, *"The President Has Been Shot,"* 99.

339. Abrams, *"The President Has Been Shot"*; Untermeyer, "Looking Forward: George Bush"; Deaver, *Behind the Scenes*; Ronald Reagan Library, "David M. Alpern, Thomas DeFrank, Eleanor Clift, and James Doyle, *Newsweek*, 'Who's Minding the Store,'" dated April 13, 1981, Box 1, Cabinet Affairs, Ronald Reagan Library.

340 / Notes to Chapter 4

340. Bush, *Barbara Bush: A Memoir*.

341. Ronald Reagan Library, "David M. Alpern, Thomas DeFrank, Eleanor Clift, and James Doyle."

342. Meacham, *Destiny and Power*, 279.

343. Ronald Reagan Library, "George J. Church, Time, 'Business as Usual—Almost,'" dated April 13, 1981, Box 1, Cabinet Affairs, Ronald Reagan Library.

344. Abrams, *"The President Has Been Shot."*

345. Abrams, *"The President Has Been Shot,"* 186.

346. Abrams, *"The President Has Been Shot,"* 187.

347. Abrams, *"The President Has Been Shot,"* 187.

348. Ronald Reagan Library, "William J. Casey to James A. Baker III," dated April 10, 1981, Box 1, Cabinet Affairs, Ronald Reagan Library.

349. Deaver, *Behind the Scenes*, 28.

350. Clayton Yeutter, in conversation with the author, October 2008; Teeley, in conversation with the author.

351. Abrams, *"The President Has Been Shot,"* 244.

352. Bush, *Looking Forward: An Autobiography*, 226.

353. Craig Fuller, in conversation with the author, April 2009.

354. Ed Meese, in conversation with the author, June 2008.

355. Baker, *"Work Hard, Study,"* 244–45.

356. Meacham, *Destiny and Power*, 282.

357. Untermeyer, in conversation with the author.

358. Ronald Reagan Library, "George J. Church, Time."

359. Abrams, *"The President Has Been Shot"*; Regan, *For the Record*; Bush, *Barbara Bush: A Memoir*; Baker, *"Work Hard, Study*; Reagan, *Ronald Reagan: An American Life*.

360. Witcover, *American Vice Presidency*.

361. Fitzwater, *Call the Briefing!*, 285.

362. Goldstein, *White House Vice Presidency*.

363. Untermeyer, "Looking Forward: George Bush," 162.

364. Goldstein, *White House Vice Presidency*, 108.

365. Meacham, *Destiny and Power*, 282.

366. Meacham, *Destiny and Power*, 282.

367. Goldstein, *White House Vice Presidency*, 108.

368. Frank Carlucci, in conversation with the author, June 2008.

369. Untermeyer, "Looking Forward: George Bush."

370. Witcover, *American Vice Presidency*.

371. Meacham, *Destiny and Power*, 261.

372. Baker, *"Work Hard, Study."*

373. Witcover, *American Vice Presidency*.

374. Witcover, *American Vice Presidency*, 450.

375. Bush, *All the Best, George Bush*, 312.

Notes to Chapter 4 / 341

376. Goldstein, *White House Vice Presidency*, 111.

377. Goldstein, *White House Vice Presidency*, 107.

378. Goldstein, *White House Vice Presidency*, 107.

379. Michael Deaver, in conversation with the Miller Center, September 2002.

380. Goldstein, *White House Vice Presidency*, 108.

381. Untermeyer, "Looking Forward: George Bush"; Teeley, in conversation with the author; Green, in conversation with the author.

382. Fitzwater, in conversation with the author.

383. Meese, in conversation with the author.

384. Bush, *All the Best, George Bush*.

385. Cribb, in conversation with the author.

386. Skinner et al., *Reagan, In His Own Hand* (New York: The Free Press, 2001).

387. Untermeyer, "Looking Forward: George Bush."

388. Memo, January 21, 1981. George H. W. Bush Library, "Thaddeus Garrett, Jr. to Admiral Murphy," dated January 21, 1981, Box 5, Thaddeus Garrett Files, George H. W. Bush Library.

389. Untermeyer, "Looking Forward: George Bush."

390. Skinner, et al., *Reagan, In His Own Hand*.

391. State of the Union, "Address before a Joint Session of the Congress on the State of the Union," dated January 25, 1984, in *Public Papers of the Presidents of the United States: Ronald Reagan, 1984* (Washington, DC: Government Printing Office, 1984).

392. Reagan, *Ronald Reagan: An American Life*, 298.

393. Meacham, *Destiny and Power*, 268.

394. Meacham, *Destiny and Power*, 268.

395. Untermeyer, "Looking Forward: George Bush"; Fitzwater, in conversation with the author; Craig Fuller, in conversation with the author, April 2009; Teeley, in conversation with the author; Meese, in conversation with the author; Green, in conversation with the author.

396. Untermeyer, "Looking Forward: George Bush," 163.

397. Untermeyer, "Looking Forward: George Bush"; Goldstein, *White House Vice Presidency*.

398. Untermeyer, "Looking Forward: George Bush."

399. Untermeyer, "Looking Forward: George Bush."

400. Untermeyer, "Looking Forward: George Bush."

401. Fuller, in conversation with the author.

402. Memo, July 20, 1985.

403. Memo, July 20, 1985.

404. Ronald Reagan Library, "News Briefing, George Bush," dated March 6, 1986, ID #377752, FG258, WHORM: Subject File, Ronald Reagan Library.

342 / Notes to Chapter 4

405. Ronald Reagan Library, "News Briefing, James L. Holloway, III," dated March 6, 1986, ID 377752, FG258, WHORM: Subject File, Ronald Reagan Library.

406. George H. W. Bush Library, "Don Gregg and Doug Menarchik to George Bush," dated June 1, 1987, Box 9, Donald P. Gregg Files, OA/ID 41622, George H. W. Bush Library.

407. George H. W. Bush Library, "Don Gregg and Doug Menarchik."

408. George H. W. Bush Library, "Don Gregg and Doug Menarchik."

409. George H. W. Bush Library, "Task Force on Terrorism," dated December 20, 1985, Box 1, OA/ID 41061, Task Force on Combatting Terrorism, George H. W. Bush Library.

410. Ronald Reagan Library, "News Briefing, James L. Holloway, III."

411. Goldstein, *White House Vice Presidency*.

412. Paul Kengor, "The Vice President, Secretary of State, and Foreign Policy," *Political Science Quarterly* 115 (2): 175–99; Kengor, *Wreath Layer or Policy Player?*

413. Goldstein, *White House Vice Presidency*; Baumgartner, with Crumblin, *The American Vice Presidency: From the Shadow to the Spotlight*.

414. Meese, in conversation with the author; Gregg, in conversation with the author.

415. Carlucci, in conversation with the author; Green, in conversation with the author.

416. Goldstein, *White House Vice Presidency*, 109.

417. Goldstein, *White House Vice Presidency*; Fuller, in conversation with the author.

418. Untermeyer, "Looking Forward: George Bush."

419. Goldstein, *White House Vice Presidency*; Teeley, in conversation with the author; Gregg, in conversation with the author.

420. Goldstein, *White House Vice Presidency*; Baumgartner, with Crumblin, *American Vice Presidency*; Untermeyer, "Looking Forward: George Bush."

421. Goldstein, *White House Vice Presidency*, 110.

422. Thomas Risse-Kappen, "Did 'Peace through Strength' End the Cold War?: Lessons from INF," *International Security* 16, no. 1 (1991): 162–88; Fitzwater, in conversation with the author; Peter, in conversation with the author.

423. Bush, *All the Best, George Bush*, 329.

424. Meacham, *Destiny and Power*, 285.

425. Kengor, *Wreath Layer or Policy Player?*, 155.

426. Kengor, *Wreath Layer or Policy Player?*, 153.

427. Kengor, *Wreath Layer or Policy Player?*, 153.

428. Kengor, *Wreath Layer or Policy Player?*, 153–54.

429. Meacham, *Destiny and Power: The American Odyssey of George Herbert Walker Bush*, 286.

430. Kengor, *Wreath Layer or Policy Player?* Gregg, in conversation with the author.

Notes to Chapter 4 / 343

431. Teeley, in conversation with the author.

432. Baumgartner, with Crumblin, *American Vice Presidency*120; Fuller, in conversation with the author.

433. Untermeyer, "Looking Forward: George Bush."

434. Bush, *Barbara Bush: A Memoir*.

435. Bush, *Barbara Bush: A Memoir*, 337.

436. Bush, *All the Best, George Bush*; Brinkley, *The Reagan Diaries*; Reagan, *Ronald Reagan: An American Life*.

437. Bush, *All the Best, George Bush*, 332.

438. Gregg, in conversation with the author.

439. Untermeyer, in conversation with the author.

440. Untermeyer, "Looking Forward: George Bush."

441. Goldstein, *White House Vice Presidency*.

442. Craig Fuller, in conversation with the author, April 2009.

443. Baumgartner, with Crumblin, *American Vice Presidency*, 123.

444. Friedersdorf, in conversation with the author.

445. Goldstein, *White House Vice Presidency*.

446. Goldstein, *White House Vice Presidency*, 109.

447. Goldstein, *White House Vice Presidency*, 109.

448. Baumgartner, with Crumblin, *American Vice Presidency*, 126.

449. Goldstein, *White House Vice Presidency*, 113.

450. Beckwith, in conversation with the author.

451. Beckwith, in conversation with the author.

452. Carnes Lord, in conversation with the author, July 2008.

453. Kengor, *Wreath Layer or Policy Player?*; Baumgartner, with Crumblin, *American Vice Presidency*; Goldstein, *White House Vice Presidency*; Witcover, *American Vice Presidency*.

454. Baumgartner, with Crumblin, *American Vice Presidency*.

455. David S. Broder and Bob Woodward, *The Man Who Would Be President: Dan Quayle* (New York: Simon & Schuster, 1992), 18.

456. Baumgartner, with Crumblin, *American Vice Presidency*; Scowcroft, in conversation with the author.

457. Lord, in conversation with the author.

458. Beckwith, in conversation with the author.

459. Meacham, *Destiny and Power*.

460. Kengor, *Wreath Layer or Policy Player?*; Dan Quayle, in conversation with the author, November 2008; Colin Powell, in conversation with the author, June 2008.

461. Kengor, *Wreath Layer or Policy Player?*

462. Kengor, *Wreath Layer or Policy Player?*

463. Kengor, *Wreath Layer or Policy Player?*, 170.

464. Kengor, *Wreath Layer or Policy Player?*, 170.

344 / Notes to Chapter 4

465. Powell, in conversation with the author.

466. Dan Quayle, in conversation with the author, November 2008.

467. Joseph DeSutter, in conversation with the author, September 2008.

468. Sam Skinner, in conversation with the author, August 2008.

469. Nicholas Calio, in conversation with the author, August 2008.

470. Scowcroft, in conversation with the author.

471. Lord, in conversation with the author.

472. Kengor, *Wreath Layer or Policy Player?*, 171.

473. Kengor, *Wreath Layer or Policy Player?*, 171.

474. Kengor, *Wreath Layer or Policy Player?*, 171.

475. Kengor, *Wreath Layer or Policy Player?*, 171.

476. Kengor, *Wreath Layer or Policy Player?*, 171.

477. Broder and Woodward, *Man Who Would Be President*, 96.

478. George H. W. Bush, *A World Transformed* (New York: Alfred A. Knopf, 1998), 24.

479. Kengor, *Wreath Layer or Policy Player?*

480. Broder and Woodward, *Man Who Would Be President*, 89.

481. Baumgartner, with Crumblin, *The American Vice Presidency: From the Shadow to the Spotlight*; Broder and Woodward, *Man Who Would Be President*; George H. W. Bush Library, "Sara Fritz, *Los Angeles Times*, 'Quayle: He Tries Harder,'" dated May 9, 1991, Box 19, Council on Competitiveness Files, OA/ID 41240, George H. W. Bush Library.

482. Broder and Woodward, *Man Who Would Be President*, 89.

483. Broder and Woodward, *Man Who Would Be President*, 90.

484. Lord, in conversation with the author.

485. Broder and Woodward, *Man Who Would Be President*; News Article, *Richmond Times-Dispatch*, October 11, 1989; News Article, *Los Angeles Times*, May 9, 1991; Lord, in conversation with the author; Dan Quayle, in conversation with the author.

486. Baumgartner, with Crumblin, *American Vice Presidency*; Lord, in conversation with the author; Clayton Yeutter, in conversation with the author, October 2008; Marlin Fitzwater, in conversation with the author, June 2008.

487. Yeutter, in conversation with the author.

488. Beckwith, in conversation with the author.

489. Joseph DeSutter, in conversation with the author, September 2008.

490. Dan Quayle, *Standing Firm* (New York: HarperCollins, 1994); Dick Cheney, in conversation with the author, December 2011; Yeutter, in conversation with the author; Green, in conversation with the author.

491. Beckwith, in conversation with the author,; Lord, in conversation with the author; Quayle, in conversation with the author.

492. Quayle, *Standing Firm*.

493. Beckwith, in conversation with the author.

494. Yeutter, in conversation with the author.

495. Quayle, in conversation with the author.

496. Quayle, in conversation with the author.

497. Baker, in conversation with the author.

498. Calio, in conversation with the author.

499. John Sununu, in conversation with the author, October 2008.

500. Meacham, *Destiny and Power*, 507.

501. Fitzwater, in conversation with the author, June 2008; Brent Scowcroft, in conversation with the author.

502. Quayle, *Standing Firm*, 165.

503. Lord, in conversation with the author.

504. Yeutter, in conversation with the author.

505. Meacham, *Destiny and Power*, 509; Dick Cheney, in conversation with the author, December 2011.

506. Broder and Woodward, *Man Who Would Be President*, 90.

507. Lord, in conversation with the author.

508. Broder and Woodward, *Man Who Would Be President: Dan Quayle*.

509. George H. W. Bush Library, "Sara Fritz, *Los Angeles Times*."

510. Broder and Woodward, *Man Who Would Be President*, 92.

511. Quayle, in conversation with the author.

512. Quayle, in conversation with the author.

513. Thomas M. DeFrank, *Write It When I'm Gone: Remarkable Off-the-Record Conversations with Gerald R. Ford* (New York: G. P. Putnam's Sons, 2007); Bush, *Decision Points*; Baker, "Work Hard, Study"; Fitzwater, *Call the Briefing!*; Meacham, *Destiny and Power:*; Beckwith, in conversation with the author; Lord, in conversation with the author; Cheney, in conversation with the author.

514. Beckwith, in conversation with the author.

515. Baker, in conversation with the author.

516. Baker, in conversation with the author.

517. Skinner, in conversation with the author.

518. Jim McGrath, *Heartbeat: George Bush in His Own Words* (New York: Lisa Drew, 2001), 290.

519. Fitzwater, in conversation with the author.

520. Beckwith, in conversation with the author.

521. Scowcroft, in conversation with the author.

522. Witcover, *American Vice Presidency*, 455.

523. Dan Quayle, "A New Framework: Walter Mondale as Vice President," in *At the President's Side: The Vice Presidency in the Twentieth Century*, ed. Timothy Walch (Columbia: University of Missouri Press, 1997), 171.

524. Baumgartner, with Crumblin, *American Vice Presidency*; Meacham, *Destiny and Power*; Beckwith, in conversation with the author; DeSutter, in conversation with the author.

346 / Notes to Chapter 4

525. Baumgartner, with Crumblin, *American Vice Presidency*, 110.

526. Kengor, *Wreath Layer or Policy Player?*, 166.

527. Kengor, *Wreath Layer or Policy Player?*, 166.

528. Baker, *"Work Hard, Study,"* 246.

529. Meacham, *Destiny and Power*, 336.

530. Beckwith, in conversation with the author.

531. Witcover, *American Vice Presidency*, 455–56.

532. Untermeyer, in conversation with the author.

533. George H. W. Bush Library, "Sara Fritz, *Los Angeles Times*"; George H. W. Bush Library, "William Boot, Columbia Journalism Review, 'Dan Quayle: The Sequel,'" dated September/October 1991, Box 8, Kristol, William, Files, OA/ID 40794, Office of Vice President Dan Quayle, George H. W. Bush Library; Nicholas Calio, in conversation with the author, August 2008.

534. Broder and Woodward, *Man Who Would Be President*, 30.

535. Quayle, *Standing Firm*, 24.

536. Lord, in conversation with the author; Quayle, in conversation with the author.

537. DeSutter, in conversation with the author.

538. Baumgartner, with Crumblin, *American Vice Presidency*.

539. Broder and Woodward, *Man Who Would Be President*.

540. Broder and Woodward, *Man Who Would Be President*.

541. Broder and Woodward, *Man Who Would Be President*, 25.

542. Quayle, *Standing Firm*.

543. Broder and Woodward, *Man Who Would Be President*; Beckwith, in conversation with the author.

544. Goldstein, *White House Vice Presidency*; Quayle, in conversation with the author.

545. Quayle, in conversation with the author.

546. George H. W. Bush Library, "John Sununu to George Bush," dated March 30, 1989, OA/ID 40689, Office of Vice President Dan Quayle, George H. W. Bush Library.

547. Witcover, *American Vice Presidency*.

548. Goldstein, *White House Vice Presidency*.

549. Broder and Woodward, *Man Who Would Be President*, 125.

550. Broder and Woodward, *Man Who Would Be President*, 126; George H. W. Bush Library, "President's Plan for Reducing the Burdens of Regulation through Admin. Action," dated January 30, 1992, Box 1, Gattuso, James, Files, OA/ID 41269, Domestic Policy and the Council on Competitiveness, Office of Vice President Dan Quayle, George H. W. Bush Library; George H. W. Bush Library, "Competitive Council, n.d., folder "Council on Competitiveness," n.d., Box 2, Hubbard, Allan B., Subject Files, OA/ID 41207, George H. W. Bush Library.

Notes to Chapter 4 / 347

551. Quayle, *Standing Firm*, 275.

552. Witcover, *American Vice Presidency*.

553. George H. W. Bush Library, "Warren T. Brookes, *Washington Times*, 'Quayle's Sharper Edge: Tending the Home Turf,'" n.d., Box 1, Gattuso, James, Files, Domestic Policy and the Council on Competitiveness, George H. W. Bush Library.

554. Goldstein, *White House Vice Presidency*; George H. W. Bush Library, "The President's Council on Competitiveness," Box 1, Gattuso, James, Files, OA/ID 41269, Domestic Policy and the Council on Competitiveness, George H. W. Bush Library.

555. Broder and Woodward, *Man Who Would Be President*.

556. Quayle, *Standing Firm*, 278.

557. Quayle, in conversation with the author.

558. Quayle, *Standing Firm*, 279.

559. Broder and Woodward, *Man Who Would Be President*, 126.

560. Quayle, in conversation with the author.

561. Broder and Woodward, *Man Who Would Be President*.

562. Broder and Woodward, *Man Who Would Be President*, 127.

563. Quayle, "A New Framework: Walter Mondale"; Quayle, in conversation with the author.

564. Quayle, "A New Framework: Walter Mondale," 175.

565. Quayle, in conversation with the author.

566. Quayle, *Standing Firm*.

567. George H. W. Bush Library, "The President's Council on Competitiveness."

568. Bush, *All the Best, George Bush*, 537.

569. Kengor, *Wreath Layer or Policy Player?*; Beckwith, in conversation with the author; Sununu, in conversation with the author.

570. DeSutter, in conversation with the author.

571. Lord, in conversation with the author.

572. Quayle, in conversation with the author.

573. Quayle, *Standing Firm*, 200.

574. George H. W. Bush Library, "Sara Fritz, *Los Angeles Times*."

575. Broder and Woodward, *Man Who Would Be President*, 99.

576. Baumgartner, with Crumblin, *American Vice Presidency*.

577. Skinner, in conversation with the author.

578. Broder and Woodward, *Man Who Would Be President*.

579. Kengor, "The Vice President, Secretary of State, and Foreign Policy." *Political Science Quarterly* 115 (2): 190; Kengor, *Wreath Layer or Policy Player?*

580. George H. W. Bush Library, "Sara Fritz, *Los Angeles Times*."

581. Kengor, "The Vice President, Secretary of State," 190; Kengor, *Wreath Layer or Policy Player?*

582. Broder and Woodward, *Man Who Would Be President*, 100.

348 / Notes to Chapter 4

583. Goldstein, *White House Vice Presidency*.

584. Richard Darman, *Who's in Control? Polar Politics and the Sensible Center* (New York: Simon & Schuster, 1996).

585. George H. W. Bush Library, "Sara Fritz, *Los Angeles Times*."

586. Broder and Woodward, *Man Who Would Be President*, 100.

587. Broder and Woodward, *Man Who Would Be President*, 100.

588. Broder and Woodward, *Man Who Would Be President*, 100.

589. Baumgartner, with Crumblin, *American Vice Presidency*.

590. Quayle, "A New Framework: Walter Mondale," 177.

591. Witcover, *American Vice Presidency*.

592. Broder and Woodward, *Man Who Would Be President*, 101.

593. Quayle, "A New Framework: Walter Mondale," 174.

594. Kengor, *Wreath Layer or Policy Player?*; Sununu, in conversation with the author.

595. Kengor, "The Vice President, Secretary of State," 191; Kengor, *Wreath Layer or Policy Player?*

596. Quayle, *Standing Firm*.

597. Goldstein, *White House Vice Presidency*; DeSutter, in conversation with the author.

598. Kengor, *Wreath Layer of Policy Player?*, 193.

599. Goldstein, *White House Vice Presidency*.

600. Goldstein, *White House Vice Presidency*.

601. Beckwith, in conversation with the author.

602. Skinner Interview 2008.

603. Goldstein, *White House Vice Presidency*.

604. Quayle, *Standing Firm*, 174.

605. Quayle, "A New Framework: Walter Mondale."

606. Witcover, *American Vice Presidency*; Quayle, in conversation with the author.

607. George H. W. Bush Library, "Les Novitsky to Bill Kristol and Dave Ryder," dated October 30, 1989, Administration Office, OA/ID 40689, Office of Vice President Quayle, George H. W. Bush Library; George H. W. Bush Library, "Les Novitsky to Bill Kristol, Dave Ryder, Cece Kremer, Greg Zoeller and Tom Pernice," dated December 5, 1989, Administration Office, OA/ID 40689, Office of Vice President Quayle, George H. W. Bush Library.

608. Quayle, "A New Framework: Walter Mondale," 174.

609. Broder and Woodward, *Man Who Would Be President*.

610. George H. W. Bush Library, "Sara Fritz, *Los Angeles Times*."

611. Quayle, "A New Framework: Walter Mondale," 174.

612. Baumgartner, with Crumblin, *American Vice Presidency*.

613. George H. W. Bush Library, "FY 1992 Vice Presidential Trip Summary," dated 1992, OA/ID 40689, Office of Vice President Dan Quayle, George H. W. Bush Library.

Notes to Chapter 4 / 349

614. Quayle, *Standing Firm*, 200.

615. Broder and Woodward, *Man Who Would Be President*, 103.

616. Broder and Woodward, *Man Who Would Be President*, 103.

617. Quayle, *Standing Firm*.

618. News Article, *Los Angeles Times*, May 9, 1991.

619. Witcover, *American Vice Presidency*; Baumgartner, with Crumblin, *American Vice Presidency*.

620. Baumgartner, with Crumblin, *American Vice Presidency*; Anthony Lake, in conversation with the author, May 2009.

621. Baumgartner, with Crumblin, *American Vice Presidency*, 140.

622. Bill Clinton, *My Life* (New York: Alfred A. Knopf, 2004).

623. Sidney Blumenthal, *The Clinton Wars* (New York: Farrar, Straus and Giroux, 2003).

624. Sidney Blumenthal, *The Clinton Wars*, 41.

625. Dee Dee Myers, in conversation with the author, February 2010.

626. Witcover, *American Vice Presidency*; Baumgartner, with Crumblin, *American Vice Presidency*.

627. Bob Woodward, *Plan of Attack* (New York: Simon & Schuster, 1994).

628. Witcover, *American Vice Presidency*; Clinton, *My Life*.

629. Baumgartner, with Crumblin, *American Vice Presidency*.

630. Witcover, *American Vice Presidency*; Baumgartner, with Crumblin, *American Vice Presidency*; Myers, in conversation with the author.

631. David Maraniss and Ellen Nakashima, *The Prince of Tennessee: Al Gore Meets His Fate* (New York: Touchstone, 2000); Roy Neel, in conversation with the author, May 2008.

632. Woodward, *Plan of Attack*.

633. Myers, in conversation with the author.

634. Maraniss and Nakashima, *Prince of Tennessee*, 271–72.

635. Woodward, *Plan of Attack*, 53.

636. Witcover, *American Vice Presidency*; Baumgartner, with Crumblin, *American Vice Presidency*; David Beier, in conversation with the author, April 2009; Mack McLarty, in conversation with the author, May and June 2010.

637. Witcover, *American Vice Presidency*, 472.

638. Baumgartner, with Crumblin, *American Vice Presidency*; Mike McCurry, in conversation with the author, June 2009; Neel, in conversation with the author.

639. Hillary Rodham Clinton, *Living History* (New York: Simon & Schuster, 2003), 113.

640. Kay Casstevens, in conversation with the author, October 2008.

641. Carol Rasco, in conversation with the author, June 2009.

642. McCurry, in conversation with the author.

643. Baumgartner, with Crumblin, *American Vice Presidency*.

644. Beier, in conversation with the author.

645. Beier, in conversation with the author.

350 / Notes to Chapter 4

646. Terry Sullivan, *The Nerve Center: Lessons in Governing from the White House Chiefs of Staff* (College Station: Texas A&M University Press, 2004); McLarty, in conversation with the author; Neel, in conversation with the author.

647. Sullivan, *Nerve Center: Lessons in Governing*, 82.

648. Maraniss and Nakashima, *Prince of Tennessee*, 278.

649. George Stephanopoulos, *All Too Human: A Political Education* (New York: Little, Brown, 1999), 205.

650. Woodward, *Plan of Attack*, 59.

651. Stephanopoulos, *All Too Human*, 206.

652. Woodward, *Plan of Attack*; Greg Simon, in conversation with the author, February 2009.

653. Simon, in conversation with the author.

654. McLarty, in conversation with the author.

655. McLarty, in conversation with the author.

656. Stephanopoulos, *All Too Human*.

657. Stephanopoulos, *All Too Human*.

658. Witcover, *American Vice Presidency*.

659. Baumgartner, with Crumblin, *American Vice Presidency*.

660. Neel, in conversation with the author.

661. Baumgartner, with Crumblin, *American Vice Presidency*, 143.

662. Goldstein, *White House Vice Presidency*, 119.

663. Witcover, *American Vice Presidency*; Beier, in conversation with the author; Neel, in conversation with the author.

664. McCurry, in conversation with the author.

665. Baumgartner, with Crumblin, *American Vice Presidency*.

666. Clinton, *My Life*, 466.

667. Kengor, *Wreath Layer or Policy Player?*

668. Kengor, *Wreath Layer or Policy Player?*, 213.

669. Kengor, *Wreath Layer or Policy Player?*, 213.

670. Kengor, *Wreath Layer or Policy Player?*, 213.

671. Kengor, *Wreath Layer or Policy Player?*, 213.

672. Leon Fuerth, in conversation with the author, April 2009.

673. Roy Neel, in conversation with the author, May 2008.

674. Kengor, *Wreath Layer or Policy Player?*

675. Goldstein, *White House Vice Presidency*.

676. Kengor, *Wreath Layer or Policy Player?*, 223.

677. Kengor, *Wreath Layer or Policy Player?*, 223.

678. Zbigniew Brzezinski, *Second Chance: Three President's and the Crisis of American Superpower* (New York: Basic Books, 2007), 87.

679. Kengor, *Wreath Layer or Policy Player?*

680. Kengor, *Wreath Layer or Policy Player?*

681. Kengor, *Wreath Layer or Policy Player?*, 223.

682. Kengor, *Wreath Layer or Policy Player?*, 223.

683. Kengor, *Wreath Layer or Policy Player?*, 223.

684. Kengor, *Wreath Layer or Policy Player?*; Fuerth, in conversation with the author; Lake, in conversation with the author; Simon, in conversation with the author, February 2009; Roy Neel, in conversation with the author.

685. Lake, in conversation with the author.

686. DeSutter, in conversation with the author.

687. Fuerth, in conversation with the author.

688. Kengor, *Wreath Layer or Policy Player?*, 214.

689. Kengor, *Wreath Layer or Policy Player?*, 214.

690. Clinton, *My Life*, 507.

691. Baumgartner, with Crumblin, *American Vice Presidency*.

692. Kengor, *Wreath Layer or Policy Player?*

693. Kengor, *Wreath Layer or Policy Player?*, 234.

694. Baumgartner, with Crumblin, *American Vice Presidency*.

695. Kengor, *Wreath Layer or Policy Player?*

696. Goldstein, *White House Vice Presidency*.

697. Kengor, *Wreath Layer or Policy Player?*, 224.

698. Kengor, *Wreath Layer or Policy Player?*, 224.

699. Goldstein, *White House Vice Presidency*.

700. Kengor, *Wreath Layer or Policy Player?*, 225.

701. Kengor, *Wreath Layer or Policy Player?*, 225.

702. DeSutter, in conversation with the author.

703. DeSutter, in conversation with the author.

704. Fuerth, in conversation with the author.

705. Kengor, *Wreath Layer or Policy Player?*.

706. Kengor, *Wreath Layer or Policy Player?*, 238.

707. David Gergen, *Eyewitness to Power: The Essence of Leadership* (New York: Simon & Schuster, 2000), 283.

708. Stephanopoulos, *All Too Human*, 221.

709. Baumgartner, with Crumblin, *American Vice Presidency*; Witcover, *American Vice Presidency*; Gergen, *Eyewitness to Power*; Blumenthal, *The Clinton Wars*.

710. Kengor, *Wreath Layer or Policy Player?*; Goldstein, *White House Vice Presidency*; Lake, in conversation with the author; McLarty, in conversation with the author.

711. Baumgartner, with Crumblin, *American Vice Presidency*.

712. Kengor, *Wreath Layer or Policy Player?*

713. Kengor, *Wreath Layer or Policy Player?*

714. Goldstein, *White House Vice Presidency*; Gergen, *Eyewitness to Power*.

715. Goldstein, *White House Vice Presidency*.

716. Stephanopoulos, *All Too Human*.

717. Woodward, *Plan of Attack*.

352 / Notes to Chapter 4

718. Goldstein, *White House Vice Presidency.*

719. Goldstein, *White House Vice Presidency.*

720. Joel K. Goldstein, "Reshaping the Model: Clinton, Gore, and the New Vice Presidency," in *The Clinton Presidency and the Constitutional System*, ed. Rosanna Perrotti (College Station: Texas A&M University Press).

721. Maraniss and Nakashima, *Prince of Tennessee*, 283.

722. Casstevens, in conversation with the author.

723. Casstevens, in conversation with the author.

724. Kenneth T. Walsh and Matthew Cooper, "A Vice President Who Counts," *U.S. News & World Report* 115, no. 3 (July 19, 1993); Lawrence Haas, in conversation with the author, December 2008; Myers, in conversation with the author; Neel, in conversation with the author.

725. Woodward, *Plan of Attack*, 216.

726. Gergen, *Eyewitness to Power*, 293.

727. Gergen, *Eyewitness to Power*; Simon, in conversation with the author; Neel, in conversation with the author.

728. McCurry, in conversation with the author; Casstevens, in conversation with the author.

729. Simon, in conversation with the author.

730. McCurry, in conversation with the author.

731. Tal Kopan, "Emails: Hillary Clinton Campaign Stressed about Al Gore before Endorsement," *CNN*, October 21, 2016; Myers, in conversation with the author; Maraniss and Nakashima, *The Prince of Tennessee*, 281.

732. Myers, in conversation with the author.

733. Witcover, *American Vice Presidency*, 472.

734. Darren Samuelson, "Why Al Gore Won't Endorse Hillary Clinton," *Politico*, November 17, 2015.

735. Goldstein, *White House Vice Presidency*; Gergen, *Eyewitness to Power.*

736. Stephanopoulos, *All Too Human*, 402.

737. Goldstein, "Reshaping the Model: Clinton, Gore," 96.

738. McCurry, in conversation with the author.

739. Goldstein, *White House Vice Presidency.*

740. Joseph Lockhart, in conversation with the author, May 2009.

741. Goldstein, *White House Vice Presidency.*

742. Lockhart, in conversation with the author.

743. Joseph Lockhart, in conversation with the Miller Center, September 2005; Myers, in conversation with the author.

744. Woodward, *Plan of Attack*, 281.

745. Goldstein, *White House Vice Presidency.*

746. Goldstein, *White House Vice Presidency*; Witcover, *American Vice Presidency.*

747. Beier, in conversation with the author.

Notes to Chapter 4 / 353

748. Beier, in conversation with the author.

749. Simon, in conversation with the author.

750. George Tenet, *At the Center of the Storm: My Years at the CIA* (New York: HarperCollins Publishers, 2007); Blumenthal, *The Clinton Wars*; Clinton, *My Life*; Fuerth, in conversation with the author.

751. Tenet, *At the Center of the Storm*, 137.

752. Tenet, *At the Center of the Storm*, 137.

753. Tenet, *At the Center of the Storm*, 137.

754. Goldstein, *White House Vice Presidency*; Powell, in conversation with the author; McCurry, in conversation with the author; McLarty, in conversation with the author; Myers, in conversation with the author.

755. Woodward, *Plan of Attack*.

756. Goldstein, *White House Vice Presidency*.

757. Stephanopoulos, *All Too Human*, 207.

758. Rasco, in conversation with the author.

759. Goldstein, *White House Vice Presidency*.

760. Clinton, *My Life*, 488.

761. Goldstein, *White House Vice Presidency*; Witcover, *American Vice Presidency*.

762. Witcover, *American Vice Presidency*.

763. Witcover, *American Vice Presidency*.

764. Baumgartner, with Crumblin, *American Vice Presidency*; Clinton, *Living History*, 380.

765. Clinton, *My Life*, 648.

766. Powell, in conversation with the author; McLarty, in conversation with the author.

767. Baumgartner, with Crumblin, *American Vice Presidency*.

768. Goldstein, *White House Vice Presidency*.

769. Gergen, *Eyewitness to Power*; Stephanopoulos, *All Too Human*; Woodward, *Plan of Attack*; Clinton, *My Life*; Goldstein, "Reshaping the Model: Clinton, Gore"; Myers, in conversation with the author.

770. Clinton, *My Life*.

771. Sullivan, *Nerve Center: Lessons in Governing*, 82.

772. Sullivan, *Nerve Center: Lessons in Governing*, 82.

773. Clinton, *My Life*, 516.

774. Lockhart, in conversation with the author.

775. Clinton, *My Life*, 589.

776. Goldstein, "Reshaping the Model: Clinton, Gore," 96.

777. Goldstein, "Reshaping the Model: Clinton, Gore," 98.

778. Blumenthal, *The Clinton Wars*.

779. Blumenthal, *The Clinton Wars*.

780. Blumenthal, *The Clinton Wars*, 284.

354 / Notes to Chapter 4

781. Bob Woodward, "Gore Was 'Solicitor-In-Chief' in '96 Reelection Campaign," *Washington Post*, March 2, 1997.

782. Maraniss and Nakashima, *The Prince of Tennessee*, 288.

783. Maraniss and Nakashima, *The Prince of Tennessee*, 290.

784. Blumenthal, *The Clinton Wars*, 293.

785. Blumenthal, *The Clinton Wars*, 520.

786. Blumenthal, *The Clinton Wars*.

787. McLarty, in conversation with the author.

788. Maraniss and Nakashima, *Prince of Tennessee*, 291–22.

789. McCurry, in conversation with the author.

790. Baumgartner, with Crumblin, *American Vice Presidency*:; Myers, in conversation with the author; Simon, in conversation with the author.

791. Simon, in conversation with the author.

792. McCurry, in conversation with the author, June 2009; Dee Dee Myers, in conversation with the author.

793. Witcover, *The American Vice Presidency*, 475–76.

794. Baumgartner, with Crumblin, *American Vice Presidency*.

795. Clinton, *Living History*, 487.

796. Goldstein, *White House Vice Presidency*; McCurry, in conversation with the author; Myers, in conversation with the author.

797. Witcover, *American Vice Presidency*, 475–76.

798. Casstevens, in conversation with the author.

799. Robert E. Rubin, *In an Uncertain World* (New York: Random House, 2003).

800. Witcover, *American Vice Presidency*, 476.

801. Maraniss and Nakashima, *The Prince of Tennessee*.

802. Maraniss and Nakashima, *The Prince of Tennessee*.

803. Blumenthal, *The Clinton Wars*, 716.

804. Lockhart, in conversation with the author.

805. Blumenthal, *The Clinton Wars*.

806. McCurry, in conversation with the author; Maraniss and Nakashima, *Prince of Tennessee*.

807. Blumenthal, *The Clinton Wars*.

808. Blumenthal, *The Clinton Wars*, 716.

809. Witcover, *American Vice Presidency*.

810. Haas, in conversation with the author.

811. Clinton, *My Life*, 873.

812. Blumenthal, *The Clinton Wars*.

813. Lockhart, in conversation with the author.

814. Blumenthal, *The Clinton Wars*, 716.

815. Witcover, *American Vice Presidency*; Blumenthal, *The Clinton Wars*.

816. Blumenthal, *The Clinton Wars*.

Notes to Chapter 4 / 355

817. Clinton, *My Life*, 872–73.

818. Blumenthal, *The Clinton Wars*.

819. Blumenthal, *The Clinton Wars*.

820. Domenico Montanaro, "Why President Obama Campaigning for Clinton Is Historic," *NPRPolitics*, July 5, 2016.

821. Blumenthal, *The Clinton Wars*, 752.

822. Simon, in conversation with the author.

823. Baumgartner, with Crumblin, *American Vice Presidency*; Haas, in conversation with the author; Neel, in conversation with the author.

824. Goldstein, "Reshaping the Model: Clinton, Gore, and the New Vice Presidency," 99.

825. Myers, in conversation with the author.

826. Gergen, *Eyewitness to Power*, 297.

827. McLarty, in conversation with the author.

828. Witcover, *American Vice Presidency*, 503.

829. Baumgartner, with Crumblin, *American Vice Presidency*.

830. John Heilmann and Mark Halperin, *Game Change* (New York: HarperCollins, 2010), 336.

831. Richard Yon, "The Biden Vice Presidency: Perpetuating Influence or Restoring Historical Insignificance?" in *The Obama Presidency*, eds. Robert P. Watson, Jack Covarrubias, Tom Lansford, and Douglas M. Brattebo (New York: SUNY Press, 2012).

832. Richard Yon, "The Biden Vice Presidency," 367.

833. Heilmann and Halperin, *Game Change*, 338.

834. James Traub, "After Cheney," *New York Times*, November 24, 2009.

835. Heilmann and Halperin, *Game Change*.

836. Heilmann and Halperin, *Game Change*.

837. Baumgartner, with Crumblin, *American Vice Presidency*.

838. Yon, "The Biden Vice Presidency."

839. Cady Lang, "Barack Obama and Joe Biden's Great American Bromance," *Time*, November 16, 2016.

840. Heilmann and Halperin, *Game Change*.

841. Yon, "Biden Vice Presidency."

842. Ed Hornick and Josh Levs, "What Obama Promised Biden," *CNN*, December 11, 2008.

843. Baumgartner, with Crumblin, *American Vice Presidency*.

844. Edward-Isaac Dovere and Darren Samuelsohn, "The Biden Factor," *Politico*, September 5, 2012.

845. Michael Hirsch, "Joe Biden: The Most Influential Vice President in History?" *The Atlantic*, December 31, 2012.

846. Ed Henry, "Biden Starting to Raise Profile," *CNN*, December 22, 2008.

847. Traub, "After Cheney."

848. Witcover, *American Vice Presidency.*

849. Yon, "Biden Vice Presidency"; Baumgartner, with Crumblin, *American Vice Presidency*; Witcover, *The American Vice Presidency.*

850. Yon, "The Biden Vice Presidency."

851. Witcover, *American Vice Presidency.*

852. Hornick and Josh Levs, "What Obama Promised Biden"; Lee 2008; Witcover, *American Vice Presidency.*

853. David Rothkopf, "The Bidenization of America," *Foreign Policy*, January 14, 2013.

854. Yon, "The Biden Vice Presidency"; Baumgartner, with Crumblin, *The American Vice Presidency*; Dovere and Darren Samuelsohn, "The Biden Factor."

855. Dovere and Darren Samuelsohn, "The Biden Factor."

856. Traub, "After Cheney."

857. Yon, "The Biden Vice Presidency"; Baumgartner, with Crumblin, *American Vice Presidency*; Goldstein, *White House Vice Presidency.*

858. Bob Woodward, *Obama's Wars* (New York: Simon & Schuster, 2010).

859. Woodward, *Obama's Wars.*

860. Evan Osnos, "The Biden Agenda," *New Yorker*, July 28, 2014.

861. Baumgartner, with Crumblin, *American Vice Presidency*, 191.

862. Witcover, *American Vice Presidency*, 506.

863. Goldstein, *White House Vice Presidency.*

864. Baumgartner, with Crumblin, *American Vice Presidency*; Osnos, "The Biden Agenda."

865. Yon, "The Biden Vice Presidency: Perpetuating Influence or Restoring Historical Insignificance?"; Jules Witcover, *Joe Biden: A Life of Trial and Redemption* (New York: William Morrow, 2010).

866. Robert M. Gates, *Duty: Memoirs of a Secretary at War* (New York: Alfred A. Knopf, 2014), 152; Witcover, *American Vice Presidency.*

867. Osnos, "The Biden Agenda."

868. Osnos, "The Biden Agenda."

869. Osnos, "The Biden Agenda."

870. Yon, "The Biden Vice Presidency."

871. Yon, "The Biden Vice Presidency.

872. Rothkopf, "The Bidenization of America."

873. Johnathan Allen and Carrie Budoff Brown, "Power Play: Reid Sidelined Biden," *Politico*, October 8, 2013.

874. Allen and Brown, "Power Play: Reid Sidelined Biden."

875. Allen and Brown, "Power Play: Reid Sidelined Biden."

876. Glenn Thrush, "Joe Biden in Winter," *Politico*, March/April 2014.

877. Allen and Brown, "Power Play: Reid Sidelined Biden."

878. Allen and Brown, "Power Play: Reid Sidelined Biden."

879. Osnos, "The Biden Agenda."

880. Allen and Brown, "Power Play: Reid Sidelined Biden"; Thrush, "Joe Biden in Winter."

881. Thrush, "Joe Biden in Winter."

882. Thrust, 2014.

883. Peter Baker and Jeff Zeleny, "Emanuel Wields Power Freely, and Faces the Risks," *New York Times*, August 15, 2009.

884. Helene Cooper, "As the Ground Shifts, Biden Plays a Bigger Role," *New York Times*, December 11, 2010.

885. Peter Nicholas, "Biden in Linchpin of Obama's Presidency," *Los Angeles Times*, December 31, 2010.

886. Yon, "The Biden Vice Presidency."

887. Witcover, *American Vice Presidency*.

888. Baumgartner, with Crumblin, *American Vice Presidency*, 191.

889. Osnos, "The Biden Agenda."

890. Osnos, "The Biden Agenda."

891. Osnos, "The Biden Agenda."

892. Osnos, "The Biden Agenda."

893. Thrush, "Joe Biden in Winter."

894. Gates, *Duty: Memoirs of a Secretary at War*, 288.

895. Thrush, "Joe Biden in Winter."

896. Osnos, "The Biden Agenda."

897. Osnos, "The Biden Agenda."

898. Thrush, "Joe Biden in Winter"; Dovere and Samuelsohn, "The Biden Factor."

899. Thrush, "Joe Biden in Winter."

900. Osnos, "The Biden Agenda."

901. Osnos, "The Biden Agenda."

902. Thrush, "Joe Biden in Winter."

903. Thrush, "Joe Biden in Winter."

904. Thrush, "Joe Biden in Winter."

905. Thrush, "Joe Biden in Winter."

906. Osnos, "The Biden Agenda."

907. Thrush, "Joe Biden in Winter."

908. Osnos, "The Biden Agenda."

909. Witcover, *American Vice Presidency*.

910. Witcover, *American Vice Presidency*, 496.

911. Osnos, "The Biden Agenda."

912. Mike Allen, Jonathan Martin, and Jim VandeHei, "Biden 'Intoxicated' by 2016 Run," *Politico*, January 23, 2013.

913. Dovere and Samuelsohn, "The Biden Factor."

914. Dovere and Samuelsohn, "The Biden Factor."

358 / Notes to Conclusion

Conclusion

1. Jody C. Baumgartner, *The American Vice Presidency Reconsidered* (Westport, CT: Praeger, 2006), 1.

2. Michael Turner, *The Vice President as Policy Maker: Rockefeller in the Ford White House* (Westport, CT: Greenwood Press, 1982), 3.

3. Turner, *Vice President as Policy Maker*, 22.

4. Joel K. Goldstein, *The Modern American Vice Presidency: The Transformation of a Political Institution* (Princeton, NJ: Princeton University Press, 1982), 3.

5. Jules Witcover, *Crapshoot: Rolling the Dice on the Vice Presidency* (New York: Crown, 1992), 10.

6. David McCullough, *John Adams* (New York: Simon & Schuster, 2001), 447.

7. Baumgartner, *American Vice Presidency Reconsidered*, 3.

8. Michael Nelson, *A Heartbeat Away: Report of the Twentieth Century Fund Task Force on the Vice Presidency* (Washington, DC: CQ Press, 1988), 4.

9. Goldstein, *Modern American Vice Presidency: The Transformation of a Political Institution*, 306.

10. Eli E. Nobleman, "The Delegation of Presidential Functions: Constitutional and Legal Aspects," *Annals of the American Academy of Political and Social Sciences* 307 (September 1956): 135.

11. Nobleman, "Delegation of Presidential Functions, 135–36.

12. Nobleman, "Delegation of Presidential Functions, 142.

13. Goldstein, *Modern American Vice Presidency*, 140–41, 184; Irving F. Williams, *The American Vice Presidency: New Look* (Garden City, NY: Doubleday, 1954), 69.

14. Paul C. Light, *Vice-Presidential Power: Advice and Influence in the White House* (Baltimore, MD: Johns Hopkins University Press, 1984).

15. David Willer, Michael J. Lovaglia, and Barry Markovsky, "Power and Influence: A Theoretical Bridge," *Social Forces* 76 (1997): 571.

16. Talcott Parsons, "On the Concept of Political Power," *Proceedings of the American Philosophical Society* 107 (1963): 338.

17. Robert J. Mokken and Frans N. Stokman, "Power and Influence and Political Phenomena," in *Power and Political Theory: Some European Perspectives*, ed. Brian Barry (Hoboken, NJ: John Wiley, 1976), 37.

18. Mokken and Stokman, "Power and Influence and Political Phenomena."

19. David Willer, Michael J. Lovaglia, and Barry Markovsky, "Power and Influence: A Theoretical Bridge," *Social Forces* 76 (1997): 573.

20. Willer, Lovaglia, and Markovsky, "Power and Influence: A Theoretical Bridge," 572.

21. Nelson, *A Heartbeat Away: Report*; Light, *Vice-Presidential Power*; Goldstein, *Modern American Vice Presidency*; Baumgartner, *American Vice Presidency Reconsidered*; Walter Mondale, in conversation with the author, February 2008;

Dick Cheney, in conversation with the author, December 2011; Dan Quayle, in conversation with the author, November 2008.

22. Kimberly H. Conger, "A Matter of Context: Christian Right Influence in U.S. State Republican Politics," *State Politics & Policy Quarterly* 10 (2010): 69, 254.

23. Joel K. Goldstein, "The Rising Power of the Modern Vice Presidency," *Presidential Studies Quarterly* 38 (2008): 374–389.

24. Goldstein, *Modern American Vice Presidency*, 100.

25. Baumgartner, *American Vice Presidency Reconsidered*, 142.

26. Baumgartner, *American Vice Presidency Reconsidered*, 142.

27. Joel K. Goldstein, "The Contemporary Presidency: Cheney, Vice Presidential Power, and the War on Terror," *Presidential Studies Quarterly* 40 (2010): 102–39; Goldstein, "Rising Power."

28. Nelson Rockefeller, in discussion with Mike Turner, December 1977.

29. Nelson Rockefeller, in discussion with Hugh Morrow, February 1978.

30. Joseph E. Persico, *The Imperial Rockefeller* (New York: Simon and Schuster, 1982), 277.

31. Rockefeller, in discussion with Hugh Morrow.

32. Rockefeller, in discussion with Hugh Morrow.

33. Rumsfeld, in conversation with the author.

34. Melvin Laird n.d., in discussion with Trevor Armbrister.

35. Turner, *Vice President as Policy Maker*, 175.

36. Turner, *Vice President as Policy Maker*.

37. Cheney, in conversation with the author.

38. Cheney, in conversation with the author.

39. Roger Hooker, in conversation with the author, May 2008.

40. James Cannon, in conversation with the author, May 2008.

41. Rumsfeld, in conversation with the author; Karl Rove, in conversation with the author, December 2011; Condoleezza Rice, in conversation with the author, September 2010.

42. Dan Bartlett, in conversation with the author, June 2010.

43. Cheney, in conversation with the author.

44. Andy Card, in conversation with the author, October 2010.

45. Cheney, in conversation with the author.

46. Ari Fleischer, in conversation with the author, May 2009.

47. Peter Baker, *Days of Fire: Bush and Cheney in the White House* (New York: Doubleday, 2013).

48. Stephen Hadley, in conversation with the author, November 2010; Cheney, in conversation with the author.

49. Card, in conversation with the author; Cheney, in conversation with the author.

50. Dana Perino, in conversation with the author, April 2009; Bartlett, in conversation with the author; Hadley, in conversation with the author.

360 / Notes to Conclusion

51. Peter Baker, Days of Fire, Bush and Cheney in the White House (New York: Doubleday, 2013), 640.

52. Card, in conversation with the author.

53. Robert M. Gates, *Duty: Memoirs of a Secretary at War* (New York: Alfred A. Knopf, 2014), 97–98.

54. Condoleezza Rice, *No Higher Honor* (New York: Crown Publishers, 2011).

55. Rice, *No Higher Honor*, 490–91.

56. Dick Cheney. *In My Time: A Personal and Political Memoir* (New York: Threshold, 2011).

57. Hadley, in conversation with the author.

58. Cheney, *In My Time.*

59. Cheney, *In My Time.*

60. Peter Baker, *Days of Fire: Bush and Cheney in the White House.*

61. Fleischer, in conversation with the author.

62. Rove, in conversation with the author.

63. Cheney, in conversation with the author.

References

Abrams, Herbert L. 1992. *"The President Has Been Shot"*: *Confusion, Disability, and the 25th Amendment in the Aftermath of the Attempted Assassination of Ronald Reagan*. New York: W. W. Norton.

Ackerman, Bruce. October 2, 2008. "Abolish the Vice Presidency." *Los Angeles Times*.

Activities, Competitive Council, n.d., folder "Council on Competitiveness," Box 2, Hubbard, Allan B., Subject Files, OA/ID 41207, Domestic Policy and the Council on Competitiveness, Office of Vice President Dan Quayle, George H. W. Bush Library.

Adkinson, Danny M. 1982. "The Electoral Significance of the Vice Presidency." *Presidential Studies Quarterly* 12 (3): 330–36.

Agenda, Meeting between Nelson Rockefeller and Gerald Ford, June 12, 1975, folder "VP 6/75," Box 11, James Cannon Papers (Domestic Council), Gerald R. Ford Library.

Agenda, Meeting between Nelson Rockefeller and Gerald Ford, September 25, 1975, folder "VP 8/75–9/75," Box 12, James Cannon Papers (Domestic Council), Gerald R. Ford Library.

Agenda, Meeting between Nelson Rockefeller and Gerald Ford, January 8, 1976, folder "VP 12/75–1/76," Box 12, James Cannon Papers (Domestic Council), Gerald R. Ford Library.

Agenda, Meeting between Nelson Rockefeller and Gerald Ford, January 15, 1976, folder "VP 12/75–1/76," Box 12, James Cannon Papers (Domestic Council), Gerald R. Ford Library.

Agenda Meetings, June 19, 1975–January 21, 1976, folders "Vice President's Memos for the President (1) and Vice President's Memos for the President (4)," Box 6, Dorothy E. Downton Files, 1974–1977, Gerald R. Ford Library.

Agenda Meetings, December 27, 1974–September 10, 1975, Rockefeller Family Collection, Record Group 26, Series 18, Vol. 27: Meetings with the President December 27, 1974 to September 10, 1975, Rockefeller Archive Center.

Albright, Madeleine. 2003. *Madame Secretary: A Memoir*. New York: Miramax.

362 / References

Alford, John R. 2001. "We're All in This Together: The Decline of Trust in Government, 1958–1996." In *What Is It about Government that Americans Dislike?* Edited by John R. Hibbing and Elizabeth Theiss-Morse. New York: Cambridge University Press.

Allen, Jonathan, and Carrie Budoff Brown. "Power Play: Reid Sidelined Biden." *Politico*, October 8, 2013. http://www.politico.com/story/2013/10/joe-biden-government-shutdown-debt-ceiling-097969. Date accessed October 10, 2013.

Allen, Mike, Jonathan Martin, and Jim VandeHei. "Biden 'Intoxicated' by 2016 Run." *Politico*, January 23, 2013. http://www.politico.com/story/2013/01/no-joke-joe-biden-makes-2016-moves-086600. Date accessed October 10, 2013.

Baker, James A., III. 2006. *"Work Hard, Study . . . and Keep Out of Politics!"* New York: G. P. Putnam's Sons.

Baker, Peter. 2013. *Days of Fire: Bush and Cheney in the White House.* New York: Doubleday.

Baker, Peter, and Jeff Zeleny. August 15, 2009. "Emanuel Wields Power Freely, and Faces the Risks." *New York Times.* http://www.nytimes.com/2009/08/16/us/politics/16emanuel.html?pagewanted=all&_r=0. Date accessed November 30, 2016.

Barber, James David. 1992. *The Presidential Character: Predicting Performance in the White House.* 4th ed. Hoboken, NJ: Prentice Hall.

Baturo, Alexander, and Johan A. Elkink. 2014. "Office or Officeholder? Regime Deinstitutionalization and Sources of Individual Political Influence." *Journal of Politics* 76: 859–72.

Baumgartner, Jody C. 2006. *The American Vice Presidency Reconsidered.* Westport, CT: Praeger.

Baumgartner, Jody C., with Thomas F. Crumblin. 2015. *The American Vice Presidency: From the Shadow to the Spotlight.* New York: Rowman & Littlefield.

Beveridge, Albert J. December 1909. "The Fifth Wheel in Our Government." *Century Magazine* 79.

Bierstedt, Robert. 1950. "An Analysis of Social Power." *American Sociological Review* 15: 161–84.

Bipartisan Leadership Meeting, January 16, 1975, folder "Bipartisan Leadership Meetings, Jan–March 1975," Box 3, Max L. Friedersdorf Files, 1974–1977, Gerald R. Ford Library.

Blumenthal, Sidney. 2003. *The Clinton Wars.* New York: Farrar, Straus and Giroux.

Brinkley, Douglas, ed. 2007. *The Reagan Diaries.* New York: HarperCollins.

Broder, David S., and Bob Woodward. 1992. *The Man Who Would Be President: Dan Quayle.* New York: Simon & Schuster.

Brzezinski, Zbigniew. 1983. *Power and Principle: Memoirs of the National Security Adviser 1977–1981.* New York: Farrar, Straus, Giroux

———. 2007. *Second Chance: Three Presidents and the Crisis of American Superpower.* New York: Basic Books.

Burke, John P. 2000. *The Institutional Presidency: Organizing and Managing the White House from FDR to Clinton*. 2nd ed. Baltimore, MD: Johns Hopkins University Press.

———. 2003. "The Bush 2000 Transition: The Historical Context." In *The White House World: Transitions, Organization, and Office Operations*. Edited by Martha Joynt Kumar and Terry Sullivan. College Station: Texas A&M University Press.

———. 2009. *Honest Broker? The National Security Advisor and Presidential Decision Making*. College Station: Texas A&M University Press.

Bush, Barbara. 1994. *Barbara Bush: A Memoir*. New York: Charles Scribner's.

Bush, George. 1987. *Looking Forward: An Autobiography*. New York: Doubleday.

———. 1999. *All the Best, George Bush: My Life in Letters and Other Writings*. New York: Lisa Drew/Scribner.

Bush, George H. W. 1998. *A World Transformed*. New York: Alfred A. Knopf.

Bush, George W. 2010. *Decision Points*. New York: Crown.

Bush, Laura. 2010. *Spoke from the Heart*. New York: Scribner.

Cabinet Meeting, 4/4/77, folder "Cabinet [CF, O/A 374] [1]," Box 7, Administration–H. Carter, Staff Offices, Jimmy Carter Library.

Cabinet Meeting, January 9, 1978, folder "Cabinet Meeting Minutes–10/3/77–2/27/78," Box 7, Vertical File, WHCF, Jimmy Carter Library.

Cabinet Meeting, February 6, 1978, folder "Cabinet Meeting Minutes–10/3/77–2/27/78," Box 7, Vertical File, WHCF, Jimmy Carter Library.

Cannon, James. 1994. *Time and Chance: Gerald Ford's Appointment with History*. Ann Arbor: University of Michigan Press.

———. 1997. "Gerald R. Ford and Nelson A. Rockefeller." In *At the President's Side: The Vice Presidency in the Twentieth Century*. Edited by Timothy Walch. Columbia: University of Missouri Press.

Cannon, Lou. 1991. *President Reagan: The Role of a Lifetime*. New York: Public Affairs.

Caro, Robert. 2013. *The Passage of Power: The Years of Lyndon Johnson*. New York: Knopf.

Carter, Jimmy. 1982. *Keeping Faith: Memoirs of a President*. New York: Bantam Books.

———. 2010. *White House Diary*. New York: Farrar, Straus and Giroux.

Cheney, Dick. 2011. *In My Time: A Personal and Political Memoir*. New York: Threshold.

Clift, A. Denis. 1993. *With Presidents to the Summit*. Fairfax, Virginia: George Mason University Press.

Clinton, Bill. 2004. *My Life*. New York: Alfred A. Knopf.

Clinton, Hillary Rodham. 2003. *Living History*. New York: Simon & Schuster.

Clymer, Adam. "Thomas F. Eagleton, 77, a Running Mate for 18 Days, Dies." *New York Times*, March 5, 2007.

364 / References

Cohen, David B. 2002. "From the Fabulous Baker Boys to the Master of Disaster: The White House Chief of Staff in the Reagan and G. H. W. Bush Administrations." *Presidential Studies Quarterly* 32 (3): 463–83.

Cohen, David B., and George A. Krause. 2000. "Presidents, Chiefs of Staff, and White House Organizational Behavior: Survey Evidence from the Reagan and Bush Administrations." *Presidential Studies Quarterly* 30 (3): 421–42.

Cohen, David B., and Charles E. Walcott. "Serving Our Country in Historic Times: The Chiefs of Staff in the George W. Bush White House." Paper presented to the Annual Meeting of the American Political Science Association, Washington, DC, September 2–5, 2010.

Commission on the Organization of the Government for the Conduct of Foreign Policy, n.d., folder "Rockefeller Role in the Ford Administration," Box 2, James Cannon Papers (Domestic Council), Gerald R. Ford Library.

Comstock, Donald E. 1980. "Dimensions of Influence in Organizations." *Pacific Sociological Review* 23: 67–84.

Conger, Kimberly H. 2010. "A Matter of Context: Christian Right Influence in U.S. State Republican Politics." *State Politics & Policy Quarterly* 10: 248–69.

Conley, Richard S. 2006. "Reform, Reorganization, and the Renaissance of the Managerial Presidency: The Impact of 9/11 on the Executive Establishment." *Politics & Policy* 34: 304–42.

Cooper, Helene. "As the Ground Shifts, Biden Plays a Bigger Role." *New York Times*, December 11, 2010. http://www.nytimes.com/2010/12/12/us/politics/12biden.html. Date accessed January 2, 2011.

Cornell, Saul. 1999. *The Other Founders: Anti-Federalism and the Dissenting Tradition in America, 1788–1828.* Chapel Hill: University of North Carolina Press.

Darman, Richard. 1996. *Who's in Control?: Polar Politics and the Sensible Center.* New York: Simon & Schuster.

Deaver, Michael K. 1987. *Behind the Scenes.* New York: William Morrow.

Michael Deaver Interview, Miller Center, University of Virginia, Ronald Reagan Presidential Oral History Project, September 12, 2002.

DeFrank, Thomas M. 2007. *Write It When I'm Gone: Remarkable Off-the-Record Conversations with Gerald R. Ford.* New York: G. P. Putnam's.

Dolce, Philip C., and George H. Skau. 1976. *Power and the Presidency.* New York: Charles Scribner's.

Dovere, Edward-Isaac, and Darren Samuelsohn. "The Biden Factor." *Politico*, September 5, 2012. http://www.politico.com/blogs/media/2015/08/the-biden-factor-211758. Date accessed 9/13/12.

Draft Speech in Oval Office by President and Vice President, March 3, 1975, folder "VP 3/75-5/75," Box 11, James Cannon Papers (Domestic Council), Gerald R. Ford Library.

Dubose, Lou and Jake Bernstein. 2006. *Vice: Dick Cheney and the Hijacking of the American Presidency.* London: Pimlico.

Dur, Andreas, and Dirk De Bievre. 2007. "The Question of Interest Group Influence." *Journal of Public Policy* 27: 1–12.

Edwards, George C. 1991. "Presidential Influence in Congress: If We Ask the Wrong Questions, We Get the Wrong Answers." *American Journal of Political Science* 35: 724–29.

Edwards, George C., and Stephen J. Wayne. 2006. *Presidential Leadership: Politics and Policy Making.* 7th ed. Belmont, CA: Thomson Wadsworth.

Edwards, George C., J. H. Kessel, and Burt A. Rockman. 1993. *Researching the Presidency: Vital Questions, New Approaches.* Edited by George C. Edwards, J. H. Kessel and Burt A. Rockman. Pittsburgh, PA: University of Pittsburgh Press.

Executive Order 11828, 1/4/75, folder "Rockefeller Role in the Ford Administration," Box 2, James Cannon Papers (Domestic Council), Gerald R. Ford Library.

Fact Sheet, The President's Council on Competitiveness, n.d., folder "Defense on Hill, General: Fact Sheets on Council," Box 1, Gattuso, James, Files, OA/ID 41269, Domestic Policy and the Council on Competitiveness, Office of Vice President Dan Quayle, George H. W. Bush Library.

Fitzwater, Marlin. 1995. *Call the Briefing!* New York: Times Books.

Fleischer, Ari. 2005. *Taking Heat: The President, the Press, and My Years in the White House.* New York: William Morrow.

Ford, Gerald R. 1979. *A Time to Heal: The Autobiography of Gerald R. Ford.* New York: Harper and Row.

Frum, David. 2003. *The Right Man: The Surprise Presidency of George W. Bush.* New York: Random House.

FY 2020 Congressional Budget Submission. https://www.whitehouse.gov/wpcontent/uploads/2019/03/EOP_FY20_Congressional_Budget_Submission.pdf. Date accessed July 13, 2020.

Gates, Robert M. 2014. *Duty: Memoirs of a Secretary at War.* New York: Alfred A. Knopf.

Gellman, Barton. 2008. *Angler: The Cheney Vice Presidency.* New York: Penguin.

Genovese, Michael. 2001. *The Power of the American Presidency 1789–2000.* New York: Oxford University Press.

Gergen, David. 1992. "Enter the New Deputy President." *U.S. News & World Report*, August 24, 42.

———. 2000. *Eyewitness to Power: The Essence of Leadership.* New York: Simon & Schuster.

Gillon, Steven M. 1992. *The Democrats' Dilemma: Walter F. Mondale and the Liberal Legacy.* New York: Columbia University Press.

———. 1997. "A New Framework: Walter Mondale as Vice President." In *At the President's Side: The Vice Presidency in the Twentieth Century.* Edited by Timothy Walch. Columbia: University of Missouri Press.

Glad, Betty. 1980. *Jimmy Carter: In Search of the Great White House.* New York: W. W. Norton.

366 / References

Gleiber, Dennis W., and Steven A. Shull. 1992. "Presidential Influence in the Policymaking Process." *Western Political Quarterly* 45: 441–67.

Goldstein, Joel K. 1982. *The Modern American Vice Presidency: The Transformation of a Political Institution*. Princeton, NJ: Princeton University Press.

———. 2008. "The Rising Power of the Modern Vice Presidency." *Presidential Studies Quarterly* 38: 374–89.

———. 2010. "The Contemporary Presidency: Cheney, Vice Presidential Power, and the War on Terror." *Presidential Studies Quarterly* 40: 102–39.

———. 2012. "Reshaping the Model: Clinton, Gore, and the New Vice Presidency." In *The Clinton Presidency and the Constitutional System*. Edited by Rosanna Perotti. College Station: Texas A&M University Press.

———. 2016. *The White House Vice Presidency: The Path to Significance, Mondale to Biden*. Lawrence: University Press of Kansas.

Haig, Alexander. 1984. *Caveat: Realism, Reagan, and Foreign Policy*. New York: Macmillan.

Handwritten Note, Nelson Rockefeller to Gerald R. Ford, n.d., folder "FG Vice President (1)," Box 16, Presidential Handwriting File, Gerald R. Ford Library.

Hargrove, Erwin C. 1993. "Presidential Personality and Leadership Style." In *Researching the Presidency: Vital Questions, New Approaches*. Edited by George C. Edwards, J. H. Kessel, and Burt A. Rockman. Pittsburgh, PA: University of Pittsburgh Press.

Hayes, Stephen F. 2007. *Cheney: The Untold Story of America's Most Powerful and Controversial Vice President*. New York: HarperCollins.

Heilemann, John, and Mark Halperin. 2010. *Game Change*. New York: HarperCollins.

Henry, Ed. "Biden Starting to Raise Profile." *CNN*, December 22, 2008. http://politicalticker.blogs.cnn.com/2008/12/22/biden-starting-to-raise-profile/. Date accessed November 10, 2010.

Hess, Stephen. 2002. *Organizing the Presidency*. 3rd ed. Washington, DC: Brookings Institution Press.

Hirschfield, Robert S. 1976. "The Scope and Limits of Presidential Power." In *Power and the Presidency*. Edited by Philip C. Doce and George H. Skau. New York: Charles Scribner's.

Hirsh, Michael. "Joe Biden: The Most Influential Vice President in History?" *The Atlantic*, December 31, 2012. http://www.theatlantic.com/politics/archive/2012/12/joe-biden-the-most-influential-vice-president-in-history/266729/. Date accessed January 4, 2013.

Hornick, Ed, and Josh Levs. "What Obama Promised Biden." *CNN*, December 11, 2008. http://www.cnn.com/2008/POLITICS/12/21/transition.wrap/index.html?eref=ib_to. Date accessed December 10, 2010.

Huckfeldt, Robert, and John Sprague. 1991. "Discussant Effects on Vote Choice: Intimacy, Structure, and Interdependence." *Journal of Politics* 53: 122–58.

Hughes, Karen. 2004. *Ten Minutes from Normal.* New York: Viking Penguin.

Interview with Gerald R. Ford, 1977, folder "Interview with Gerald R. Ford by Trevor Armbrister," Box 34, James Cannon Papers (Domestic Council), Gerald R. Ford Library.

Interview with Gerald R. Ford, 1979, folder "Interview with Gerald R. Ford by Hugh Morrow (1979)," Box 34, James Cannon Papers (Domestic Council), Gerald R. Ford Library.

Interview with Melvin Laird, n.d., folder "Interview with Gerald R. Ford by Trevor Armbrister," Box 34, James Cannon Papers (Domestic Council), Gerald R. Ford Library.

Interview with Nelson Rockefeller by Hugh Sidey and Bonnie Angelo, January 8, 1975, folder "Rockefeller, Nelson–Media Interviews," Box 25, Ron Nessen Papers, 1974–1977, Gerald R. Ford Library.

Interview with Nelson A. Rockefeller, October 21, 2017, folder "Interview with Nelson A. Rockefeller by Trevor Armbrister 10/21/77," Box 35, James Cannon Papers (Domestic Council), Gerald R. Ford Library.

Interview with Nelson Rockefeller, November 22, 1977, Rockefeller Family Collection, Record Group 4, Series Q: Morrow Interviews, Sub-Series 1, Box 1, Folder 12, Rockefeller Archive Center.

Interview with Nelson A. Rockefeller, December 2, 1977, folder "Interview with Nelson A. Rockefeller by Bob Hartmann 12/2/77," Box 35, James Cannon Papers (Domestic Council), Gerald R. Ford Library.

Interview with Nelson A. Rockefeller Conducted by Hugh Morrow, February 2, 1978, folder "Interview with Nelson A. Rockefeller by Bob Hartmann, 2/2/78," Box 35, James Cannon Papers (Domestic Council), Gerald R. Ford Library.

Interview with Nelson Rockefeller, March 4, 1976, Rockefeller Family Collection, Record Group 26, Series 13, Box 13, Folder 694, Rockefeller Archive Center.

Interview with Nelson A. Rockefeller, December 21, 1977, folder "Nelson A. Rockefeller Interview with Mike Turner 12/21/77," Box 35, James Cannon Papers (Domestic Council), Gerald R. Ford Library.

Interview with Donald Rumsfeld, n.d., folder "Interview with Donald Rumsfeld by Trevor Armbrister, "Box 34, James Cannon Papers (Domestic Council), Gerald R. Ford Library.

Jacobs, Lawrence R., and Robert Y. Shapiro. 2000. "Conclusion." In *Presidential Power: Forging the Presidency for the Twenty-First Century.* Edited by Robert Y. Shapiro, Martha Joynt Kumar, and Lawrence R. Jacobs. New York: Columbia University Press.

Johnson, Clay, III. 2003. "The 2000–2001 Presidential Transition: Planning, Goals, and Reality." In *The White House World: Transitions, Organization, and Office Operations.* Edited by Martha Joynt Kumar and Terry Sullivan. College Station: Texas A&M University Press.

368 / References

Journal Article, William Boot, *Columbia Journalism Review*, "Dan Quayle: The Sequel," *Columbia Journalism Review*. September/October 1991, folder "October 1991 [3 of 4]," Box 8, Kristol, William, Files, OA/ID 40794, Office of Vice President Dan Quayle, George H. W. Bush Library.

Kaper, Stacy, and Cheyenne Hopkins. November 23, 2010. "ABA Names Frank Keating New CEO." *American Banker*.

Katzenbach, Nicholas deB. March 9, 1961. "Participation by the Vice President in the Affairs of the Executive Branch." Memo to Vice President Lyndon Johnson from the Assistant Attorney General, Office of Legal Counsel, Washington, DC. March 1961.

Kengor, Paul. 2000. "The Vice President, Secretary of State, and Foreign Policy." *Political Science Quarterly* 115 (2): 175–99.

———. 2002. *Wreath Layer or Policy Player? The Vice President's Role in Foreign Policy*. New York: Lexington Books.

Kenny, Christopher, and Eric Jenner. 2008. "Direction versus Proximity in the Social Influence Process." *Political Behavior* 30: 73–95.

Kernell, Samuel, and Samuel L. Popkin, eds. 1986. *Chief of Staff: Twenty-five Years of Managing the Presidency*. Los Angeles: University of California Press.

King, Larry. December 28, 2008. "Interview with Joe Biden." *Larry King Live*. http://transcripts.cnn.com/TRANSCRIPTS/0812/28/lkl.02.html. Date accessed December 28, 2010.

Kopan, Tal. October 21, 2016. "Emails: Hillary Clinton Campaign Stressed About Al Gore before Endorsement." *CNN*. http://www.cnn.com/2016/10/21/politics/wikileaks-hillary-clinton-podesta-emails-al-gore/index.html. Date accessed October 21, 2016.

Kurland, Philip B., and Ralph Lerner, eds. 2000. The Founders' Constitution. http://press-pubs.uchicago.edu/founders/. Date accessed December 8, 2016.

Lang, Cady. November 16, 2016. "Barack Obama and Joe Biden's Great American Bromance." *Time*. http://time.com/barack-obama-joe-biden-friendship-photos/. Date accessed November 18, 2016.

Learned, H. B. 1912. "Some Aspects of the Vice-Presidency." *Proceedings of the American Political Science Association* 9: 162–77.

Lee, Carol E. December 21, 2008. "Biden to Head New Middle Class Task Force." *Politico*, http://www.politico.com/story/2008/12/biden-to-head-new-middle-class-task-force-016778. Date accessed January 2, 2011.

Lemert, Charles. 2004. *Social Theory: The Multicultural and Classic Readings*. 3rd ed. Boulder, CO: Westview Press.

Letter, Jimmy Carter to Walter Mondale, December 22, 1978, folder "FG 38 12/1/78–12/31/78," Box FG-161, Federal Government-Organizations, Subject File, WHCF, Jimmy Carter Library.

Letter, Jimmy Carter to Nelson Rockefeller, November 9, 1976, Rockefeller Family Collection, Record Group 26, Series 18, Vol. 38: 217–24, Rockefeller Archive Center.

References / 369

Letter, Gerald R. Ford to Nelson Rockefeller, January 27, 1976, folder "Domestic Council–Vice President's Role, 1/75–12/75," Box 3, Richard Cheney Files, 1974–77, Gerald R. Ford Library.

Letter, Walter Mondale to Charlie Schultze, May 17, 1978, folder "Memos from Vice-President," Box 55, Staff Office–CEA (Council on Economic Advisers), Jimmy Carter Library.

Letter, Nelson Rockefeller to Gerald R. Ford, March 11, 1975, folder "VP 10/75–11/75," Box 12, James Cannon Papers (Domestic Council), Gerald R. Ford Library.

Letter, Nelson Rockefeller to Gerald R. Ford, December 16, 1975, folder "Domestic Council–Vice President's Role, 1/75–12/75," Box 3, Richard Cheney Files, 1974–77, Gerald R. Ford Library.

Light, Paul C. 1984. *Vice-Presidential Power: Advice and Influence in the White House.* Baltimore, MD: Johns Hopkins University Press.

Joseph Lockhart Interview, Miller Center, University of Virginia, William J. Clinton Presidential Oral History Project, September 19–20, 2005.

Lott, Jeremy. April 19, 2009. "Why We Should Get Rid of the Vice Presidency." *Washington Post.*

Maier, Pauline. 2010. *Ratification: The People Debate the Constitution, 1787–1788.* New York: Simon & Schuster.

Mann, James. 2004. *Rise of the Vulcans: The History of Bush's War Cabinet.* New York: Penguin.

Maraniss, David, and Ellen Nakashima. 2000. *The Prince of Tennessee: Al Gore Meets His Fate.* New York: Touchstone.

Maslin-Wicks, Kimberly. 1998. "Two Types of Presidential Influence in Congress." *Presidential Studies Quarterly* 28: 108–26.

Masters, Johnathan. June 29, 2016. "The U.S. Vice President and Foreign Policy." *Council on Foreign Relations,* 2016. http://www.cfr.org/united-states/us-vice-president-foreign-policy/p38104. Date accessed June 30, 2016.

Mayer, Kenneth R. 2001. *With the Stroke of a Pen: Executive Orders and Presidential Power.* Princeton, NJ: Princeton University Press.

McClellan, Scott. 2008. *What Happened: Inside the Bush White House and Washington's Culture of Deception.* Philadelphia, PA: Public Affairs.

McCullough, David. 1992. *Truman.* New York: Simon & Schuster.

———. 2001. *John Adams.* New York: Simon & Schuster.

McGrath, Jim, Editor. 2001. *Heartbeat: George Bush in His Own Words.* New York: Lisa Drew.

Meacham, Jon. 2015. *Destiny and Power: The American Odyssey of George Herbert Walker Bush.* New York: Random House.

Meeting, Walter Mondale with Jewish Leaders, October 27, 1978, folder "FG 38 10/13/78–11/30/78," Box FG-161, Federal Government-Organizations, Subject File, WHCF, Jimmy Carter Library.

370 / References

Meetings with Congressional Leaders, January 1975–September 1975; October 1976–June 1976, folders 290: "Meetings with Congressional Leaders, Jan–Sept 1975 and 290.1: Meetings with Congressional Leaders, Oct–June 1976," Box 11, Rockefeller Family Collection, Record Group 26, Series 19, Rockefeller Archive Center.

Memo, Dick Allison to Nelson Rockefeller, February 18, 1976, Rockefeller Family Collection, Record Group 26, Series 18, Vol. 38: "Office of the Vice President 1975–1977 General Book II," Rockefeller Archive Center.

Memo, Roy Ash to Gerald R. Ford, 1/13/75a, folder "Domestic Council–Vice President's Role, 1/75–12/75," Box 3, Richard Cheney Files, 1974–77, Gerald R. Ford Library.

Memo, Mike Berman to Denis Clift, Al Eisele, Jim Johnson, Bill Smith, and Gail Harrison, July 25, 1977, folder "V.P.–Six Month Assessment," Box 2, Locator: 154.J.8.7B, Administrative Assistant to President of the Senate, Vice Presidential Files, Walter F. Mondale Papers, Minnesota Historical Society Library.

Memo, Zbigniew Brzezinski to Jimmy Carter, November 3, 1977, File 3, Box 4, Brzezinski Material: President's Daily Report File, Jimmy Carter Library.

Memo, Landon Butler to Walter Mondale, May 25, 1979, folder "VP Calls, 5/25/79–6/25/80," Box 141, Landon Butler Files, Jimmy Carter Library.

Memo, Spofford Canfield to James Cannon and Roger Hooker, January 10, 1975, folder "Rule XXII (Senate Cloture Rule) Changes," Box 2, James Cannon Papers (Domestic Council), Gerald R. Ford Library.

Memo, Spofford Canfield to Nelson Rockefeller through Jon Howe, February 4, 1976, folder "Howe, Jon," Box 1515, WHCF, Name File, Howe, Jon, Gerald R. Ford Library.

Memo, James Cannon to Nelson Rockefeller, January 10, 1975b, folder "Rule XXII (Senate Cloture Rule) Changes," Box 2, James Cannon Papers (Domestic Council), Gerald R. Ford Library.

Memo, James Cannon to Nelson Rockefeller, March 5, 1975, folder "Vice Presidential Memoranda, March 5–20, 1975," Box 86, James Cannon Files, Gerald R. Ford Library.

Memo, James Cannon to Nelson Rockefeller, April 14, 1975, folder "Vice Presidential Memoranda, April 1–21, 1975," Box 86, James Cannon Files, Gerald R. Ford Library.

Memo, James Cannon to Nelson Rockefeller, April 23, 1975, folder "Vice Presidential Memoranda, April 22–30, 1975," Box 86, James Cannon Files, Gerald R. Ford Library.

Memo, Tom Cantrell to Nelson Rockefeller, January 8, 1975, folder "Rockefeller Role in the Ford Admin.," Box 2, James Cannon Papers (Domestic Council), Gerald R. Ford Library.

Memo, Jimmy Carter to Walter Mondale, Cyrus Vance, Griffin Bell, Zbigniew Brzezinski, Stansfield Turner, and Robert Lipshutz, March 5, 1977, folder

"The Vice President 2/1/77–1/16/78," Box 226, Handwriting File, Office of Staff Secretary, Staff Offices, Jimmy Carter Library.

Memo, William J. Casey to James A. Baker III, April 10, 1981, folder "Assassination Attempt on Pres. March 30, 1981 (OA9620)," Box 1, Cabinet Affairs, White House Office of: "Records," Ronald Reagan Library.

Memo, Dick Cheney to Gerald R. Ford through Donald Rumsfeld, January 20, 1975, folder "Domestic Council–Vice President's Role, 1/75–12/75," Box 3, Richard Cheney Files, 1974–77, Gerald R. Ford Library.

Memo, Dick Cheney to Gerald R. Ford, May 18, 1975, folder "Rockefeller, Nelson," Box 19, Richard Cheney Files, 1974–1977, Gerald R. Ford Library.

Memo, Jeanne W. Davis to Jon Howe, August 28, 1975, folder "Howe, Jon," Box 1515, WHCF, Name File, Howe, Jon, Gerald R. Ford Library.

Memo, Jeanne W. Davis to Jon Howe, January 16, 1976, folder "Howe, Jon," Box 1515, WHCF, Name File, Howe, Jon, Gerald R. Ford Library.

Memo, Al Eisele to Dick Moe, Mike Berman, Jim Johnson, Denis Clift, Gail Harrison, and Bill Smith, February 6, 1979, folder "1979 Memo + Follow-ups," Box 2, Locator: 154.J.8.7B, Administrative Assistant to President of the Senate, Vice Presidential Files, Walter F. Mondale Papers, Minnesota Historical Society Library.

Memo, Jim Fallows through Jody Powell to Jimmy Carter, January 22, 1977, folder "FG 38 1/20/77–2/15/77," Box FG-157, Federal Government–Organizations, Subject File, WHCF, Jimmy Carter Library.

Memo, Thaddeus Garrett, Jr. to Admiral Murphy, January 21, 1981, folder "[Memoranda–January 1981]," Box 5, Thaddeus Garrett Files, Domestic Policy Office, Office of Vice President George Bush, George H. W. Bush Library.

Memo, Don Gregg and Doug Menarchik to George Bush, June 1, 1987, folder "Vice President's Task Force on Combatting Terrorism–Thursday, July 25, 1985, The Roosevelt Room, 4:15 p.m. to 5:15 p.m.," Box 9, Donald P. Gregg Files, OA/ID 41622, Office of Vice President, George Bush, George H. W. Bush Library.

Memo, Jon Howe to Nelson Rockefeller, March 22, 1975, Rockefeller Family Collection, Record Group 26, Series 19, Box 11, Folder 299, Rockefeller Archive Center.

Memo, Jerry Jones to Nelson Rockefeller, January 13, 1975, folder "Vice President," Box 31, James E. Connor Files, 1974–1977, Gerald R. Ford Library.

Memo, Jack Marsh to Gerald R. Ford, December 20, 1974, folder "Rockefeller, Nelson–Role as V.P., 12/20/74," Box 10, Richard Cheney Files, 1974–77, Gerald R. Ford Library.

Memo, Robert C. McFarlane to George Bush, et al., July 20, 1985, folder "Vice President's Task Force on Combatting Terrorism–Thursday, July 25, 1985, The Roosevelt Room, 4:15 p.m. to 5:15 p.m.," Box 9, Donald P. Gregg Files, OA/ID 41622, Office of Vice President George Bush, George H. W. Bush Library.

372 / References

Memo, Richard Moe to Walter Mondale January 29, 1978, folder "Review of Vice Presidency Folder 2," Box 3, Locator: 154.J.9.6F, Chief of Staff Richard Moe Files, Walter F. Mondale Papers, Minnesota Historical Society Library.

Memo, Walter Mondale to Jimmy Carter, December 9, 1976, folder "V.P.–Role & Functions," Box 2, Locator: 154.J.8.7B, Administrative Assistant to President of the Senate, Vice Presidential Files, Walter F. Mondale Papers, Minnesota Historical Society Library.

Memo, Walter Mondale to Jimmy Carter, February 16, 1977, folder "Vice President–HJ," Box 7, Gerald Rafshoon Subject Files, Jimmy Carter Library.

Memo, Walter Mondale to Jimmy Carter, April 1, 1977, folder "Presidential Agenda," Box 1, Locator 154.J.8.6F, Administrative Assistant to President of the Senate, Vice President Files, Walter F. Mondale Papers, Minnesota Historical Society Library.

Memo, Walter Mondale to Jimmy Carter, April 19, 1978, folder "Memos from the VP to the President, [1/1–6/30/1978]," Box 205, Papers of Walter F. Mondale, Donated Material, Collection #133, Jimmy Carter Library.

Memo, Walter Mondale to Secretaries Miller, Marshall, Chair Schultze, Jim McIntyre, Stu Eizenstat, and Fred Kahn, January 28, 1979, folder "Memos from Vice-President," Box 55, Staff Office–CEA (Council of Economic Advisers), Jimmy Carter Library.

Memo, Walter Mondale to Charlie Schultze, April 11, 1977, folder "Memos from Vice-President," Box 55, Staff Office–CEA (Council of Economic Advisers), Jimmy Carter Library.

Memo, Walter Mondale, Stu Eizenstat, and Executive Committee to President, August 15, 1979, folder "[Office of the Vice President–Legislative Agenda], 8/15/79," Box 109, Lisa Bourdeaux Files, Office of Congressional Liaison, Jimmy Carter Library.

Memo, Hugh Morrow to Nelson Rockefeller, March 5, 1975a, Rockefeller Family Collection, Record Group 26, Series 13: Press Releases, Box 13, Filefolder 713, Rockefeller Archive Center.

Memo, Hugh Morrow to Nelson Rockefeller, October 2, 1975, Rockefeller Family Collection, Record Group 26, Series 13, Box 14, Folder 741, Rockefeller Archive Center.

Memo, Robert Mosbacher to Nelson Rockefeller, March 17, 1976, folder "Hughes Subject File–Staff Memoranda–Rockefeller, Nelson," Box B10, President Ford Committee Records, 1975–1976, Gerald R. Ford Library."

Memo, Al Moses to Walter Mondale, August 21, 1980, folder "Foreign Policy Breakfast, [7/80–12/80]," Box 1, Papers of Walter F. Mondale, Donated Material, Collection #133, Jimmy Carter Library.

Memo, Les Novitsky to Bill Kristol and Dave Ryder, October 30, 1989, folder "VP Administrative Files," Administration Office, OA/ID 40689, Office of Vice President Quayle, George H. W. Bush Library.

Memo, Les Novitsky to Bill Kristol, Dave Ryder, Cece Kremer, Greg Zoeller, and Tom Pernice, December 5, 1989, folder "VP Administrative Files," Administration Office, OA/ID 40689, Office of Vice President Quayle, George H. W. Bush Library.

Memo, Patrick E. O'Donnell to Max Friedersdorf through William Kendall, January 9, 1975, folder "Rule XXII (Senate Cloture Rules) Changes, Box 2, James Cannon Papers (Domestic Council), Gerald R. Ford Library.

Memo, Frank R. Pagnotta to John O. Marsh Jr., December 5, 1974, folder "VP Office–Administration and Personnel," Box 2, James Cannon Papers (Domestic Council), Gerald R. Ford Library.

Memo, Nelson Rockefeller for his records, January 19, 1975, folder "Vice President's Memos for the President (1)," Box 6, Dorothy E. Downton Files, 1974–1977, Gerald R. Ford Library.

Memo, Nelson Rockefeller to Gerald R. Ford, January 8, 1975a, folder "Rockefeller, Nelson–General (1)," Box 60, Philip Buchen Files, 1974–77, Gerald R. Ford Library.

Memo, Nelson Rockefeller to Gerald R. Ford, January 10, 1975a, folder "Rule XXII (Senate Cloture Rule) Changes," Box 2, James Cannon Papers (Domestic Council), Gerald R. Ford Library.

Memo, Nelson Rockefeller to Gerald Ford, April 30, 1975, folder "Vice President," Box 31, James E. Connor Files, 1974–1977, Gerald R. Ford Library.

Memo, Nelson Rockefeller to Gerald Ford, May 8, 1975, folder "Rockefeller, Nelson," Box 19, Richard Cheney Files, 1974–1977, Gerald R. Ford Library.

Memo, Nelson Rockefeller to Gerald Ford, June 19, 1975, folder "Vice President's Memos for the President (1)," Box 6, Dorothy E. Downton Files, 1974–1977, Gerald R. Ford Library.

Memo, Nelson Rockefeller to Gerald Ford, August 26, 1975, Rockefeller Family Collection, Record Group 26, Series 18, Vol. 37: 60, Rockefeller Archive Center.

Memo, Nelson Rockefeller to Gerald Ford, December 16, 1975, Rockefeller Family Collection, Record Group 26, Series 18, Vol. 9: 166–69, Rockefeller Archive Center.

Memo, Nelson Rockefeller to Gerald Ford, December 16, 1975a, folder "Domestic Council–Vice President's Role, 1/75–12/75," Box 3, Richard Cheney Files, 1974–77, Gerald R. Ford Library.

Memo, Nelson Rockefeller to Walter Mondale, November 5, 1976, Rockefeller Family Collection, Record Group 26, Series 18, Vol. 38: 217–24, Rockefeller Archive Center.

Memo, Senior Staff to Walter Mondale, n.d., folder "V.P. Yearly Assessment," Box 2, Locator: 154.J.8.7B, Administrative Assistant to President of the Senate, Vice Presidential Files, Walter F. Mondale Papers, Minnesota Historical Society Library.

374 / References

Memo, Bill Smith to Dick Moe, February 16, 1978, folder "V.P. Yearly Assessment," Box 2, Locator: 154.J.8.7B, Administrative Assistant to President of the Senate, Vice Presidential Files, Walter F. Mondale Papers, Minnesota Historical Society Library.

Memo, Bill Smith to Dick Moe, November 13, 1978, folder "Chronological File–Oct.78 to Jul 79, Box 2, Locator: 154.J.8.7B, Administrative Assistant to President of the Senate, Vice Presidential Files, Walter F. Mondale Papers, Minnesota Historical Society Library.

Memo, Bill Smith to Walter Mondale, February 1, 1979, folder "1979 Memo + Follow-ups," Box 2, Locator: 154.J.8.7B, Administrative Assistant to President of the Senate, Vice Presidential Files, Walter F. Mondale Papers, Minnesota Historical Society Library.

Memo, Stu Spencer to Nancy Towell, September 1, 1976, Rockefeller Family Collection, Record Group 26, Series 18, Vol. 31: 16–24, Rockefeller Archive Center.

Memo, John Sununu to George Bush, March 30, 1989, folder "Competitiveness Council," Administration Office, OA/ID 40689, Office of Vice President Dan Quayle, George H. W. Bush Library.

Memo, Jack Veneman to Jim Cannon, April 18, 1975, folder "VP 3/75–5/75," Box 11, James Cannon Papers (Domestic Council), Gerald R. Ford Library.

Memo, Vice-Presidential Activities, February 5, 1976, folder "Rockefeller, Nelson," Box 20, Ron Nessen Papers, 1974–1977, Gerald R. Ford Library.

Memo, Peter J. Wallison to Nelson Rockefeller, April 28, 1975, folder "Vice President," Box 31, James E. Connor Files, 1974–1977, Gerald R. Ford Library.

Memo, Jack Watson and Landon Butler to Walter Mondale, September 4, 1980, folder "Memos: Watson to Vice President Mondale," Box 21, Jack Watson Files, January 1977–January 1981, Personal Correspondence (A-K), Carter Presidential Papers–Staff Offices: Cabinet Secretary & Intergovernmental Affairs, Jimmy Carter Library.

Memo, Jack Watson and Larry Gilson to Walter Mondale, January 15, 1978, folder "Memos: Watson to Vice President Mondale," Box 21, Jack Watson Files January 1977–January 1981, Personal Correspondence (A-K), Carter Presidential Papers–Staff Offices: Cabinet Secretary & Intergovernmental Affairs, Jimmy Carter Library.

Moe, Terry M. 2003. "The Presidency and the Bureaucracy: The Presidential Advantage." In *The Presidency and the Political System*. Edited by Michael Nelson. Washington, DC: CQ Press.

Moe, Terry M. 2015. "Vested Interests and Political Institutions." *Political Science Quarterly* 130: 277–318.

Mokken, Robert J., and Frans N. Stokman. 1976. "Power and Influence and Political Phenomena." In *Power and Political Theory: Some European Perspectives* edited by Brian Barry. Hoboken, NJ: John Wiley.

References / 375

Mondale, Walter F. 2010. *The Good Fight: A Life in Liberal Politics*. New York: Scribner.

Montanaro, Domenico. "Why President Obama Campaigning for Clinton Is Historic." *NPRPolitics*, July 5, 2016. http://www.npr.org/2016/07/05/484817706/looking-back-at-a-century-of-presidents-not-campaigning-for-their-successor. Date accessed July 5, 2016.

Morin, Richard. "18%?" *Washington Post*, March 5, 2006. http://www.washingtonpost.com/wp-dyn/content/article/2006/03/03/AR2006030302045.html. Date accessed June 30, 2016.

Nash, Bradley D. 1980. Organizing and Staffing the Presidency. *Proceedings/Center for the Study of the Presidency* 3 (1).

Natoli, Marie D. 1980. "The Vice Presidency: Gerald Ford as Healer?" Editorial. *Presidential Studies Quarterly* 10 (4): 662–64.

Nelson, Michael. 1988. *A Heartbeat Away: Report of the Twentieth Century Fund Task Force on the Vice Presidency*. New York: Priority Press.

———. 2003. The Psychological Presidency. In *The Presidency and the Political System*. Edited by Michael Nelson. Washington, DC: CQ Press.

Neustadt, Richard E. 1960. Presidential Power. New York: John Wiley.

———. 1990. *Presidential Power and the Modern Presidents: The Politics of Leadership from Roosevelt to Reagan*. New York: The Free Press.

———. 1997. Vice Presidents as National Leaders: Reflections Past, Present, and Future. In *At the President's Side: The Vice Presidency in the Twentieth Century*. Edited by Timothy Walch. Columbia: University of Missouri Press.

News Article, David M. Alpern, Thomas DeFrank, Eleanor Clift, and James Doyle, April 13, 1981. *Newsweek*, "Who's Minding the Store," folder "Assassination Attempt on Pres. 3/30/81 OA9620," Box 1, Cabinet Affairs, White House Office of: "Records," Ronald Reagan Library.

News Article, Fred Barnes, July 25, 1975, *Washington Star*, "Is Divorce the Next Step for Ford and Rockefeller?," folder "Callaway Subject File–Rockefeller, Nelson," Box A4, President Ford Committee Records, 1975–1976, Gerald R. Ford Library.

News Article, Dom Bonafede, August 23, 1975, *National Journal*, "White House Report/Rockefeller's Role Fails to Match Ford Promise," Rockefeller Family Collection, Record Group 26, Series 18, Vol. 38, Rockefeller Archive Center.

News Article, Dom Bonafede, February 14, 1976, *National Journal*, "The Forgotten Man," folder "VP 2/76–3/76," Box 12, James Cannon Papers (Domestic Council), Gerald R. Ford Library.

News Article, Warren T. Brookes, n.d. *Washington Times*, "Quayle's Sharper Edge: Tending the Home Turf," folder "Defense on Hill, General: Clips, Box 1, Gattuso, James, Files, Domestic Policy and the Council on Competitiveness, Office of Vice President Dan Quayle, George H. W. Bush Library.

376 / References

News Article, Lou Cannon, *Washington Post*, "Rockefeller Aiming at Major Role in Administration," February 2, 1975, Rockefeller Family Collection, Record Group 26, Series 13, Box 14, Folder 724, Rockefeller Archive Center.

News Article, George J. Church, April 13, 1981, *Time*, "Business as Usual—Almost," folder "Assassination Attempt on Pres. 3/30/81 OA9620," Box 1, Cabinet Affairs, White House Office of: "Records," Ronald Reagan Library.

News Article, Rowland Evans and Robert Novak, July 28, 1975, *Washington Post*, "Deepening the Rocky Dilemma," folder "Callaway Subject File–Rockefeller, Nelson," Box A4, President Ford Committee Records, 1975–1976, Gerald R. Ford Library.

News Article, Saul Friedman, February 17, 1975, *Detroit Free Press*, "Rockefeller Power a Rarity in V-Ps," folder "Vice President's Memos for the President (4)," Vertical File of Clippings on Rockefeller, Box 6, Dorothy E. Downton Files, 1974–1977, Gerald R. Ford Library.

News Article, Sara Fritz, May 9, 1991, *Los Angeles Times*, "Quayle: He Tries Harder," folder "VP Clips," Box 19, Council on Competitiveness Files, OA/ID 41240, Office of Vice President Dan Quayle, George H. W. Bush Library.

News Article, Louis Harris, September 11, 1975, *Washington Post*, "Rockefeller Opposed for No. 2 Spot," folder "Rockefeller, Nelson," Box 27, Robert A. Goldwin Papers, 1973–1978, Gerald R. Ford Library.

News Article, May 16, 1972, *Philadelphia Inquirer*, "Rockefeller: Suddenly Back as a Kingmaker," Rockefeller Family Collection, Record Group 26, Series 13, Box 13, Filefolder 694, Rockefeller Archive Center.

News Article, *Richmond Times-Dispatch*, "Dan Quayle, Heavyweight," October 11, 1989, folder "October 1989," Box 2, Kristol, William, Files, OA/ID 40788, Office of Vice President Dan Quayle, George H. W. Bush Library.

News Article, October 13, 1975. *U.S. News & World Report*, "Rockefeller Talks about His Job and Future," Rockefeller Family Collection, Record Group 26, Series 13, Box 10, Folder 632, Rockefeller Archive Center.

News Article, October 26, 1975, *Washington Star*, "A Revised Seal for Rockefeller," Rockefeller Family Collection, Record Group 26, Series 13, Box 14, Folder 741, Rockefeller Archive Center.

News Article, Jim Squires, February 5, 1976, *Chicago Tribune*, "Rocky Hopes for Last Laugh," folder "Callaway Subject File–Rockefeller, Nelson," Box A4, President Ford Committee Records, 1975–1976, Gerald R. Ford Library.

News Article, Richard A. Viguerie and Steven Allen, n.d., *Newsday*, "Quayle's Got What It Takes to Take Over," folder "May 1991 [4 of 6]," Box 7, Kristol, William, Files, OA/ID 40793, Office of Vice President Dan Quayle, George H. W. Bush Library.

News Article, Jules Witcover, December 25, 1974, *Washington Post*, "Rocky to Speak Out if He Disagrees with Ford," folder "Vice President Rockefeller," Box 29, Gwen A. Anderson Files, 1974–1977, Gerald R. Ford Library.

News Briefing, George Bush, March 3, 1986, ID #377752, FG258, WHORM: Subject File, Ronald Reagan Library.

News Briefing, James L. Holloway III, March 6, 1986, ID 377752, FG258, WHORM: Subject File, Ronald Reagan Library.

Nicholas, Peter. December 31, 2010. "Biden Is a Linchpin of Obama's Presidency." *Los Angeles Times*, http://articles.latimes.com/2010/dec/31/nation/la-na-joe-biden-20110101. Date accessed January 2, 2011.

Nobleman, Eli E. September 1956. "The Delegation of Presidential Functions: Constitutional and Legal Aspects." *Annals of the American Academy of Political and Social Sciences* 307: 134–43.

NPR Commentary, National Public Radio Commentary on Bush, n.d., "The Bush Strategy," folder "Polls/Press (VP)," Office of Policy, OA/ID 41202, Office of Vice President George Bush, George H. W. Bush Library.

Osnos, Evan. July 28, 2014. "The Biden Agenda." *New Yorker*. http://www.newyorker.com/magazine/2014/07/28/biden-agenda. Date accessed November 30, 2016.

Parsons, Talcott. 1963. "On the Concept of Political Power." *Proceedings of the American Philosophical Society* 107: 232–62.

Patterson, Bradley H. Jr., 2000. *The White House Staff: Inside the West Wing and Beyond*. Washington, DC: Brookings Institution Press.

Persico, Joseph E. 1982. *The Imperial Rockefeller*. New York: Simon and Schuster.

Pfiffner, James P. 1993. "The President's Chief of Staff: Lessons Learned." *Presidential Studies Quarterly* 23 (1): 77–102.

Poll, Harris Poll, September 11, 1975, folder "Vice President Rockefeller," Box 29, Gwen A. Anderson Files, 1974–1977, Gerald R. Ford Library.

Polsby, Nelson W., and Aaron B. Wildavsky. 1968. Presidential Elections: Strategies of American Electoral Politics. 2nd ed. New York: Charles Scribner's.

Presidential Meetings with House Members, January 31, 1975–August 4, 1976, folders "Presidential Meetings with House Members, Jan. 1975; Feb. 1975; March 1975; April 1975; June 1975; July 1975; April–June 1976; July 1976–January 1977," Box 6, Max L. Friedersdorf Files, 1974–1977, Gerald R. Ford Library.

Presidential Meetings with Senate Members, January 27, 1975–September 6, 1976, folders "Presidential Meetings with Senate Members, January 1975; February 1975; September 1975; March–December 1976," Box 7, Max L. Friedersdorf Files, 1974–1977, Gerald R. Ford Library.

Press Conference with Nelson Rockefeller, July 9, 1975, folder "Rockefeller, Nelson–General," Box 25, Ron Nessen Papers, 1974–1977, Gerald R. Ford Library.

Press Conference with Nelson Rockefeller, November 6, 1975, folder "VP 10/75–11/75," Box 12, James Cannon Papers (Domestic Council), Gerald R. Ford Library.

Press Guidance, Task Force on Terrorism, December 20, 1985, folder "News Clippings/Media Clippings," Box 1, OA/ID 41061, Task Force on Combatting Terrorism, Office of Vice President George Bush, George H. W. Bush Library.

378 / References

Press Release, President's Plan for Reducing the Burdens of Regulation through Admin. Action, January 30, 1992, folder "Defense on Hill, General: Fact Sheets on Council," Box 1, Gattuso, James, Files, OA/ID 41269, Domestic Policy and the Council on Competitiveness, Office of Vice President Dan Quayle, George H. W. Bush Library.

Quayle, Dan. 1994. *Standing Firm*. New York: HarperCollins.

———. 1997. "A New Framework: Walter Mondale as Vice President." In *At the President's Side: The Vice Presidency in the Twentieth Century*. Edited by Timothy Walch. Columbia: University of Missouri Press.

Rakove, Jack N. 1996. *Original Meanings: Politics and Ideas in the Making of the Constitution*. New York: Alfred A. Knopf.

Reagan, Nancy. 1989. *My Turn: The Memoirs of Nancy Reagan*. New York: Random House.

Reagan, Ronald. 1990. *Ronald Reagan: An American Life*. New York: Simon and Schuster.

Reeves, Richard. 1975. *A Ford, Not a Lincoln*. New York: Harcourt Brace Jovanovich.

Regan, Donald T. 1988. *For the Record: From Wall Street to Washington*. Orlando, FL: Harcourt Brace Jovanovich.

Remarks of William J. Clinton. 1994. "Teleconference Remarks to the National Association of County Officials," July 19, 1993, *Public Papers of the Presidents of the United States: William J. Clinton, 1993*. Washington, DC: Government Printing Office.

Remarks of the President, Remarks of the President upon His Announcing Nelson Rockefeller as Vice President-Designate, August 20, 1974, folder "Rockefeller, Nelson (1)," Box 2689, WHCF, Gerald R. Ford Library.

Remarks of the President, Remarks of Ford at the Salute to the Vice President Dinner at the Waldorf Astoria, February 13, 1975, Rockefeller Family Collection, Record Group 26, Series 13: Press Releases, Box 13, Filefolder 713, Rockefeller Archive Center.

Remarks of Press Secretary Ronald H. Nessen Following a Meeting between the President and Vice President, Week Ending Friday, December 27, 1974, The Role of Vice President Rockefeller, December 27, 1974, folder "Rockefeller Role in the Ford Administration," Box 2, James Cannon Papers (Domestic Council), Gerald R. Ford Library.

Report, Murphy Commission, January 5, 1977, Rockefeller Family Collection, Record Group 26, Series 19, Box 6, Folder 120, Rockefeller Archive Center.

Republican Leadership Meetings, January 14, 1975–August 5, 1976, folders "Republican Leadership Meetings, January–March 1975; April–August 1975; September–December 1975; January–April 1976; May–December 1976," Box 8, Max L. Friedersdorf Files, Gerald R. Ford Library.

Rice, Condoleezza. 2011. *No Higher Honor*. New York: Crown.

Ricks, Thomas E. 2006. *Fiasco: The American Military Adventure in Iraq*. New York: Penguin.

Riker, William H. 1986. *The Art of Political Manipulation*. New Haven, CT: Yale University Press.

Risse-Kappen. 1991. "Did 'Peace through Strength' End the Cold War? Lessons from INF." *International Security* 16 (1): 162–88.

Rosen, Elliot A. 1997. "Not Worth a Pitcher of Warm Piss": John Nance Garner as Vice President. In *At the President's Side: The Vice Presidency in the Twentieth Century*. Edited by Timothy Walch. Columbia: University of Missouri Press.

Rosen, James. 2015. *Cheney One on One: A Candid Conversation with America's Most Controversial Statesman*. Washington, DC: Regnery.

Rossiter, Clinton L. 1948. "The Reform of the Vice-Presidency." *Political Science Quarterly* 63 (3): 383–403.

———, ed. 1961. *The Federalist Papers*. New York: Mentor.

Rothkopf, David. January 14, 2013. "The Bidenization of America." *Foreign Policy*. http://foreignpolicy.com/2013/01/14/the-bidenization-of-america/. Date accessed January 17, 2023.

Rove, Karl. 2010. *Courage and Consequence: My Life as a Conservative in the Fight*. New York: Threshold.

Rubin, Robert E. 2003. *In an Uncertain World*. New York: Random House.

Rumsfeld, Donald. 2011. *Known and Unknown*. New York: Sentinel.

Samuelsohn, Darren. November 17, 2015. "Why Al Gore Won't Endorse Hillary Clinton." *Politico*. http://www.politico.com/story/2015/11/al-gore-hillary-clinton-215957. Date accessed April 20, 2016.

Schattschneider, E. E. 1960. *The Semisovereign People*. New York: Holt, Rinehart & Winston.

Schedule for Friday, December 20, 1974, folder "Rockefeller Schedule 12/20/74," Box 2, James Cannon Papers (Domestic Council), Gerald R. Ford Library.

Schlesinger, Arthur M., Jr. 1974. "On the Presidential Succession," *Political Science Quarterly* 89 (3): 475–505.

Skinner, Kiron K., Annelise Anderson, and Martin Anderson, eds. 2001. *Reagan, In His Own Hand*. New York: The Free Press.

Skowronek, Stephen. 1993. *The Politics Presidents Make: Leadership from John Adams to George Bush*. Cambridge, MA: Harvard University Press.

———. 2003. "Presidential Leadership in Political Time." In *The Presidency and the Political System*. Edited by Michael Nelson. Washington, DC: CQ Press.

Smith, Virginia W. 1979. "How Interest Groups Influence Legislators." *Social Work* 24: 234–39.

Stephanopoulos, George. 1999. *All Too Human: A Political Education*. New York: Little, Brown.

380 / References

State of the Union Address, Ronald Reagan. 1984. "Address before a Joint Session of the Congress on the State of the Union," January 25, 1984, *Public Papers of the Presidents of the United States: Ronald Reagan, 1984*. Washington, DC: Government Printing Office.

Sullivan, Terry. 2004. *The Nerve Center: Lessons in Governing from the White House Chiefs of Staff*. College Station: Texas A&M University Press.

Tabulations and Summaries for VP, 1974, file "Vice Presidential Vacancy, 1974 Tabulations and Summaries of Suggestions (1)," Box 21, Robert T. Hartmann Files, 1974–1977, Gerald R. Ford Library.

Talking points for meeting with W. Clement Stone, January 20, 1976, folder "Vice President," Box 31, James E. Connor Files, 1974–1977, Gerald R. Ford Library.

Tenet, George. 2007. *At the Center of the Storm: My Years at the CIA*. New York: HarperCollins.

terHorst, Jerald F. 1974. *Gerald Ford and the Future of the Presidency*. New York: Third Press.

Century Foundation. 2010. "About the Century Foundation." https://tcf.org/about/. Date accessed February 6, 2017.

Thrush, Glenn. "Joe Biden in Winter." *Politico,* March/April 2014. http://www.politico.com/magazine/story/2014/02/joe-biden-profile-103667. Date accessed November 30, 2016.

Traub, James. November 24, 2009. "After Cheney." *New York Times.* http://www.nytimes.com/2009/11/29/magazine/29Biden-t.html. Date accessed December 1, 2010.

Trip Summaries, FY 1992 Vice Presidential Trip Summary, folder "1992 Trip Summaries," Administration Office, OA/ID 40689, Office of Vice President Dan Quayle, George H. W. Bush Library.

Tulis, Jeffrey K. 2003. "The Two Constitutional Presidencies." In *The Presidency and the Political System*. Edited by Michael Nelson. Washington, DC: CQ Press.

Turner, Michael. 1982. *The Vice President as Policy Maker: Rockefeller in the Ford White House*. Westport, CT: Greenwood Press.

United States Senate. Vice Presidents' Profiles. http://www.senate.gov/artandhistory/history/common/generic/VP_Dan_Quayle.htm. Date accessed October 11, 2016.

Untermeyer, Chase. 1997. "Looking Forward: George Bush as Vice President." In *At the President's Side: The Vice Presidency in the Twentieth Century*. Edited by Timothy Walch. Columbia: University of Missouri Press.

Vice Presidential Organizational Chart, January 18, 1976, Rockefeller Family Collection, Record Group 26, Series 18, Vol. 39: 6–10, Rockefeller Archive Center.

Vice Presidential Staff Descriptions, n.d., Rockefeller Family Collection, Record Group 25, Series 18, Vol. 39: 11–34, Rockefeller Archive Center.

Walcott, Charles E., Shirley Anne Warshaw, and Stephen J. Wayne. 2001. "The Chief of Staff." *Presidential Studies Quarterly* 31 (3): 464–89.

Walsh, Kenneth T., and Matthew Cooper. July 19, 1993. "A Vice President Who Counts," *U.S. News & World Report* 115, no. 3.

Warshaw, Shirley Anne. 2009. *The Co-Presidency of Bush and Cheney*. Stanford, CA: Stanford University Press.

Watson, Robert P., and Richard M. Yon. 2006. "Vice Presidential Selection: A Model." White House Studies 6 (2): 163–77.

Weekly Briefing/Report for the Vice President August 9, 1974–March 31, 1975, filed "MC 4-9 Weekly Briefing/Report for the Vice President 8/9/74–3/31/75," Box 21, WHCF, Subject File, MC: Meetings-Conferences, Gerald R. Ford Library.

Willer, David, Michael J. Lovaglia, and Barry Markovsky. 1997. "Power and Influence: A Theoretical Bridge." *Social Forces* 76: 571–603.

Willer, Robb, Lisa Troyer, and Michael J. Lovaglia. 2005. "Influence over Observers of Structural Power: An Experimental Investigation." *Sociological Quarterly* 46: 263–77.

Williams, Irving G. 1954. *The American Vice-Presidency: New Look*. Garden City, NY: Doubleday.

———. 1976. The Vice-Presidency. In *Power and the Presidency*. Edited by Philip C. Dolce and George H. Skau. New York: Charles Scribner's.

Witcover, Jules. 1992. *Crapshoot: Rolling the Dice on the Vice Presidency*. New York: Crown.

———. 2007. *Very Strange Bedfellows: The Short and Unhappy Marriage of Richard Nixon and Spiro Agnew*. New York: Public Affairs.

———. 2010. *Joe Biden: A Life of Trial and Redemption*. New York: William Morrow.

———. 2014. *The American Vice Presidency: From Irrelevance to Power*. Washington, DC: Smithsonian Books.

Woodward, Bob. 1994. *The Agenda: Inside the Clinton White House*. New York: Simon & Schuster.

———. March 2, 1997. "Gore Was 'Solicitor-in-Chief' in '96 Reelection Campaign." *Washington Post*. https://www.washingtonpost.com/archive/politics/1997/03/02/gore-was-solicitor-in-chief-in-96-reelection-campaign/db76cc99-8616-44c5-96cc-1cea8ac271d8/. Date accessed November 1, 2016.

———. 2004. *Plan of Attack*. New York: Simon & Schuster.

———. 2006. *State of Denial*. New York: Simon & Schuster.

———. 2008. *The War Within*. New York: Simon & Schuster.

———. 2010. *Obama's Wars*. New York: Simon & Schuster.

Wrong, Dennis H. 1980. *Power: Its Forms, Bases and Uses*. New Brunswick, NJ: Transaction Publishers.

Yon, Richard. 2012. "The Biden Vice Presidency: Perpetuating Influence or Restoring Historical Insignificance?" In *The Obama Presidency*. Edited by Robert P. Watson, Jack Covarrubias, Tom Lansford, and Douglas M. Brattebo. New York: SUNY Press.

382 / References

Zimbardo, Philip G., and Michael R. Leippe. 1991. *The Psychology of Attitude Change and Social Influence.* New York: McGraw-Hill.

Index

Aaron, David, 176
Abbot, Steve, 135, 142
Abourezk, James, 56
Abraham, Spencer, 119
Acheson, Dean, 226
Adams, John, 254
Addington, David, 113, 118, 121–122
  Congress circumvented by, 129
  GAO battled by, 123
  Iraq War not believed in by,
    165–166
  Powell circumvented by, 151
  THREATCON checked by, 137–
    138
  Twenty-Fifth Amendment
    examined by, 133
  war on terror shaped by, 149–150
  White House staff and, 166
affirmative action, 182
Afghanistan, 144, 240
Agnew, Spiro, 41
Ailes, Roger, 216, 217
Air Force One, 138
Albright, Madeleine, 226
Allbaugh, Joe, 93
Allen, Richard, 191
Allison, Richard, 81
alternatives, defining of, 8, 21–22
Andropov, Yuri, 206–208

Appropriations Committee, for
  Senate, 56
Armed Services committee, for
  Senate, 210
Armey, Dick, 127
Armitage, Richard, 158
Armstrong, Anne, 53
Armstrong Ranch, 158–159
Ash, Roy, 68
Ashcroft, John, 119, 161–162
Aspen Lodge, at Camp David, 142
authority, vice presidential, 114–115

Baker, James "Jim," 32, 191, 194, 199,
  208
  Bush, G. H. W., helped by, 246,
    269–270
  Quayle clashing with, 211–212
  Reagan, R., choosing, 29, 203
Baker, Peter, 106
Baldridge, Malcolm, 194
Barber, James David, 19–20
Bartlett, Dan, 104, 152, 159, 162
Beckwith, David, 209, 216
Beier, David, 231
Bell, Griffin, 182
Bellinger, John, 162
Berenson, Bradford, 115
Berger, Sandy, 228

383

384 / Index

Bergland, Robert, 176
Biden, Joe
  economic recovery plan
    championed by, 239–240
  electoral dynamics of, 243–244
  Emanuel dismissing, 31
  foreign policy prioritized by,
    240–241
  gaffes impacting, 243
  institutional dynamics impacting,
    242–243
  interpersonal dynamics of, 238–349
  line assignments reduced by, 239
  McConnell negotiated with by, 241
  presidency sought by, 244
  presidential transition developed
    by, 239
  Republicans lobbied by, 27
  vice presidency considered by,
    25–26
  vice presidential influence of, 27,
    238, 250, 274
Big Eight (foreign policy team), 210–
    211, 248
bin Laden, Osama, 128, 143–145
Blair, Tony, 112, 149
Blount, Red, 103
Blumenthal, Werner, 176
Bolten, Joshua, 118, 120, 140
  Card replaced by, 33, 166–167
  on Cheney, D., 107, 141
  vice presidential influence reduced
    by, 171, 266
Bosnia, 149, 228–229
Brown, Jerry, 189
Brzezinski, Zbigniew, 178–179, 182–
    183, 185
budget, federal, 74–75, 77
Budget Review Board, for White
  House, 115, 167
Burke, John, 33

Bush, Barbara, 193
Bush, G. H. W., model, of vice
  presidency, 195, 247, 271
Bush, George H. W., 5, 22, 29, 96,
  103, 109
  archival research at presidential
    library of, 261
  Baker, J., helping, 246, 269–270
  ceremonial functions attended by,
    206–208
  on Cheney, D., 164
  congressional relations improved
    by, 208
  foreign affairs impacted by, 206–207
  foreign policy impacted by, 198
  institutional dynamics of, 202–209
  interpersonal dynamics tempering,
    247, 270–271
  line assignments embraced by, 169,
    203, 246
  loyalty prioritized by, 201–202, 215,
    246–247, 270
  Mondale advising, 193
  Mondale model expanded by, 203,
    246, 269
  politics avoided by, 221–222
  Quayle and, 213–214
  Reagan, R., and, 191–193, 195–200
  South Florida Task force led by, 205
  Task Force on Combatting
    Terrorism led by, 205
  Task Force on Regulatory Relief
    headed by, 204
  terrorism combated by, 205
  vice presidential influence of, 197–
    198, 203–204, 208–209
  vice presidential selection by, 47,
    215–216
  Western Europe visited by, 206–207
  White House staff not trusting,
    194–195, 202–203

Index / 385

Bush, George W., 21, 29, 104, 211–212
  advice sought by, 109
  Card emphasized by, 118
  ceremonial functions enjoyed by, 104
  Cheney, D., and, 95–99, 104–108,
    111–112, 116–117, 146–148
  enhanced interrogation authorized
    by, 151
  gay marriage opposed by, 153–154
  Gore *versus*, 260
  Iraq War announced by, 149
  Kyoto Protocol opposed by, 124–125
  Libby not pardoned by, 154–155, 170
  national security brushed up on
    by, 98
  Office of Homeland Security
    announced by, 142–143
  presidential transition to, 105,
    117–118
  reelection campaign of, 153
  Rumsfeld fired by, 155, 170
  State of the Union address by, 148,
    154
  strengths and weaknesses of,
    102–104
  White House staff changed by, 167
Bush, Laura, 95
Bush (2001–2009) administration
  Cheney, D., filling out, 119–120
  Congress pressured by, 126–127
  energy crisis faced with, 121
  terrorists and nations supporting
    them not distinguished by, 143
Bush Tax Cuts, 131–133, 241
business community, Quayle in,
  218–219

Califano, Joseph, 176
California, brownouts plaguing, 121
Calio, Nicholas, 163
Callaway, Bo, 77, 84

Camp David, 142, 144, 186, 225
Camp David peace accords, 186
Canfield, H. Spofford, 55
Cannon, James, 65, 75, 79, 81–82, 89
  Cavanaugh not fired by, 66
  Domestic Council directed by, 64
  on Ford, 44–45, 68
  on Rockefeller, 264
Card, Andy, 171
  Bolten replacing, 33, 166–167
  Bush, G. W., emphasizing, 118
  Cheney, D., enabled by, 162
Carlucci, Frank, 197
Carp, Bert, 176, 182
Carter, Jimmy, 10, 178
  archival research at presidential
    library of, 10, 261
  Democrats disillusioned with, 188
  details bogging down, 184–185
  "malaise speech" by, 185, 245, 269
  Mondale and, 3, 176, 180–182,
    185–186
  presidential transition to, 176
  reelection efforts by, 187–190
  Rose Garden strategy taken by, 189,
    245
  vice presidential selection by,
    173–174
Casey, William, 194
Casstevens, Kay, 229
Cavanaugh, James, 66, 81–82
Central Intelligence Agency (CIA),
  for U.S., 51–53, 135–136, 146,
  148–149
ceremonial functions, of vice
  presidents, 246
  Bush, G. H. W. attending, 206–208
  Bush, G. W. enjoying, 104
  Cheney, D., minimizing, 117
  Johnson, L., diminished by, 25
  Mondale not interested in, 175

386 / Index

Cheney, Dick, 1, 22, 37, 39, 63, 196
  as advisor, 108
  Ashcroft criticizing, 161–162
  Bolten on, 107, 141
  Budget Review Board chaired by, 115
  Bush, G. H. W., on, 164
  Bush, G. W., and, 95–99, 104–108, 111–112, 116–117, 146–148
  Bush administration filled out by, 119–120
  Bush Tax Cuts championed by, 130–132
  cabinet filled by, 160
  Card enabling, 162
  ceremonial functions minimized by, 117
  as chief of staff, 30
  Congress and, 120, 132–133
  congressional relations with, 125–126
  controversial programs developed by, 149–151
  Democrats attacking, 153
  on diminished role, 28
  documents classified and declassified by, 115–116
  domestic policy avoided by, 115
  electoral dynamics impacting, 89, 169
  enhanced interrogation supported by, 127–128
  foreign policy and, 152, 172, 267
  Greenspan met with by, 110
  health of, 99–100
  homeland security focused on by, 133–135, 143, 156
  Hussein emphasized by, 149
  institutional dynamics impacting, 160–168
  intelligence community engaged by, 134
  interpersonal dynamics of, 151–156
  Iraq focused on by, 145
  Kyoto Protocol and, 161
  letter of resignation drafted by, 133
  Libby relied on by, 158, 165
  line assignments accepted by, 133
  in meetings, 109–112
  Middle East toured by, 144
  National Energy Policy Development Group led by, 121
  national security understood by, 103
  on "No New Starts," 75–76
  PDB and, 112–113
  polls not cared about by, 106
  Powell battling, 146
  presidency not sought by, 97–98, 105, 152–153
  presidential administrations worked for by, 103
  presidential power defended by, 113–114, 123–124
  presidential transition planned by, 117–120, 160
  press relations of, 116–117
  Principals Committee attended by, 110
  Republicans differed from by, 153
  résumé of, 96
  Rice and, 146–147, 168
  Rockefeller and, 71, 81–83, 85–86, 264
  Rove arguing against, 100–101
  Rumsfeld on, 102, 113
  Russert interviewing, 142
  scandals impacting, 157–159
  second term of, 108, 153, 167–168, 170–171
  secretary of defense considered as position for, 105
  Senate meeting with, 132–133
  September 11 impacting, 21, 137–139, 156

situational dynamics of, 156–160
staff of, 164
strengths and weaknesses of,
102–104
Tenet on, 128, 145
terrorism concerning, 135
TSP architected by, 129
unpopularity of, 157
VFW spoken at by, 146–147
vice presidency of, 104–109
vice presidential influence
demonstrated by, 9, 124, 142–
143, 151–152, 156–157, 165–166,
170–172, 261, 265
vice presidential search committee
headed by, 92–93
vice presidential selection of,
92–102
on vice presidents, 91
war on terror impacted by, 151,
266
White House staff informing, 111
Whitman, C., circumvented by,
124–125
Whittington shot by, 158–159
Cheney, Lynne, 95
Cheney, Mary, 153–154
Cheney One on One (Rosen), 91
Chernenko (Soviet leader), 207–208
Chernomyrdin, Viktor, 227
chiefs of staff, 39. *See also* Card,
Andy; Kristol, William; Libby,
Scooter; Rumsfeld, Donald
Cheney, D., as, 30
management styles of, 30–31
vice presidential influence impacted
by, 29–30, 33
for vice presidents, 162
China, 206, 232
Christopher, Warren, 226–228
Churchill, Winston, 11
CIA. *See* Central Intelligence Agency

CIA Commission. *See* Commission
on CIA Activities within the
United States
Clean Air Act, of U.S., 124
Clift, A. Denis, 180
Clinton, Bill, 114–115, 223, 260, 272
Democrats redefined by, 223
foreign policy challenging, 225–226
Gore and, 28, 36, 233–238, 273–274
Lewinsky and, 234–235, 249–250
Supreme Court and, 231
Clinton, Hillary, 223, 230, 232, 241
Clinton fatigue theory, 236, 250
Cohen, David, 29–30
Cohen, William, 229
Cole, Ken, 49, 64
Commission on Aviation Safety and
Security, for White House, 231
Commission on CIA Activities
within the United States (CIA
Commission) (Rockefeller
Commission), 51–52, 53
Commission on Critical Choices,
70–71
Commission on the Organization of
the Government for the Conduct
of Foreign Policy (Murphy
Commission), 49, 53–55
Competitiveness Council. *See*
President's Council on
Competitiveness
Congress (U.S.), 2, 62, 70–71, 103. *See
also* House of Representatives;
Senate
Addington circumventing, 129
Bush administration pressuring,
126–127
Cheney, D., and, 120, 132–133
Gore investigated by, 234
lame-duck, 27, 241
Mondale impacting, 183
Quayle, Dan lobbying, 220

388 / Index

Congress (U.S.) *(continued)*
Republicans in, 234
Rockefeller not impacting, 55–56
congressional relations
Bush, G. H. W., improving, 208
with Cheney, D., 125–126
of Quayle, 218–219, 247–248, 271
of Rockefeller, 54–57
vice presidents managing, 55
Constitution, of U.S., 253, 257
Twelfth Amendment of, 92, 100
Twenty-Fifth Amendment of, 133
vice presidents not limited by, 4
contingent influence, vice presidential
influence as, 23, 258
Corpus Christi Caller-Times
(newspaper), 159
Counterproliferation Division, of CIA,
148
Counterterrorist Center, 147
Cox, Christopher, 120
Cuomo, Andrew, 229

Damm, Helene von, 201
Danforth, John, 220
Daniels, Mitch, 115
Darman, Richard G., 213, 220
Darth Vader (character), 134
Deaver, Michael, 200, 202
Defense Intelligence Agency (DIA), of
U.S., 135
defining of alternatives, 8, 21–22
Democratic Caucus, 241
Democratic Party Convention, 25
Democrats. *See also specific Democrats*
Carter disillusioning, 188
Cheney, D., attacked by, 153
Clinton, B., redefining, 223
House of Representatives lost by,
27, 31, 225
Mondale connecting with, 175,
187–188

Quayle working with, 220–221
Rockefeller, Nelson appealing to,
263
Senate lost by, 225
Department of Defense, for U.S., 1
Department of Education, for U.S.,
186
Department of Health, Education, and
Welfare, of U.S., 40
Department of Homeland Security,
for U.S., 136, 156, 158
Department of Justice, of U.S., 161
DeSutter, Joseph, 211, 228
Detroit Free Press (newspaper), 48
DIA. *See* Defense Intelligence Agency
Dilulio, John, 164–165
Dingell, John, 123
directional model, vice presidential
influence considered through, 18
Disarmament Committee, of UN,
206
Domestic Council (U.S.), 49–50, 56,
62–63, 65–66, 74, 80–81
Cannon directing, 64
Energy and Resource Policy and
Finance within, 58–59, 61
NSC compared with, 68
Rockefeller on, 9, 67–69, 73, 262
vice presidential influence and, 57
domestic policy, of U.S.
Cheney, D., avoiding, 115
Gore involved in, 231
presidents controlling, 2
Quayle advancing, 217
Rockefeller and, 46–48, 64–65, 68,
74–75
Don't Ask, Don't Tell (policy), 27,
240, 274
Dora Farms (complex), 149
Dorn, Nancy, 163
Duberstein, Kenneth, 202, 204
Dunham, Richard, 65

Eagleton, Thomas, 173
economic recovery plan, Biden
  championing, 239–240
Egyptian Islamic Jihad, 147
EIA. *See* Energy Independence
  Authority
Eisenhower, Dwight, 40, 57
Eisenhower, Milton, 40
Eizenstat, Stuart, 186
electoral dynamics, of vice
  presidential influence, 7, 8, 9,
  34–37, 259
  of Biden, 243–244
  Cheney, D., impacted by, 89, 169
  of Mondale, 186–190, 245, 269
  of Quayle, 215–222
  Rockefeller and, 84–87, 264
Emanuel, Rahm, 31, 241–242, 250,
  274
Energy and Resource Policy and
  Finance (review group), within
  Domestic Council, 58–59, 61
energy crises, 57–58, 121
Energy Independence Authority
  (EIA), of U.S., 57–58, 60, 63,
  80–81, 264
  ERFCO renamed, 59
  Rockefeller lobbying for, 54, 61–62
  Rumsfeld on, 60
energy market, wholesale contrasted
  with retail, 121
Energy Resources Finance
  Corporation (ERFCO), 59
enhanced interrogation, 127–128,
  150–151
Environmental Protection Agency
  (EPA), for U.S., 120, 134
Equal Rights Amendment (proposed
  legislation), 191
ERFCO. *See* Energy Resources
  Finance Corporation
Europe, 170, 206–207

executive branch. *See also* presidents;
  vice presidents
  increase in size of, 1, 12
  legislative branch encroaching on,
  113
  New Deal enlarging, 2
executive orders, OVP reviewing,
  114–115

FAA. *See* Federal Aviation
  Administration
FACA. *See* Federal Advisory
  Committee Act
FBI. *See* Federal Bureau of
  Investigation
Federal Advisory Committee Act
  (FACA), 122, 157
Federal Aviation Administration
  (FAA), of U.S., 139
federal budget, for U.S., 74–75, 77
Federal Bureau of Investigation (FBI),
  of U.S., 135
Federal Emergency Management
  Agency, for U.S., 135
Federal Energy Administration, for
  U.S., 59
Federal Reserve, of U.S., 110
Ferrell, Will, 116
FISA. *See* Foreign Intelligence
  Surveillance
Flanigan, Timothy, 167
Fleischer, Ari, 93, 146, 152, 267
Flemming, Arthur, 40
Ford, Gerald, 9, 30, 35, 63, 89, 103, 190
  archival research at presidential
  library of, 10, 261
  Cannon on, 44–45, 68
  CIA Commission established by,
  51–52
  energy crisis faced by, 57–58
  House of Representatives known
  by, 55

390 / Index

Ford, Gerald (*continued*)
  management style of, 71–72, 88,
    262–263
  Nixon choosing, 41
  presidency of, 73–74
  Rockefeller and, 11, 45–46, 48–51,
    60–61, 65–66, 69–72, 76–79,
    84–87
  Rumsfeld on, 263
  strengths and weaknesses of, 43
  vice presidential influence
    emphasized by, 78–79
  vice presidential selection by, 43–44
  White House staff convincing, 61
Ford Library, 50
foreign affairs, Bush, G. H. W.,
  impacting, 206–207
Foreign Intelligence Surveillance
  (FISA), of U.S., 128–129
foreign policy, of U.S., 49, 53–55, 98,
  214, 248, 272
  Biden prioritizing, 240–241
  Bush, G. H. W., impacting, 198
  Cheney, D., and, 152, 172, 267
  Clinton, B., challenged by, 225–226
  Gore impacting, 225–227
  Kristol on, 210
  Mondale impacting, 181–183
  Quayle and, 209–212
  vice presidents and, 2–3
founding fathers, of U.S., 253
Fox, Vincente, 108
Fox News (broadcast network), 159
Friday breakfasts (meetings), 178
Friedersdorf, Max, 190, 208
Frist, Bill, 131, 153
Frum, David, 106
Fuerth, Leon, 228
Fuller, Craig, 201

gang of eight (congressional leaders),
  130

GAO. *See* General Accounting Office
Garner, John Nance, 1, 24, 254
Gates, Robert, 108, 210, 241, 242
gay marriage, 153–154
General Accounting Office (GAO),
  123, 157, 266
Geneva Convention, 127, 150–151
Gergen, David, 200, 229–230
Germany, 206–207
Gingrich, Newt, 219
Goldschmidt, Neil, 176
Goldstein, Joel, 106, 140, 253
Gonzales, Alberto, 129, 150, 167
Gorbachev (Soviet leader), 208
Gore, Al, 5, 100, 110, 120
  Bush, G. W., *versus*, 260
  Christopher meeting with, 227–228
  Clinton, B., and, 28, 36, 233–238
  Clinton, H., competing with, 230
  Clinton and, 273–274
  Congress investigating, 234
  domestic policy involved in by, 231
  foreign policy impacted by, 225–227
  fundraising scandal impacting, 234
  Kyoto Protocol championed by, 232
  line assignments embraced by, 225
  Mondale model differed from by, 225
  NAFTA championed by, 228
  presidency sought by, 235–236
  REGO led by, 231–232
  situational dynamics of, 222–238
  State Department superseded by, 227
  Stephanopoulos undercutting, 224
  Tenet on, 231
  vice presidential influence of, 225–
    226, 233–234
  vice presidential selection of, 222–
    223, 249, 272
  White House Commission on
    Aviation Safety and Security
    chaired by, 231
  White House staff placed by, 229

Gore-Chernomyrdin Commission, 227
Gore-Mbecki Commission, 227
Gore-Mubarak Commission, 227
Graham, Lindsey, 240
Gramm, Phil, 125
Grassley, Charles, 131
Gray, Boyden, 205
Greenspan, Alan, 58–61, 96, 110, 121
Gulf War, 103, 144–145, 220–221, 248, 271
Gurney, Edward, 103

Habitation Clause, of Twelfth Amendment, 92, 100
Hadley, Stephen, 120, 267
Hagel, Chuck, 124
Haig, Alexander, 80, 194, 198
Haiti, 228–229
Halliburton (firm), 92, 94, 99, 121
Hammond, Darrell, 116
Hannah, John, 148
Harlow, Bryce, 43, 44–46
Hastert, Dennis, 120, 132, 138
Hayden, Michael, 128–130
Hersh, Seymour, 51
Hess, Stephen, 33
Hills, Roderick, 61
homeland security, Cheney, D., focusing on, 133–136, 143, 156
House Intelligence Committee, 133
House of Representatives (U.S), 120
  Commission on Critical Choices and, 70
  Democrats losing, 27, 31, 225
  Ford knowing, 55
  Intelligence Committee for, 133
  Ways and Means Committee for, 132
Hughes, Karen, 95, 116, 139, 162
Hume, Brit, 159
Humphrey, Hubert, 26–27, 40

Hussein, Saddam, 127, 143
  Cheney, D., emphasizing, 149
  al Qaeda not linked to, 126
  uranium sought by, 148
  WMDs possessed by, 144–145

INF. *See* intermediate range nuclear forces
influence, 169–172. *See also* vice presidential influence
  contingent, 23, 258
  definition of, 22
  diminished, 12–13, 28, 74, 87–88, 171, 210, 234, 262
  marginalized, 12–13, 202, 209, 243, 245, 248–249, 257, 269, 272
  as multidimensional, 16–17
  power and, 15–17, 256–258
  proximity model of, 16, 19
  social cohesion model of, 16, 19
  of staff, 233
institutional dynamics, of vice presidential influence, 7, 8, 9, 19, 28–34, 259
  Biden impacted by, 242–243
  of Bush, G. H. W., 202–209
  Cheney, D., impacted by, 160–168
  of Quayle, 209–215, 272
intelligence community, Cheney, D., engaging in, 134
intermediate range nuclear forces (INF), 206
interpersonal dynamics, of vice presidential influence, 7–9, 8, 19–20, 24–27, 88, 258–259
  of Biden, 238–349
  Bush, G. H. W. tempered by, 247, 270–271
  of Cheney, D., 151–156
  Mondale impacted by, 173, 186, 188–189, 245–246, 268
  of Rockefeller, 69–73

392 / Index

interrogation, enhanced, 127–128,
150–151
Iran, 189, 206
Iraq, 240, 266
Cheney focusing on, 145
al Qaeda connected to, 147
Resolution 1441 responded to by,
148–149
U.S concerned with, 144–145
Iraq War
Addington not believing in, 165–
166
authorization for, 126–127
Bush, G., announcing, 149
Israel, Lebanon invaded by, 267

Jeffords, Jim, 130
Johnson, Clay, 118–119
Johnson, Lyndon
ceremonial functions diminishing,
25
Humphrey bullied by, 26
Kennedy not trusting, 24–25
Space Council chaired by, 2
Joint Committee on National Security,
52
Jordan, Hamilton, 174, 182
Justice Department, 150–151, 182

Kennedy, Edward "Ted," 173, 189
Kennedy, John F., 24–25
Khalid Sheikh Mohammed (KSM),
128
Khalilzad, Zalmay, 119, 120
Kissinger, Henry, 42, 48, 49, 54
Klain, Ron, 110
Kristol, William "Bill," 31, 212–213,
220, 248–249, 272
Baker, J., discussed by, 211
on foreign policy, 210
on Quayle, 181

KSM. *See* Khalid Sheikh Mohammed
Kyoto Protocol
Bush, G. W., opposing, 124–125
Cheney, D., and, 161
Gore championing, 232

Laird, Melvin, 88, 263
Lake, Anthony, 228
Landrieu, Maurice, 176
Larry King Live (TV program), 228
Laxalt, Paul, 191
leadership succession, formal
procedures for, 133
Lebanon, Israel invading, 267
legislative branch, executive branch
encroached on by, 113
Lemann, Nicholas, 135
Lewinsky, Monica, 234–235, 249–250,
273
Libby, Scooter, 29, 118, 141, 266
as assistant to the president, 163
Bush, G. W., not pardoning, 154–
155, 170
Cheney, D., relying on, 158, 165
OVP filled out by, 119
Lieberman, Joe, 220–221
line assignments, 204–205, 217–218,
231–232. *See also specific line
assignments*
Biden reducing, 239
Bush, G. H. W., embracing, 169,
203, 246
Cheney, D., accepting, 133
Gore embracing, 225
Mondale, W., avoiding, 177
Lodge, Cabot, 40
Lord, Carnes, 212
Lott, Trent, 130
lunches meetings, between presidents
and vice presidents, 19, 111
Lynn, James, 58–59

"malaise speech," by Carter, 185, 245, 269

Manhattan Project, 11

Mansfield, Mike, 70

Marine Two, 141–142, 181

Marsh, Jack, 52, 78

Marshall, Thomas, 254

Matalin, Mary, 29, 159, 162, 163

McBride, Lea, 145

McCain, John, 127–128, 132, 241

McClellan, Scott, 146

McConnell, John, 136, 163

McConnell, Mitch, 241

McCrystal, Stanley, 240

McFarlane, Robert, 204

McGovern, George, 173

McLarty, Mack, 229

Meese, Ed, 199, 201

Meet the Press (TV program), 143

Messina, Jim, 243

Middle East, Cheney, D., touring, 144

Mineta, Norm, 139

minimum wage bill (1989), 220

Minnesota State Historical Society, 10, 261

modern vice presidencies, 7–8, 9, 186

Moe, Richard, 178

Mondale, Walter "Fritz," 10, 19, 35, 89
as advisor, 178, 257
Bush, G. H. W., advised by, 193
Carter and, 3, 176, 180–182, 185–186
ceremonial functions not interesting, 175
Congress impacted by, 183
Democrats connected with by, 175, 187–188
electoral dynamics of, 186–190, 245, 269
foreign policy impacted by, 181–183

interpersonal dynamics impacting, 173–186, 188–189, 245–246, 268
line assignments avoided by, 177
"malaise speech" opposed by, 185
national security and, 178–179
NATO allies visited by, 180–181
vice presidency considered by, 173–174
vice presidential influence expanded by, 176–177, 244–245

Mondale model, for vice presidency, 176–178, 275
Bush, G. H. W., expanding on, 203, 246, 269
Gore differing from, 225
vice presidential influence ensured by, 180–181

Moore, Frank, 183

Morrow, Hugh, 73

Murphy, Daniel, 207

Murphy Commission. *See* Commission on the Organization of the Government for the Conduct of Foreign Policy

Murtha, John, 126

Myers, Dee Dee, 222–223, 237

NAFTA. *See* North American Free Trade Agreement

National Economic Council, of U.S., 110

National Energy Policy Development Group (energy task force), for U.S., 121–122

National Intelligence Estimate (NIE), for U.S., 148

National Partnership for Reinventing Government (REGO), of U.S., 231–232

National Reconnaissance Office, for U.S., 135

394 / Index

national security, 52
  Bush, G. W., brushing up on, 98
  Cheney, D., understanding, 103
  Mondale and, 178–179
National Security Administration, for
  U.S., 135
National Security Agency (NSA), of
  U.S., 128–129
National Security Council (NSC), 49,
  110, 164, 168, 206, 210
  Domestic Council compared with,
    68
  Powell on, 226
  vice presidents sitting on, 2
National Security Directive 179, for
  U.S., 205
National Security Reorganization Act,
  for U.S., 179
NATO, 180–181, 206
NATO allies, Mondale visiting,
  180–181
NBC News/Wall Street Journal, polling
  by, 157
Neustadt, Richard, 4, 255
New Deal, executive branch enlarged
  by, 2
New START Treaty, of U.S., 27
New York Times (newspaper), 51, 102,
  121
New Yorker (magazine), 135
NIE. *See* National Intelligence
  Estimate
Niger, 148
9/11. *See* September 11
Nixon, Richard, 40–41, 63, 73, 103,
  193
"No New Starts" (policy), 75–76,
  264–265
North American Free Trade
  Agreement (NAFTA), 149, 228,
  273
North Korea, 267
Northern Mariana Islands, 56

Novak, Bob, 158
NSA. *See* National Security Agency
NSC. *See* National Security Council
Nuclear Nonproliferation Treaty,
  229
nuclear weapons, 206, 229, 267
Nunn, Sam, 220

Obama, Barack, 10, 27, 238
Office of Homeland Security, for U.S.,
  142–143, 156
Office of Inter-American Affairs, for
  U.S., 40
Office of Legal Counsel (OLC), of
  Justice Department, 150–151
Office of Management and Budget
  (OMB), of U.S., 60, 115, 120
Office of National Preparedness, for
  U.S., 135
Office of the Vice President (OVP), 1,
  33–34, 166
  Adams frustrated by, 254
  executive orders reviewed by,
    114–115
  Libby filling out, 119
  vice presidential influence shaped
    by, 11–12
  in West Wing, 18–19, 179
Offutt Air Force Base, 138
oil embargo, against U.S., 57–58
O'Keefe, Sean, 102, 120, 136
OLC. *See* Office of Legal Counsel
OMB. *See* Office of Management and
  Budget
O'Neill, Paul, 119, 120
OPEC (oil producers), 57
Osborne, Kathy, 199
OVP. *See* Office of the Vice President

Panama Canal Treaty, 181, 186
Panetta, Leon, 241
passenger planes, order to shoot
  down, 139–140

Patel, Neil, 148
PDB. *See* President's Daily Brief
Pena, Federico, 229
Pentagon, 137–138
PEOC. *See* Presidential Emergency
    Operations Center
Perino, Dana, 145
Perot, Ross, 214, 215, 228
Persian Gulf War, 212
Petraeus, David, 240
Plame Wilson, Valerie, 148, 154, 158,
    165, 266
Plouffe, David, 238, 243
Podesta, John, 224, 230–231
Point Four Program, 40
The Politics Presidents Make
    (Skowronek), 18
Powell, Colin, 119, 125, 161, 210
    Addington circumventing, 151
    Cheney, D., battling, 146
    on NSC, 226
Powell, Jody, 180
power, influence and, 10, 15–17,
    256–258
power, presidential, 2, 113–114, 119–
    120, 123–124, 254
presidency (U.S.)
    Biden seeking, 244
    Cheney, D., not seeking, 97–98,
        105, 152–153
    of Ford, 73–74
    Gore seeking, 235–236
    public aspects of, 188
    Rockefeller seeking, 40–43
    Truman on, 254
    vice presidents seeking, 36, 260
presidential character, 20
Presidential Emergency Operations
    Center (PEOC), 137–138
presidential power, 2, 113–114, 119–
    120, 123–124, 254
presidential transition (U.S), 193, 197
    Biden developing, 239

to Bush, G. W., 105, 117–118
to Carter, 176
Cheney, D., planning, 117–120, 160
presidents (U.S.). *See also* Biden,
    Joe; Bush, George H. W.; Bush,
    George W.; Carter, Jimmy;
    Clinton, Bill; Ford, Gerald;
    Reagan, Ronald; Truman, Harry
assistants to, 163
demands on, 1–2
domestic policy controlled by, 2
lunches meetings between vice
    presidents and, 19, 111
management styles of, 26
personalities of, 26
reelection campaigns by, 259–260
vice presidents and relationship
    with, 3, 11, 69, 254–255
President's Council on
    Competitiveness
    (Competitiveness Council), 217–
    219, 248, 271
President's Daily Brief (PDB), 112–
    113
press relations, of Cheney, D., 116–117
Principals Committee, 110, 163
proximity model, of influence, 16, 19

al Qaeda, 144
    Hussein not linked to, 126
    Iraq connected to, 147
    NSA monitoring, 129
Quayle, Dan, 31, 95, 96, 107, 162
    Baker, J., clashing with, 211–212
    Bush, G. H. W., and, 213–214
    in business community, 218–219
    Congress lobbied by, 220
    congressional relations of, 218–219,
        247–248, 271
    Democrats worked with by, 220–
        221
    domestic policy advanced by, 217
    electoral dynamics of, 215–222

396 / Index

Quayle, Dan (*continued*)
  foreign policy and, 209–212
  institutional dynamics of, 209–215,
    272
  Kristol damaging, 213
  Kristol on, 181
  Republicans fundraised for by,
    221–222, 247
  State Department obstructing,
    211–212
  vice presidential selection of, 271
  White House staff not trusting,
    212–213, 248–249, 272

Reagan, Nancy, 190, 195, 202, 204
Reagan, Ronald, 76, 84–85, 89, 102–
    103, 246–248
  archival research at presidential
    library of, 10, 261
  assassination attempt against,
    198–200
  Baker, J., chosen by, 29, 203
  Bush, G. H. W., and, 191–193,
    195–200
  INFs banned by, 206
  State of the Union address by, 204
  vice presidential selection by,
    190–191
Reagan Revolution, 204
Regan, Donald, 31, 195
*Regents of the University of California
    v. Bakke*, 182
Reid, Harry, 241
Republican National Committee
    (RNC), 43, 191, 192
Republican National Convention, 86
Republicans, 131. *See also specific
    Republicans*
  Biden lobbying, 27
  Cheney, D., differing from, 153
  in Congress, 234
  conservative wing of, 219, 221, 271

Jeffords threatening to leave, 130
  liberal wing of, 74, 76, 84, 263
  presidential primaries of 1980, 29,
    202, 204
  Quayle fundraising for, 221–222,
    247
  in Senate, 132, 220
Resolution 1441, by UN Security
    Council, 147–149
Resources Policy and Finance
    Corporation (RPFC), 58
Rice, Condoleezza, 108, 125, 162, 167,
    267
  Afghanistan discussed by, 144
  Cheney, D., and, 146–147, 168
  State Department elevating, 168
  United Airlines Flight 93 discussed
    by, 141
Ridge, Tom, 142
RNC. *See* Republican National
    Committee
Robb, Chuck, 220–221
Rockefeller, Nelson, 8, 10, 30, 37, 179
  Callaway mistrusted by, 84
  Cannon on, 264
  Cheney, D., and, 71, 81–82, 85–86,
    264
  Cole replaced by, 64
  Congress not impacted by, 55–56
  congressional relations of, 54–57
  Democrats appealed to by, 263
  on Domestic Council, 9, 67–69, 73,
    262
  domestic policy and, 46–48, 64–65,
    68, 74–75
  EIA lobbied for by, 54, 61–62
  electoral dynamics and, 84–87, 264
  Ford and, 11, 45–46, 48–51, 60–61,
    65–66, 69–72, 76–79, 84–87
  Harlow on, 44–45
  institutional obstacles faced by,
    83–84

interpersonal dynamics of, 69–73
Kissinger defended by, 54
"No New Starts" impacting, 264–265
presidency sought by, 40–43
role of, 47–51
Rumsfeld in conflict with, 52, 64–66, 74–75, 81–82
situational dynamics impacting, 88–89, 263–264
strengths and weaknesses of, 43
Truman appointing, 40
vice presidency of, 261–262
vice presidential influence of, 62–63, 87–88, 263–264
vice presidential selection of, 40–42, 46, 69
on vice presidents, 39
White House staff and, 46–47, 50, 71–72, 262
Rockefeller Archive Center, 10, 261
Rockefeller Commission. *See* Commission on CIA Activities within the United States
Roosevelt, Franklin D., 1, 11, 24, 40
Rose Garden strategy, by Carter, 189, 245
Rosen, James, 91
Rove, Karl, 93, 100–101, 116, 153–154
RPFC. *See* Resources Policy and Finance Corporation
Rumsfeld, Donald, 39, 71, 84–85, 87, 103, 119, 167
  Bush, G. W., firing, 155, 170
  on Cheney, D., 102, 113
  on EIA, 60
  on Ford, 263
  Haig replaced by, 80
  Rockefeller in conflict with, 52, 64–66, 74–75, 81–82
Russert, Tim, 142, 143, 158
Russia, 227

sanctions, 16–18, 22, 256–257
Saturday Night Live (TV show), 116
Savage, Charlie, 115
Schattschneider, E. E., 21–22
Schmidt, Steve, 163
Schmitt, Eric, 142
Schneiders, Greg, 174
Scott, Hugh, 70
Scowcroft, Brent, 126, 210
Secret Service, of U.S., 135, 137
secular time, 18
secure video teleconferencing system (Secvid) (SVTS), 109
Security Council, of UN, 147–148
Secvid. *See* secure video teleconferencing system
selection, vice presidential. *See* vice presidential selection
Senate (U.S.), 219
  Appropriations Committee for, 56
  Armed Services committee for, 210
  Cheney, D., meeting with, 132–133
  Democrats losing, 225
  Republicans in, 132, 220
September 11, 136, 140–142, 144, 265
  changes following, 145
  Cheney, D., impacted by, 21, 137–139, 156
  U.S. responding to, 143
Shanahan, Kathleen, 106
Shriver, Sargent, 173
Shultz, George, 204
Simon, William, 58–59
Situation Room, 199
situational dynamics, of vice presidential influence, 7, *8*, 9, 19, 27–28, 259
  of Cheney, D., 156–160
  of Gore, 222–238
  Rockefeller impacted by, 88–89, 263–264
Skowronek, Stephen, 18

398 / Index

Smith, William, 187
Snowe, Olympia, 131
social cohesion model, of influence, 16, 19
South Florida Task force, Bush, G. H. W., leading, 205
South Lawn, of White House, 141, 181, 199
Soviet Union, 206, 246, 270
Space Council, 2
Speaker of the House, 1
Specter, Arlen, 240
Spellings, Margaret, 167
staff, of vice presidents
   of Cheney, D., 164
   influence of, 233
   White House staff mingling with, 162–165, 175
Stalin, Joseph, 11
START Treaty, 240, 241
State Department (U.S.), 120, 124, 164
   Gore superseding, 227
   Quayle obstructed by, 211–212
   Rice elevated within, 168
State of the Union addresses, 148, 154, 204
Stephanopoulos, George, 224, 228
Stone, Roger, 222
Strategic Command (Stratcom), U.S., 138
Summers, Larry, 229
Sunday Morning (TV program), 215
Sununu, John, 109, 210, 212–213, 220
Supreme Court (U.S.), 124
   Clinton, B., and, 231
   on presidential power, 2, 254
   Thomas, C., nominated to, 220, 248
SVTS. *See* secure video teleconferencing system
Syria, 267

Taiwan, 206

Task Force on Combatting Terrorism, for U.S., 205
Task Force on Regulatory Relief, for U.S., 204
Task Force on Working Families, for White House, 239
Teeley, Pete, 198
Teeter, Robert, 217
Telecommunications Act, of U.S., 231
Tenet, George, 128–129, 146–147
   on Cheney, D., 128, 145
   on Gore, 231
   Laden blamed by, 144–145
terrorism, 145–147. *See also* Hussein, Saddam; al Qaeda; September 11
   Bush, G. H. W., Combatting, 205
   Cheney, D., concerned with, 135
   U.S combating, 205
"Terrorism Wednesdays" (presidential meetings), 110
Terrorist Surveillance Program (TSP), of U.S., 128–130
This Week (news show), 26
Thomas, Bill, 125, 131, 248
Thomas, Clarence, 220, 248
THREATCON, Addington, D., checking, 137–138
ticket, balancing of, 24, 34–35, 102–103, 215–216, 222–223, 249
Today Show (TV show), 51
Tower, John, 220
transition, presidential. *See* presidential transition
Truman, Harry, 1–2
   Manhattan Project not told to, 11
   on presidency, 254
   Rockefeller appointed by, 40
TSP. *See* Terrorist Surveillance Program
Turner, Michael, 253
Twelfth Amendment, of Constitution, 92, 100

Index / 399

Twenty-Fifth Amendment, of Constitution, 133

United Airlines Flight 93, 141
United Airlines Flight 175, 137
United Nations (UN), 145–146, 147–148, 206
United States (U.S). *See also* Congress; Constitution; Domestic Council; domestic policy; foreign policy; House of Representatives; presidents; Senate; State Department; Supreme Court; vice presidents
  CIA for, 51–53, 135–136, 146, 148–149
  Clean Air Act of, 124
  Commission on CIA Activities within the, 51–52
  Department of Defense for, 1
  Department of Education for, 186
  Department of Health, Education, and Welfare of, 40
  Department of Homeland Security for, 136, 158
  Department of Justice of, 161
  DIA of, 135
  EPA for, 120, 134
  FAA of, 139
  FBI of, 135
  federal budget for, 74–75, 77
  Federal Emergency Management Agency for, 135
  Federal Energy Administration for, 59
  Federal Reserve of, 110
  FISA for, 128–129
  founding fathers of, 253
  Iraq concerning, 144–145
  National Economic Council of, 110

  National Energy Policy Development Group for, 121–122
  National Reconnaissance Office for, 135
  National Security Administration for, 135
  National Security Directive 179 for, 205
  National Security Reorganization Act for, 179
  New START Treaty of, 27
  NIE for, 148
  NSA of, 128–129
  Office of Homeland Security for, 142–143, 156
  Office of Inter-American Affairs for, 40
  Office of National Preparedness for, 135
  oil embargo against, 57–58
  OMB of, 60, 115, 120
  REGO of, 231–232
  Secret Service of, 135, 137
  September 11 responded to by, 143
  Stratcom, 138
  Task Force on Combatting Terrorism for, 205
  Task Force on Regulatory Relief for, 204
  Telecommunications Act of, 231
  terrorism combated by, 205
  TSP of, 128–130
  VFW of, 146
United States-China Policy Forum on Environment and Development, 232
uranium, Hussein seeking, 148
U.S. *See* United States

Vance, Cyrus, 176, 182
Veterans of Foreign Wars (VFW), of U.S., 146

400 / Index

vice presidency (U.S.), 3–4, 10–11.
 See also Bush, G. H. W., model;
 Mondale model
Barber analyzing, 19–20
Biden considering, 25–26
Bush, G. H. W., model of, 195, 247,
 271
of Cheney, D., 104–109
modern, 7–8, 9, 186, 260–261
Mondale considering, 173–174
Mondale model for, 176–178
of Rockefeller, 261–262
vice presidential authority, 114–115
vice presidential influence, 4–5, 8,
 36–37, 119, 251. *See also* electoral
 dynamics; institutional dynamics;
 interpersonal dynamics;
 situational dynamics
archival research on, 10
of Biden, 27, 238, 250, 274
Bolten reducing, 171, 266
of Bush, G. H. W., 203–204, 208–
 209
of Bush, George H. W., 197–198
capacity contrasted with exercise of,
 17–18
Cheney, D., demonstrating, 9, 124,
 142–143, 151–152, 156–157,
 165–166, 170–172, 261, 265
chiefs of staff impacting, 29–30, 33
as contingent influence, 23, 258
decline over administration of, 11,
 171, 266
directional model considering, 18
Domestic Council and, 57
Ford emphasizing, 78–79
framework for understanding,
 22–24
of Gore, 225–226, 233–234
modern era increase in, 23, 258
Mondale expanding, 176–177,
 244–245

Mondale model ensuring, 180–181
origins of, 256
OVP shaping, 11–12
relationships enabling, 73
of Rockefeller, 62–63, 87–88,
 263–264
studies not addressing, 253
trajectory of, 7
variation in, 6, 255
vice presidential selection
 impacting, 169
White House staff surveying, 182
vice presidential search committee,
 Cheney, D., heading, 92–93
vice presidential selection (U.S.), 29, 34
by Bush, G. H. W., 47, 215–216
by Carter, 173–174
of Cheney, D., 92–102
by Ford, 43–44
of Gore, 222–223, 249, 272
original process of, 253
of Quayle, 271
by Reagan, R., 190–191
of Rockefeller, 40–42, 46, 69
vice presidential influence
 impacting, 169
vice presidents (U.S.). *See also*
 Biden, Joe; Bush, George H. W.;
 ceremonial functions; Cheney,
 Dick; Gore, Al; Mondale, Walter;
 Office of the Vice President;
 Quayle, Dan; Rockefeller, Nelson;
 staff, of vice presidents
Cheney, D., on, 91
chiefs of staff for, 162
congressional relations managed
 by, 55
Constitution not limiting, 4
evolution of, 1–2
federal budget including, 77
foreign policy and, 2–3
governing abilities of, 47

informal powers enabling, 17, 255
lunches meetings between
    presidents and, 19, 111
NSC sat on by, 2
personalities of, 26
presidency sought by, 5
presidential election sought by, 36,
    260
presidents and relationship with, 3,
    11, 69, 254–255
Rockefeller on, 39
role of, 47–51, 107
sanctions not exerted by, 16–18, 22,
    256–257
as senior advisers, 17, 203, 239, 257
White House traveled from by,
    35–36
Vietnam War, 26–27, 53, 127
Voinovich, George, 131
Vulcans (foreign policy advisory
    team), 98

Walker, David, 123
Walker, Lundquist, 123
Wall Street Journal, polling by, 157
Wallace, Henry, 41, 42
Wallace, Nicolle, 159
Wallison, Peter, 62
war on terror, 134, 143–151, 156, 266
Warshaw, Shirley Anne, 106
Washington Post (newspaper), 46, 157,
    234
Watergate Crisis, 41
Waxman, Henry, 123
Ways and Means Committee, for
    House of Representatives, 132
weapons of mass destruction
    (WMDs), 126, 135–136, 144–145,
    148–149
Weber, Max, 16
West Wing, of White House, 18–19,
    179

Western Europe, 170, 206–207, 270
White House, 29–31. *See also*
    presidents
Budget Review Board for, 115,
    167
Commission on Aviation Safety and
    Security for, 231
South Lawn of, 141, 181, 199
structure of, 162
Task Force on Working Families
    for, 239
vice presidents traveling from,
    35–36
West Wing of, 18–19, 179
White House staff, 29, 49, 230–231,
    242–243. *See also* chiefs of staff
Addington and, 166
Bush, G. H. W., not trusted by,
    194–195, 202–203
Bush, G. W., changing, 167
Cheney, D., informed by, 111
Ford convinced by, 61
Gore placing, 229
Quayle not trusted by, 212–213,
    248–249, 272
Rockefeller and, 46–47, 50, 71–72,
    262
staff of vice presidents mingling
    with, 162–165, 175
vice presidential influence surveyed
    by, 182
Whitman, Ann, 79
Whitman, Christine Todd, 120,
    124–125
Whittington, Harry, 158–159
Wilson, Joe, 154
Wilson, Woodrow, 1–2, 254
Witcover, Jules, 253
WMDs. *See* weapons of mass
    destruction
Wolff, Candida, 164–165
Wolfowitz, Paul, 120, 144, 167

402 / Index

Woodward, Bob, 234
World Trade Center, 136–137
World War II, 11
Wrong, Dennis, 15–16

Xiaoping, Deng, 206

Yeutter, Clayton, 213
Yoo, John, 151, 167

Zarb, Frank, 59–61
al Zawahiri, Ayman, 147
Zoellick, Robert, 120